COMMUNICATE!

5th Edition

Rudolph F. Verderber

University of Cincinnati

Wadsworth Publishing Company
Belmont, California
A Division of Wadsworth, Inc.

Communication Editor: Kristine M. Clerkin
Production Editor: Leland Moss
Editorial Associate: Naomi Brown
Designer: Merle Sanderson
Print Buyer: Barbara Britton
Copy Editor: Ellen Setteducati
Cartoonist: Tony Hall
Compositor: Thompson Type
Cover: Merle Sanderson
Cover Illustration: Ken and Denis Parkhurst

Photo Credits

pp. 6, 40, 168: Marshall Rheiner; **p. 35**: H. Kubota, Magnum; **p. 71**: Bob Clay, Jeroboam; **p. 95**: Paul Fusco, Magnum; **p. 96**: Jane Scherr, Jeroboam; **p. 127**: Mary Ellen Mark, Archive; **p. 140**: Joan Liftin, Archive; **p. 150**: Kit Hedman, Jeroboam; **p. 158**: Ken Gaghan, Jeroboam; **p. 165**: Randy Matusow, Archive; **p. 166**: Raymond Depardon; **p. 171**: Abigail Heyman, Archive; **p. 173**: Helga Maaser, Archive; **p. 199, 276**: Laimute E. Druskis, Jeroboam; **p. 201**: Frank Siteman, Jeroboam; **p. 217**: Bill Owens, Jeroboam; **p. 245**: Avidson, Magnum; **p. 247**: Erich Hartmann, Magnum; **pp. 325, 328, 341**: Stephen Rapley

Printed in the United States of America   **34**

3 4 5 6 7 8 9 10—91 90 89 88 87

ISBN 0-534-07170-8

Library of Congress Cataloging in Publication Data
Verderber, Rudolph F.
  Communicate!

  Includes bibliographies and index.
  1. Communication.   1. Title.
P90.V43   1987   001.51   86-13180
ISBN 0-534-07170-8

COMMUNICATE!

CONTENTS

P R E F A C E

Because you spend more time communicating than doing almost anything else, it is important that you learn to communicate as effectively as possible. This fifth edition of *Communicate!* has been revised to maximize its value in helping you become a better communicator. I hope that you find this book both informative and interesting.

Organization

The material in *Communicate!* is presented in five parts:

Part One ("Introduction") provides a perspective to the study of communication.

Part Two ("Establishing a Communication Foundation") provides a base for communicating in all settings. It covers the fundamentals of communication: perception, verbal communication, nonverbal communication, and listening.

Part Three ("Interpersonal Communication") Part Four, ("Decision-Making Group Communication") and Part Five ("Public Speaking") present information to help you develop communication competence in each of these three communication formats.

Fifth Edition Features

Although the parts of the book are essentially the same as in the last edition, material has been added, deleted, and rearranged with your ability to learn and apply the material kept firmly in mind. Let's take a detailed look at both the contents of the book and the ways the materials differ from the last edition.

The first chapter, "Communication Perspective," is essentially the same as in the last edition. Part Two, however, has been substantially revised. The key change has been the addition of a separate chapter on listening skills. This foundation unit now consists of the material that is truly basic to all three sections that follow. As a result, Parts Three, Four, and Five can be covered in any order. Nevertheless, because skills are cumulative, the established organization provides the most unified and coherent approach to the study of communication.

Part Three ("Interpersonal Communication") begins with two chapters on responding skills and communicating ideas and feelings.

These two chapters cover more than ten of the most important skills necessary to improving your interpersonal communication. The next chapter on building and maintaining relationships has been totally revised to put emphasis on skills necessary to help you achieve the most from your communication relationships. The final chapter is on interviewing.

Part Four ("Decision-Making Group Communication") includes the same material found in the last edition, but organized into two chapters instead of three. The key chapters on participation and leadership have been reorganized to give you a step-by-step procedure for maximizing your effectiveness in groups.

Part Five ("Public Speaking") has received the most dramatic revision. Because finding material and organizing material are so important to speech preparation, material on preparation is now covered in two chapters instead of one. The chapter on speech presentation has also been expanded; the final two chapters on informative and persuasive speaking have been totally revised. Again, the emphasis has been placed on steps of preparation that will enable you to prepare and present the best speeches possible.

The appendices include a sample of an interpersonal conversation, two speeches with analyses, various analysis checksheets, and a form for self-contracts based upon results from self-analyses.

Exercises

Any study of fundamental skills calls not only for clear explanation but also for well-conceived ideas directed toward helping you put those fundamentals into practice. Throughout the text realistic, workable exercises are included for practice of the skills discussed. This edition features many revisions of exercises and a number of newly created exercises. In each exercise some behavioral objective is sought; and there are convenient tearout sheets in Appendix B for use in interpersonal, group, and public speaking analyses.

Through the practice, observation, and analysis model, you can help yourself to learn quickly and efficiently. You will also find, particularly in the public-speaking chapters, exercises including performance assignments that give you different kinds of practical application of the various communication skills.

Acknowledgments

This fifth edition could not have been completed without the help of many people. Mostly, I would like to acknowledge the help of my colleagues at various colleges and universities who offered prerevision suggestions or who read the completed manuscript for the fifth edition and offered many valuable suggestions: Professors Martin H. Brodey, Montgomery Community College; Rudolph E. Busby, San Francisco State University; Martha Cooper, Northern Illinois University; Elizabeth Coughlin, Northern Virginia Community College; Carley H. Dodd, Abilene Christian University; Joan Holm, Northern Virginia Community College; Melba Kop, Chaminade University; Sylvia Malone, Jacksonville State University; James Mancuso, Mesa Community College; Lois Roach, Spokane Community College; V. A. Smith, Texas A&I University; and Charlotte Toguchi, Kapiolani Community College.

COMMUNICATE!

PART *ONE*

- -

▶ *Successful communi-
cation is important in nearly
every aspect of your life.
This chapter gives insight
into the communication
process.*

1 COMMUNICATION PERSPECTIVE

INTRODUCTION

COMMUNICATION
PERSPECTIVE

OBJECTIVES

After you have read this chapter, you should be able to:

1 Define communication

2 List and show the interrelationships among the seven elements of the communication process

3 Explain the differences between the social and the decision-making functions of communication

4 Identify the goals of interpersonal communication, group communication, and public speaking

Whether you are just out of high school and taking your first college class, a senior looking toward graduation, or a person starting or returning to college after raising a family or changing a career, you are likely to realize that a college education will help improve your professional life. The fact is that in many fields a college education may well be the *only* way you can hope to achieve at the highest level.

You may be less aware of the value of this particular course to your education; yet competence in *communication*—expertise with the skills that we will be considering in this textbook—continues to be far and away the most important ability for a student to master. For instance, employers of liberal arts graduates continue to prize five kinds of skills: verbal communication skills, responsibility, interpersonal skills, initiative, and decision-making skills.[1] Three of these five are featured in this book; the other two—responsibility and initiative—are often implemented by communication skills. And whether you aspire to a leadership position in business, industry, government, education, or almost any field you can name, these same communication skills are often prerequisites to success. Moreover, in social interaction, family relations, and every aspect of your daily lives, communication competence is a must.

Yet although communication skills are clearly valuable to understand and master, most people take them for granted. When something goes wrong due to an unfortunate misunderstanding, all too often we hear someone glibly remark, "What we have here is a communication problem"—a statement that suggests no way to resolve the situation. In this first chapter we will focus on what communication is, what purposes it serves, and what kinds of communication settings you will be studying.

Despite the presence of more definitions than most of us can count, I continue to consider **communication** as a transactional process of sharing meaning. If we get meaning, ideas, and feelings from a person, an action, a painting, a building, a room, or whatever we are dealing with, we say that it *communicated*. In this book, however, we are not as concerned with the ideas and feelings we get from inanimate objects as with those we receive from people—like your family, your classmates, and *you*.

Simply stimulating ideas and feelings will not always result in *effective* communication. One person may communicate with another in such a way that the communication has a different meaning for each person. **Effective communication** is communication in which the meaning that is stimulated is similar to or the same as that within the communicator; in short, effective communication is shared meaning—shared ideas and feelings. The goal of this book is not just to explore communication but to discover what makes communication *effective*.

ELEMENTS OF THE PROCESS

Communication is a dynamic, ongoing, transactional process. It is dynamic because it is constantly active and changing; it is ongoing because it has no fixed beginning or end; and it is transactional because those communicating are mutually responsible for the success of the communication, which involves the interaction of many elements.

To get a mental picture of the dynamic, ongoing, and transactional nature of communication, envision yourself at a mixer, a fraternity or sorority rush party, a department gathering, or a club meeting. From the time the event begins until it ends, communication takes place. For purposes of analysis let's isolate the elements of communication that occur as you chat with three or four people:

- the *context* in which the people are communicating
- the *people* involved
- the *rules* that guide their communication
- the *messages* that are being communicated
- the *channels* through which the communication occurs
- the presence or absence of *noise*
- the verbal and nonverbal responses that communication scholars call *feedback*

Context

The interrelated conditions of communication make up what we term **context**. One aspect of context is the *physical setting* in which the communication episode occurs. The components of physical context include location, time, light, temperature, distance between communicators, and any seating arrangements. Each one of these affects the communication. The context of the room in which your mixer is taking place is likely to be different from the context of a conversation held in a quiet restaurant. The interaction of a decision-making group in a seminar room is different from the interaction between a politician and an audience in a large auditorium. In Chapter 4, "Communicating Nonverbally," we will demonstrate that every aspect of the physical environment has the potential to affect communication and the meanings understood by the participants.

A second aspect of context is *historical*—the previous communication episodes that have occurred affect the meanings currently being shared. For instance, suppose that this morning Marcie tells Phil that she will go to the cleaner for the suit that he needs the next day. As Phil enters the apartment that evening he sees Marcie and says, "Did you get it?" Another person listening to the conversation would have no idea what Phil is talking about. Yet Marcie may well reply, "It's in the closet." What is *it*?

The suit, of course: The subject, which was determined in a different context, still affects the nature of this communication event. At your mixer, on the other hand, because the people are probably meeting for the first time, the context holds no historical aspect.

A third aspect of context is *psychological*. The manner in which people perceive themselves—as well as how they perceive those with whom they communicate—will affect the meaning that is shared. For instance, suppose Randy has had a really rough day. The typist he hired to do his term paper couldn't get it done, so he has to do it himself, even though he still has to finish studying for a test. If his roommate bounds into the apartment and jokingly suggests that he take a speed-typing course, Randy might lose his normally good sense of humor and explode. Why? Because the feelings of the people involved have created a psychological context for the interpersonal interaction.

People

The people in a communication transaction play the roles of **sender** and **receiver**, sometimes—as in interpersonal communication—simultaneously. As senders we form messages and attempt to communicate them to others through symbols. As receivers we process the messages that are sent to us and react to them both verbally and nonverbally.

The five people depicted in this photo are all involved in some form of communication. How does your interpretation of this photo change if (a) you know nothing more about the photo than what you see; (b) you are told that the man looking at you is the father of the sleeping woman; (c) you discover the photo is a still from a new movie; (d) you learn that the amorous couple met thirty minutes earlier. Each bit of information elaborates on the *context* of the communication.

Each person is a product of individual experiences, feelings, ideas, moods, sex, occupation, religion, and so forth. As a result, the meaning sent and the meaning received may not be exactly the same for each. For instance, when Art speaks of a good job, he means one that is highly paid; to Joan, the person to whom he is talking, a good job may be one that is stimulating, regardless of pay.

Moreover, the people in a communication transaction have some relationship with each other that further affects perceptions of the ideas and feelings communicated. Friends may have much more latitude than strangers or enemies in how they say something in order to be understood correctly. That's why communication in a friend-to-friend relationship differs qualitatively from communication in a relationship between public speaker and audience. A successful communicator must take advantage of every skill available to present and interpret ideas and feelings as clearly as possible.

Rules

Rules are the guidelines that we establish (or perceive as established) for conducting transactions. Rules exist at the beginning of a communication encounter and grow, change, or solidify as people get to know each other better. Rules tell us what kinds of messages and behavior are

proper in a given context or with a particular person or group of people. For instance, students who pepper their conversations with four-letter words when talking with friends in a dorm are likely to use a much different vocabulary when giving a speech to their class.

Sometimes we don't know the rules; we have to learn them through experience. People who are used to breaking in to speak at an informal group meeting may find it difficult to raise their hands to be recognized at a business meeting.

The rules for communication may be formal (such as parliamentary procedures for organizational meetings), may be accepted social guidelines ("Never discuss religion or politics at the dinner table"), or may simply develop within the context of a particular setting.

Messages

Communication takes place through the sending and receiving of **messages**. These messages have at least three elements: meanings, the symbols used to communicate the meanings, and form or organization.

Meanings, as we said earlier, are the ideas and feelings communicated. You have ideas about how to study for your next exam, where to go for lunch, and whether taxes should be raised or lowered. You also have feelings such as hunger, anger, and love. Meanings may start with or from one person, but they grow, change, and take form as a result of the interaction with another person. As we discover almost daily, the meanings we have cannot be moved magically to another person's mind.

These ideas and feelings are expressed through *symbols*—words, sounds, or actions that represent meaning. Symbols can be communicated with both voice and body. As you speak, you choose words to convey your meaning. At the same time, facial expressions, gestures, and tone of voice—all nonverbal cues—accompany your words and affect the meaning that is received. As you listen, you take both the verbal symbols and the nonverbal cues and assign meanings to them. The process of transforming ideas and feelings into symbols is called **encoding**; the process of transforming symbols and the accompanying nonverbal cues into ideas and feelings is called **decoding**.

You have been communicating for so long that you probably don't consciously think about either the encoding or the decoding process. When your eyes grow bleary and you say, "I'm tired," you don't think, "I wonder what symbols will best express the feeling I am now having." When you hear the words "I'm tired" and see the bleary eyes of the other person, you are not likely to think: "*I* stands for the person doing the talking, *am* means that the *I* is linked to some idea, and *tired* means growing weary or feeling a need for sleep; therefore, the person is feeling a need for sleep and the bleary eyes confirm the accuracy of the statement." At the same time, you are not likely to consider whether you have the same mental picture of "tired" as the person using the word. You are probably aware of the encoding process only when you must grope for words, especially when you feel the right word is just "on the tip of your tongue." Similarly, you are aware of the decoding process when you figure out the meaning of an unfamiliar word by the way it is used in a sentence.

Meanings may be communicated intentionally or unintentionally. When meaning is intentional, the person communicating makes a conscious, purposeful effort to select the symbols that will communicate. Yet, at the same time, that person may be unintentionally sending a conflicting message through nonverbal cues. For instance, if someone says, "Yes, I'm very interested in your story," the meaning you actually receive depends upon whether the person looks engaged or whether the person's nonverbal cues say "I'm bored stiff." Both the intentional and the unintentional aspects of the communication are important to the meaning.

When meaning is complicated or complex, people may need to communicate it in sections or in a certain order to convey the meaning. In this case the meaning must be organized. Message *form* is especially important in the public-speaking setting when one person talks without interruption for a relatively long time. But even in the give-and-take of interpersonal conversation, form can affect message understanding. For instance, when Julia tells Connie about the apartment she looked at yesterday, her symbols take a certain form. If Julia's description moves logically from room to room, Connie is likely to have a clearer picture than if she has to piece together impressions Julia communicates in a random order.

Channels

The **channel** is both the route traveled by the message and the means of transportation. Words are carried from one person to another by air waves; facial expressions, gestures, and movement travel by light waves. Usually the more channels used to carry a message, the more likely the communication will succeed. Although human communication has basically two channels—light and sound—people can and do communicate by any of the five sensory channels. A fragrant scent or a firm handshake may be as important as what is seen or heard.

Noise

A person's ability to interpret, understand, or respond to symbols is often hurt by noise. **Noise** is any stimulus that gets in the way of sharing meaning. Much of your success as a communicator depends on how you cope with external, internal, and semantic noises.

External noises are the sights, sounds, and other stimuli that draw people's attention away from intended meaning. For instance, during a friend's explanation of how a food processor works, your attention may be drawn to the sound of an airplane overhead: external noise. However, external noise does not have to be a sound. Perhaps during the explanation you notice a photograph of a particularly attractive person on the wall and for a moment your attention turns to that image. Such visual distraction to your attention is also external noise.

Internal noises are the thoughts and feelings that interfere with meaning. Have you ever found yourself daydreaming when a person was trying to tell you something? Perhaps you let your mind wander to thoughts of the good time you had at a party last night or to the argument you had with someone this morning. If you have tuned out the words of your friend and tuned in a daydream or a past conversation, then you have created internal noise.

Semantic noises are those alternate meanings aroused by certain symbols that inhibit meaning. Suppose a friend describes a forty-year-old secretary as "the girl in the office." If you think of *girl* as a condescending term for a forty-year-old woman, you might not even hear the rest of what your friend has to say. Rather, you might dwell on the chauvinistic message you perceive in such symbol use. Symbols that are derogatory to a person or group, such as ethnic slurs, often cause semantic noise; profanity can have the same effect. Because meaning depends on your own experience, at times others may decode a word or phrase differently from the way you intended; this is semantic noise.

Feedback

Whether receivers decode the meaning of messages properly or not, they have some mental or physical response to the messages; this response—called **feedback** in most communication books—tells the person sending a message whether that message was heard, seen, or understood. If the verbal or nonverbal response tells the sender that the communication was not received, was received incorrectly, or was misinterpreted, the person can send the message again, perhaps in a different way, so that the meaning the sender intends to share is the same meaning received by the listener.

During this course you will be involved in different kinds of communication situations. The situations or settings themselves determine the differing amounts and types of response. Stop reading right now and draw a rectangle resting on one of its longer sides. Did you do it? Obviously I have no way of knowing whether you understood what I was talking about, whether you actually drew the rectangle, or, if you drew it, whether you drew it correctly. As the source of that message—as well as the other messages in this textbook—I cannot know for certain if I am really communicating. A *zero-feedback* situation is said to exist when it is virtually impossible for the sender to be aware of a receiver's response. The lack of direct feedback is one weakness of any form of mass communication. The source has little or no immediate opportunity to test the impact of his or her message.

Suppose, however, that instead of being the author of a book, I am your instructor in a class of twenty students. Now suppose that I say, "Draw a rectangle resting on one of its sides." Even if you said nothing in response, my presence would enable me to monitor your nonverbal feedback directly. If you drew the rectangle, I could see it; if you refused, I would know; in some cases I could see exactly what you were drawing. A person in a public-speaking setting must be sensitive to this type of basically nonverbal feedback.

Now suppose that when I ask you to draw the rectangle, you are free to ask me any direct questions and I am equally free and willing to respond. The free flow of interacting communication that would take place represents the highest level of feedback. This type of feedback is most likely in a personal communication setting.

How important is feedback to effective communication? Leavitt and Mueller conducted an experiment similar to the one just described.[2] They reported that communication improved markedly as the situation moved from zero feedback to complete interaction. In our communication, whether interpersonal, small-group, or public speaking, we want to stimulate as much feedback as the situation will allow.

As we will discover, feedback can be more useful than as a simple test of the understanding of the message; it can help us gain insight into ourselves as people, stimulate personal growth, and verify or validate our perceptions.

A MODEL OF THE PROCESS

Let's look at a pictorial representation to see how the elements of communication interrelate. Figure 1.1 illustrates the communication process in terms of a one-to-one relationship, that is, one sender to one receiver. The left-hand circle represents the sender. In the center of that circle is a message, a thought, or a feeling that the person sends. The nature of that thought or feeling is created, shaped, and affected by the speaker's total field of experience, represented in the outer circle by such specific factors as values, culture, environment, experiences, occupation, sex, interests, knowledge, and attitudes. The bar between the circles represents the channel. The person sends the message through the sending channel (upper half of the bar) by words and actions.

The right-hand circle represents the receiver. Into the center of the circle comes the message. The message is turned into meaning for the receiver through the decoding process. This decoding process is affected by the receiver's total field of experience—that is, by the same factors of values, culture, environment, experiences, occupation, sex, interests, knowledge, and attitudes. Upon decoding and interpreting the message, the receiver sends verbal and nonverbal reactions back to the sender through the receiving or feedback channel (lower half of the bar). The sender receives and decodes the feedback in order to interpret the response he or she is getting from the receiver.

The area around the sender and the receiver represents the physical and psychological context, which includes the formal and informal rules in operation during the communication. At the same time this process is taking place, external, internal, and semantic noise may be occurring at various places in the model. These noises may affect the ability of sender and receiver to share meanings.

In a group or public-speaking situation this model operates simultaneously—and differently—for every person in the group or in the audience. Let us trace the variables in operation in a simple communication act. When the professor looks at her watch she sees she has only five minutes left. She frowns because she still has one major point to cover, but, aware that time is too short, she says, "That's enough for today." In response, various members of the class look surprised; many smile; a few even cheer. Most students gather their books, pencils, paper, and coats, and begin filing out—all except for Kim, who has been lost in thought over tomorrow's big game.

The professor and her students exist in a classroom *context*. Be-

FIGURE 1 · 1

A model of communication
between two individuals

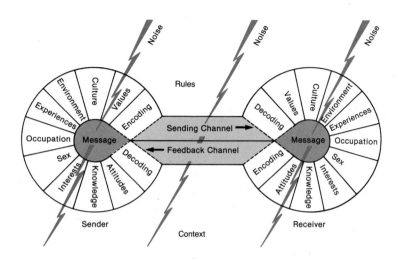

havior in that context is determined by *rules*—in this case, that class continues for the assigned time, unless the professor determines otherwise. As
the *sender*, the professor conveys her *message* in verbal symbols and
nonverbal signs. Her language ("That's enough for today") is the verbal
representation of her thoughts; her frown and dejected tone are the nonverbal representation of her frustration at not having more time. Her words
and tone of voice are carried by air waves and her facial expression and
bodily action by light waves (the *channels*) to each member of the class.
As *receivers*, the class members record the sound and light waves and
then interpret (decode) the verbal symbols and nonverbal signs that carried the message. As a result of their interpretation of the message, the
students respond, give *feedback*, by looks of surprise, smiles, and a few
cheers; they further respond by gathering materials and leaving. Most of
the class experienced no barriers to the satisfactory completion of the
communication, but Kim—distracted by *internal noise*—could not understand why most of the class was leaving early.

PRACTICE

*Identifying
Variables*

Identify the communication elements in the following example.

▶   With a look of great anticipation Rita says, "That's a beautiful dress.
Can I have it?" Ted frowns, shrugs his shoulders, and says hesi-

tantly, "Well . . . yes . . . I guess so." Rita continues, "And it's only thirty dollars!" Ted brightens and says, "Yes, it is a beautiful dress. Go ahead and buy it."

FUNCTIONS OF COMMUNICATION

We have seen what communication is; now let's consider what it does for us. We study communication because it fulfills several very important functions. All communication has social and decision-making functions that touch and affect every aspect of our lives.

Social Functions

Communication serves a number of social functions.

1. *We communicate to meet psychological needs.* Psychologists tell us that people are by nature social animals; that is, just as they need food, water, and other biological necessities, people need other people. Without at least some social interaction, most people hallucinate, lose their motor coordination, and become generally maladjusted.[3] Of course we all have heard of hermits who choose to live and function alone, but they are an exception. Most of us need to talk to people and have them talk to us. Often the topic of conversation is unimportant. Two people may sit and enjoy talking for hours about relatively inconsequential matters. When they part, they may have exchanged little real information, but they may carry away a pleasant feeling simply by having communicated with another human being.

2. *We communicate to fulfill social obligations.* Why do you say "How are you doing?" to a person you sat next to in class last quarter but haven't seen since? Why do you say such things as "What's happening?" or simply "Hi" when you walk by people you know? People use such statements to meet social obligations. When you recognize people, you feel a need to let them know that you recognize them. By saying, "Hi, Skip, how's it going?" you conform to societal norms: You acknowledge a person you recognize with one of the many statements you have learned to use under these circumstances. Not speaking is perceived as a slight; the person may think you are stuck-up or unfeeling. Recognition efforts serve to demonstrate your ties with people.

3. *We communicate to build and to maintain relationships.* When you do not know a person at all, you may communicate with that person to try out the relationship. If you find that you have things in common, the relationship may grow. Depending upon the results of the interaction, you may

be content with an acquaintance relationship or a school-friend relationship, or you may seek a deeper, more intimate relationship. Some conversation is conducted for purposes of moving the relationship to a higher level of intimacy, some for reinforcing the satisfactory nature of the relationship that has been achieved. Few relationships stay the same—especially during college years. Even within a single term you may find yourself moving into and out of a variety of relationships; this is part of living.

4. *We communicate to define the nature of our relationships.* Through communication, people in relationships are continually defining and redefining the power and affection between them by what they say and how they say it. As a result of their communication, people's relationships are likely to be perceived as complementary or symmetrical.[4]

In a **complementary relationship**, one person lets the other define who is to have greater power. For instance, most student-teacher relationships are complementary, with the teacher in the higher power/status position. A teacher assigns Joan to complete a certain task. The assignment is made in a way that implies that the teacher expects Joan to do it. Joan, in turn, responds in a way that shows that she accepts the professor's right to make such an assignment.

In a **symmetrical relationship**, the people involved challenge each other's attempts to control, or strive to equalize power. For example, the communication of Don and Barbara, a married couple, may define their relationship as symmetrical in one of two ways. In one instance, Don and Barbara will behave in ways that indicate that each believes himself or herself to be in charge. In a conversation about budget, Don says, "Don't worry, Barbara, I'm reworking the budget," to which Barbara replies, "I think I'd better make the revision; I know how much we need for household expenses." Another scenario between Don and Barbara indicates that they share power: In the conversation about budget, Don says, "I think we need to sit down together and revise our household budget, don't you?" And Barbara responds, "I know, I've been thinking the same thing. What do you say we start working on it after dinner?"

Which type of relationship is preferable? Complementary relationships exhibit less open conflict than do symmetrical ones, but in symmetrical relationships power is more evenly shared. The feelings of the individuals involved determine the appropriateness of the relational type.

5. *We communicate to enhance and maintain our sense of self.* Through our communication we seek approval for who and what we are. How do you know what you are good at? Mostly through your communication—people tell you. Did you conduct that meeting well? Did you do the job as you were expected? Do you have the right to feel happy? angry? guilty? You learn the answers to such questions partially from what others say to you.

6. *We communicate to manage conflict.* Conflict is a reality of life; we can't, or at least we shouldn't, always avoid it. Conflict can be constructive— but we must be able to manage conflict. Through communication we can manage conflict by sharing important information and by solving problems.

Decision-Making Functions

Along with being social animals, humans are also decision makers. Starting with whether or not to get up this morning, through what to eat for breakfast, to whether or not to go to class, you have made countless decisions already today. Some of these decisions you made alone; others you made in consultation with one or more people. Even more important, every decision involved some kind of language use. Decision making involves *information* and *influence*.

1. *We communicate to share information.* Information is a key ingredient in effective decision making. It is impossible to function in our society without data. You get some data through observation, some through reading, some through television, and a great deal through interpersonal communication. Jeff runs out to get the morning paper. As he comes hurriedly through the door, Tom asks, "What's it like out there?" Jeff replies, "Wow, it's cold! It couldn't be more than twenty degrees." Tom says, "I was going to wear my jacket, but I guess I'd better break out the old winter coat." Such a conversation is typical of countless exchanges that send and receive information. Because decisions are generally better when they are based on information, anything that you can do to improve the accuracy of your information exchange is to your benefit in decision making.
2. *We communicate to influence others.* Since many of the decisions we make involve other people's agreement, a second goal of decision making is that of changing attitudes and behaviors. Examples include convincing your friends to go to a play rather than to a movie; campaigning door-to-door for a political candidate; persuading your father to let you use the car this weekend; or (an old favorite) trying to get an instructor to change your course grade. These are but a few examples of attempts to influence people in decision making. Some communication scholars even argue that the primary purpose of all communication is to influence the behavior of others.

Just as a direct relationship exists between communication and human relations, so does one exist between communication and decision making. The better you understand the means of processing information, sharing information, and persuading, the more likely you will make good decisions. Likewise, the more you understand the problem-solving method, the more likely you will be able to cope with your problems systematically and to arrive at the best decisions possible.

PRACTICE

Communication Functions

1. List five people you talked with yesterday. For each, indicate the social level on which you communicated: (a) meeting psychological needs; (b) fulfilling social obligations; (c) developing relationships; (d) defining relationships; (e) enhancing sense of self; (f) managing conflict.

2. Consider the last decision you made today. What part, if any, did communication have in that decision?

COMMUNICATION SETTINGS

The final three major sections of this textbook will focus on communication in three major settings: interpersonal, decision-making group, and public speaking.

Interpersonal Communication

Interpersonal communication involves the kind of interaction that most of us refer to as *conversation*, which is the person-to-person interaction with one other person or with a small informal aggregate of people. Talking to a friend on campus, talking on the phone with a classmate about an upcoming test, and discussing a movie with the gang over a beer are all interpersonal communication. Intimate relationships and friendships are formed and maintained through interpersonal communication. In this setting, feedback is immediate; total interaction is the rule.

How we relate to others is strongly influenced by our ability to use the communication skills most associated with conversation: shaping messages, listening and responding, understanding nonverbal cues, and forming relationships. Although personal communication is spontaneous, fast, and at times difficult to recall accurately, it can be analyzed, and how we communicate in personal informal settings can be changed and improved.

We generally think of interpersonal communication as involving two or more persons. But just think of the time you spend talking to yourself! Sometimes the conversation is a silent one, but sometimes you actually speak aloud. Were you ever embarrassed by someone pointing out that you were mumbling to yourself? This communication that takes place within you is often called *intra*personal communication. Because the skills are the same for the most part, we will group communication both with self and with others under the heading of *interpersonal*.

Decision-Making Groups

Another large portion of our communication occurs in decision-making group settings. Each of us belongs to many groups: the family, social organizations, church organizations, work committees, and others. Although our communication in these groups is basically interpersonal in nature, when several persons formalize their relationships by meeting to combine talents to solve a problem or make a decision, they form a **decision-making group**.

The purpose of a decision-making group—achieving a goal that represents and is shaped by the thinking of the entire group—introduces additional variables that are not found in interpersonal communication: elements of group structure, the need for task and maintenance functions by group members, leadership, and formalized methods of group problem-solving and decision making.

Still, decision-making group communication is not a separate, un-related activity. Think of group communication as a format that builds on interpersonal communication skills.

Public Speaking

At times, on both formal and informal levels, we address others not as interacting participants but as an audience. All the variables of communication are present in a one-to-many model, but their use in public speaking is much different from their use in the other settings. For most people, **public speaking** is more difficult than personal or small-group interaction because it requires careful message preparation, willingness and ability to face a large group, and sensitivity to what are often very subtle feedback responses.

Unfortunately, most people are not very effective public speakers. Their speeches are often long, tedious, and easily forgotten. However, the true value of public speaking should not be measured by the average or even the typical effort. Because public speaking can serve both to disseminate information and to act as a catalyst for change, it is important to master the fundamentals and learn to apply them effectively. In this text we will consider the skills of preparation, presentation, information exchange, and persuasion that you can use to become a more effective speaker.

SUMMARY

We have defined effective communication as the transactional process of sharing ideas and feelings. Although the dynamic nature of the process is very difficult to isolate, it involves sending and receiving messages through various channels within a specific context while competing with noise. Upon receiving a message a person may or may not feed back verbal or nonverbal responses.

Communication serves both social and decision-making functions. We communicate to meet psychological needs, to fulfill social obligations, to build and to maintain relationships, to define the nature of our relationships, to enhance and maintain our sense of self, and to manage conflict. We also communicate to share information and to influence others.

Communication takes place interpersonally with one or more people in informal settings, in decision-making groups, and in public-speaking settings.

SUGGESTED READINGS

Arnold, Carroll C., and John Waite Bowers, eds. *Handbook of Rhetorical and Communication Theory*. Boston: Allyn & Bacon, 1984. This volume stands as the most complete summary of current research on communication theory.

Devito, Joseph A. *The Communication Handbook*. New York: Harper & Row, 1986. This dictionary of communication words and concepts is an invaluable addition to the library of any student of communication.

Littlejohn, Stephen W., *Theories of Human Communication*. 2nd ed. Belmont, Calif.: Wadsworth, 1983. Littlejohn does an amazingly comprehensive analysis of major communication theories, focusing on the strengths and weaknesses of each.

Spitzberg, Brian H., and William R. Cupach, *Interpersonal Communication Competence*. Beverly Hills, Calif.: Sage Publications, 1984. An excellent, up-to-date analysis of interpersonal competence research, with a comprehensive bibliography.

*P*ART *T*WO

▶ *This four-chapter unit contains information on perception, language, nonverbal communication, and listening that will enable you to build a solid foundation for your skill development in interpersonal communication, decision-making groups, and public speaking.*

*E*STABLISHING A *C*OMMUNICATION *F*OUNDATION

Self-Analysis

In the first chapter of this textbook we defined communication as the transactional process of sharing meaning. In this unit we look at four fundamentals of communication: perception, verbal communication, nonverbal communication, and listening. These four fundamentals are the building blocks of effective communication.

How strong is your communication foundation? Are your perceptions always accurate? Is your verbal communication clear and honest? Do your nonverbal cues go along with or go against what you say? Do you really listen to what others say to you? The following analysis looks at ten specifics that are basic to a communication fundamentals profile.

For each of the paired statements listed below, circle the number that best indicates how you see your behavior. The numbers 1 and 2 represent the negative behavior; the numbers 4 and 5 represent the positive behavior. The number 3 represents the midpoint between the extremes. It may also say you are not sure of your behavior.

When I speak, I tend to present a negative image of myself.	1 2 3 4 5	When I speak, I tend to present a positive image of myself.
In my behavior toward others I rely heavily on my first impressions.	1 2 3 4 5	In my behavior toward others I look for more information to confirm or negate my first impressions.
My conversation is limited by a small vocabulary.	1 2 3 4 5	My conversation is helped by a large vocabulary.

I have trouble wording my ideas clearly in ways that people understand.	1 2 3 4 5	I speak clearly using words that people readily understand.
I tend to look away when I talk with people.	1 2 3 4 5	I tend to look at people when I talk with them.
Many of my sentences contain meaningless expressions like "uh," "well," and "you know."	1 2 3 4 5	Most of my sentences are free from such expressions as "uh," "well," and "you know."
I don't consider the effect of my dress and grooming on others.	1 2 3 4 5	I consider the effect of my dress and grooming on others.
I am unaware of ways that I can control my environment to help my communication.	1 2 3 4 5	I try to control my environment in ways that help my communication.
I am unaware of or I ignore the nonverbal cues that people give while they talk.	1 2 3 4 5	I look for and try to understand the meaning of people's nonverbal behavior.
I listen in much the same way regardless of the purpose of my listening.	1 2 3 4 5	I change the way I listen depending on the purpose of my listening.
If I lose interest in the person or the ideas, I tend to quit listening.	1 2 3 4 5	I listen attentively, regardless of my interest in the person or the ideas.

First, consider your analysis. Is the number you circled indicative of where you would like to be in that category? If not, using a different color of ink or pencil, circle the number that represents your goal for this term. Then select one of the areas in which your goals are farthest from your current behavior. Write a communication improvement contract similar to the sample contract in Appendix C.

Why a written contract? Because there is often a great deal of truth to the old adage "The road to hell is paved with good intentions." It is easy to resolve, "I'm going to listen better in the future," but it is also easy to ignore that resolution. Without a clear plan and a written commitment, you are less likely to follow through.

One way to verify the accuracy of your analysis is to ask two or three persons whom you know and have worked with to complete the same analysis sheets about you. On the basis of the responses you receive, you can validate your self-analysis, making any necessary modifications.

PERCEPTION AND **Y**OUR **C**OMMUNICATION

OBJECTIVES

After you have read this chapter, you should be able to:

1   Define perception

2   Explain the processes of selection, organization, and interpretation

3   Explain how a self-concept develops

4   Explain how self-concept affects your communication

5   List factors that affect the accuracy of your perceptions of others

6   Discuss three methods of improving perceptions of self and others

As you begin reading the first major unit of this textbook, you are likely to expect to find discussions of speaking and listening. You may not realize that speaking and listening both are based or dependent upon perception. Indeed, understanding of perception underlies understanding of any form of communication. For instance, your communication with the person who shares a microscope with you in biology class depends in part on your perception of him or her; likewise, how far your communication goes depends on that person's perception of you! What you say in the speech you give at your company's sales meeting may depend on your perception of the people listening to you, while the success of your speech may depend on the audience's perception of you as a speaker.

Perception is the process of gathering sensory information and assigning meaning to it. Your eyes, ears, nose, skin, and taste buds gather information; your brain selects from among the items of information gathered, organizes the information, and finally interprets and evaluates it. The result is perception.

Perception does not necessarily provide an accurate representation of the event being perceived, but it does offer a unique portrait on which a behavioral response can be based. Some people have very accurate perceptions of their world; others, for one reason or another, distort what comes to them through their senses so much that their perceptions of self and others have very little to do with reality. We'll begin this chapter by taking a brief look at the process of perception; then we'll focus on how perception of self and others affects our communication; and finally we'll consider methods of improving self-perception and perception of others.

PERCEPTION PROCESS

We can think of the process of perception as occurring in three stages:

- selection of stimuli
- organization of stimuli
- interpretation of stimuli

Although the three stages of perception happen almost simultaneously, let's consider them one at a time.

Selection

You are subject to a variety of sensory stimuli every second, yet you focus attention on relatively few of them. For instance, right now, as you read this book, you are focusing your attention on making sense out of the visual information on this page rather than on the various sights and sounds around you. If your concentration lapses for a moment, the barking of a dog, the buzz of a lamp, or a song in the background may capture your attention, making it difficult for you to concentrate. If you are able to refocus your attention on this book, the noise again blends into the background. On what bases are these **selections** made?

Limitations of the senses   Selection is determined in part by **physiological limitations of our senses**. If you are nearsighted, you have trouble selecting visual stimuli that are far away; your eyes just can't see them. But even when the senses are keen, they have limitations. For example, human eyes perceive only certain wavelengths; you do not see the infrared or ultraviolet ends of the color spectrum. Likewise, human ears are limited to a range of between 20 and 20,000 cycles per second. This is why you cannot hear some dog whistles.

Interest   **Interest** also affects selection. What do people see when they walk on your campus for the first time? A person interested in architecture may see the beauty (or ugliness) of the buildings; a person in a wheelchair sees the steps and curbings that have to be negotiated to get from building to building; a person interested in nature sees the trees and shrubs that grace the campus.

Need   Another factor in the selection process is **need**. If you drive to school, you focus on traffic lights; cars in front of, behind, and next to you; people darting across streets; and potholes in the road. Passengers in the car, however, may be oblivious to any of these because they have no need to notice these particular sights.

Expectation   We form **expectations** on the basis of past experience. Read the phrases in the triangles (Fig. 2.1). If you are not familiar with this test, you probably read the three triangles as "Paris in the springtime," "Once in a lifetime," and "Bird in the hand." But if you look closely you will see something different. We tend not to see the repeated words because we

FIGURE 2 · 1

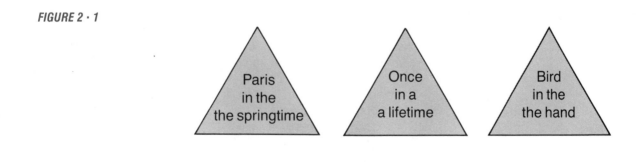

don't expect them to be there. We are so familiar with the phrases that our active perception stops once we recognize the phrase.

Whether because of sensory capability, interest, need, expectation, or any number of other potential factors, you consciously and unconsciously focus on certain stimuli.

Organization

Information is received from the senses by the brain. The brain selects from that information and then organizes its selections. Although the principles of perceptual organization are not universally agreed upon, Gestalt psychologists, who first introduced various rules of organization, consider the following as some of the most important.

Rule of simplicity   We tend to simplify a relatively complex perception into some recognizable form. Look at Figure 2.2. You are likely to see two overlapping squares (rather than an eight-sided figure) and a triangle on two posts or a covered bridge.

Rule of pattern   When people look at sets of shapes, they tend to group them along common lines. Thus, instead of perceiving a number of individual human beings, you may think of them as males and females, marrieds and singles, or young, middle-aged, and elderly. Visually, patterning is illustrated by Figure 2.3.

Rule of proximity   We tend to group those things that are physically close together. In a classroom, if you see a group of five students sitting apart from the rest of the class, you may decide they have something in common. Visually, proximity is illustrated by Figure 2.4.

Rule of good form   If a perception has a gap in it, you are likely to see it as a closed figure. We will perceive three lines that seem to join each other as a triangle even if part of a line is missing. This phenomenon explains why you may read a neon sign correctly when a portion is burned out and why you may finish a sentence correctly when a speaker leaves out a word. Visually, good form is illustrated by Figure 2.5.

Factors affecting organization   How you organize perceptions is a result of many factors, including the degree of ambiguity and your emotional state. The more ambiguous or the more complicated the information, the more difficulty there will be in organizing it. Most people have been startled by something they saw from the corner of their eye, only to discover that what they thought they saw was far different from what was actually there. Similarly, most people have mistakenly recognized a stranger as someone they knew because they saw what seemed to them a familiar coat or

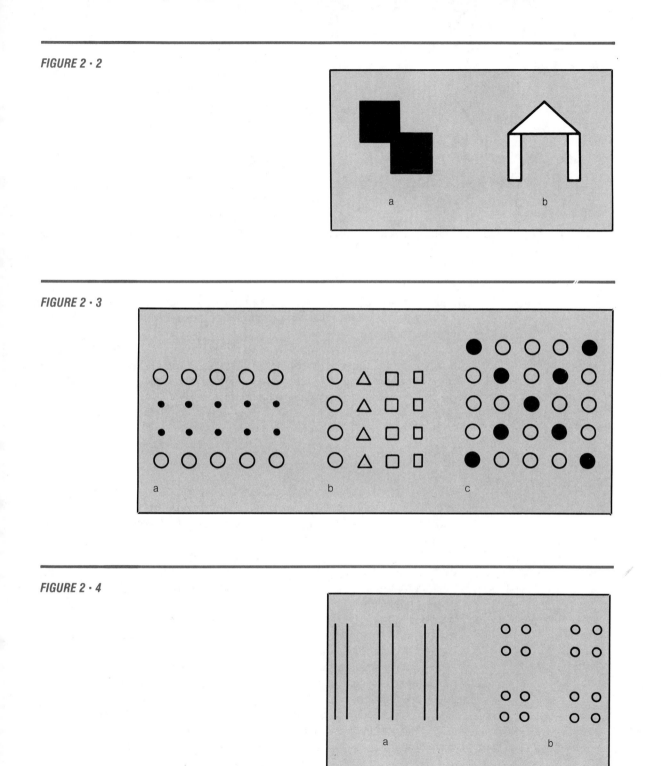

FIGURE 2 · 5

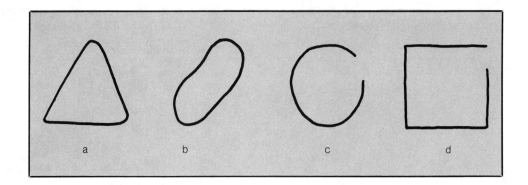

hair style or gesture. The more ambiguous the information, the more time it takes to go through the organizational process and the more likely the chance for error.

Especially important is that how you organize will be affected by how you feel at the moment of perception. When you are really hungry, you will often see everything in terms of food. You may walk down a street and be oblivious to nearly everything but places to eat.

Interpretation

As the mind selects and organizes, it completes its perception by interpreting the information it receives. **Interpretation** is the process of explaining what has been selected and organized. Because two or more people seldom select the same stimuli or organize stimuli the same way, they are unlikely to arrive at the same interpretation of events or other people. Yet the unique portrait you derive from a situation directly affects your communication. Selection and organization identify. Interpretation gives an evaluation. For instance, two people driving down a highway crowded with neon signs each identify an object as a logo for a fast-food restaurant (McDonald's golden arches, perhaps). One person may get excited about the sign; the other may not.

Figure 2.6 demonstrates the link between perception and communication; examine it very closely, and describe aloud the person you see. Talk about her age, her features, how attractive she is, what she is wearing, and what you believe she is thinking.

If you saw a young woman, your description was much different from what it would be if you saw an old woman. Which did you see? Look

FIGURE 2 · 6

again. Keep looking at the picture until you have seen both women. "Ah," you say, "but this is just a trick. No real-life situation could possibly fool me like this one." Don't believe it. People are fooled every day. People see shadows or reflections and momentarily believe they are being threatened; people see balloons, flashes of light, or cloud formations and swear they saw flying saucers.

Perception is a result of selecting, organizing, and interpreting information. Although we have great belief in the accuracy of our senses, our perceptions may well be inaccurate. Sometimes the level of inaccuracy is insignificant, but more often than we would like to believe, our perceptions are totally inaccurate. All of our communication is based on our perceptions. When our perceptions are distorted, our interpersonal communication, our decision-making communication, and our public speaking are likely to be distorted as well. Misperception leads to communication that will be inaccurate, misleading, and, at times, dangerous.

In the remainder of this chapter we want to consider the relationships between perception and self-concept and between perception and communication with others. In both cases communication may be a source of problems of self-concept and person perception; however, communication can also be a major force in strengthening self-concept and correcting inaccurate perceptions.

PRACTICE

Perceiving

1. Look around at the place where you are reading this material. Now close your eyes. What did you "see"? Open your eyes. What did you miss? What factors of selection or organization caused you to perceive what you did?

2. On a day that there are cloud formations, let your mind react to the forms the clouds are taking. What caused you to interpret your perceptions as you have?

PERCEPTION AND COMMUNICATION ABOUT SELF

In the next two sections we will study perception and communication about self and others. Why start with self? Primarily because much of the way we communicate is directly related to self-concept. We'll start with a look at the interrelationship between perception and self-concept; then we'll see how the self reveals itself through communication.

Formation of the Self-Concept

Your **self-concept** is a collection of perceptions of every aspect of your being: your appearance, physical and mental capabilities, vocational potential, size, strength, and so forth. Your self-concept is formed through self-appraisal and the reactions and responses of others; it is then presented to others through the roles you play.

Self-appraisal　You form impressions about yourself partly from what you see. You look at yourself in the mirror and make judgments about your weight and size, the clothes you wear, and your smile. These judgments affect how you feel about yourself. If you like what you see, you may feel good about yourself. If you don't like what you see, you may try to change. Perhaps you will go on a diet, buy some new clothes, get your hair styled differently, or begin jogging. If you don't like what you see and you cannot or are unwilling to change, you may begin to develop negative feelings about yourself.

Your impressions of yourself may result from your reactions to your experiences. Through experience you learn what you are good at and what you like. If you discover that you can throw a ball or a stone from twenty or thirty feet and hit your target, you are likely to see yourself as having a powerful arm. If you can strike up a conversation with a stranger and get that person to talk with you, you will probably consider yourself friendly, engaging, or interesting. Keep in mind that a single satisfying experience may not give you a positive perception of your throwing or conversational ability—just as a single negative experience may not give you a negative perception—but if additional experiences produce similar results, then the initial perception will be strengthened. People are more likely to draw conclusions based on what they choose to do rather than what they choose not to do. For instance, people who sketch may see themselves as artistic. But people who do not sketch do not necessarily think of themselves as nonartistic.[1]

In general, the greater the number of positive experiences you have—whether as a cook, lover, decision maker, student, worker, or parent—the more positive your self-concept and your communication about yourself become. Likewise, the more negative experiences you have, the more negative your self-concept and your communication about yourself become.

Reactions and responses of others   In addition to your self-perceptions, your self-concept is a result of how others react and respond to you. Suppose a colleague says to you, "You have a really friendly smile." Or suppose that after you've given your plan for developing alternate marketing strategies one of your co-workers tells you, "You're a logical thinker and convincing speaker." One comment from another person might convince you that you have a friendly smile or that you are a logical and influential speaker. Moreover, the greater your respect for the person making the comment, the greater the effect of such a comment on your perception of self. Just as positive comments may have a great impact, so also may negative comments.

You are likely to use other people's comments to validate, reinforce, or alter your perception of who and what you are. The more positive comments you receive about yourself, the more positive your total self-concept becomes.

Presenting the self   Although your self-concept is well formed by the time you are an adult, you continue to present it publicly through roles you play. As a result of how you appraise yourself and how others respond to you, you may choose or be expected to play various roles. A **role** is a pattern of behavior that characterizes a person's place in a given context. Roles are products of the value systems of society, or groups, and of the self. Society's value systems are easy to illustrate. Even today when women and men share many of the same roles, some people still expect little girls to play with dolls and homemaking toys to prepare them for the nurturing roles of wife and mother. Likewise, little boys are expected to hold back tears, to be aggressive in sports, and to play with mechanical toys in preparation for their roles as husband, father, and breadwinner.

In addition to social values, the value system of a specific group may also define your role. Your family, your social and service organizations, and every other group you belong to help shape the kind of person you are. For instance, if you are the oldest in a large family, your parents may cast you in the role of disciplinarian, brothers' and sisters' keeper, or housekeeper, depending on how they see family relationships. Or your peers may look upon you as a "joker"; you may go along by playing your role, laughing and telling stories when you really feel hurt or imposed upon.

Other roles you play are products of your own value system. You may portray yourself as "easygoing," a "fashion model," or a "bookworm" to fit your perception of self based on your own experience, to conform with impressions of others, or to reflect a role you have chosen to play.

We all play a number of roles; those we play in one context may be considerably different from those we play in another. For instance, Samantha, who is perceived as a shy, quiet, aloof person in private, may become enthusiastic, energetic, and outgoing when giving a public speech. In each new encounter you may test a role you have been playing or decide to play a new role.

How real or accurate is your self-concept? The answer depends on the accuracy of your perceptions, and accuracy varies from person to person. Yet even inaccurate perceptions of self can have a far greater effect on your behavior than reality, assuming that one can determine some objective reality.

Functions of Self-Concept

Your self-concept serves at least four communication functions:

1. It expresses predictions of behavior.
2. It filters messages received from others.
3. It influences word selection and tone of voice.
4. It moderates competing internal messages.

Predicting behavior   An important communication function of your self-concept is to express predictions of behavior. The higher your self-concept is, the more likely you are to talk in ways that predict positive experiences. The lower your self-concept is, the more likely you are to talk in ways that predict negative experiences. Soon your self-concept begins to shape reality—you begin to profit or lose by what are called "self-fulfilling prophecies." A self-fulfilling prophecy is a prediction that comes true *because* you predicted it. For example, Ed sees himself as a good public speaker; he says, "I'm going to do well on the speech assignment." Then, as a result of his positive self-concept, he remains relaxed, prepares carefully, gives the speech confidently, and, just as he predicted, does really well. On the other hand, Jeff believes himself to be a poor public speaker; he says, "I just know I'll blow the speech!" Then, because he fears speaking, his preparation is interrupted by negative thoughts; he goes into his speech tired, irritable, and worried; and, just as he predicted, he does poorly. Positive thoughts and positive language do, in fact, often produce positive results, and, unfortunately, negative thoughts and negative language may produce negative results.

Filtering evaluations   Self-concept may also affect your listening by filtering evaluations others make of you or your behavior. Even though you may receive all messages adequately (that is, your ears receive the messages and your brain records them), you do not *listen* equally to each. Moreover, what you choose to listen to is likely to be those messages that reinforce your self-concept. If someone says something that contradicts your perception, you are likely to act as if it had never been said. For example, you prepare an agenda for your study group, and someone comments that you're a good organizer. Because this remark contradicts your self-concept, you may ignore it, not really hear it, or perhaps reply, "Thanks for being kind, but it really wasn't that good" or "Anyone could have done that—it was nothing special." On the other hand, if you think you are a good organizer, you will seek out those messages that reinforce this positive view and screen out those that don't.

Perhaps you have spotted what appears to be a contradiction in this analysis of self-concept. Earlier we said that your self-concept is formed partly by listening to other people's statements. Now we are saying that the self-concept determines whether you listen to those statements or screen them out. The fact is that your self-concept is *both* a result of others' comments and a filter of others' comments. Certain comments seem to help form a self-concept. Then the self-concept begins to work as a filter, screening out certain messages. At times, however, comments will get past the filter and change the self-concept, and then the newly changed self-concept begins to filter other comments. As a result, change in self-concept does occur.

Influencing word selection and tone of voice   Your self-concept is likely to affect both your word selection and your tone of voice.[2] People with low self-concepts overuse self-criticism and self-doubt. Constant statements like "I never was any good at . . .," "I don't know why I'm even trying; I know it won't work," and "I know you're disappointed with me; I just can't seem to get it right" are examples of such self-criticism. On the other hand, people with high self-concepts are likely to speak with confidence. "I know it will be tough, but I look forward to trying," "You can count on me; I'll be giving it my best," or "I'll get the job done and you'll be pleased" are examples of the positive approach.

People with low self-concepts are more likely to put the burden of their behavior on others with such statements as "I might have done better if Tom started better" or "Sally gets A's because she butters up the instructor." Moreover, people with low self-concepts frequently adopt a whining voice when they are asked to explain their thoughts, feelings, or behavior.

Moderating competing internal messages   A fourth, particularly interesting function of self-concept is to moderate internal messages. When you are thinking, you are, in fact, talking to yourself (some people even do much of their thinking aloud). When you are faced with a difficult decision, you may be especially conscious of the different and often competing voices in your head. Perhaps this morning when your alarm went off you had a conversation much like Carl's: "There goes that blasted alarm. I'm so tired—maybe if I lie here just a few more minutes. . . . Hold on—if I don't get up now, I'll go back to sleep. Oh, who cares—I need sleep! If I slept just another fifteen minutes. . . . No! It's already later than I wanted to get up—come on, Carl, move it." What determines which of these competing voices Carl listens to? Self-concept is a moderator in the choice. If Carl feels good about himself and the day he has in store, he will probably get up right away. If, on the other hand, things aren't going well for him or there are important decisions to be made, Carl might seek to escape reality through sleep.

The psychologist Eric Berne developed a system of analyzing these internal messages, a system he called **Transactional Analysis (TA)**.[3] In brief, TA says that the kinds of thoughts that Carl experienced come from three ego states: the *Parent*, the *Child*, and the *Adult*. Statements from the Parent ego state are critical evaluative statements, the voice of conscience. They are the kinds of statements that your parents were likely to have made when you were young, such as "Don't touch the stove; you'll get burned," "Cheating on tests is wrong," and "Eat your vegetables; they're good for you." Statements from the Child ego state are emotional reactions. If you are being criticized and you burst into tears and say, "Don't say another thing—I don't want to hear it," or if you are on a roller coaster and you scream as you start down the steepest dip, you're giving voice to pure emotional reaction—you're becoming childlike. Statements from the Adult ego state encourage rational decision making. Statements like "Let me examine this carefully" or "I could go either way on this; I've got to see both sides clearly" are Adult statements.

Everyone listens to all three types of statements on occasion. If we find, however, that we almost always react emotionally or we almost always fall back on parental guidelines, we may not be meeting our personal needs best. Especially when what we're deciding is very important, we need to pay attention to those Adult voices of reason.

Although Transactional Analysis is not the only way to explain these voices in the head, many students have found some of its concepts helpful to understanding or identifying certain communication events. Knowing what kind of statements you are inclined to listen to and under what circumstances can be useful.

PRACTICE

Self-Concept

1. On a blank sheet of paper list as many of your personal characteristics as you can think of. Finish the statement "I am _____" for each characteristic. When you can think of no more, go back through the list. How many statements are positive? How many are negative?

2. On what basis did you determine each item? How many were based on perception of experience? How many on the reactions of others?

3. What roles do you play in your family? With your friends? What determines these roles?

PERCEPTION AND COMMUNICATION ABOUT OTHERS

People select, organize, and interpret observations, experiences, and opinions of others to form social perceptions. Your social perceptions lay the groundwork for the kind of relationship you are likely to have with others. In this section we'll first consider the influence of self-concept on perception of others; then we'll consider the effects of snap judgments, expectation of further interaction, halo effect, and stereotyping on the formation of these perceptions.

Influence of Self-Concept on Perception of Others

Your self-concept is a major influence on how you perceive others. Research suggests three ways your self-concept influences your perception of others.[4] First, the more accurate your self-concept, the more accurately you perceive others. Second, the more you accept yourself—that is, the more positive your self-concept—the more likely you perceive others favorably. Studies have shown that people who accept themselves are more likely to accept others; similarly, those with low self-concepts are more likely to find fault in others. Third, your own personal characteristics influence the type of characteristics you are likely to perceive in others. For example, people who are secure tend to see others as warm rather than cold.

Snap Judgments

Snap judgments are opinions you form on the basis of initial and often limited information. For instance, after a party in which Jack meets Marty for the first time at the buffet table, Jack may decide, "Marty's a jerk," or perhaps "That Marty's really got it together." Such snap judgments are often made on the basis of only a one- or two-sentence interchange! In fact, people don't even need an in-person encounter to form a snap judgment. For instance, merely looking at a photograph may cause a person to have a strong perception. Haven't you often formed an opinion on the basis of a photo alone?

Expectation of Further Interaction

You are likely to think highly of a person that you would like to be with. If Donna sees Nick as a man with whom she would like to develop a strong relationship, Donna will give weight to her positive perceptions of Nick. Donna will look only at the positive side of Nick's personality and overlook or ignore the negative side that is apparent to others. When we are in love, we are oblivious to a person's faults. Once two people have married, however, they may begin to see the negative traits of their partners, traits that may have been apparent to others all along.

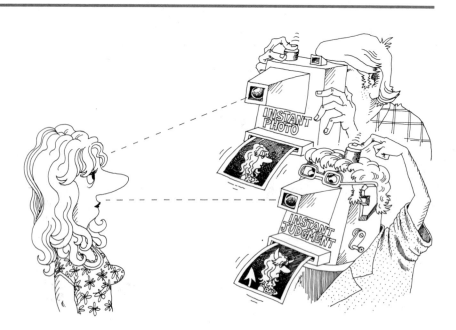

Halo Effect

You may often find yourself forming complex perceptions of someone based on a single central trait and then allowing that cue to influence your impressions of that person's other characteristics without further verification. This tendency is known as the **halo effect**. For instance, Nancy sees Marsha as a "warm" person. To Nancy "warmth" may also be correlated with "good." Because Nancy sees Marsha as "warm," she projects that Marsha is also friendly, easygoing, likeable, and supportive, whether or not Marsha actually has these qualities. Moreover, because Nancy sees warmth as good, she may also project that Marsha is honest.

Because people recognize a strong, dominating trait, they allow that trait to influence their perceptions of other traits and qualities, whether such perceptions are warranted or not. For instance, Marsha may be warm, but she may also be dishonest. If someone accuses Marsha of some dishonest act, Nancy is likely to defend Marsha because of her positive perception of Marsha. A halo effect can work to a person's advantage or disadvantage depending on whether the perception was positive or negative. But Hollman has found that negative information about people more strongly influences impressions of others than does positive information.[5]

Halo effects seem to occur most frequently under one or more of three conditions:

- when the perceiver is judging traits with which he or she has limited experience
- when the traits have strong moral overtones
- when the perception is of a person that the perceiver knows well

Stereotyping

Perhaps the greatest barrier to our accurate judgment of others is our tendency to stereotype. **Stereotyping** is maintaining a set of beliefs about the personal attributes of a group of people. Secord, Backman, and Slavitt suggest that stereotyping has four aspects or stages.

1. A person distinguishes some category or class of people—economists, for example.
2. The person observes that one or more of the individuals in this category exhibits a certain trait, such as dullness.
3. The person generalizes from this observation and perceives that everyone in this category possesses this characteristic—all economists are dull.
4. When confronted with an individual the person is not acquainted with but knows to be a member of the category, the person stereotypes this individual: She is an economist, so she is dull.[6]

Stereotyping is making a judgment about an entire group with little or no regard for individual differences within the group. You are likely to develop generalized opinions about any group you come in contact with. Your opinions may be true in a very broad sense, partially true, or totally false, depending on the accuracy and breadth of your perceptions. When you learn that a person is a member of a given group (recognition may come as a result of perception of a foreign-sounding name, a religious medal, gray hair, or any number of other signs), you may automatically project your general opinions onto the individual person. If Allen stereotypes a group as pushy, greedy, and insensitive, as soon as he learns that Dave is a member of that group, he automatically perceives Dave as pushy, greedy, and insensitive.

Stereotyping is a major problem for two obvious reasons. First, it is extremely likely that the original stereotype of a group is wrong. That one person or five people who happen to belong to a group are greedy does not mean that all members of the group are greedy. Yet we perceive some

Does this photograph depict a man or a woman? How do stereotypes that you hold influence your perception of this portrait?

characteristic of one or two people and assume that the entire group has those characteristics. Second, those who stereotype compound the problem by assuming that a different person has the same characteristics just because that person is a member of the same group. So even if 90 percent of a group were greedy, that does not mean that Dave is greedy just because he is a member of that group.

If stereotypes are often inaccurate, why do they persist? One reason is that people look for shortcuts: It is easier to work with an inaccurate stereotype of a person or group of people than to take the time to really learn about the individuals involved. Another reason is that people believe stereotypes are helpful. In unfamiliar social settings general guidelines help people interpret what is happening. Stereotypes help people classify others and thus guide their behavior in what they hope are socially acceptable responses. For example, a young man may stereotype an older, well-dressed woman as being old-fashioned. Not wanting to offend her, he may use his stereotype of older women to guide his behavior. Thus, he quickly steps ahead to open the door for her when she is ready to leave. Stereotyping is hard to combat because a person can always find in a group one or more members with characteristics that gave rise to the stereotype. Throughout this text we will try to remind you that opinions about people must be formed on data about each individual, not on stereotypes of groups.

Accuracy of Perceptions

We know that we will form perceptions about people; we also know that these perceptions will form the bases of our interaction with these people. How accurate are our perceptions of others likely to be? Research results are inconclusive. Some people make reasonably accurate judgments rather consistently; others make judgments that are neither consistent nor accurate. Given the inconclusive nature of the research, we believe that you are better off not relying solely on your impressions to determine how another person feels or what that person is really like.

PRACTICE

Social Perceptions

1. Your instructor will ask for three volunteers, who will leave the classroom. One at a time they will reenter the room and describe to the class a full-page magazine ad that the instructor has given

them. On the basis of their descriptions, try to visualize the picture as clearly as you can. Then, again using the three descriptions, determine your perception of the person or persons in the ad. When the three volunteers have finished, your instructor will show you the ad.

2. What were the differences among the three descriptions? How did your image differ from the actual picture? How can you account for the differences? Did your perception of the person or persons in the picture change after you actually saw the picture? How?

IMPROVING PERCEPTION OF SELF AND OTHERS

Because inaccuracies in perception are common and influence how you communicate, improving your perceptual accuracy will help you start to become a competent communicator. In addition to information we have already covered, the following suggestions can help you improve the accuracy of your social perceptions.

1. *Always actively question the accuracy of your perceptions before you act.* Too often people accept their perceptions without question and behave accordingly. People persist in making such statements as "I was there—I know what I saw." Instead, you need to say to yourself, "I know what I *think* I saw, heard, tasted, smelled, or felt, but I *could* be wrong." By accepting the possibility of error, you may be motivated to seek further verification. Increased accuracy of perception is worth the few seconds it takes to double-check.

   In later chapters we will consider the important skills of paraphrasing and perception checking that you can use to ensure the accuracy of your perceptions. A **paraphrase** is a verbal statement of your understanding of the meaning of what another person has said; a **perception check** is a verbal statement of your understanding of the meaning of a person's nonverbal behavior.

2. *Keep a lookout for information that tests your perceptions.* Once you have drawn a conclusion about yourself or others, you begin to behave in accordance with that conclusion. As a competent communicator, you must continue to collect information to test the accuracy of your perceptions. Try to make a mental note that any and all perceptions are tentative and subject to change.

   It takes strength of character to say to yourself or others, "I was wrong." But communicating on the basis of outdated, inaccurate perceptions can be more costly than revising your perceptions.

3. *Learn to separate inferences from facts.* Perception involves selecting, organizing, and interpreting information. Interpretation often involves drawing an inference from a set of observed facts. Yet we sometimes forget that the inference we draw may not be a fact. Let's consider the difference.

Ellen tells a friend that she saw a Bob's TV Repair truck in her neighbor's driveway for the fifth time in the last two weeks. Ellen is reporting only what she saw; she is relating a perception of fact. A **fact** is a verifiable statement—usually a statement about something that can be or has been directly observed. If, however, Ellen adds, "She's having a terrible time getting her TV fixed," she would be making an **inference**—a conclusion about what has been observed. Ellen would be concluding—without actually knowing—that the truck was at her neighbor's house because someone was trying to repair a television set. This inference drawn from the fact may be true, but it may not be. The driver of the truck might be a friend of Ellen's neighbor, or they may be having an affair, or perhaps a special system is being installed, or whatever. The reporting of the presence of the truck is fact; the explanation for the presence of the truck is inference. Separating fact from inference means being able to tell the difference between a verifiable observation and an opinion related to that observation.

There is nothing wrong with drawing inferences; they are necessary to make sense of the world. However, you would be wise to remember these three things:

1. You should know when you are inferring and when you are reporting factual observation.
2. You should recognize that your inferences may or may not be true,— and inferences should not be stated as if they were.
3. You should not act as though your inferences are facts.

PRACTICE

Separating Inferences from Facts

Read the following statement. Assume that all information presented is accurate and true.

▶ The only vehicle parked in front of 725 Main Street is a red truck. The words "Bob Jones TV Repair" are spelled in large letters across the side panels of the truck.

Indicate whether the following statements made in reference to the preceding statement are F (fact) or I (inference).

_____ a. "Tom, there's a red truck parked in front of 725 Main."
_____ b. "Yes, I see it. It belongs to Bob Jones, the TV repair man."
_____ c. "Looks like the people living at 725 need their TV fixed."
_____ d. "Well, if it can be fixed, Bob Jones will fix it."

ANSWERS: **a.** Fact. **b.** Inference. (Beware of inferences in fact clothing! If someone says, "I see it," don't be fooled. Bob Jones may have just sold this truck and the new owner may not have had time to change the lettering.) **c.** Inference. (Someone may need a TV repaired, but from the statements we don't know that as a fact.) **d.** Inference. (If there is something wrong, the repairman may fix it—the repairman may or may not be Bob Jones.)

2. Now here's another statement. Read it and label the comments referring to it as you did previously.

▶ Two people came hurrying out of a bank with several large bundles, hopped into a long black car, and sped away. Seconds later, a man rushed out of the bank waving his arms and looking quite upset.

_____ a. "The bank's been robbed!"
_____ b. "Yes, indeed—we saw the robbers hurry out of the bank, hop into a car and speed away."
_____ c. "It was a long black car."
_____ d. "The men were carrying several large bundles."
_____ e. "Seconds after they left a man came out of the bank after them— but he was too late; they'd already escaped."

ANSWERS: **a.** Inference. **b.** Inference. **c.** Fact. **d.** Inference (men?). **e.** Inference.

SUMMARY

Perception is the process of assigning meaning to sensory information. Our perceptions are a result of our selection, organization, and interpretation of sensory information. Inaccurate perceptions cause us to see the world not as it is but as we would like to see it or as we want it to be.

A person's self-concept is a collection of perceptions that relate to every aspect of that person's being. The self-concept is formed by views of self and experiences and by other people's comments about self and behavior. The self-concept is presented publicly through roles played. The self-concept serves at least four basic communication functions: It predicts behavior, it filters evaluations from others, it influences word selection and tone of voice, and it moderates competing internal messages.

Perception also plays an important role in forming impressions of others. Because research shows that the accuracy of people's perceptions and judgments varies considerably, you will have more successful communication if you do not rely entirely on your impressions to determine how another person feels or what that person is really like. You will improve (or at least better understand) your perception of others if you will take into account self-concept, snap judgments, expectation of further interaction, the halo effect, and stereotyping.

You can learn to improve perception if you question the accuracy of your perceptions, seek more information to verify perceptions, and learn to separate inferences from facts.

SUGGESTED READINGS

Centi, Paul. *Up with the Positive: Out with the Negative.* Englewood Cliffs, N.J.: Prentice-Hall, 1981. This relatively short book gives very readable insight into the development of the self-concept. As the title suggests, throughout the book Centi emphasizes the positive aspects of dealing with self-concept. Contains many interesting self-tests and exercises.

Deaux, Kay, and Lawrence S. Wrightsman. *Social Psychology in the '80s.* 4th ed. Monterey, Calif.: Brooks/Cole, 1984. One of the many excellent social psychology books available.

Goldstein, E. Bruce. *Sensation and Perception.* 2nd ed. Belmont, Calif.: Wadsworth, 1984. See especially Chapters 7 and 14 on perception of speech.

Schneider, David J., Albert H. Hastorf, and Phoebe C. Ellsworth. *Person Perception.* 2nd ed. Reading, Mass.: Addison-Wesley, 1979. An excellent, relatively short work that puts emphasis on perception of people. Draws together some of the best research findings available.

Suls, Jerry, and Anthony G. Greenwald, eds. *Psychological Perspectives on the Self.* Vol. 2. Hillsdale, N.J.: Lawrence Erlbaum Associates, 1983. A collection of articles on self-concept that summarize recent research.

3 **C**OMMUNICATING **V**ERBALLY

OBJECTIVES

After you have read this chapter, you should be able to:

1   List and discuss five principles of language development

2   Explain the difference between denotation and connotation

3   Prepare a semantic differentiation

4   Use precise words

5   Use specific and concrete words

6   Use provisional words

7   Date generalizations

8   Index generalizations

Many serious students of our culture are concerned by modern Americans' apparent lack of sophistication with the use of the English language. This problem occurs with young and old alike. Although family members and close friends often seem to understand each other intuitively regardless of their word selection or grammar, failure to communicate clearly with words is a major problem in the marketplace. In such important contexts as interviewing for a job, giving a speech, talking with your professor at school or your boss at work, or coping with conflict, a premium is placed on word choice and sentence construction.

The English language is a system of symbols used for communicating. This system consists of known words (vocabulary) arranged in certain learned ways (grammar and syntax). How well you communicate depends in part on your vocabulary and your grammar and syntax. In this chapter we'll review the relationship between language and meaning and the important differences between word denotation and word connotation. We'll also consider several specific skills you can develop to help you improve your communication performance.

LANGUAGE AND MEANING

The collections of sounds we call words are only symbols; they have no intrinsic meaning. It's the users who give meaning to them. Learning how words come to have meaning helps us understand how language works to communicate. The competent communicator understands these five points:

1. Language is creative.
2. Language is purposeful.
3. Language is arbitrary.
4. Language is learned.
5. Language and perception are interrelated.

Language Is Creative

When you speak, you use language to create new sentences that represent ideas you are thinking or feelings you are having. Although you may on occasion repeat other people's constructions to represent what you are thinking or feeling, most of your speech is significantly different from what anyone else has said. To test this out, have three people witness the same event, and then have each in turn tell the class about it. Although there will be many similarities in what was said, each person will present a unique, creative approach to the material witnessed.

Language Is Purposeful

You usually have a reason to say something. More often than not, when you speak you are expecting the other person to react to you or to your message. You may be expecting them to acknowledge information or to think or act a certain way.

Language Is Arbitrary

Word meaning is a matter of choice. Whether the word is *chair, sister,* or *predilectory,* we know that someone at some time had to choose to use those letters (sounds) in that order for the first time. But, even though someone chose to use "sister," for example, to convey the idea of a female sibling, the use of the word *sister* as a symbol with some specific meaning wasn't possible until others agreed to use that word when they wanted to express the idea of a female sibling.

Frequently people form new words using certain sound patterns to stand for meaning; the word does not become a part of the language until other people have used the word often enough to make it conventional.

Language Is Learned

Each new generation must learn the language anew. Children's brains enable them to think, and they have a vocal mechanism that allows them to form any number of sounds. But how to determine which sounds go together to form which words must be taught from generation to generation.

By the time children are between three and five years old, they have learned enough vocabulary to communicate almost all their basic ideas and feelings and have mastered enough grammar to be understood. From then on, they enlarge their vocabulary and sharpen their understanding of grammar.

How do people learn? Blaine Goss states four principles that guide language learning.[1] First, development proceeds from simple to complex. Specific and concrete one-syllable words that denote familiar objects and people are likely to be learned first.

Second, language acquisition is overgeneralized. Notice how children will say "I *goed* (rather than *went*) to the store." They hear play/played, walk/walked, and so on, and they generalize that all verbs become past tense by adding -ed. Later in the learning process they learn to differentiate verbs that do not follow this rule.

Third, our listening capabilities exceed our speaking capabilities. We all understand more than we can verbalize—our reading vocabulary, for instance, is much larger than our speaking vocabulary. This principle of language learning is at the heart of the teaching philosophy expressed in this book. For instance, you may already *know* many of the skills we will discuss, but you are likely to find that you do not *use* them very well or that in some cases you do not use them at all.

Fourth, people pay attention to the nonverbal as well as to the verbal aspects of communication. Even though we emphasize the verbal aspect of meaning in this chapter, as we discuss various communication skills we will stress both the language and the sound of voice, the gestures, and the facial expressions that accompany the words.

The implication of the point that meanings are learned is that people do not learn exactly the same meanings for words or exactly the same words. We should never assume, therefore, that another person will know what we are talking about just because we have used the "right" word.

Language and Perception Are Interrelated

It is easy to see that perception affects language. For instance, if we encounter a situation that no word in our vocabulary can describe, we are likely either to form a new word or to use an old word in a new way to describe the situation. Likewise, if we see an object different from any other known object, we choose a new word to label it.

That the words in our language shape our perceptions is a far more controversial assertion. The idea that language shapes perception was developed by Benjamin Lee Whorf with suggestions from Edward Sapir. In the early 1950s Whorf presented what is now called the Sapir–Whorf hypothesis. The gist of the hypothesis is that your perception of reality is determined by the language system that controls your thought system. For instance, Eskimos have different words for different kinds of snow, such as *gana* (falling snow) and *akilukak* (fluffy fallen snow). These two words are different from each other. In English we say simply *snow*. We can add words (fallen, fluffy, hard-packed), but in each case the word *snow* is included. The Sapir–Whorf hypothesis suggests that, when confronted with many different samples of frozen moisture, the American will perceive all the different sizes, shapes, and densities as *snow*. Eskimos, on the other hand, perceive snow in many different ways because they have the language flexibility to do so.

The Sapir–Whorf hypothesis allows us to see how different people from different places will *think* differently and *communicate* differently because of differences in both language and perception. Although you are not likely to be communicating much with Eskimos unless you live in Alaska, a lot of your communicating does cross cultural and socioeconomic boundaries. As a result, you must not assume either that the words you use will mean the same to others or that you will even see the same realities that others see.

PRACTICE

Creating New Words

As an experiment, create a nonsense word. Use it in your conversation. Who understands? Do any others begin to use the word? When? Under what circumstances?

COMPLICATIONS IN USING WORDS

Science fiction writers have worked for years on the premise that advanced societies will develop some form of telepathy so that a person will be able to share meanings directly with another. But until such a time, we must share our ideas and feelings indirectly through a system of symbols—through words. This symbol system is often an imperfect means of sharing. Since words carry both denotative and connotative meanings, you need to be able to distinguish between them and understand the complications related to each.

Denotation

Denotation is the direct, explicit meaning people give to a word; in short, denotation is the meaning given in a dictionary. Although dictionary definitions contribute to our ability to communicate accurately, even with a dictionary at hand, we can still encounter many problems with meaning. Let's examine a few.

Dictionary differences   Very few words are defined exactly the same way in each of the most popular American dictionaries. And even though most of the differences are minor, they illustrate the problems we face when we rely on their information. Let's take the word *dog*. *Webster's New World Dictionary* says a dog is "any of a large and varied group of domesticated animals related to the fox, wolf, and jackal."[2] *Webster's New Intercollegiate Dictionary* (published by another company even though the word *Webster's* is in both titles) says a dog is "a carnivorous domesticated mammal, type of the family Canidae."[3]

Why do these differences occur? Most dictionaries are compiled in the same way. Companies survey printed materials to see how people use words. Then, based on these surveys, someone writes a definition. Depending on what written work is surveyed and who writes the definition, some differences are bound to occur. Both definitions of *dog* quoted above classify and differentiate. Nevertheless, if the only knowledge you had about a dog was from these two dictionary definitions, you can see the confusion that might result in your understanding.

Multiple meanings   An even more confusing fact is that a great many words we use daily have more than one distinct meaning. If we looked up the 500 most commonly used American words in any dictionary, we'd be likely to find more than 14,000 definitions. Some of these definitions would be similar, but some would be much different. Take the word *low*, for instance. *Webster's New World Dictionary* offers 26 meanings for *low*. Number 1 is "of little height or elevation"; number 8 is "near the equator"; and number 16 is "mean; despicable; contemptible."[4] No matter how we look at these three definitions, we have to admit that they are quite different.

As words get more difficult we begin to find fewer and fewer definitions. Thus, it is with the use of our most common words that we have the greatest number of choices. These common words have so many different meanings that unless we carefully examine context, we may get (or give) the wrong idea. On the other hand, if we use the more precise word, there may be some in our audience who are not familiar with it.

Changes in meanings   As time goes on, words both acquire and lose meanings. According to W. Nelson Francis, in the 700 years *nice* has been in the English language, it "has been used at one time or another to mean the following: foolish, wanton, strange, lazy, coy, modest, fastidious, refined, precise, subtle, slender, critical, attentive, minute, accurate, dainty, appetizing, agreeable."[5]

We all know some words that have changed their meaning over a relatively short period of time. Our communication is most affected when these changes are quick and/or dramatic. Take the word *gay*. In the fifties and sixties, people spoke of having a "gay old time," of Jack being a "gay blade," and of the state of "being gay" as being happy. In each case *gay* meant joyous, merry, happy, or bright. Today, the state of "being gay" is most likely to refer to a person's sexual preference. Although *gay* as joyous is still heard sometimes, it is becoming obsolete. If you describe another person as "gay" and you mean happy or joyous, you will probably be totally misunderstood.

Influence of context   The position of a word in a sentence and the other words around it may change the denotation. When a young girl says, "Dad, you owe me a dime," the meaning is somewhat different from when she says, "Dad, I need a dime for the machine." In the first case, she is looking for two nickels, ten pennies, five pennies and a nickel, or a single ten-cent piece. In the second case, she is looking specifically for that small coin that we call a dime.

Examples of influence of context abound. Think of the difference between "George plays a really *mean* drum" and "The way George talked to Sally was downright *mean*."

PRACTICE

Word Denotation

1. Make a list of current "slang" or "in" words. How do the meanings you assign to these words differ from the meanings your parents or grandparents assign?

2. Write your own definition of each of the following words. Then go to a dictionary and check to see how closely your definition matches the dictionary's.

rabbit	building	love
cloud	career	justice
freedom	pride	peace
glass	ring	success

Connotation

Whereas denotation refers to the standard dictionary meaning given to a word, **connotation** refers to the feelings or evaluations associated with a word.

Earlier, we noted that the word *dog* denotes a domesticated animal. But because at some time in your life you have had experiences with dogs, you have feelings and attitudes that define *dog* for you in a way that may be much different from the way another person defines *dog*. Suppose that as a child you had a dog that was a constant companion, slept with you at night, licked you when you came home from school, lay at your feet as you watched television, and wagged its tail at the sight of you. Your meaning for *dog* would be far different from the meaning of *dog* for a person who never had one for a pet, had been bitten six times by dogs for "no reason," and is allergic to dog hair.

So when Carl says to Paul, "I'm buying a dog this week," Carl must understand that his sentence denotes the purchase of a domesticated mammal—a denotation that Paul is likely to share. But the statement also carries a connotation that will be shared only if Carl and Paul have had similar experiences with dogs and, as a result, feel much the same way about them. In short, the meaning when Carl says *dog* may be different from the meaning when Paul says *dog*, because Carl and Paul are likely to have different connotations for *dog*.

As an effective communicator you must take into account both the denotative meaning and the potential connotative meaning of words to the specific person or persons with whom you are communicating.

Semantic differentiation   Since people's feelings about words do vary considerably, scientists have been trying to find ways of measuring the nature and intensity of those feelings. Let us briefly describe one method that has gained wide use among psychologists and communication scholars. Charles Osgood and his associates developed an approach to word connotation that focuses on dimensions of meaning.[6] Each dimension of meaning is part of a total feeling a person has about a word. The method used by Osgood involves describing feelings about words through *bipolar adjectives* (adjectives that are opposites of each other).

Why did Osgood and his associates focus their study on adjectives? If you list the responses that come to your mind when someone says words like *dog, camp,* or *home,* you will see that many, if not all, of the words you choose are adjectives. You may think of *dog, camp,* or *home* in terms of pleasant, big or small, happy or sad, attractive or unattractive.

As they studied the various responses, Osgood and his associates grouped them in identifiable categories called *dimensions.* There are many of these dimensions, but the three most common are adjectives of evaluation, adjectives of potency or intensity, and adjectives of activity or movement. They found that good–bad, awful–nice, ugly–beautiful, and valuable–worthless are pairs that can be used to measure the *evaluation dimension.* Strong–weak, light–heavy, and large–small are used to measure the *potency dimension.* And hot–cold, active–passive, and fast–slow are used to measure the *activity dimension.* Their work resulted in a semantic differentiation test that can be administered to groups and individuals alike.[7] A test using only the ten pairs just cited can be used to compare how one person or one group feels in comparison to another person or another group on a specific word like *dog, camp,* or *home.*

The value of such a test is that it gives us the ability to compare one person's feelings with another's. For example, is one person's feeling about the word *home* more or less positive? Stronger or weaker? More or less active? Second, it enables us to compare a person's reaction to several different words. Does the person see *home* differently from *resort, farm, camp,* or *trailer?* Third, the test enables us to compare a person's feelings about a word at different times. Does a person feel differently about *camp* after spending six weeks at one?

When is the value of this kind of knowledge to you in your communication? If you know how others feel about the words they use, you can better understand and communicate with them. Consider a schoolteacher who wants to develop a teaching unit on the theme "A community is a group of people who help one another." It would be useful for that teacher to discover how the class feels about such words as *community, home, police,* and *businessperson* before beginning the unit. Or consider the value of semantic differentiation to the congresswoman who would like to know how the people in her district feel about words like *busing, schools,* and *taxes* before she begins preparing campaign speeches.

PRACTICE

Word Connotation

Working in groups, construct a test using five pairs of bipolar adjectives. Use at least five check points between the words to represent variations in reactions (*good . . . . . bad*). Then select a word to test (*dog, home, class, textbook,* and so on). Each member of the group should take the test. Then compute the results for the group. On which pairings were reactions similar? On which were they different? Discuss the results.

GUIDELINES FOR IMPROVING YOUR VERBAL COMMUNICATION

In nearly every chapter in this textbook, we consider verbal skills that you can use to communicate more effectively. The following skills are equally applicable to interpersonal, group, and public-speaking settings.

Select the Most Precise Word

For any idea or feeling you wish to communicate, you have many words from which to choose. Speaking **precisely** requires that you select the words that best represent your ideas. Although you can never be completely sure that the words you choose will create a meaning for others that is exactly what you intended, the less precise your word choice, the greater the chance for misunderstanding. Suppose that you told a friend that you had just finished a snack. Your friend would most likely picture a small amount of food. If, however, you had eaten two sandwiches, a large bag of potato chips, a bowl of soup, and three glasses of milk, the word *snack* would hardly be the most precise word for describing what you ate.

Many times we use the first word that comes to mind, whether it is precise or not. Yet the words you choose may make large differences in what another person envisions. Consider the sentence "'I'll be there in a minute,' Donna said." Notice the difference in meaning you get when you replace *said* with *growled, shouted, purred, whispered, whined,* or *cried.*

To communicate more precisely, you may need to enlarge your vocabulary. Your vocabulary, as well as the vocabulary of those with whom you communicate, affects the degree of your communication success. In general, the smaller your vocabulary, the greater the potential difficulty in communicating effectively. As a speaker you will have fewer choices from which to select the word that you want; as a listener you will be limited in your ability to understand the words used. Recall that it is the most common words in our language that have the greatest number of meanings.

One way to enlarge your vocabulary is to work through a basic vocabulary book such as Agel's *Test Your Word Power,* noted in the suggested readings at the end of this chapter. Another way is to take a more active role in working with the words you hear and read every day. Begin by noting words that people use in their conversations with you that you are *not* able to define precisely. For instance, suppose Jackie says, "I was *inundated* with phone calls today!" If you can't give a precise definition for *inundated*, you could ask Jackie what she meant by that word. But if for some reason you don't wish to ask Jackie, you can still make a note of the word, look up its meaning at the first opportunity, and then review what Jackie said to see whether the dictionary meaning seems to be what Jackie meant. Most dictionaries define *inundated* with synonyms such as *overwhelmed* and *flooded*. If you then say to yourself, "Jackie was inundated— overwhelmed or flooded—with phone calls today," you will tend to remember that meaning and apply it the next time you hear the word. You can follow the same procedure in your reading. As you are reading today's assignment in one of your courses, circle any words about which you have any question. After you have finished the assignment, go back to those words and look them up.

Most of us are confronted with several words each day for which we are unable to supply precise meanings. By following the practice of noting those words and then looking them up, you can increase your vocabulary tremendously. The better your vocabulary, the more precise your communication is likely to be. Although precise wording does not ensure effective communication (the person to whom you are speaking may not understand that word, or contextual factors may interfere), you are more likely to communicate effectively if your word choice is precise.

Select the Most Specific and/or Concrete Word

Precision helps sharpen meaning by giving the best or most correct image; being specific and concrete helps to sharpen meaning by limiting the number of choices in a category. People who don't discipline themselves to think sharply fill their conversations—and their writing—with words that are too general or abstract to limit choices. General and abstract words allow the listener the choice of many possible images rather than a single intended image. The more listeners are called on to provide their own images, the more likely their images will be different from the meaning you intended.

General means an entire category; **specific** means one item within a category. What do you picture when someone says "car"? It may be any number of four-wheeled vehicles used primarily to transport people. You may picture a large car or a small one, a sedan or a coupe, a Buick or a Datsun. If, on the other hand, someone says "small red sedan," the number of choices of image you can picture is reduced. If the person says "small, red, two-door Ford Escort," the likelihood that you and the person doing the talking will be picturing a similar image is considerably better.

Whereas "*general* versus *specific*" deals with object language, "*abstract* versus *concrete*" deals with ideas or values. **Concrete** language turns an abstract idea or value into clearly pictured behavior. When people say they are loyal, for instance, you may think they mean faithful. However, what *loyal* means in a particular situation is hard to say. What is an act of loyalty to Jim or to Sarah may not be an act of loyalty to you. To avoid ambiguity and confusion, instead of saying that "Bill is loyal," a person might say, "Bill always buys his company's products." On hearing such a statement you would have a sharper image of the speaker's meaning.

Semanticists speak of levels of abstraction. Meaning can be moved from general to specific (abstract to concrete) through a series of words. For example, from the general word *building* we can move to increasingly more specific words: *domestic structures, houses, two-story houses, Cape Cods.*

When you select a general or abstract word to carry your meaning, you are inviting confusion. A listener may take the time to ask you questions to help sharpen the meaning of your message. But it is more likely that he or she will be satisfied with his or her *own* meaning, whether or not it coincides with yours. On the other hand, if you select specific or concrete language to carry your meaning, a person will more likely share your meaning without having to question you. In summary, then, speaking in specific and concrete language means using words that indicate a single item within a category or a single representation of an abstract concept or value.

Although you can and should work to improve word selection in conversation, you will find it especially important in public speaking, where people seldom have a chance to question you about what you meant.

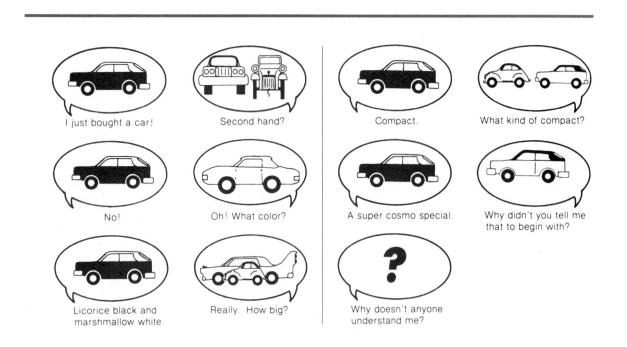

I just bought a car!

Second hand?

Compact.

What kind of compact?

No!

Oh! What color?

A super cosmo special.

Why didn't you tell me that to begin with?

Licorice black and marshmallow white.

Really. How big?

Why doesn't anyone understand me?

State Beliefs Provisionally

Competent communicators use provisional rather than dogmatic language to express beliefs. **Provisional** wordings suggest that the ideas are thought to be—but may not be—correct; **dogmatic** wordings leave no room for discussion. Whereas provisional language helps create or maintain a good communication climate, dogmatic statements stop discussion and usually create defensiveness.

The following paired sentences illustrate the differences between provisional and dogmatic statements:

▶ *If I remember rightly*, Dalton holds the record for most sales in a month.

I'm telling you, Dalton holds the record for most sales in a month.

▶ *It's my opinion that* this is no time to buy a house.

Everybody knows this is no time to buy a house.

Why is the first sentence of each pair, stated provisionally, more likely to result in better communication? First, the tone is different. Although we can't see a difference in vocal tone, the tentative phrasing is likely to result in a less certain tone of voice than in the second sentence; also, the tone of the phrasing is better. The words themselves convey a tentativeness that is less antagonizing. Second, both cases demonstrate the recognition that the words come from the speaker—and that the speaker may be wrong. "I'm telling you" leaves no room for possible error; on the other hand, "If I remember rightly" not only leaves room for error but also shows that it is the speaker's recollection and not a statement of universal certainty. Both sets of statements are asserting the "truth." Although the first set considers facts that are a matter of record (they can be validated by looking at company records), neither, as stated, is *necessarily* true. The other set of statements are matters of opinion—they are inferences drawn from facts, but, again, they are not necessarily true.

Speaking provisionally allows for different opinions and acknowledges that something that seems to be true under certain circumstances may not be entirely true—or may not be true at all under different circumstances. On occasion, speaking provisionally may seem unassertive and wishy-washy; if carried to an extreme, it may be. But there is a world of difference in stating what you think is true and stating it in a way that is likely to arouse hostility.

Speaking dogmatically suggests superiority. How do you feel when people say something that you interpret as meaning that they know more or are better than you are? If you are like most people, you get angry, especially when you are not convinced of the superiority.

Date Generalizations When Appropriate

Dating generalizations means including a specific time reference in your statements that indicates when a given fact was true. When we share information we can unintentionally create mistaken impressions by failing to date the information. For instance, Park says, "I'm going to be transferred to Henderson City." Bill replies, "Henderson City—they've had some real trouble with their schools." On the basis of Bill's statement Park is likely to be concerned about what this move might mean to his family. What Park doesn't know is that Bill was talking about a problem that Henderson City had *five years ago*! Henderson City still may have problems, but it may not. Had Bill replied, "Five years ago they had some real trouble with their schools, but I don't know what the situation is now," Park would look at the information differently.

Conclusions we draw are based on information we have or get. When the information is accurate, the conclusions we draw from that information are more likely to be accurate.

The fact is that nearly everything changes with time. Some changes may be nearly imperceptible, but others are so great as to make a person, idea, place, or thing nearly unrecognizable. Include a time reference that specifies *when* the statement was true and if it is still likely to be true: for example, "When we were in Palm Springs *two years ago*, it was really popular with the college crowd," or "Powell brings great enthusiasm to her teaching—at least she did *last quarter* in communication theory."

Index Generalizations

Indexing is a companion skill to dating. Dating accounts for differences caused by the passing of time. **Indexing** is the verbal practice of accounting for individual differences among groups of people, objects, or places.

Indexing is a verbal effort to counter the effect of overgeneralizing. *Generalizations* are the conclusions about classes of objects, people, or behaviors that allow you to apply what you have learned from one experience to another. For instance, when Glenda learns that fertilization helped both of her neighbors' tomatoes and squash grow better, she generalizes that fertilizing will help all vegetables to grow better, including hers. When Sam's girlfriend says she likes the fragrance of the new after-shave he is wearing, he is likely to generalize and believe that she will always like it, so he wears the same after-shave all the time.

Yet generalizations by their nature have exceptions. For instance, that men (a class) *in general* have greater strength than women (a class) does not mean that Max (one man) is stronger than Barbara (one woman).

Likewise, that one Chevrolet goes 50,000 miles without a brake job does not mean that *all* Chevrolets can or that *my* Chevrolet can.

Technically, indexing would call for you to assign numbers to each member of a class in order to differentiate man[1] from man[2] from man[3] and so forth. But how you can index generalizations in a conversation? For comparison we will pair a generalization with a similar statement that is properly indexed.

GENERALIZATION
Since men are stronger than women, Max is stronger than Barbara.

INDEXED
Men are *in general* stronger than women, so Max *is probably* stronger than Barbara, but not necessarily.

GENERALIZATION
Your Chevrolet should go 50,000 miles before you need a brake job; Jerry's did.

INDEXED
Your Chevrolet may well get 50,000 miles before you need a brake job; Jerry's did, *but of course, all Chevrolets aren't the same.*

As you make generalized statements about an object, person, or place, index your statement to show your listener that the generalization is not necessarily accurate.

Avoid Statements That May Have Double Meanings

Much of our metaphoric language carries the potential for opposite connotations. For instance, if in referring to Alice's work habits you say "Alice is a real workhorse," some people may think you are referring to Alice's appearance.

Even more likely is the potential for double meaning in your message resulting from differences between what you say and how you say it. When you say, "Ouch!" you are likely to have a pained expression on your face and a pained sound in your voice. But our verbal and nonverbal messages are not always complementary. For example, a person may answer the question "Do you still love me?" with the words "Of course I do," but nonverbal signals may contradict the words. In this situation the listener is more likely to pay attention to the nonverbal cue than to the words. Why? Because words can be controlled much more easily than facial expression or tone of voice. We'll explore ways nonverbal cues affect meaning in the next chapter.

Avoid Sexist or Racist Language

Not only do words hurt us as much as "sticks and stones"; language may also have accidental repercussions. We should be especially careful to avoid any language that could be termed sexist or racist. *Sexist* or *racist* language is any language perceived as negative and that occurs solely because of differences in sex, race, or national origin. As you monitor your speaking, be on the lookout for the following:

1. Using words with built-in sexism, such as *policeman, mailman, chairman*. More acceptable are such labels as *police officer, mail carrier,* and *chairperson*.
2. Modifying generic labels with the words *black* or *female*, such as *black doctor* or *female professor*. Instead of saying "Roberts is a highly respected black surgeon" or "Carson is a good female professor," just leave out the modifiers. In each case, the modification takes away from the value of the praise: "Carson is a good female professor" means "Carson is a good professor for a woman, although compared to men she's nothing special."
3. Using masculine pronouns when no sexual reference is intended. A sentence such as "A doctor is an important member of a community; he is respected and deferred to and stands as a role model" is grammatically correct. Nevertheless, many people feel that the generic use of *he* excludes women and find such usage offensive. It would be better to cast this sentence in the plural: "Doctors are important members of their community; they are respected and deferred to and stand as role models."

Recognize the Effects of Pressure

When you are relaxed and confident, your communication usually flows smoothly and is most effective. When you are under pressure, however, the effectiveness of your communication is likely to deteriorate. Your greatest problems with language will occur when you are under pressure. For instance, you may have heard parents of a large family run through the names of all the children before getting the right name when they felt pressure.

Your brain is like a computer: It is a marvelous instrument, but it does fail to work well sometimes. More often than not, the failures happen when you are under pressure or when you speak before you think. People sometimes think one thing and say something entirely different. Consider a familiar scene: The math professor says, "We all remember that the numerator is on the bottom of the fraction and the denominator is on the top, so when we divide fractions—" "Professor," a voice from the third row interrupts, "You said the numerator is on the bottom and—" "Is that what I said?" the professor replies. "Well, you know what I meant!" Did everyone in the class know? Probably not.

PRACTICE

Language Skills

1. Which of the language skills mentioned causes you the greatest difficulty? Why?

2. For each word listed below, try to find three words or phrases that are more specific or more concrete.

happiness	education	clothes
colors	chair	bad
implements	stuff	things

3. Working with two or more individuals, discuss a topic from the list below. The rest of the group should observe when dating and indexing are used, how well they are being used, and when they should have been used. Each person in the group should have an opportunity to practice.

cars	equal opportunity laws
food preferences	college course requirements
job interviewers	wedding rituals
politicians	minority groups in college

SUMMARY

Language is a system of symbols used for communicating. Language communicates when words are arranged in certain learned ways. Even though you have worked years to develop a good vocabulary and to understand the grammar of the English language, you are still likely to have some communication problems.

You will be a more effective communicator if you recognize that language is creative, purposeful, arbitrary, learned, and related to perception.

A word's denotation is its dictionary meaning. Despite the ease with which we can check a dictionary meaning, word denotation can still present problems. Most words have more than one dictionary meaning, changes in meanings occur faster than dictionaries are revised, words take on different meanings when they are used in different contexts, and meanings can become obscured as words become more abstract.

A word's connotation is the emotional and value significance the word arouses. Regardless of what a dictionary says a word means, we carry with us meanings that are a result of our experience with the object, thought, or action the word represents. Connotations can be quantified and tested by comparing scores achieved on a semantic differentiation test.

Students of language can improve their use by speaking precisely, using specific and concrete words, speaking provisionally, dating generalizations, indexing generalizations, avoiding double meanings, avoiding sexist and racist language, and recognizing the effect of pressure on word selection.

SUGGESTED READINGS

Agel, Jerome B. *Test Your Word Power*. New York: Ballantine, 1984. This book is typical of many of the vocabulary-building books on the market that are short and inexpensive.

Chase, Stuart. *The Power of Words*. New York: Harcourt Brace Jovanovich, 1953. A pioneer work in general semantics. A good place to begin the study of problems with meaning.

Fromkin, Victoria, and Robert Rodman. *An Introduction to Language*. 3rd ed. New York: Holt, Rinehart and Winston, 1983. An excellent introduction to linguistics.

Goss, Blaine. *Processing Communication*. Belmont, Calif.: Wadsworth, 1982 (paperback). This short book has two excellent chapters on meaning and language.

Lewis, Norman, ed. *Roget's Thesaurus Newly Revised*. New York: Berkley, 1978. A book of synonyms that can be very useful in vocabulary building.

Newman, Edwin. *On Language*. New York: Warner, 1980. This is a combination of his books *Strictly Speaking: Will America Be the Death of English?* and *Civil Tongue.*

Rothwell, J. Dan. *Telling It Like It Isn't.* Englewood Cliffs, N.J.: Prentice-Hall, 1982. A well-written and quite entertaining look at major language problems.

COMMUNICATING **N**ONVERBALLY

OBJECTIVES

After you have read this chapter, you should be able to:

1   Explain the differences between verbal and nonverbal communication

2   List and explain three functions of nonverbal communication

3   Identify the use of emblems, illustrators, affect displays, regulators, and adaptors

4   Identify two categories of paralanguage

5   Discuss how your clothing, touching behavior, and use of time affect self-presentation

6   Explain how use of space, color, temperature, and lighting affect communication

7   Verbally check perceptions

We have all heard—and said—that actions speak louder than words. Actions (nonverbals) are so important to our communication that researchers have estimated that in face-to-face communication as much as 90 percent of the social meaning may be carried in the nonverbal message.[1] Moreover, how you are perceived as a communicator is based in part on your ability to use nonverbal skills appropriately. Yet using and interpreting nonverbal cues are not always easy to do. Most of what we know about nonverbal usage and understanding is instinctive—a result of what you might call "doing what comes naturally." In this chapter we provide you with a framework for analysis. We begin by studying both the differences between verbal and nonverbal messages and the way verbal and nonverbal communication interrelate. We then look at the elements of nonverbal communication. Finally, we consider the skill of perception checking.

VERBAL AND NONVERBAL COMMUNICATION

Verbal and nonverbal communication differ qualitatively in at least three ways. First, nonverbal communication is continuous. Whereas speech communication begins when sound comes from the mouth and ends when that sound stops, nonverbal communication continues for as long as a person is in another's presence.

Second, nonverbal communication is multichanneled. Verbal symbols—words—come to us one at a time, in sequence; we hear the spoken words, see the printed or written words. Nonverbal signals, however, may be seen, heard, felt, smelled, or tasted—or several of these senses may be used simultaneously. For instance, when you say the word *please*, it occurs in a context of nonverbals that include sound of voice, facial expression, hand movement, and possibly touch. With our nonverbals, we communicate more than most of us realize.

Third, nonverbal communication may occur with no conscious effort. You are likely to think about what you want to say, but you are probably unaware of the various nonverbal signals you are sending constantly.

These contrasts are not meant to give the impression that you have two communication systems, verbal and nonverbal, operating totally apart from each other. Actually, verbal and nonverbal communication are usually both operating as you send and receive messages.

Your nonverbal behavior may take the place of words. Sometimes meaning is generated through nonverbal behavior alone. When a team comes into the dressing room after a game, the looks, posture, and tones of voice tell who won the game; no one needs to ask. And when the umpire jerks his thumb into the air, you know the runner is out.

Your nonverbal behavior may supplement words. When you point to show the direction a car went, when you frown as you say, "I lost," or when you grip your sister's arm as you say, "It's up to you—we need you!" each nonverbal cue supplements the verbal meaning.

Your nonverbal behavior may contradict your words. When you slam the door behind you but say you don't care, when you perspire profusely but claim you are not nervous, and when you shout that you are not angry, your verbal and nonverbal messages are contradictory. Which is to be believed? In these circumstances the nonverbal messages you send are likely to override the verbal meaning. Observers are more inclined to believe what is expressed nonverbally because it is less subject to conscious control. You are not likely to fool anyone if, when you say, "Oh, I'm sorry!" your eyes are dancing and a smile is twitching at the corners of your mouth. The contradiction of verbal statements is carried to an art when the tone of voice is sarcastic. Such statements as "Great play, George!" are always perceived as negative when said in a sarcastic tone, regardless of the positive nature of the words themselves.

In the remainder of this chapter we will examine elements of nonverbal communication under the headings *body motions, paralanguage, self-presentation,* and *managing the environment.*

BODY MOTIONS

Of all the kinds of nonverbal behavior, you are probably most familiar with **body motions**, *kinesics* by its technical name. After we identify the types of body motions, we will look at the way people use them to communicate.

Types of Body Motions

The major types of body motions are *eye contact, facial expression,* and *gesture.*

Eye contact   When people look directly at each other's eyes while talking, **eye contact** occurs. In addition to meeting psychological needs, eye contact helps monitor the effect of people's communication. For instance, through eye contact you can tell when a person is paying attention to your words, when a person is really involved in what you are saying, whether what you are saying is causing anxiety, or whether the person you are talking with has something to hide.

The amount of eye contact used differs from person to person and from situation to situation. Studies show that people are likely to look at each other 50 to 60 percent of the time as they talk. For the talker the average amount of eye contact is about 40 percent; for the listener the average is nearer 70 percent.[2]

You are likely to have better eye contact when you are discussing topics that are easy for you to talk about, when you are really interested in a person's comments or reactions, or when you are trying to influence the other person. Your eye contact is likely to be less when you are discussing topics that are difficult for you, when you lack interest in the topic or the person, or when you are embarrassed, ashamed, or trying to hide something.

Facial expression **Facial expression** involves the arrangement of facial muscles to communicate emotional state or reaction to a message. Your facial expression is likely to mirror your thoughts or feelings. A person's facial expression becomes difficult to read when it gives either no cues or totally inaccurate cues to thoughts and feelings.

The significance of the role your facial expression plays in the communication of your ideas and feelings may depend on the intensity of those ideas and feelings. For instance, if you cannot see the sadness in a situation, you are not likely to register any sadness facially, but if you truly feel sadness, you are likely to show an appropriate facial expression.

Gesture **Gestures** are movements of hands, arms, and fingers. We use gestures consciously to describe or to emphasize. When a person says "about this high" or "nearly this round," we expect to see a gesture accompany the verbal description. Likewise, when a person says, "Put that down"

What does this woman's facial expression communicate?

or "Listen to me," we look for a pointing finger, a pounding fist, or some other gesture that reinforces the point.

People vary in the amount of gesturing that accompanies their speech. Some people "talk with their hands" far more than others. People from expressively gesturing families gesture more than people from families whose gestures are more sedate or controlled.

Use of Body Motions

Even more important to your understanding of nonverbal communication is how body motions are used. To the unobservant, all body motion may appear to be random movement; however, body movements serve important communication functions. Ekman and Friesen[3] discuss these movements under the headings of *emblems, illustrators, affect displays, regulators,* and *adaptors.*

Emblems   Body motions or gestures that take the place of a word or phrase are termed **emblems**. Just as we learn what words mean, so we learn what various body motions or gestures mean. A North American dictionary of emblems would include such definitions as thumbs up for "everything is go"; extension of first and second finger in a V shape for "peace"; shaking the head from side to side for "no" and nodding for "yes"; and shrugging the shoulders for "maybe" or "I don't care."

Our nonverbal vocabulary includes the same three classifications as our verbal vocabulary: emblems that we know and use regularly in our daily speech, emblems that we can recognize if others use them but that are not in our working vocabulary, and emblems that we have to discover meaning for. For instance, nearly everyone in our culture nods for "yes"; this is an example of a nonverbal emblem that each of us knows and uses regularly. On the other hand, people may recognize or understand certain obscene gestures but may not use them themselves. And we may run across many gestures that have no meaning for us. Many groups develop certain emblems whose meaning is known only to group members.

People use emblems when they are too far apart for speech to be heard and when there is so much noise present that they cannot hear or when they just don't feel like verbalizing. Emblems are also used by the deaf (sign language is an elaborate language) or when people are trying to exclude someone who is not a member of their group.

Illustrators   Movements or gestures used to accent or emphasize what is being said are termed **illustrators**. When we say, "He talks with his hands," we mean that the person's speech and body movement are totally complementary. We use gestures to illustrate in at least five ways.

1. Illustrators can be used to *emphasize* speech: People may pound the table in front of them when they say, "Don't bug me."

2. Illustrators can show the *path or direction* of thought: People may move their hands on an imaginary continuum when they say, "The papers went from very good to very bad."
3. Illustrators can show *position*: People may point when they say, "Take that table."
4. Illustrators can be used *to describe*: People may use hands to show the size as they say, "The ball is about three inches in diameter."
5. Illustrators can be used to *mimic*: People may nod as they say, "Did you see the way he nodded?"

Like emblems, illustrators are socially learned and can be taught. We are not advocating that you learn and put into practice a set of illustrators. Our goal is to raise your awareness of their use. If you use them inappropriately or if your use calls attention to them rather than adding to meaning, you should try to correct their use.

Affect displays   When your feelings have been touched, you are likely to display the nature of that feeling through **affect displays**, that is, through some facial reaction and/or body response. For instance, if you get out of bed in the morning and stub your toe as you walk sleepy-eyed to the bathroom, you are likely to show the pain with some verbal comment (do you have a pet word for these occasions?) and with some accompanying grimace. More often than not, these spur-of-the-moment emotional displays are not intended as conscious communication. One of the apparent reasons for labeling such reactions as "displays" is that the reaction will take place automatically whether you are alone or whether someone else is present, and it will probably be quite noticeable.

Despite the automatic nature of these displays, most of us have developed patterns of usage of these displays:

1. Some people *deintensify* the *appearance of clues*. When they are afraid, happy, or hurt, they attempt to look less afraid, happy, or hurt than they really are. For instance, when people who deintensify bang their heads so hard that a bump appears, they may act as if the bang was only a minor injury.
2. Some people may *overintensify or amplify*. When they are only slightly afraid, happy, or injured, they are likely to display a much greater amount of emotion than they really feel. Children who suffer a little pain but are trying to get attention may scream as if they've been maimed.
3. Some people may take a *neutral position*. Whether they are happy, afraid, sad, or angry, we see no real difference. We call a neutral expression a "poker face," the kind a poker player will show to bluff successfully.
4. Some people may *mask the clues*. They use a totally different expression from what we would expect. When people who mask are hurt, they may smile.

These display patterns may be learned at home or in a social group and may be in keeping with a self-image a person is trying to project. For instance, if in your family it is considered bad form to show fear, then you may learn to deintensify your display, to show a "poker face," or perhaps to mask your response. Of course, the stronger the stimulus the harder it is to follow your personal rule. When you step sleepily out of bed and stub your toe, the display is likely to be directly proportional to the degree of pain.

Because of the patterns of displays people adopt, we need to be very careful about the conclusions we draw from them. We can be fooled.

Regulators   Nonverbal communication cues that are meant to control the flow of conversation are termed **regulators**. Regulators tell a person when to continue, to repeat, to elaborate, to hurry up, and to finish. We pick up such communication clues from movements such as shifting eye contact, slight head movements, shifts in posture, raising of the eyebrows, and nodding of the head. (You may have noticed that nodding the head has been used to exemplify an emblem meaning "yes" and a regulator meaning "good, go on." Like words, nonverbal responses have different meanings in different contexts.)

Regulating occurs on the periphery of our awareness. We usually do not know when we are using nonverbal cues to regulate, and we are not necessarily conscious of others' using them. Yet we expect and need these regulators. Regulators penetrate our awareness when their usage reaches a state that we describe as rudeness. For instance, if other people gather up their things, put on their coats, and start to leave while you are in the middle of what you think is a good conversation, you would probably be upset. Yet we do regulate communication on a subtler level constantly.

Adaptors   The most difficult classification of body motion cues to define is the adaptors, because, unlike other cues, they change not only from person to person but from situation to situation. Researchers view **adaptors** as efforts to satisfy personal needs that arise as people relate to each other. Just as you may change the manner in which you verbally communicate to another person based on previous conversations, so you change your body posture, gestures, facial expressions, and eye contact based on previous talks.

You may be familiar with one or more of the popular books that trade on the mystery of adaptors. Some years ago everyone who read Fast's *Body Language*[4] was trying to "psych out" the hidden messages that people were unaware of or were trying to repress. A close reading of these books shows that how people cross their legs may (or may not) indicate their attitude toward the people they are with; how they cross their arms may (or may not) indicate their rejection of others' ideas. Usually we just are not aware of our adaptive behavior.

Yet communication is greatly affected if people believe they sense something in our nonverbal behavior. When we talk with people we often get an instinctive feeling of what they are like, what they are thinking, or what they are feeling. For instance, when the bosses take off their coats, roll up their sleeves, and pitch in, they are telling something about themselves that is different from other bosses who dress rather formally, stand apart from their workers, and look disgusted at the thought of getting their hands dirty. Many times we say we are attracted to people because they exude sexuality or have a kind of grace or just seem comfortable. Sometimes we are repelled by people because they seem stern, strict, formal, uptight. Many of these impressions are projected by adaptive behaviors on the part of the people in question.

In the following exercises, your goal is to determine your own reactions to nonverbal behavior. Of course, in normal conversation you should check out the accuracy of your perception. We will consider the subject of perception checking later in the chapter.

PRACTICE

Body Motions

1. Do you use many gestures when you speak? With the aid of a friend, list:

   a. the emblems most common to your usage
   b. the illustrators you use most frequently
   c. the nonverbal reactions you use most frequently to show your emotions
   d. the nonverbal cues you give to show others that you have finished talking

2. Observe others' nonverbal behavior in the same categories.

3. Determine the kinds of facial expression, posture, gesture, or movement that are suggestive of being "sexy," "fun-loving," "boring," and "pushy." What is it about these cues that give these meanings?

PARALANGUAGE

In contrast to kinesic behavior, which relates to the bodily movements we see, **paralanguage** relates to the sounds we hear. Paralanguage concerns *how* something is said, not *what* is said. We have all developed some sensitivity to the clues people give through their voices. Let's consider two major categories of paralanguage.

Vocal Characteristics

The four major characteristics of voice are *pitch* (highness or lowness of tone), *volume* (loudness), *rate* (speed), and *quality* (the sound of the voice). Each of these, by itself or in concert with one or more others, complements, supplements, or contradicts the words used. People talk loudly when they wish to be heard over greater distances, but some people also talk louder when they are angry and softer when they are being loving. People tend to raise and lower their pitch to accompany changes in volume. They may also raise pitch when they are nervous or lower pitch when they are trying to be forceful. People may talk more rapidly when they are happy, frightened, or nervous; they will talk more slowly when they are unsure or trying to emphasize a point.

In addition to combined changes in volume, pitch, and rate, each of us uses a slightly different quality of voice to communicate a particular state of mind. We may associate complaints with a whiny, nasal quality; seductive invitation with a soft, breathy quality; and anger with a strident, harsh quality. To each of these different qualities we assign some kind of a value judgment about how people are feeling or what they are thinking.

None of these particular differences in voice quality necessarily has the meaning we assign. Some people have high-pitched or breathy or nasal or strident voices all the time. Perhaps some people use these different qualities for reasons other than what we assign. Nevertheless, *how* people say what they say does convey meaning, whether intended or not. Our purpose here is to make you more aware of the meanings received through paralanguage than to suggest the need for change of your own paralanguage. If you have concerns about your vocal characteristics, talk them over with your professor.

Vocal Interferences

Sounds that interrupt or intrude into fluent speech, causing distraction and, occasionally, total communication breakdown are termed **vocal interferences**. Excessive vocal interferences are bad speech habits that we develop over a period of time. The most common interferences are the "uh's," "er's" "well's," and "OK's" that creep into our speech, as well as that nearly universal interrupter of thought, "you know."

Vocal interferences are sometimes difficult to eliminate from our speech, but they can be reduced through a program of awareness and practice. Vocal interferences are often caused by a fear of momentary silence. Americans have been taught that it is impolite to interrupt another person until the flow of sound stops. A problem occurs for people when they pause for the right word or idea: The second or two it takes for them to come up with the word may be perceived by others as "dead air time." For fear that another person may perceive the pause as a full stop, people often fill that dead air time with sound. More often than not, the sound has no meaning. For some, the customary filler sound is "uh" or "er"; for others, it may be "well," "uh," or "um." Although the fear of being interrupted may be justified (some people will seek to interrupt at any pause), the intrusion of an excessive number of fillers is a terrible price to pay for occasional interruption.

Equally prevalent, and perhaps even more irritating than "uh" and "um," is the incessant use of "you know." The "you know" habit may begin as a way people seek to find out whether what they are saying is already known by others. For some, "you know" may be a source of identification; some people seek to show that they and those to whom they are talking have common knowledge as a binding element. For most people, however, the flooding of sentences with "you know" is just a bad habit.

Curiously, no matter how irritating the use of "you know" may be, listeners are unlikely to acknowledge their irritation. Seldom, if ever, do people say openly to others anything like "Your use of 'you know' at every break in thought is really very annoying to me." Yet passages like the following are quite common: "You know, Maxwell is, you know, a good, uh, a good, you know, lecturer." In addition to one "uh" and one repetition, the short sentence contains three "you knows"! We wish such uses were ex-aggerations. Unfortunately, they are not. If it seems appropriate, you might start pointing out this irritant in others' speech; most important, you should request others to tell you whether you are an offender.

In the normal give and take of conversation, even the most fluent speakers may use an occasional "uh" or "you know"; few people can completely avoid their use at all times. Interferences become a problem when they are perceived by others as "excessive," when they begin to call attention to themselves and prevent a person from concentrating on mean-ing. These interferences become especially detrimental to public-speaking effectiveness. With some practice you can limit their occurrence in your speech. Remember, although people may not be willing to tell you, they are likely to be distracted or irritated by your interferences. So what do you do? Try these suggestions:

1. *Train yourself to hear your interferences.* Even people with a major prob-lem seem unaware of the interferences they use. You can train your ears in at least two ways:

   ■ Tape-record yourself talking for several minutes about any subject— the game you saw yesterday, the course you plan to take next term, or anything else that comes to mind. Before you play it back, estimate the number of times you used interferences. Then compare the actual number with your estimate. As your ears become trained, your estimates will be closer to the actual number.

■ Have a close friend listen to you and raise a hand every time you say "uh" or "you know." You may find the experience traumatic or nerve-racking, but your ear will soon start to pick up the interferences as fast as the listener.

2. *Practice to see how long you can go without using a vocal interference.* Start out by trying to talk for fifteen seconds. Continue to increase the time until you talk for two minutes without using an interference. Meaning may suffer; you may spend a disproportionate amount of time avoiding interferences. Still, it is good practice.

3. *Mentally note your usage of interferences in conversation or public speaking.* You will be making real headway when you can recognize your own interferences in normal conversation or in the midst of a speech *without* affecting the flow. When you reach this stage, you will find yourself beginning to avoid or limit the use of interferences.

Ridding yourself of these habits is hard work. You will have to train your ear to catch your usages. But the work is worth it. Conversation and public speaking both would be a lot more pleasant if everyone would work to reduce vocal interferences by just 50 percent.

PRACTICE

Paralanguage

1. What happens to your voice in stress situations? When does your pitch go up? down? When do you talk loudly? softly? When are you likely to talk fast? slowly?

2. Are there any vocal interferences that you use frequently? Are you always aware of their use? Are you making some effort to reduce or eliminate their use?

3. Working in groups, have two persons of the group role-play various situations. For instance, a student has received a low grade on her theme, which she worked on for hours, and she wishes to confront her instructor, a person who does not have much patience when talking with students. The rest of the group should listen for paralanguage.

4. Working in groups, have each person try to talk continuously for two minutes on a topic of his or her choice. You can talk about such matters as a movie you saw recently, the success of your school team, difficulties you are having with a particular course, and so forth. Whenever the speaker uses an interference, one of the other members of the group will raise a hand. At the end of each two minutes, count the number of times hands were raised. Give everyone two chances. See who can use the fewest interferences.

SELF-PRESENTATION

People learn a great deal about you from the way you choose to present yourself. Elements over which you have some control are choice of *clothing, touch,* and the way you treat *time.*

Clothing

Although people's reactions to your dress will vary, people will draw conclusions about you based on the way you dress. You need to determine what you are trying to say and then to dress appropriately.

There are times when it is in your best interest to meet the expectations of others. Business managers are likely to have a clear idea of the images they want their businesses to portray. If you want to prosper with those businesses, you will want to dress in a way that is in line with those images. Likewise, audiences expect public speakers to dress appropriately for the audience and occasion.

The man who goes into an interview with a major oil company in a rumpled sweatshirt, Levis, and tennis shoes had better have a lot going for him if he expects even to be heard, let alone hired. A defendant charged with assault and battery runs a risk of alienating the jury if he shows up in the courtroom wearing a black leather jacket with chains, jeans, and boots. Lawyers are very careful to tell their clients exactly how to dress in order to favorably impress judge and jury.

People have the right to their individual differences, and we believe society is moving in the right direction in allowing persons to express themselves as individuals. Nevertheless, your clothes are still perceived by others as clues to your attitudes and behaviors. Clothes do communicate, however accurate or inaccurate you may believe that communication to be.

Touch

Touch is often considered the most basic form of communication and, as such, is a fundamental aspect of self-presentation. Americans use their hands to pat, slap, pinch, stroke, hold, embrace, and tickle. We use these and other touching behaviors for a variety of reasons, from impersonal and random to very intimate and purposeful. We shake hands to be social and polite, we pat a person on the back for encouragement, and we hug a person to show love.

But whether people touch and like to be touched is a matter of personal preference and cultural background. Although Americans as a group are relatively non-contact-oriented, the levels and amounts of individual touching behavior vary widely. Behavior that seems impersonal for one person may be very intimate and threatening for another. Appropriateness of touch will vary with context. A normally touch-oriented person may act totally differently in public or with a large group of people. Your own behavior will at times have to be tempered by the expectations of those with whom you interact.

Time

How we manage our time and how we react to others' use and management of time are important aspects of self-presentation. The amount of time that we regard as appropriate for certain events is one consideration. For instance, people are likely to expect a sermon to be twenty to thirty minutes, a class to be fifty minutes, and a movie to be roughly two hours long. When the length of an event does not meet our expectations, that time becomes an obstacle to communication. We get angry with the professor who holds us beyond normal class time; we become hostile if someone asks us to cut short our lunch hour or coffee break.

A second consideration is the time of day that is appropriate for things to happen. We work during the day, sleep at night, eat at noon, and so on. As a result of these habits, we make judgments about people who consistently do things at times that differ from our perception of what is natural. Joe is regarded as strange if he gets up at 4:30 A.M. daily. The Martins would be regarded as peculiar if they ate dinner at midnight. *When* people do things also affects communication.

A third consideration is punctuality: We draw conclusions about people based on the way they treat time designations. If your professor asks you to stop by the office at 10 A.M., she is likely to have different perceptions of you if you were to knock on her door at 9:45, at 10:00, at 10:10, or at 10:30. Likewise, your perception of your professor will differ depending on whether she is in her office when you get there.

Since time does communicate, we must be sensitive to our own perceptions of time, as well as those of others, so that the variable of time helps—or at least does not hurt—our communication.

PRACTICE

Self-Presentation

1. Take a clothing inventory. Divide your clothes into three groups: those you wear for special occasions, those you wear for everyday activities, and those you wear for grubbing around. Over the next week note how your interactions with others are affected by your clothing. Do you act differently when wearing one type of clothing? Do others treat you differently?

2. Next time you go to class, dress completely differently from your normal dress. Notice what effect, if any, this has on your communication with those around you.

3. Analyze your reaction to people's time behavior. Describe an incident in which someone's violation of your time behavior caused communication problems with you.

COMMUNICATING THROUGH MANAGEMENT OF YOUR ENVIRONMENT

In addition to the way you use body motions, paralanguage, and self-presentation, you also communicate nonverbally through your management of your physical environment. The principal elements of your environment over which you can exercise control are *space, color, temperature,* and *lighting.*

Space

How much control you have over space varies with the kind of space, which may be *fixed-featured, semi-fixed-featured,* or *informal.*[5]

Fixed-featured space   The elements of your environment that are relatively permanent—the buildings that you live and work in and the parts of those buildings that cannot be moved—are all **fixed-featured**. Although you may not have much control over the creation of such elements, you do exercise control in your selection. For instance, when you rent an apartment or buy a condominium or home, you consider whether or not the structures are in tune with your life-style. People who select a fourth-floor loft may see themselves differently from those who select one-room efficiencies. Business people, doctors, and lawyers usually search with care to find surroundings that fit the image they want to communicate.

Elements of your choice affect your communication within that environment. People who live in apartment buildings tend to become better acquainted with neighbors who live across the hall and next door than with those who live on other floors. Also, your chances of knowing people who live in your building are greatly enhanced if you live near an elevator, a staircase, or a door.

Semi-fixed-featured space　You manage your **semi-fixed-featured space**—objects that remain in a fixed position unless they are moved—by arranging and rearranging objects until they create the kind of atmosphere you wish. In general, the more formal the arrangement, the more formal the communication setting.

Whether the semi-fixed-featured space is a dormitory room, a living room, a seminar room, or a classroom, you can arrange the furnishings to create the kind of effect you want. In a living room you can arrange

furniture in a way that will contribute to conversation or will encourage attention to, say, a television set. A room with Victorian furniture and hard-backed chairs arranged formally will produce an entirely different kind of conversation from a room with a thick carpet, pillows, beanbag chairs, and a low, comfortable sectional sofa.

Your professor's office will tell you a lot about the kind of climate he or she is trying to establish just by the arrangement of the office and where you are expected to sit. A professor who shows you to a chair opposite from the desk may be saying, "Let's talk business—I'm the professor and you're the student." Such a formal arrangement (the desk between you and the professor) lends itself to formal conversation. On the other hand, a professor who shows you to a chair at the side of the desk may be saying, "Don't be nervous—let's just chat." In this case the lack of any formal barrier between you and the relatively small space is designed to lead to much more informal conversation. Although such conclusions should be tentative, the use of space is, nevertheless, a pretty good index of how people are going to treat you and how they expect you to treat them.

This relationship between semi-fixed-featured space and communication can be seen by examining your various classrooms. The communication atmosphere of a classroom in which several rows of chairs face the lectern differs from that of a classroom in which chairs are grouped into one large circle or one in which there are four or five smaller circles. In the first environment most students anticipate a lecture format. In the second they might expect a give-and-take discussion, with the instructor and members of the class participating. In the third setting they might expect the class to work on group projects.

Regardless of the nature of arrangements, you can change them to create a particular communication atmosphere.

Informal space   The space around us or the space we are occupying at the moment is termed **informal space**. The study of informal space is called *proxemics*. Managing your informal space requires some understanding of attitudes toward space around us and attitudes toward our territory.

You are probably aware that communication is influenced by the distances between people. Edward T. Hall, a leading researcher in nonverbal communication, has discussed the four different distances that most people perceive.[6] Intimate distance, up to eighteen inches, is appropriate for intimate conversation with close friends. Personal distance, from eighteen inches to four feet, is the space in which casual conversation occurs. Social distance, where impersonal business is conducted (a job interview, for instance), is the range of from four to twelve feet, and public distance (for public speaking) is a distance of more than twelve feet. Determining these four distances was not done arbitrarily; these are descriptions of what most people consider appropriate in various situations. Individuals do, of course, vary.

By far the most important to us is the intimate distance, which we regard as appropriate for intimate conversation with close friends, parents, and younger children. People usually become uncomfortable when "outsiders" violate this intimate distance. Consider your last ride in a crowded elevator, for example. Most people get rather rigid, look at the floor or the indicator above the door, and pretend that they are not touching when they are forced into such intimate space.

Intrusions into our intimate space are only acceptable when all involved follow the "rules." When there is no apparent good reason for your intimate space to be intruded upon, you may be alarmed. In a movie theater that is less than one-quarter full, couples will tend to leave a seat or more between them and another couple. If you are in such a setting and a stranger sits right next to you, you are likely to be upset and may move away instinctively.

Interpersonal problems occur when a person violates the behavioral expectations of someone who follows a different standard. For instance, Paul may come from a family that conducts informal conversations with others at a range closer than the eighteen-inch limit that most Americans place on intimate space. So when Paul talks to Dan or Mary for the first time, he may move in closer than eighteen inches for his conversation. He then may be very much surprised when both Dan and Mary back away from him during the conversation.

Normally our intimate or personal space moves when we move, for we are likely to define these spaces as distances from us. Yet in many situations we seek to put claim to a given space whether we are occupying it currently or not—that is, we are likely to look at certain space as our **territory**. Territory is space over which a person claims possession. If Marcia decides to eat lunch at the school cafeteria, the space at the table she selects becomes her territory. Let's say that during lunch Marcia leaves her territory to go back to the food area to get butter for her roll. The chair she left, the food on the table, and the space around that food are "hers," and she will expect others to stay away. If, when she returns, she finds that someone at the table has moved a glass or a dish into the area that Marcia sees as her territory, she is likely to feel resentful.

Many people stake out their territory with markers. George is planning to eat in the cafeteria. Before he gets his food he finds an empty table and puts his books on the table and his coat on a chair. Markers are indicators of occupied territory. If someone comes along while George is gone and puts his books and coat on the floor and occupies his space, that person is breaking the rules and will be in big trouble when George returns.

As a student of nonverbal communication, you must understand that others may not look at either the space around you or your territory in quite the same way as you do. That the majority of Americans have learned the same basic rules does not mean that everyone has or will treat either the respect for the rules or the consequences of breaking the rules in the same way.

Temperature, Lighting, and Color

Three other elements of environment that people seem sensitive to and over which you are likely to have considerable control are *temperature, lighting,* and *color.*

Temperature　Temperature acts as a stimulant or deterrent to communication. Americans seem most comfortable when the temperatures are in the 70s. To verify the negative effect of temperature on communication, recall when the June or September heat made listening to the teacher in a stuffy classroom especially difficult. Or, if you live in the northern part of the country, think of how a sudden cold snap causes a similar drop in communication efficiency in buildings that are much colder than normal.

Lighting　Lighting can also act as a stimulant or deterrent to communication. In lecture halls and reading rooms, bright light is expected—it encourages good listening and comfortable reading. In a chic restaurant, a music-listening room, or a television lounge, you expect the lighting to be soft and rather dim, which makes for a cozy atmosphere and leads to intimate conversation.

Color　Differences in color seem particularly important to how we behave. For instance, many people see red as exciting and stimulating; blue as comfortable, soothing, calming, peaceful; yellow as cheerful, jovial. As a result, interior designers who are trying to create a peaceful, serene atmosphere will decorate in blues rather than in reds and yellows. On the other hand, they will use reds and yellows to create a stimulating atmosphere, as for a playroom.

The effect of color is most noticeable when the color violates our expectations. Mashed potatoes tinted green in honor of Saint Patrick's Day may nauseate diners who are not color-blind, even before they attempt to eat.

You can create a communication climate by adjusting the variables of temperature, lighting, and color.

PRACTICE

Environment

1. Are you territorial? Make a list of territories that you "own." What do you do when those territories are invaded?

2. Analyze your use of personal space. What are your expectations about space when you are talking with an instructor? When you are talking with a good friend? When you are talking with a stranger? How do they differ?

3. Change the arrangement of furniture in your dorm room or a room of your home. How do these changes affect conversations?

4. Visit six different restaurants in your city. Choose several that specialize in fast food and several that specialize in more leisurely dining. Make notes on semi-fixed-featured space as well as on color and lighting. What conclusions can you draw?

5. Enlist the aid of a friend. Starting on the opposite sides of the room (at least twenty feet apart), begin to walk toward each other. Stop at twelve feet apart and hold a conversation. Stop at seven feet apart and hold a conversation. Stop at one or two feet apart and hold a conversation. Then continue until you feel too close. Step back until the distance seems comfortable. Notice how far apart you are. Compare reactions with your friend.

PERCEPTION CHECKING

We have shown the potential for creating meaning through nonverbal means of communication alone. You can be sure that people will ascribe meaning to your nonverbal cues. But how can you be sure that the meanings you get from others' nonverbal cues are accurate? The skill that you can develop to help you clarify the meaning of nonverbal communication is perception checking. A **perception check** is a verbal statement that reflects *your* understanding of the meaning of another person's nonverbal cues.

Because some people do not verbalize what they are thinking or feeling and because what they do say sometimes seems at odds with other clues they are sending, we as receivers must interpret not only the words but also the actions. There is no way of judging the accuracy of our perceptions without putting them to the test.

The procedure for perception checking is quite simple:

1. Watch the behavior of another.
2. Describe the behavior to yourself or aloud.
3. Ask yourself, "What does that behavior mean to me?"
4. Put your interpretation of the nonverbal behavior *into words* to verify whether your perception is accurate.

Examine the following situations and the efforts at using perception checking.

▶   Vera comes walking into the room with a completely blank expression. She neither speaks to Ann nor even recognizes that Ann is in the room. Vera sits on the edge of the bed and stares into space. Ann says: "Vera, I sense that something has happened that put you in some kind of a shock. Am I right? Is there something I can do?"

▶   George, speaking in short, precise sentences with a sharp tone of voice, gives Bill his day's assignment. Bill says, "From the sound of your voice, George, I can't help but get the impression that you're upset with me."

▶   Ted, the company messenger, delivers a memo to Mary. As Mary reads the note her eyes brighten and she breaks into a smile. Ted says: "Hey, Mary, you certainly seem pleased. That must have been good news. Am I right?"

In each of the above examples, the response is a perception check that is intended to test the receiver's perceptions of the nonverbal communication of the sender. Notice that sometimes it is the body language that provides the clues; at other times it is the paralanguage—the sound of the voice—that provides the clues. Also notice that the perception-checking statements do not express approval or disapproval of what is being received—they are purely descriptive statements of the perceptions.

You should check your perceptions whenever the accuracy of your understanding is important to your current communication or to the relationship you have with that other person. Most of us use this skill far too little, if at all. People *assume* that they have a perfectly accurate understanding of another's nonverbal cues; too often they are wrong. Both verbal and nonverbal meanings are determined, in part, by the relationship. Thus, especially in new relationships you will find perception checking an important skill to use.

Let's see what might happen when we respond without checking the accuracy of our perceptions. We'll examine a rather typical conversation based on the situation described in one of the examples just given.

If, in place of the descriptive perception check ("I get the impression that you're upset with me. Are you?"), Bill were to say, "Why are you so upset with me?" Bill would not be describing his perception—he would be making a judgment based on his perception. Replying as if your perception is "obviously" accurate involves reliance on mind reading, and few of us can read minds that well all the time. When mind reading is substituted for perception checking, trouble results all too often. Perhaps you are thinking, "Well, I know when another person is upset (or happy) with me." Perhaps you are correct in your certainty that you can properly identify such feelings as anger or happiness most of the time. But if you do not check it out, you are still guessing that you know how the other person is feeling or that his or her anger or happiness is centered on you. If you choose the judgmental reply, people so spoken to would be inclined to be rather defensive about their feelings that you appear to be challenging. In response people might say, "Who said I'm upset?" or, more harshly, "What the hell are you talking about?" Such responses might soon lead to further emotional outbursts, and very little communication takes place when communicators lose their tempers.

Because a perception check is descriptive rather than judgmental, the original sender will be less likely to become defensive. The purpose of checking out any perception of behavior is to give a person the opportunity to deal with that perception—to verify it or to correct it. Let's carry through with George and Bill's conversation. When Bill says, "I get the impression that you're upset with me, George. Am I right?" George may say:

1. "No, whatever gave you that impression?" Bill can then further describe the clues that he received.
2. "Yes, I am." Bill can then get George to specify what has been the cause of the upset.
3. "No, it's not you, it's just that three people on my team didn't show up for this shift." If George is not upset, then Bill can deal with what caused him to misinterpret George's feelings; if George is upset, then he is given the opportunity to explain why in more detail, and Bill has the opportunity to change the behavior that caused George to be upset.

A perception check will not always eliminate defensive behavior. There are times when the emotional stress is so great that calm, logical communication is nearly impossible. Through the selective use of perception checking, however, you can reduce the likelihood of misinterpreting another's nonverbal cues and thus the likelihood of defensiveness.

PRACTICE

Perception Checking

1. Respond to the following situations with well-phrased perception checks:

   ▶ Marsha comes rushing into her room, throws her books on the floor, and sits at her desk with her head in her hands. What do you say?

   ▶ Bob comes come from the doctor's office with pale face and slumped shoulders. Glancing at you with a forlorn look, he shrugs his shoulders. What do you say?

▶ As you return the tennis racket you borrowed from Jim, you smile and say, "Here's your racket." Jim stiffens, grabs the racket, and starts to walk away. What do you say?

▶ In the past your advisor has told you that almost any time would be all right for working out your next term's schedule. When you tell him you'll be in Wednesday afternoon at 4 P.M., he pauses, frowns, sighs, says "Uh," and nods. What do you say?

2. With others in groups of three, A talks with B and C observes. A role-play situation is developed in which A gives various clues to his or her feelings through words and actions. B uses perception checking to test his or her perception of A's feelings. C discusses the conversation. The exercise continues until everyone in the group has a chance at being sender, receiver, and observer. After the exercise, each person discusses how it feels to check out perceptions. Did the perception checking help or hinder the communication? How?

SUMMARY

Although verbal and nonverbal communication work together best when they are complementary, nonverbal communication may take the place of or even contradict verbal communication.

Perhaps the most obvious of the nonverbal means is what and how a person communicates through body motions and paralanguage. Eye contact, facial expression, and gestures are three major types of body motions. Body motions act as emblems, illustrators, affect displays, regulators, and adaptors. Likewise, a person's vocal characteristics and vocal interferences affect the meaning communicated.

Self-presentation, manifested by clothing, touching behavior, and use of time, further affects communication. The environment is one aspect of nonverbal communication that is often overlooked. Yet the way people arrange and react to space and the way they control or react to color, temperature, and lighting contribute to the nature of the communication that will occur.

A skill that you can use to test your understanding of nonverbal meanings is perception checking, a verbal statement that indicates your interpretation of nonverbal cues.

SUGGESTED READINGS

Burgoon, Judee K., and Thomas Saine. *Unspoken Dialogue.* Boston: Houghton Mifflin, 1978. This book provides a comprehensive analysis of nonverbal communication.

Hall, Edward T. *The Silent Language.* Garden City, N.Y.: Doubleday, 1959 (paperback). This classic work by Hall is fundamental to any comprehensive study of the roles of time and space in communication.

Hickson, Mark L., III, and Don W. Stacks. *NVC Nonverbal Communication: Studies and Applications.* Dubuque, Iowa: Wm. C. Brown Publishers, 1985 (paperback). A well-organized presentation of current research.

Knapp, Mark L. *Essentials of Nonverbal Communication.* New York: Holt, Rinehart and Winston, 1980 (paperback). Excellent analysis and summary of research studies.

Mehrabian, Albert. *Silent Messages.* 2nd ed. Belmont, Calif.: Wadsworth, 1981 (paperback). A short, highly readable book focusing on the role of nonverbal communication in social interaction.

5 ▶ *LISTENING SKILLS*

OBJECTIVES

After you have read this chapter, you should be able to:

1 Explain the difference between hearing and listening

2 Identify five faulty listening behaviors

3 List and explain the differences among four different types of listening

4 Identify six steps for improving listening

5 Listen actively and take notes effectively

You may be surprised to know that in your daily communication you spend more time listening than speaking, reading, or writing. One study of college student communication habits shows that college students spend 22 percent of their time speaking, 20 percent reading, 8 percent writing, and 50 percent listening.[1] Yet of these four skills, you are likely to be least effective as a listener. In this chapter, we show you how to become a more skillful listener in interpersonal, group, and public-speaking contexts.

LISTENING BEHAVIOR

As important as listening is to communication, most of us are not very good at it. Research studies have shown that most people listen with only 25 to 50 percent efficiency even if they hear very well.[2] And there is an important difference between hearing and listening. Whereas *hearing* is the ability to receive the sound vibrations that are transmitted, **listening** is making sense out of what you hear.

Faulty Listening Behaviors

Suppose your boss is giving you instructions for a report you are to prepare on the pattern of sales over the last three years. There are at least five different things that can happen to you to prevent you from listening efficiently.

1. *You may totally miss what a person is saying.* Many times you miss key ideas and even long sections of speaking because of a physical or psychological problem of the moment. Something as small as a simple head cold can be a distraction; if you've had some deep emotional trauma like a death in the family, the loss of a friendship, or a low grade on an assignment you can be completely distracted at the time your boss is trying to explain the task.
2. *You may hear what is said but be unable to understand it.* You might hear every word the person is saying, but if the instructions are given with words that you don't know or that are used in a way that you don't recognize, then the result is the same: You don't understand. Suppose, for instance, you are told that "your implementation is obfuscatory"; you may not understand you're being told that what you're doing gets in the way.
3. *You may hear what is said, but you may assign a meaning different from what was intended.* Recall that language can only represent what a person is thinking or feeling. If your boss tells you that the convention hotel you'll be staying at is "within walking distance" of the convention

center, when you get to the hotel you may discover that your understanding of "walking distance" is much different from your boss's.

4. *You may listen accurately, but your mind may later change the meaning.* Your boss may say that the report is due on the fifth. You listen and understand. But a few days later you may think you heard the fifteenth.

5. *You may listen accurately and then forget.* You may hear the boss say that the report is due on the fifth, but by the end of the instruction session you have no memory of the statement—and later you may deny that it was ever mentioned.

In situations like this, putting the entire burden of effective communication on the speaker can be unfair. You, as the listener, have as much responsibility, and in some cases more, than the speaker.

Factors that Affect Your Ability to Listen

How well you listen depends on many factors; you have only minimal control over some, but others you can change if you want. Let us first consider three factors that grow from your heredity and your environment: hearing acuity, vocabulary, and an "ear for language." Then we'll discuss ways to improve your listening.

Hearing acuity   Nearly 15 million Americans suffer some hearing impairment that may be significant enough to affect their ability to listen.[3] If you are among this number, you may now wear a hearing aid, or you may have learned to adapt to the problem. If you are not aware of the problem, however, poor hearing alone may limit your listening effectiveness.

If you suspect you may have a hearing problem, have a complete hearing test. Most schools have facilities for testing hearing acuity. It is painless and is usually provided at minimal, if any, cost to the student.

Vocabulary   Listening effectiveness and vocabulary are definitely related. In Chapter 3 we emphasized the importance of building vocabulary to increase the precision of messages you send. Similarly, it is important to increase your vocabulary so you will understand the words you hear better and retain more. Many who have a reputation as poor students have average or better intelligence but are handicapped by a poor vocabulary. If you have a below-average vocabulary, you will have to take steps to ensure your understanding of what people are saying.

What do you do when a person uses a word you do not understand? For many poor listeners, the answer is "nothing." People are often shy about calling attention to their lack of understanding of a particular word. Since they do not want to appear foolish, they hide the fact that they don't know the meaning of a word. But isn't it "foolish" to respond to a person as if you understand when you really do not? If your professor told you your term paper reached the 'nadir' and you smiled because you didn't know what he or she was talking about, *that* behavior would be foolish. *Nadir* means the low point—the pits. Although you may feel embarrassed when you need to ask what a word means, you are likely to *behave* foolishly if you do not ask.

An ear for the English language   If you and members of your family carry on meaningful conversations about world events, the arts, and what is happening around you, you probably have a natural "ear for language," a grasp of good language structure, and experience in a variety of kinds and levels of listening. If you have not developed an ear for language at home, then your ear may not be tuned in to the more difficult kinds of listening that you may encounter in adult relationships. Although an adult cannot suddenly make up for years of lack of practice with language, you can use your classroom experiences to help you improve, even if your former environment has been a source of your listening problems.

IMPROVING LISTENING

Assuming that your listening is about average, what can you do to improve? You can almost double listening effectiveness in a few months. In fact, by following a few simple steps, you will note improvement in your listening immediately.

1. *Adopt a positive listening attitude.* There's no reason why you cannot improve your listening *if you want to.* It's up to you to decide that listening is important and that you are going to do whatever it takes to listen better.
2. *Recognize differences in types of listening and in listening difficulty.* Listening is similar to reading in that you should listen differently depending on the goal and degree of difficulty of the material. Yet many people "listen" about the same to all kinds of material. Listening intensity differs depending on the goal.

    The majority of your listening is done for pleasure or appreciation, for learning or understanding, for critiquing, or for enabling you to respond helpfully.

    Listening for pleasure is, of course, the least demanding of the kinds of listening we do. Listening to music on the car radio while you are driving to school or to work is one example of listening for pleasure; listening to what Tom and Paul have to say about the game they saw on television is another. When we listen to music while we are driving, we are aware of the "background" sound—we find it soothing, relaxing, and generally pleasant; likewise, when we listen to people talk about the game they saw, we are involved in the fun of the interaction, and the details of the conversation are likely to be soon forgotten.

Unfortunately, many people approach all situations as if they were listening for pleasure. Yet how you listen should change qualitatively when you listen to understand, to evaluate, or to give helpful responses.

A more difficult challenge is listening to understand. Effective listening to understand requires you to develop greater intensity. Your classroom lectures require this type of listening. Likewise, listening to directions (how to get to a restaurant), listening to instructions (how to shift into reverse in a foreign car), and listening to explanations (a recounting of the new dorm rules) also require listening to understand. In this chapter we consider several skills to help you with this kind of listening.

By far the most demanding challenge is listening to evaluate. Daily we are flooded with messages designed to influence our behavior, from the advertisements we hear on the radio or on television to the political speeches we hear calling for our vote. Critical, evaluative listening requires us to be able to recognize the facts, weigh them, separate them from emotional appeals, and determine the soundness of the conclusions presented. The remaining recommendations in this section are

What does the body language of these children tell you about their listening skills?

directed toward helping you in your listening efforts to understand and to evaluate.

A very special challenge is listening to respond helpfully. Every day you are likely to talk with people who seek to share their problems and concerns. Sometimes their only goal is to have someone there to listen. At other times the people are coming to you for help. Many of the skills we cover in the next chapter are response skills that will work for you in helping situations. In this type of listening more than in any other you must be conscious of nonverbal cues, since very often those nonverbal cues will tell you much more than what the person is expressing in words.

3. *Get ready to listen.* Your listening potential improves immediately when you become physically and mentally alert. Since physical alertness often encourages mental alertness, you need to stand or sit in a way that will help you listen. Moreover, you will want to look people in the eye when they talk with you. The visual bond you establish between you and the speaker helps form a mental bond that improves listening effectiveness.

Mentally, you need to direct all your attention to what a person is saying; you need to stop thinking about any of the thousands of miscellaneous thoughts that constantly pass through your mind. When people are talking with you, their ideas and feelings are in competition with the various thoughts and feelings going through your mind at the moment. Anticipation of an exciting evening, thoughts about a game, a test,

When people become emotional, their listening abilities become impaired.

a date, or dinner, and memories of scenes from a movie or television show may be more pleasant to tune into than what people are saying to you, yet attention paid to such competing thoughts and feelings is one of the leading causes of poor listening.

4. *Make the shift from speaker to listener a complete one.* In the classroom, where you listen continuously for long stretches, it is relatively easy to develop a listening mood. In conversation, however, you are called upon to switch back and forth from speaker to listener so frequently that you may find it hard to make the necessary shifts. If, instead of listening, you spend your time *thinking about what you're going to say* when you talk, your listening effectiveness will take a nose dive. We have all experienced situations in which two people talked right past each other—each participant broadcasting with no one receiving! Especially when you are in a heated conversation, take a second to check yourself—are you preparing speeches instead of listening? Although making the shift from speaker to listener may be difficult for you to put into practice consistently, it is especially important.

5. *Hear a person out before you react.* Far too often, because we think we know what someone is saying, we may stop listening before the person has finished. Always let a person complete his or her thought before you stop listening or before you try to respond.

In addition, we often let certain words turn us off. Are there any words or ideas that act as red flags for you? Does the mere utterance of

Being able to shift from speaker to listener is a useful skill in group interactions.

these words cause you to lose any desire to listen attentively? For instance, do you have a tendency to get derailed when people use any of these words?

racist	yuppie
communist	abortion
gay	AIDS
Jew	gun control
Arab	feminist

Would any of these or similar words turn you off? Often, poor listeners (and, occasionally, even good listeners) are given an emotional jolt by a speaker who touches a nerve. At this point all you can do is be wary. When a speaker trips the switch to your emotional reaction, let a warning light go on before you go off. Instead of tuning out or getting ready to fight, work that much harder at being objective. If you can do it, you will improve your listening.

6. *Listen actively.* Instead of letting your mind wander or preparing what you are going to say when you have a chance, you can practice and use active listening skills. **Active listening** includes repeating important details to yourself; questioning; paraphrasing; distinguishing among governing idea, main points, and detail; and, in some situations, note taking. Active listening involves you in the process of determining meaning. Too often people think of the listening experience as a passive activity in which what they remember is largely a matter of chance. In reality, good listening is hard work that requires concentration and willingness to mull over and, at times, verbalize what is said. Good listening requires using mental energy. If you really listen to an entire 50-minute lecture, for instance, when the lecture is over you will feel tired because you will have put as much energy into listening as the lecturer put into talking.

There are several mental methods for improving your listening.

Repeating Information

Repeat items of information to help you remember. For instance, when a person says, "Go two blocks east, turn left, turn right at the next light, and it's in the next block," an active listener might mentally repeat, "two blocks east, turn left, turn right at light, next block."

Using Mnemonic Devices

A **mnemonic device** is any artificial technique used as a memory aid. Some of the most common rules for forming mnemonics are taking the first letters of items that you are trying to remember and forming a word. For example, a very easy mnemonic for remembering the five great lakes is HOMES, standing for **H**uron, **O**ntario, **M**ichigan, **E**rie, and **S**uperior. When you are trying to remember some items in sequence, you can form a sentence with the words themselves or you can assign words using the first letters of the words in sequence to form some easy-to-remember statement. For instance, when you first studied music you may have learned the notes of the scale in the following way: For the notes on the treble clef lines (E-G-B-D-F) you may have learned "**e**very **g**ood **b**oy **d**oes **f**ine," and for the notes of the treble clef spaces (F-A-C-E) you may have remembered the word *face*.

Asking Questions

Ask yourself questions to help you anticipate material. For instance, if a person says, "There are four steps to coding data," you might ask yourself, "What are the four steps?" If the person goes on to tell you the steps, asking the question will help you emphasize the steps. If the person doesn't give you the steps, you ask the person. Good silent questioning also helps you test the soundness of the material. For instance, when a person says, "An activity that provides exercise for almost every muscle is swimming," active listeners might inwardly question "How?" and then pay attention to the supporting material offered.

Paraphrasing

Silently paraphrase to help you understand. A **paraphrase** is a statement of what the person's words meant to you. After a person has talked for a few minutes, you can say to yourself, "In other words, how the mixture is put together may be more important than the ingredients used." This silent paraphrase can be used verbally to have the person verify the accuracy of your understanding. In the next chapter we will provide an opportunity for you to study and practice verbal paraphrases as a means of ensuring shared meaning. But if you cannot paraphrase, either something was missing from the explanation or you weren't listening carefully enough.

Separating Message Parts

Separate the governing idea (or purpose), key points, and details to help you understand the totality of the message. Some people mistakenly think that their listening is at its best when they can feed back most of the words that were communicated. But good listening goes beyond that. Good listening means understanding the relationship of the words to each other. For instance, during a conversation with friends Gloria brings up the subject of teenage crime. As Gloria talks, she mentions three apparent causes—poverty, permissiveness, and broken homes—and she includes some information she read or heard that relates to each of the points. When Gloria finishes you can determine that she was stating her view of the causes of teenage crime (her purpose), three specific causes (her main ideas), and information about each (details).

Taking Notes

When feasible, take notes. Note taking is especially useful during classroom lectures, telephone conversations, briefing sessions, interviews, and business meetings. Whereas poor listeners may fidget, doodle, or look about the room, good listeners often make notes on the points being discussed. Repeating, asking questions, paraphrasing, and separating governing idea, key points, and details aid you in taking good notes. Most college students take notes in classes. Yet the quality of the notes that students take can vary tremendously. Just sitting down with a pen or pencil and a piece of paper does not guarantee good note taking; neither does leaving class with pages of writing.

Good notes provide a brief outline of what the speaker has said, including the overall idea, the main points of the message, and key developmental material. Good notes are not necessarily very long. In fact, many excellent lectures can be reduced to a short outline of notes.

Suppose you were listening to a supervisor instruct staff about the importance of clear writing in their reports. In the instructions the supervisor discussed the importance of testing the readability of the report by computing a Fog Index. The supervisor might say:

> The brass is really concerned with the quality of the report writing that is coming from the major divisions. The word is that reports just aren't as readable as they should be. In the future every report will be required to include a Fog Index, with a summary of the figures used for the computation.
>
> A Fog Index is one of the most common tests of readability. It's an easy one to use and generally reliable. Like most readability tests it is based on computations of sentence length and word length. The theory is that the shorter the sentences and words, the easier the reading.
>
> Computing a Fog Index for a report involves six easy steps.
>
> First, select five random sections of at least 100 words

each. In a five-page report, this would be one passage per page. Begin at the start of a paragraph and count off 100 words and then continue to count until the end of that sentence.

Second, compute the average sentence length of each passage. If a 116-word passage has 5 sentences, then the average sentence length of that passage would be 23.2 words.

Third, compute the number of difficult words per hundred. The beauty of this test is that "difficult" words are easily identified as any word of more than two syllables except proper names and verbs that become three syllables by adding *-es*, *-ed*, or *-ing*. So if that 116-word passage has 12 difficult words, you would divide 12 by 116. That passage then would have 10.3 difficult words per hundred. For both steps two and three, round off the figures to the nearest whole number.

Fourth, add the average sentence length and the number of difficult words per hundred. In the case of the example you would add 23 and 10.

Fifth, multiply the answer by .4. The result is the Fog Index. This figure stands for the number of years of schooling required to read the passage *easily*.

Sixth, since you will have done five passages, you will then compute the average Index for the five passages. Write the figure at the end of the report and include computations.

We have been instructed to rewrite reports until we achieve a Fog Index of between 10 and 13 for each.

This short passage includes a great deal of specific detail, much more than you will find in most instructions. Yet the 379 words of explanation can be outlined in just 127 words:

Notes

Computing a Fog Index (F I)

I. Include F I on future reports.

F I, a readability test based on sentence and word length.

Short sentences and words make for easier reading.

II. Computing Index involves six steps.

1. Select five random sections of at least 100 words each.

2. Compute average sentence length of each passage.

3. Compute number of difficult words per hundred.

    Count words three syllables or more

    Don't count proper names and verbs that become three syllables by adding -es, -ed, or -ing.

    Round off figures.

4. Add two figures.

5. Multiply answer by .4 to get FI.

    Number of years of schooling required to read the passage easily.

6. Compute average Index for the five passages.

    Write figure at end of the report with computations.

III. Rewrite reports until FI is between 10 and 13.

    Good note taking may range from 10 percent to as high as 30 percent (the amount in our example). The point is not the number of words but the accuracy of the notes in reflecting the sense of what the speaker said.

    Now let's test your listening.

PRACTICE

Listening

1. Under what circumstances do you really listen? Can you tell when you are really listening and when you are not?

2. The following are two separate analyses of listening behaviors. Answer each question honestly. It is important for you to know what you do well and what you need to work on. For each of the analyses there are five questions. For each question score 5 for "almost always," 4 for "usually," 3 for "some," 2 for "seldom," and 1 for "almost never." Write your score for each question in the "score" column. Then add your scores.

ANALYSIS A	ALMOST ALWAYS	USUALLY	SOME	SELDOM	ALMOST NEVER	SCORE
I listen *differently* for enjoyment, understanding, evaluation.						
I consciously recognize the speaker's purpose.						
When people talk, I differentiate between their main points and supporting details.						
At various places in a speech, I paraphrase what the speaker has said to check my understanding.						
When I am listening for information or to evaluate, I take good notes of major points and supporting details.						

Analysis A focuses on positive listening behaviors, and Analysis B focuses on negative listening behaviors. If your score for the first analysis is much higher than your score for the second (20 points or more for the first, 10 points or less for the second), your listening behaviors are positive and should yield good results. If your scores for the two analyses are very similar

ANALYSIS B	ALMOST ALWAYS	USUALLY	SOME	SELDOM	ALMOST NEVER	SCORE
I stop listening when what a person is saying isn't interesting to me.						
I pretend to listen to people when I'm really thinking about other things.						
When people's way of speaking annoys me (such as muttering, stammering, or talking in a monotone), I stop listening carefully.						
When I perceive the subject matter as very difficult, I stop listening carefully.						
When people use words that I react to negatively, I stop listening and start preparing responses.						

(15 points for each, say), you need to work on limiting negative behaviors and perfecting skills that will raise your level of positive behaviors. If your score for the *second* analysis is much higher than for the first (20 points or more for the second, 10 points or less for the first), you are likely to need a great deal of work on developing skills designed to improve your listening.

3. Each person in class will prepare a two-minute reading of a newspaper or a magazine article. As each reading progresses, everyone in class will take notes. At the end of each reading, members of the class will compare their notes.

4. Ask someone to read the following information to you once, at a normal rate of speech. Then give yourself the test that follows. Although the temptation is great to read this item to yourself, try not to—you will miss both the enjoyment and the value of the exercise if you do.

A 23-year-old Stafford woman remained in serious condition at the St. Eli Hospital after she was shot in the chest at the Black Watch Motorcycle Clubhouse, 2726 Main St., Stafford, early Saturday.

Police said Miss Olga White, 23, 621 Crescent Ave., Stafford, was shot once in the chest.

Inside the clubhouse at the time of the shooting, officers said, were Gill Bower, 20, Bishopville; Ron Lister, 23, Stafford; L. W. McShane, 25, Bishopville; and Timothy Berton, 23, 414 Ottawa St., Elmira.

The four witnesses told police they were all seated at a table. Miss White was sitting on a bar stool playing a pinball machine, the four said, when they heard what sounded like a "cap gun."

The door of the clubhouse "splintered," witnesses said, and Miss White fell to the floor saying she was shot.

Berton, who police said was Miss White's boyfriend, said he checked the outside of the building but saw only "a car with lights on top going north" on Main.

Miss White was rushed to St. Eli Hospital by the Stafford lifesquad. She was placed in the hospital intensive care unit.

Five holes made by bullets fired from the outside were found in the clubhouse door, investigating officers said. A 38-caliber slug was also found inside the building, officers said.

Answer the following questions either T for True, F for False, or ? for not stated in the story.

_____ a. Miss White was shot five times in the chest.
_____ b. The Black Watch Motorcycle Club is in Stafford.
_____ c. There were five men in the clubhouse with her at the time of the shooting.
_____ d. Two men and a woman were standing outside at the time of the shooting.
_____ e. Miss White was sitting on a bar stool playing a computer game at the time of the shooting.
_____ f. Miss White was killed instantly.
_____ g. Two of the men were from Bishopville.
_____ h. The witnesses said they heard what sounded like a "cap gun."
_____ i. Miss White said she was shot as she fell to the floor.
_____ j. Miss White's boyfriend could not be found.
_____ k. One of the men said he saw a car with lights on top of it going north on Main.
_____ l. The investigating officer was named Shane.

_____ m. The clubhouse door had five holes in it.
_____ n. A .45 caliber slug was also found inside the building.
_____ o. Miss White was dead on arrival.

SUMMARY

Good listening is essential to your communication competence. Whereas hearing involves receiving audio stimuli, listening means making sense out of what you hear.

Faulty listening involves such things as totally missing the message, hearing the message but not understanding it, hearing the message but assigning a different meaning, listening accurately but changing the meaning with time, and listening accurately and then totally forgetting.

Your heredity and environment influence how well you listen. Your hearing acuity, vocabulary, and ear for language will determine some of your effectiveness. Nevertheless, there are many behaviors you can put into practice to become a better listener. Some of the more important are (1) adopting a positive attitude, (2) recognizing differences in listening types and listening difficulty, (3) getting ready to listen, (4) making the shift from speaker to listener a complete one, (5) hearing a person out before you react, and (6) listening actively. Active listening involves repeating items; using mnemonic aids to remember; asking yourself questions; silently paraphrasing; separating governing ideas, key points, and details; and, when feasible, taking notes.

SUGGESTED READINGS

Hirsch, Robert O. *Listening: A Way to Process Information Aurally*. Dubuque, Iowa: Gorsuch Scarisbrick, 1979 (paperback). This 45-page booklet contains some excellent suggestions and a good bibliography.

Steil, Lyman K., Larry L. Barker, and Kittie W. Watson. *Effective Listening: Key to Your Success*. Reading, Mass.: Addison-Wesley, 1983. Provides specific procedures for different kinds of listening situations.

Wolff, Florence I., Nadine C. Marsnik, William S. Tacey, and Ralph G. Nichols. *Perceptive Listening*. New York: Holt, Rinehart and Winston, 1983. In addition to its many exercises and listening tests, this book provides lengthy analyses of all kinds of listening.

Wolvin, Andrew D., and Carolyn Gwynn Coakley. *Listening.* Dubuque, Iowa: Wm. C. Brown, 1982. Has chapters on appreciative listening, discriminative listening, comprehensive listening, therapeutic listening, and critical listening. Gives a list of skills involved in each of the types.

PART THREE

▶ By far the greatest
percentage of your
communication is
interpersonal—the day-to-
day conversations that are
so fundamental to your very
existence. This four-chapter
unit begins with the
development of important
skills: responding and
sharing ideas and feelings.
After focusing on one
of the primary goals
of interpersonal
communication—building
relationships—the unit
concludes with a discussion
of interviewing.

INTERPERSONAL COMMUNICATION

Self-Analysis

Your interpersonal communication is your informal interaction with self and others. The effectiveness of your interpersonal communication is fundamental both to your understanding of self and to the development and maintenance of your relationships with others. Most of us are excited about discovering people with whom we have a lot in common, yet sometimes our interpersonal communication fails at key places. What kind of an interpersonal communicator are you? The following analysis looks at ten specifics that are basic to an interpersonal communication profile.

For each of the statements listed below, circle the number that best indicates how you see your behavior. The numbers 1 and 2 represent the negative behavior; the numbers 4 and 5 represent the positive behavior. The number 3 represents the midpoint between the extremes. It may also say you are not sure of your behavior.

I either withhold my negative feelings about others' behavior toward me or blow up at what they've said or done.	1 2 3 4 5	I describe objectively to others my negative feelings about their behavior toward me without withholding or blowing up.
When I talk with people I don't really notice how they react.	1 2 3 4 5	When I talk with people I am very much in tune with how they react.
Whether I think I understand a person's point or not, I act as if I do.	1 2 3 4 5	When I'm not sure whether I understand, I seek clarification.

The way I respond to others makes them react defensively—they feel as if I'm attacking them.	1 2 3 4 5	The way I respond to others seems to encourage them to talk openly and honestly with me.
I have little interest in hearing about what others may think of me or my behavior.	1 2 3 4 5	I am willing to listen to what others think of me and my behavior; in fact, I often ask others for their reactions to me.
I am easily intimidated and will seldom give my opinion when I feel the likelihood of conflict.	1 2 3 4 5	I am willing to state what I think and how I feel regardless of the other person's status.
I seldom say anything that either helps others sustain their good feelings or ease their bad feelings.	1 2 3 4 5	I am likely to say something in an effort to help others sustain their good feelings or ease their bad feelings.
I am not likely to praise people for doing things well.	1 2 3 4 5	I am quick to praise people for doing things well.
I am quick to criticize people for the mistakes they make.	1 2 3 4 5	I only criticize people for their mistakes when they ask for criticism.
When I believe that others have neglected to treat me as they should, I am unlikely to confront them.	1 2 3 4 5	When I believe that others have neglected to treat me as they should, I will point it out politely but firmly.

First, consider your analysis. Is the number you circle indicative of where you would like to be in that category? If not, in a different color of ink or pencil, circle the number that represents your goal for this term. If you would like verification of your analysis, have a friend or work partner complete the same analysis for you.

Then select one of the areas in which your goals are farthest from your current behavior. Write a communication improvement contract similar to the sample contract in Appendix C.

6 ▶ *R* ESPONSE *S* KILLS

OBJECTIVES

After you have read this chapter, you should be able to:

1 List and explain steps for increasing empathy

2 Ask questions for information

3 Paraphrase information that you think you understand

4 Support positive and negative feelings

5 Give alternate interpretations

6 Praise people

7 Give constructive criticism

8 Eliminate inappropriate responses

Your interpersonal communication is your informal interaction with others. An important part of your role as an effective communicator involves responding to the person or people with whom you are conversing. The kind of response—silence, asking questions, changing the subject, arguing, showing understanding, giving opinions—influences the interpersonal relationship that exists between you and others. Both your verbal and your nonverbal responses can strengthen or weaken the effectiveness of the communication.

When you are playing the role of receiver, which skills represent a measure of communication competence? In this chapter we consider empathizing, clarifying meaning through questions and paraphrases, and helping through supporting statements, praise, and criticism.

EMPATHIZING

When you empathize, you lay the groundwork for selecting appropriate responses that help you communicate more effectively.

What Is Empathy?

Empathizing is detecting and identifying how a person is feeling and then responding in an appropriate manner. The first part of this definition shows that empathizing requires accurate perceptions.[1] The ability to detect and identify may derive from your own experiences in a similar situation, your fantasized reaction to that situation, or your experience in observing this person in similar situations. Empathizing stresses seeing a situation through the other person's eyes—empathizing is "you"-oriented rather than "I"-oriented.

Let's look at an example. George says to Jerry, "Professor Jones said my speech was a lot better, but when I got my grade, it was a C, the same as I got on the last speech!" As George talks, Jerry "reads" the look on George's face and perceives the cues that George's gestures, movements, and posture appear to be giving. As Jerry hears the words George speaks, he perceives the changes in vocal quality and pitch and the presence or absence of vocal interferences. From all these cues he is able to understand George's total meaning. If from his perception of George's words and nonverbal cues Jerry is able to feel the disappointment George experienced in getting the C, Jerry is empathizing. Even if Jerry himself had never had the same experience but could imagine the disappointment, Jerry would be empathizing. On the other hand, if Jerry had an "I" orientation—that is, if he was so wrapped up in his own thoughts, feelings, and experiences that the sense of George's words and nonverbal cues didn't reach him—then he would be unable to empathize very well.

The second part of the definition of empathy is the ability to respond in an appropriate manner. When George says, "But when I got my grade, it was a C," Jerry might well respond by saying, in a way that suggests understanding of the pain and surprise that George must have felt, "That must have really jolted you." Such a response might show George that (1) Jerry understands what happened, (2) Jerry shares in the emotions George is feeling—he knows what it is like to suffer pain or surprise—and (3) Jerry is willing to talk with George and offer what help he can.

People sometimes confuse *empathy* with *sympathy*. Although empathy and sympathy are similar, and, in fact, some dictionaries even consider them synonymous, more often than not, *sympathy* connotes pity or compassion for another person's trouble.

We can see that empathy has two clearly definable elements—the *recognition* of another's feeling, which is a perception skill, and the *response* to it, which is a communication skill. Let's talk further about achieving an empathic state of mind.

Achieving an Empathic State

Saying "I'm going to try to empathize" to yourself may help you achieve an empathic state, yet such a statement may be too general to do much good. Let's consider specific actions that you can use to increase your ability to empathize:

1. *Concentration.* Increasing empathy requires that you use your powers of selection to concentrate specifically on what is said. This can be especially difficult in the face of minor needs and small pains that gain exaggerated importance in our minds. That your eyes are open, however, does not mean that you see, and that your ears are clear does not mean that you hear. As Max recounts his frustration at being unable to remember material he had worked on during his study period, your attention to what he is saying and feeling may be distracted by a horde of competing thoughts and feelings. But you can choose to concentrate your attention *on what Max is saying* rather than on the pain in your knee, the letter you must get into the mail before noon, or the sound of the rain against the window. This concentration requires personal commitment—you must direct the senses.

2. *Caring.* Whether you can empathize is related to how much you *care* about a person. If you remind yourself that other people and their problems are important, you will be more likely to care about what is happening to them. If you care, it will be much easier for you to empathize.

   Some people are reluctant to really care for *fear of showing weakness.* Everybody has feelings, and the willingness to show feelings is not unmanly or unwomanly or "un-" anything. If we hurt, we should feel free to show it. If we empathize with another person's pain, we should feel free to show that, too. Nevertheless, many people are guided by the belief that any demonstration of feelings—besides cheering at a football game—reveals weakness. If your belief that showing empathy is a sign of weakness keeps you from empathizing, we hope that you will take time to examine that belief. If you consider your own feelings for a moment, you can see the importance of caring.

How do you feel when people you care about show that they understand when you have been hurt, frightened, angered, pleased, or amazed? People want and need the same expression of empathy from you that you want and need from them.

3. *Observing.* If you will observe the behavior of your friends and acquaintances, you will notice that some are particularly skillful in accurate recognition of others' states of mind. Observe skilled people closely. Ask them for help. What are they doing to help themselves be more perceptive? Through careful observation and discussion with empathic people, you may pick up some helpful clues.

4. *Practice.* Your skill will improve as you gain experience empathizing in real situations. Develop the habit of answering at least two questions during a conversation with another person: "What state of mind do I believe the person is in right now?" and "What are the clues the person is giving that I am using to draw this conclusion?" Asking these questions will help you focus at least some of your attention on others instead of keeping your thoughts mostly on yourself. As you gain skill in making these assessments quickly, you may find yourself much more in tune with the moods, feelings, and attitudes of those with whom you wish to communicate. As a result of such practice, you may be able to maintain or even to create a more positive communication climate.

In the remainder of this chapter we will explore several specific response skills that may help you show empathy.

PRACTICE

Empathy

1. Think of the last time you fully empathized with another person. Did you both recognize and respond? What was the outcome?

2. Work with your partner. One person tells about a recent experience. The other person tries to create an image of what it would feel like to be in the situation the person is describing. Respond

in a way that you believe recognizes the nature of the person's feeling. The other person will then comment on whether you have captured the nature of that feeling.

CLARIFYING MEANING

Perhaps the greatest barrier to effective communication is misunderstanding. As a result of such things as assuming accuracy of meaning when it is inaccurate, inattention to what is being said, or the need to hurry, we misunderstand far more often than we realize. We can use two skills to clarify meaning: questioning, a familiar skill that we use regularly, and paraphrasing.

Questioning

Your understanding of another's meaning often depends upon your having enough information to work with. When a person has not given you complete information, your most appropriate response would be a question phrased to get additional information.

Although you have been asking questions ever since you learned to talk, you may still find that the questions you ask either don't get the information you want or irritate or fluster the other person. Such reactions may result from poorly phrased questions. Let's see how questions may be phrased to get the kind of information you want.

Types of information needed   The following are some of the most common reasons for questioning.

You can question to get important details:

ANN: Nell, would you stop at the store on the way home and buy me some more paper?

NELL: What kind of paper would you like me to get, and how much will you need?

You can question to clarify the use of a term:

MARTHA: He's just so sanctimonious.

ADELLE: Could you tell me what you mean by *sanctimonious*?

You can question to bring out a person's feelings:

NORM: Billy called, but he's not coming over.

KAY: Are you disappointed that he's not coming?

Phrasing questions in a nonthreatening manner Good questions are phrased so that people will perceive them as an honest effort to discover information, not as actual or veiled attacks. Here are some guidelines to help you phrase questions in a way that lessens the likelihood of arousing defensiveness.

First, make sure that you have a good reason for asking a question. If you need information to be helpful in reply, then continue. If you have some other reason, maybe a paraphrase or some other response is more appropriate. If you are just curious (nosy?), perhaps you need to curb your urge to question.

Second, clearly identify what it is you need to know. Is it more details, how a word is used or defined, or how the person feels? Phrase the question so that it is designed to get the information you need.

Third, phrase questions in ways that do not seem abrupt. For

instance, in response to the statement, "He's so sanctimonious," the questions "What?" or "What do you mean?" are likely to be perceived as too abrupt.

Fourth, use nonverbal cues. Speak with a tone of voice that is sincere—not a tone that could be interpreted as sarcastic, cutting, superior, dogmatic, or evaluative.

Finally, if there is any possibility that the person may perceive the question as an attack, put the burden of ignorance on your own shoulders. For instance, you may say, "Martha, I know *sanctimonious* is a common word, but I never can remember what it means. Can you tell me what you meant when you said, 'He's so sanctimonious'?"

The following examples demonstrate what we will call *empathic* questions, contrasted with examples of less-than-helpful or inappropriately phrased questions.

Fred comes out of the committee room and says, "They turned down my proposal again!" Art asks:

EMPATHIC
"Did they tell you why?" (This question is a sincere request for additional information.)

INAPPROPRIATE
"Well, did you explain it the way you should have?" (This question is a veiled attack on Fred in question form.)

As Jack and Maude are driving home from a party, Maude says, "With all those executives there I really felt strange." Jack asks:

EMPATHIC
"What is it about their presence that makes you feel strange?" (Here the question is designed to get information that may help Maude.)

INAPPROPRIATE
"When you're with executives, why do you always say such stupid things?" (With this question Jack is intentionally hurting Maude. He is making no effort to be sensitive to her feelings or to understand them.)

Good questions get the necessary information but with less probability of a defensive reply. The inappropriate questions, on the other hand, seem deliberately designed to undermine or attack the person being questioned. To be effective, questions must have an empathic base. Questioning is a useful response when the information sought is relevant to the conversation and when it comes out of a spirit of inquiry and support and not from a conscious or unconscious need to make the person look bad.

Paraphrasing

When you do not understand, you ask a question. Do you need any special response skill when you *think* you understand what a person means? *Yes*, because serious communication problems can occur even when you think—or, for that matter, even when you are *certain*—you understand the meaning. Frequently, what we think a person means is far different from what the person really means. In times when understanding what was said is especially important or in times of great stress, before you respond to what you think a person has said, *paraphrase*.

Paraphrasing means putting into words your understanding of the meaning you get from a person's statement. Paraphrasing is not mere repetition. If Charley says, "I'm really going to study this time" and George replies, "This time you're really going to study," George's repetition shows that he *heard* the statement but it does not show that he necessarily *understood* it. An effective paraphrase states the meaning received in the paraphraser's own words. In fact, George could have gotten any of several meanings from Charley's statement. If George thinks Charley is talking about specific study skills, George's paraphrase might be, "I take it this time you're going to read and outline every chapter carefully." George's statement is an acceptable paraphrase because it tells Charley the meaning George got from the expression "really going to study." If George's understanding is correct, Charley might say, "Right!" But if George received a meaning different from what Charley intended, Charley has an opportunity to correct the meaning with a statement such as "Well, I'm going to read the chapters more carefully, but I doubt I'll outline them."

Perhaps you're thinking, "If I were in this situation, I'd just ask Charley the question, 'What do you mean by *really study*?'" Certainly a sincere, well-worded question is appropriate when you are looking for additional information. But in this case George thinks he knows what "really study" means. So George is not really looking for new information; he's checking to make sure that what he (George) thinks of when he says "really study" is the same as what Charley meant.

Types of Paraphrases

When you put a statement into your own words, you may concentrate on the content of the message or on the speaker's feelings about the content. Either or both are appropriate, depending on the situation. *Content* means the substance, or the denotative meaning, of the message; *feelings* are the emotions that a person is having in reference to the content. Let's go back to Charley's statement, "I'm really going to study this time." A good content paraphrase would be, "So you're going to read and outline each chapter carefully"; a good feelings paraphrase would be, "So you're pretty upset with your grade on the last test." Do you see the difference? Let's try one more, this time using a longer message.

▶ "Five weeks ago I sent the revised manuscript of my textbook to the publisher. I was excited because I felt the changes I had made were excellent. You can imagine how I felt when I got the book back yesterday and one reviewer said he couldn't see that this draft was much different from the first."

CONTENT PARAPHRASE
"If I have this correct, you're saying that the person who reviewed the manuscript saw no difference, yet you think your draft was both different and better."

FEELINGS PARAPHRASE
"You seem disappointed that the reviewer didn't recognize the changes you had made."

Of course, in real life settings we are not as likely to make clear distinctions between content and feelings paraphrases. In fact, we're likely to do both. For instance, a typical paraphrase of the preceding statement might well be "If I have this right, you're saying that the editor who read your revision could see no real differences, yet you think your draft was not only much different but better. Moreover, I get the feeling that the editor's comments really irk you."

From the examples presented you probably realize that several paraphrases would be acceptable or appropriate for any statement. Now let's see how well you can do. Suppose you were talking with your professor about his summer.

PROFESSOR JOHNSON: I don't know how things went for you, but for me the summer really flew by. And I'm afraid I didn't get nearly as much done as I'd planned, but I guess I'm not surprised. I hardly ever accomplish as much as I plan. Anyway, I'm really looking forward to the new term. I look at it as getting a fresh start.

YOU: [Write a paraphrase here.]

As with most statements people make, Professor Johnson's include several ideas. Moreover, what he said is only a small part of what he is thinking. Your paraphrase represents *your* understanding of his message in *your* words, which may be similar to one of the following:

▶ I get the feeling that not getting everything done that you intended isn't nearly as important to you as the excitement of starting a new term.

▶ It sounds like you enjoyed the summer but you're really excited about getting back to school.

▶ If I understand correctly what you're saying, you always expect to get more done during the summer than what you accomplish, but it doesn't bother you because you're always so excited about starting a new term.

You may be thinking that if people stated their ideas and feelings accurately in the first place, you would not have to paraphrase. Accurate wording might help you understand better, but we hope that our study of language has shown you that people can seldom be sure they have a perfectly accurate understanding of what others say. Therefore, as a student of communication you will need to perfect your paraphrasing ability.

When to Paraphrase

Not only must you know how to paraphrase, but also you need to consider when the paraphrase is most useful. Common sense will tell you that you wouldn't paraphrase after every sentence. In fact, there are times when paraphrases are unnecessary. The following are four guidelines you can follow for determining *when* a paraphrase is most beneficial.

Before you state your own ideas or feelings, you should paraphrase the ideas or feelings of the other person when

1. You think you understand what a person has said or how a person feels about what was said, but you are not absolutely sure.
2. A better understanding of a message is necessary before you can respond appropriately.
3. You perceive that what the person has said is controversial or was said under some emotional strain.
4. You have some strong reaction to what the person has said or how the person has said it—and your strong reaction may have interfered with your interpretation of the message.

In summary, listen carefully to the message, determine what the message means to you, and if you believe a paraphrase is necessary, restate the message using your own words to indicate the meaning you have received.

PRACTICE

Questioning and Paraphrasing

1. Try to clarify the following statements by providing an appropriate question or paraphrase. To get you started we have done the first conversation for you.

ART: It's Sally's birthday, and I've planned a big evening. Sometimes I think Sally wonders whether I take her for granted—well, I think after tonight she'll know I think she's something special!

QUESTION
What are you planning to do?

CONTENT PARAPHRASE
I get the idea you've planned a night that's totally different from what Sally expects on her birthday.

FEELINGS PARAPHRASE
From the way you're talking, I get the feeling you're really excited about your plans for the evening.

ANGIE: Brother! Another nothing class. I keep thinking one of these days he'll get excited about something. Professor Jones is a real bore!

QUESTION:

CONTENT PARAPHRASE:

FEELINGS PARAPHRASE:

GUY: Everyone seems to be talking about that movie on Channel 5 last night, but I didn't see it. You know, I don't watch much that's on the "idiot box."

QUESTION:

CONTENT PARAPHRASE:

FEELINGS PARAPHRASE:

SARAH: I don't know if it's something to do with me or with Mom, but lately she and I just aren't getting along.

QUESTION:

CONTENT PARAPHRASE:

FEELINGS PARAPHRASE:

AILEEN: I've got a report due at work and a paper due in management class. On top of that, it's my sister's birthday and so far I haven't even had time to get her anything. Tomorrow's going to be a disaster.

QUESTION:

CONTENT PARAPHRASE:

FEELINGS PARAPHRASE:

2. Work in groups of three. A and B will hold a conversation on a topic such as "Why I like the type of work I'm doing," "The advantages or disadvantages of early retirement," or "Dealing with drug and/or alcohol abuse on campus or in industry." C will observe the conversation. For this exercise speakers are not allowed to state their ideas until they paraphrase what the other person has just said. At the end of three to four minutes, the observer (C) discusses the paraphrasing of the two participants. Then for three to four minutes B and C converse and A observes; for the final three to four minutes C and A converse and B observes.

After the exercise is complete, the participants discuss how they felt about paraphrasing and how the paraphrasing affected the conversations.

HELPING OTHERS

Helping responses show approval of a person's feelings or acknowledge the person's right to have feelings; at times they may reward people or they may show people how to do something better. In this section we will consider *supporting, interpreting, praise,* and *constructive criticism.*

Supporting

When people express their feelings to you, they are often in need of some kind of supporting response. **Supporting** is saying something that soothes, approves, reduces tension, or pacifies. Supporting shows that you empathize with a person's *feelings.* The feelings you are responding to may be either positive (joy, elation, pride, satisfaction) or negative (sadness, anger, sorrow, disappointment). Supporting statements are useful whether the feeling is mild or so intense that it almost short-circuits the thinking process. Whatever the direction or intensity of the feeling, the supporting statement shows that you can empathize with that feeling, that you care about the person and what happens to him or her, and that you acknowledge the person's right to that feeling—whether a person "should" be having the feeling is not the issue.

Supporting positive feelings   People like to treasure their good feelings; they don't want them dashed by inappropriate or insensitive words. When a person's feelings are positive, your supporting statement is an attempt to share in the feelings and help sustain them.

JULIA (*hangs up the telephone and turns to Gloria*): That was my boss. He said he'd put my name in for promotion. I didn't realize he had ever really considered me promotable.

GLORIA: Julia, that's great. I'm so happy for you. You really seem excited.

Gloria perceives that Julia is very happy with the news. The statement "You really seem excited" shows that Gloria recognizes Julia's feeling; the statement "I'm so happy for you" goes on to show that Gloria *cares* about what happens to Julia.

Supporting negative feelings   When a person's feelings are negative, your supporting statement is an attempt to help the person work through the feeling without intensifying it or in some other way becoming more uncomfortable or unhappy. Your responsibility to make an·appropriate response may be most difficult in situations of high emotion and stress. When a person's feelings are highly negative, that person may need a few seconds, a few minutes, or even a few hours to calm down and think rationally. When a person expresses a highly negative emotion, you want to say something that will help defuse the emotion so the person can begin to return to normal.

JULIA (*slams down the phone*): That was my boss—he called to tell me that they're letting me go at work, but he wouldn't even tell me why!

GLORIA: Oh Julia—that must hurt. Anything I can do to help?

Gloria, empathizing with Julia, perceives her shock and anger. The statement "Oh Julia—that must hurt" verbalizes her recognition of the feeling; the statement "Anything I can do to help?" indicates that Gloria cares about what is happening to Julia and is ready to do something to help her through this moment of disbelief.

Since negative feelings and negative situations are the most difficult to handle, let's look at two more examples that deal with negative situations.

JIM (*comes out the door of his history class clutching the paper he had been so sure he would receive a B or an A on*): Jacobs gave me a D on the paper. I worked my tail off, did everything she asked, and she gave me a D.

AARON: A D! As hard as you worked I can see why you're so upset. That's a real blow.

Aaron's response is primarily an empathizing statement. It shows an understanding of why Jim is so upset. Aaron's saying "That's a real blow" further shows that he is in tune with Jim's feelings. Perhaps at this point you might be inclined to say, "Jim, I can see why you feel so bad. You deserved an A!" Although such a statement would have supporting qualities, Aaron is in no position to judge whether the paper did, in fact, *deserve* an A. The support comes with Aaron showing an understanding of how hard Jim worked and, therefore, why Jim feels especially bad. You need to be very careful about making statements that either are not true or that only tell people what they want to hear.

Sometimes there is virtually nothing you can say that will be perceived as helpful. At these times perhaps the very best way of showing your support is just being there and listening. Consider this one:

> NANCY (*with a few seconds left in the basketball game and her team trailing by one point, Nancy steals the ball from her opponent, dribbles down the court for an uncontested layup, and misses. The gun sounds, ending the game. Nancy runs to her coach with tears in her eyes.*): I blew it! I lost us the game!

A first reaction might be to say "Don't feel bad, Nancy." But Nancy obviously does feel bad, and she has a right to those feelings. Another response might be "It's OK, Nancy, you didn't lose us the game." But at that moment Nancy's miss did affect the outcome of the game. Perhaps the best thing the coach can do at that moment is to put her arm around Nancy to show that she understands. Later she could say, "Nancy, I know you feel bad—but without your steal we wouldn't even have had a chance to win." Still, for the moment Nancy is going to be difficult to console.

Making supporting statements is not always easy. Instead, you may be tempted to give advice. But if your goal is to soothe or reduce tension, then just acknowledging the feeling will most likely accomplish the purpose.

To make a supporting statement you should listen closely to what the person is saying, try to empathize with those feelings, and phrase a reply that is in harmony with the feeling you have identified. Later in the conversation you may be able to say something that will help the person overcome the particular problem involved. If it seems appropriate, you might indicate your willingness to be of service.

Interpreting

When a person sees only one possible explanation of a given event, your most helpful response may be to provide an interpretation. **Interpreting** is attempting to point out an alternative or hidden view of an event to help a person see things from a different perspective. Many times people will say something about themselves or what they are thinking or feeling that shows a very limited view of a given event. People who are depressed for some reason are often likely to read the worst into events and behaviors. Consider the following situation:

> (*After returning from his first date with Natalie, a woman he believes he might become very fond of, Ken is very concerned. He had an excellent time, yet the end of the evening was very disappointing.*)

> KEN: I take her to dinner and a great show, and when I get to her door she gives me a quick little kiss, says "Thanks a lot," and rushes into the house. We didn't even have much time to talk about the play. I guess she really didn't like me.

Ken is interpreting Natalie's behavior negatively. He sees her action as a rejection of him as a person. Martin does not know what Natalie thinks, but he sees Ken as taking a very limited view of the events.

> MARTIN: I wonder whether she might not have been afraid that if she did any more you'd get the wrong idea about what kind of girl she is.

Whose interpretation is correct? We don't know. What we do know is that behavior can frequently be interpreted in more than one way. Too often, especially when we feel slighted, angry, or hurt, we interpret events negatively. Listen carefully to what a person is saying. If there are other reasonable ways to look at the event, presenting those potential alternatives may be a useful response. When appropriate, preface the interpretive statement with a supportive one. When interpreting, remember that you are not a mind reader—you cannot know for sure why something was done or said. Your goal is to help a person look at an event from different points of view.

The following are two additional examples to show how interpreting can work:

> POLLY: I just don't understand Bill. I say we've got to start saving money, and he just gets angry with me.

> ANGIE: I can understand why his behavior would concern you [*a supportive statement prefacing an interpretation*]. Perhaps he feels guilty about not being able to save money or feels resentful that you seem to be putting all the blame on him.

> GLEN: I just don't seem to understand Aldrich. He says my work is top-notch, but I haven't got a pay raise in over a year.

> SID: I can see why you'd be frustrated, but maybe the company just doesn't have the money.

Praise

When people say or do things well, they deserve praise. Too often, however, the positive things people say and do are passed over with little comment. Yet from our earlier discussion of self-concept, you'll remember that what we are, as well as how we behave, is often shaped by how others respond to us. When people have done something you appreciate, take the time to tell them.

▶ When Gwenn makes an excellent tennis shot, you might say, "Gwenn, that ball was right into the corner. You've got a very good backhand."

▶ When Marty offers to share his lunch with a student who forgot his lunch money that day, you might say, "Marty, that was nice of you to share your lunch with Pete. You're a very warmhearted person."

▶ Or when your mother prepares an excellent dessert, you might say, "Gee, mom, I can't believe that after working all day you still had energy to make a pie. Thanks."

Praising doesn't take much time, and it is almost always appreciated.

Which expression of praise do you prefer to receive—a warm hug or simply a verbal compliment? Which do you prefer to give?

Constructive Criticism

At times people need help so they can perform better. A necessary and yet far too often misused response is constructive criticism. **Constructive criticism** is evaluation of behavior—usually negative—given to help a person identify or correct a fault. To grow, to achieve our potential, we often need corrective help. Yet, because it is so easy, most of us are far too quick to criticize. Even though some people learn faster and better through praise of what is done well rather than through criticism of what is done poorly, there are still times when criticism is useful, especially when a person asks for criticism.

Because criticism is such an abused skill, we offer several guidelines that will help you compose criticism that is both constructive and beneficial.

1. *Make sure that the person is interested in hearing criticism.* The safest rule to follow is to withhold any criticism until it is asked for. Criticism will be of no value if a person is not interested in hearing it.

   If a person has not asked for criticism but you feel that criticism would be beneficial, you might ask the person whether he or she is interested in criticism. Remember, however, that even if the person says "yes," you must proceed carefully. Look for signs of receptiveness; watch verbal or nonverbal cues indicating that some criticism would be welcomed. For instance, you might ask, "Are you interested in hearing any comments about the way you handled the meeting?"

2. *Before you criticize, make sure that you describe the person's behavior carefully and accurately.* **Describing behavior** means accurately recounting specific observable behavior without labeling the behavior good or bad, right or wrong. Because criticism alone does not inform, it may be met with defensive reactions. Describing behavior builds an informative base on which good criticism may be built. Moreover, criticism that is preceded with detailed description is less likely to be met defensively.

   If Paul asks, "What do you think of my forehand?" instead of saying, "It's terrible," it would be better to say something like "You're bringing your arm back behind you at the start of your swing. I think this is causing you to go off line with the swing and to lose much of your power."

3. *Try to preface a negative statement with a positive one whenever possible.* When you are planning to criticize, it is a good idea to start with some praise. But, of course, common sense suggests that superficial praise followed by crushing criticism will be seen for what it is. Thus, saying "Betty, that's a pretty blouse you have on, but you did a perfectly miserable job of running the meeting" will be rightly perceived as patronizing. A better approach would be "Betty, you did a good job of drawing

Sam into the discussion. He usually sits through an entire meeting without saying a word. But you seem hesitant to use the same power to keep the meeting on track. You seem content to let anybody talk about anything, even if it is unrelated to the agenda." The praise here is significant; if you cannot preface a criticism with significant praise, then don't try. Prefacing criticism with empty comments made to be nice is usually worthless.

4. *Be as specific as possible.* In the situation just discussed, it would not have been helpful to say, "You had some leadership problems." If the person wasn't in control, say so; if the person failed to get agreement on one item before moving on to another, say so. The more specific the criticism, the more effectively the person will be able to deal with the information.

5. *The criticism should concern recent behavior.* No one is helped much by hearing about something the person did last week or last month. Criticism is best when it is fresh. If you have to spend time recreating a situation and refreshing someone's memory, the criticism probably will be ineffective.

6. *Direct criticism at behavior the person can do something about.* It is pointless to remind someone of a shortcoming over which the person has no control. It may be true that Jack would find it easier to prepare arguments if he had taken a course in logic, but telling him so will not improve his reasoning. Telling him he needs to work on stating main points clearly and backing them up with good evidence is helpful because he can change these behaviors.

7. *Show the person you are criticizing what can be done to improve.* Don't limit your comments to what a person has done wrong. Tell the person how what was done could have been done better. If Gail, the chairperson of a committee, cannot get her members to agree on anything, you might suggest that she try phrasing her remarks to the committee differently; for example, "Gail, when you think discussion is ended, say something like, 'It sounds as if we agree that our donation should be made to a single agency. Is that correct?'"

PRACTICE

Helping Responses

1. Read each of the following situations. Supply responses that are supportive (S) and interpretive (I).

▶ The pie is all gone! I know there were at least two pieces left just a while ago. Kids! They can be so inconsiderate.

S:

I:

▶ My boss was really on me today. I worked hard all day, but things just didn't jell for me. I don't know—maybe I've been spending too much time on some of the accounts.

S:

I:

▶ I just got a call from my folks. My sister was in a car accident. They say she's OK, but the car was totalled. Apparently she had her seat belt fastened when it happened. But I don't know whether she's really all right or whether they just don't want me to worry.

S:

I:

2. Write out exactly what you said the last time you criticized some-one's behavior. Which, if any, of the guidelines for constructive criticism did you follow or violate? If you were to do it again, what would you say differently?

3. Consider the following two situations. Work out an appropriate phrasing of criticism for each:
   a. You have been driving to school with a fellow student whose name you got from the transportation office at school. You have known him for only three weeks. Everything about the situation is great except that he drives too fast for you.
   b. A good friend says "you know" more than once every sentence. You like her very much, but you see that others are beginning to avoid her. She is a very sensitive girl who does not usually take criticism well.

   Working in groups, share your phrasings of the criticism. Which of the wordings best meets the guidelines?

PROBLEM RESPONSES

Sometimes even the best communicators respond in ways that create problems. Good communicators are aware of when they have made mistakes and try to repair them immediately and avoid them in the future. Responses create problems when they cause people to feel a need to protect themselves, when they cause people to question their self-worth, and when they fail to achieve their goal.

We have already considered evaluation as a problem response. Four others are the *irrelevant*, the *tangential*, the *incongruous*, and the *interrupting response.*

Irrelevant Response

An **irrelevant response** is one that bears no relation to what has been said—in effect, it ignores the sender entirely.

BOB: I'm concerned with the way Paul is handling arrangements for the benefit.

TOM: Hey, the Russian gymnasts are coming to town—I've got to get tickets for that.

When peoples' statements are totally ignored, it not only causes them to question whether they were heard but may also cause them to wonder about the worth of what they were thinking or saying—because anything important will not be ignored. In this example Tom's irrelevant response is disconfirming because it is likely to cause Bob to wonder about the importance of what he was saying.

Tangential Response

A **tangential response** is really an irrelevant response in tactful language. It is better in that it at least suggests acknowledgment of what a person was saying. But the net result, changing the subject, is the same:

BOB: I'm concerned with the way Paul is handling arrangements for the benefit.

TOM: Well, you know Paul—I remember once when I was in charge of arrangements, I forgot who I was supposed to contact.

Even though Tom has acknowledged Bob's statement, by shifting emphasis to his own experience Tom appears to be saying that the issue is not important enough to discuss. Again, such responses chip away at a person's feelings of self-worth. Bob thought that he was raising an issue of great importance. Either Tom fails to see the importance of Bob's statement or Bob places too much emphasis on Paul's behavior. The problem is that Tom's response copes with neither possibility. The subject matter of Paul's behavior is left unresolved. The apparent withdrawal by Tom from discussing Paul's behavior creates a problem between Bob and Tom.

Incongruous Response

In our discussion of nonverbal communication we indicated that problems occur when nonverbal messages appear to conflict with the verbal messages. An **incongruous response** is an example of this problem:

BOB: Well, we got some things done today.

TOM: Yeah, that was a great meeting [*stated in sarcastic tones*].

On the surface Tom seems to be acknowledging and verifying Bob's statement, but his sarcastic tone causes Bob to wonder whether he is confirming Bob's ideas or making fun of them. Since nonverbal reactions are likely to override verbal meaning with most people, it is most likely that Bob will take Tom's words as sarcasm. If they are, in fact, sarcastic, a barrier begins to build through Tom's insensitivity to Bob's honest statement of feelings. If Tom's words are sincere, a barrier begins to build as a result of Bob's confusion about Tom's meaning.

Interrupting Response

An **interrupting response** occurs when a person breaks in before the other person has finished a statement.

BOB: I'm concerned with the way Paul . . .

TOM: I know—that Paul is something else, but I don't think there's any real problem.

People interrupt when they believe what they have to say is superior to what the other person is saying, when they believe they know what the other person is going to say and they want that person to know they already know, or when they are not paying careful attention. Any of these three common reasons shows a lack of sensitivity or a superior attitude. People need to be able to verbalize their ideas and feelings fully; constant interruptions are bound either to damage peoples' self-concepts or make them hostile—and possibly both. Whatever you have to say is seldom so important that it requires you to interrupt a person. When you do interrupt, you should realize that you are putting a person down and increasing chances for a defensive reaction. The more frequent the interruptions, the greater the harm.

Are you an interrupter? This behavior is so common that many of us don't even realize how often we do it. Do you like to be interrupted? Very few people can honestly say that they do. Our advice is to check personal behavior very closely. For the rest of the day, be very conscious of any time you interrupt—whatever the reason. Remember that the person you interrupt feels much the same as you do when you are interrupted.

SUMMARY

How you respond to others is vital in determining the quality of the conversation.

Empathizing is being able to detect and identify the immediate affective state of another and to respond in an appropriate manner. Empathy is promoted by concentrating on the other person's words and nonverbal reactions and by caring about that person. To ensure being able to empathize, you will have to guard against concentrating too much on your own needs and feelings.

Clarifying responses help to make sure people are holding the same meanings. Questioning and paraphrasing are two skills that you can use to ensure understanding.

Helpful responses give people information about themselves or about what they have said. By supporting, interpreting, praising, and giving constructive criticism you can be helpful. There are several guidelines that must be followed to ensure beneficial criticism: make sure the person is interested in hearing criticism; describe the person's behavior carefully and accurately; precede negative statements with positive ones, if possible; be specific; examine only recent behavior; direct criticism at behavior under the person's control; and show what a person can do to correct a problem.

Inappropriate responses hinder communication—they plant the seeds of discontent within people about themselves or about what they are thinking or feeling, and they ignore or scuttle efforts at understanding meaning. Irrelevant comments, tangential statements, incongruous replies, and interrupting are some of the most common types of responses that should be avoided.

SUGGESTED READINGS

Gazda, George, et al. *Human Relations Development: A Manual for Educators.* 3rd ed. Boston: Allyn & Bacon, 1984 (paperback). This entire book focuses on developing "helpful response" skills. It provides a good supplement to material in the chapter.

Kelly, Jeffrey A. *Social-Skills Training: A Practical Guide for Interventions.* New York: Springer, 1982. Contains an excellent discussion of skills acquisition.

Pace, R. Wayne, Brent D. Peterson, and Terrence R. Radcliffe, eds., *Communicating Interpersonally—A Reader.* Columbus, Ohio: Charles E. Merrill Publishing Co., 1973. See particularly John L. Wallen's article, "Developing Effective Interpersonal Communication," pp. 218–233. An excellent discussion of response skills.

*C*OMMUNICATING *I*DEAS AND *F*EELINGS

OBJECTIVES

After you have read this chapter, you should be able to:

1   List and explain guidelines for self-disclosure

2   Explain differences between withholding feelings, expressing feelings, and describing feelings

3   Describe your feelings accurately

4   State a point assertively without becoming aggressive

5   List and explain sources of social power

6   Credit self and others

7   Ask for criticism

8   Avoid the pitfalls of transfer stations, information overload, and hidden agenda

Do you take the time to tell others what you're really thinking and feeling? Do you do it clearly and concisely? For a lot of people the answer is a resounding *no*. In fact one study showed that many married people talk to each other only 27½ minutes per week! And little of that time involved sharing ideas and feelings.

When you are sharing ideas and feelings, which skills represent a measure of communication competence? In this chapter we consider self-disclosure, describing feelings, assertiveness, crediting, and asking for criticism. We also consider three pitfalls to avoid: transfer stations, information overload, and hidden agenda.

SELF-DISCLOSURE

Effective interpersonal communication requires some degree of self-disclosure. **Self-disclosure** means sharing biographical data, personal ideas, and feelings about yourself. The first of these, sharing biographical data, reveals facts about you as an individual. A statement like "I was five-foot-six when I was in tenth grade" discloses biographical information. Biographical disclosures are the easiest to make, for they are, in a manner of speaking, a matter of public record. "I don't believe prisons ever really rehabilitate criminals" discloses a personal idea. Sharing personal ideas reveals what and how you think. "I get scared whenever I have to make a speech" discloses feelings.

Self-disclosure enables other people to get to know you. Usually the more that people know about a person, the more likely they are to like that person. Yet self-disclosure does carry a degree of risk. For just as knowing a person better is likely to result in closer interpersonal relations, learning too much about a person *may* result in alienation. The statement "Familiarity breeds contempt" means that some people can learn too much about another person; eventually they learn something that detracts from the relationship. Because some people fear that their disclosures could have negative rather than positive consequences, they prefer not to disclose in the belief they will get no reaction at all.

A risk-free life (probably impossible to attain) might be safe, but it would not be very satisfying. Since some risk is vital to achieving a gain, but too much risk can be more costly than we wish, what should we do? The following are guidelines for determining an appropriate amount of self-disclosure in interpersonal encounters.

1. *Self-disclosure should begin with the kind of information you want others to disclose to you.* When people are getting to know others, they look for information that is generally shared freely among people, such as talking about hobbies, sports, school, and current events. These are the kinds of disclosures that you should make early in a relationship.

2. *Self-disclosure of more intimate information should come when you be-lieve the disclosure represents an acceptable risk.* There is always some risk involved in disclosing, but as you gain trust in another person, you perceive the disclosure of more revealing information as "safe." Inciden-tally, this guideline explains why some people engage in self-disclosure to bartenders or to people they meet in travel. The disclosures they make are perceived as safe (representing reasonable risk) because the per-son either does not know them or is in no position to use the information against them. It seems sad to us that these people do not trust their husbands, wives, or other members of the family enough to make the disclosures to them.

3. *Self-disclosure should move gradually to deeper levels.* Since receiving self-disclosure can be as threatening as giving it, most people become uncomfortable when the level of disclosure exceeds their expectations. As a friendship develops, the depth of disclosure increases as well.

4. *Intimate or very personal self-disclosure is most appropriate in ongoing close relationships.* Disclosures about deep feelings, fears, loves, and so forth are most appropriate in close, well-established relationships. When people disclose deep secrets to acquaintances, they are engag-ing in potentially threatening behavior. If disclosure is made before a bond of trust is established, the person making the disclosure may be risking a great deal. Moreover, people are often embarrassed by and hostile toward others who try to saddle them with personal information in an effort to establish a relationship where none exists.

5. *Intimate self-disclosure should continue only if it is reciprocated.* When people disclose, they expect disclosure in return. When it is apparent

that self-disclosure will not be returned, you should limit the amount of disclosure you make. Lack of return is likely to be a sign that a person does not feel the relationship is one in which deep self-disclosure is truly appropriate.

6. *Remember that people's attitudes about disclosure vary considerably, and what you would consider as appropriate or inappropriate may not be so to someone else.*

The following exercise is intended to help you analyze your feelings about disclosure and to show the potential for variation among even your peers.

PRACTICE

Self-Disclosure

1. Think of one secret about yourself. How many people know it? How do you decide whom to tell? What have been some of the consequences (good and bad) that have resulted from sharing that secret?

2. Label each of the following statements L (low risk, meaning you believe it is appropriate to disclose this information to people you first meet); M (moderate risk, meaning you believe it is appropriate to disclose this information to people you know pretty well and have already established a friendship with); H (high risk, meaning you would disclose such information only to the few friends you greatly trust or to your most intimate friends); or X, meaning you would disclose it to no one.

_____ a. Your hobbies—how you like best to spend your spare time
_____ b. Your preferences and dislikes in music
_____ c. Your educational background and your feelings about it
_____ d. Your personal views on politics, the presidency, and foreign and domestic policy
_____ e. Your personal religious views and the nature of your religious participation
_____ f. Habits and reactions of yours that bother you at the moment
_____ g. Characteristics of yours that give you pride and satisfaction
_____ h. The unhappiest moments in your life—in detail
_____ i. The occasions in your life when you were happiest—in detail
_____ j. The actions you have most regretted taking in your life and why
_____ k. The main unfulfilled wishes and dreams in your life

_____ l. Your guiltiest secrets

_____ m. Your views on the way a husband and wife should live their marriage

_____ n. What to do, if anything, to stay fit

_____ o. The aspects of your body you are most pleased with

_____ p. The features of your appearance you are most displeased with and wish to change

_____ q. The person in your life whom you most resent and the reasons why

_____ r. Your favorite forms of erotic play and sexual lovemaking

_____ s. The people with whom you have been sexually intimate and the circumstances of your relationship with each

3. Working with others in groups, discuss your labeling of the statements. You are not required to make any of the disclosures, only to discuss why you would or would not make them and under what circumstances, if any. The purpose of discussion is to see how people differ in what they view as acceptable disclosure.

DEALING WITH FEELINGS

One very important self-disclosure skill is describing feelings. Everyone has feelings. The question is how to deal with the feelings we have. Three ways that people deal with their feelings are (1) to withhold them, (2) to express or display them, and (3) to describe them. Although each of the three ways is appropriate under some circumstances, describing feelings is especially useful for educating others about how you want them to treat you. Let's discuss each of these behaviors.

Withholding Feelings

Withholding feelings means keeping feelings inside and not giving any verbal or nonverbal cues that might reveal those feelings to others. Withholding feelings is best exemplified by the good poker player who develops a "poker face," a neutral look that is impossible to decipher. The look is the same whether the player's cards are good or bad. Unfortunately, many people use poker faces for all their interpersonal relationships. Whether they hurt inside or are extremely excited, no one knows. For instance, Doris feels very nervous when Candy stands over her while Doris is working on her report. Then when Candy says, "That first paragraph isn't very well written," Doris begins to seethe, yet she says nothing. Her lack of response is an example of withholding feelings.

Psychologists believe that when people withhold negative feelings, they can develop physical problems, such as ulcers, high blood pressure, and heart disease, and psychological problems, such as stress, neuroses, and psychoses. When people withhold positive feelings, they are often perceived by others as cold, undemonstrative, and not much fun to be around.

Is withholding ever appropriate? When a situation is inconsequential, you may well choose to withhold your feelings. For instance, a stranger's inconsiderate behavior at a party may bother you, but since you can move to another part of the room, withholding may not be detrimental. In our example of Doris seething at Candy's behavior, however, withholding could be costly to Doris.

Expressing or Displaying Feelings

The second way of dealing with feelings is to express or to display them. **Expressing or displaying feelings** means giving an immediate non-verbal and/or verbal response to the feelings. Cheering over a great play at a sporting event, booing the umpire at a perceived bad call, patting a

Some people easily demonstrate their feelings; others are more reticent. Which type of person do you prefer to socialize with?

person on the back when the person does something well, or kicking a chair when you stub your toe are all expressions or displays of feelings.

An open expression or display of your negative feelings may be good for you psychologically but is likely to be very bad interpersonally. For instance, had Doris lashed out at Candy by saying, "Who the hell asked you for your opinion!" her display might have made Doris feel better but it would certainly create interpersonal problems with Candy. On the other hand, when you are experiencing positive feelings, a display can be very helpful. For instance, if Paul retrieves the books you left in chemistry class, a warm smile and a sincere "thanks" will be well received.

In fact, many people need to be even more demonstrative of good feelings. You've probably seen the bumper sticker "Have you hugged your kid today?" It reinforces the point that you need to demonstrate love and affection constantly to show another person that you really care.

Describing Feelings

The final way people handle their feelings is by describing them. **Describing feelings** simply means putting your immediate emotional state into words. Describing is often the best strategy for dealing with feelings, not only because it gives you the best chance for a positive outcome but also, as we said, because describing feelings teaches people how to treat you.

When you describe your feelings, people are made aware of the effect of their behavior. This knowledge gives them the information needed to determine whether they should continue or repeat that behavior. If you tell Paul that you really feel flattered when he visits you, such a statement should encourage Paul to visit you again; likewise, when you tell Cliff that you feel very angry when he borrows your jacket without asking, he is more likely to ask the next time he borrows a jacket. Describing your feelings allows you to exercise a measure of control over others' behavior toward you.

Keep in mind that describing and expressing are not the same. Many times people think they are describing when in fact they are expressing feelings. The first part of the communication practice at the end of this section focuses on your developing awareness of the difference between expressing or displaying and describing feelings.

If describing feelings is so important to communication effectiveness, why don't more people do it regularly? There seem to be at least four reasons why many people don't describe feelings.

1. *Many people have a poor vocabulary of words for describing the various feelings they are experiencing.* People can sense that they are angry; they may not know whether what they are feeling might best be described as annoyed, betrayed, cheated, crushed, disturbed, furious,

outraged, or shocked. Each of these words describes a slightly different aspect of what many people lump together as anger. The second part of the communication practice at the end of this section focuses on your developing a vocabulary that gives you the power of describing your feelings more precisely.

2. *Many people believe that describing their true feelings reveals too much about them.* If you tell people when their behavior hurts you, you risk their using the information against you when they want to hurt you *on purpose.* Although this is true, the potential benefits far outweigh the risks. For instance, if Pete has a nickname for you that you don't like and you tell Pete that calling you by that nickname really makes you nervous and tense, Pete *may* use the nickname when he wants to hurt you, but he is more likely to stop calling you by that name. If, on the other hand, you don't describe your feelings to Pete, he is probably going to call you by that name all the time because he doesn't know any better. When you say nothing, you reinforce his behavior. The level of risk varies with each situation, but you will more often improve a relationship than be hurt by describing feelings.

3. *Many people believe that if they describe feelings, others will make them feel guilty about having such feelings.* At a very tender age we all learned about "tactful" behavior. Under the premise that "the truth sometimes hurts" we learned to avoid the truth by not saying anything or by telling "little" lies. Perhaps when you were young your mother said, "Don't forget to give Grandma a great big kiss." At that time you may have blurted out, "Ugh—it makes me feel yucky to kiss Grandma. She's got a mustache." If your mother responded, "That's terrible—your grandma loves you. Now you give her a kiss and never let me hear you talk like that again!" then you probably felt guilty for having this "wrong" feeling. But the point is that the thought of kissing your grandma made you feel "yucky" whether it should have or not. In this case what was at issue was the way you talked about the feelings—not your having the feelings.

4. *Many people believe that describing feelings causes harm to others or to a relationship.* If it really bothers Max when his girlfriend, Dora, bites her fingernails, Max may believe that describing his feelings to Dora may hurt her so much that the knowledge will drive a wedge into their relationship. So it's better for Max to say nothing, right? Wrong! If Max says nothing, he's still going to be bothered by Dora's behavior. In fact, as time goes on, it is likely that being bothered by this will cause Max to lash out at Dora for other things because he can't bring himself to talk about the behavior that really bothers him. The net result will likely be that Dora will be hurt by Max's behavior. Only Dora won't understand why. The point is that how Max feels may well drive a wedge into their relationship anyway.

If Max does describe his feelings to Dora, she might quit or at least try to quit biting her nails; they might get into a discussion in which he finds out that she doesn't want to but that she just can't seem to stop, and he can help her in her efforts to stop; or they might discuss the problem and Max may see that it is a small thing really and not let it bother him as much. The point is that describing feelings has more chances of successful outcome than not describing them has.

To describe your feelings, first put the emotion you are feeling into words. Be specific. (The second part of the communication practice at the end of this unit is designed to provide the necessary vocabulary so that you will have the necessary specific words to use.) Second, indicate what triggered the feeling. Finally, make sure that you indicate that the feeling is yours. For example, suppose your roommate borrows your jacket without asking. When he returns, you describe your feelings by saying, "Cliff, I [indication that the feeling is yours] get really angry [the feeling] when you borrow my jacket without asking [trigger]." Or suppose that Carl has just reminded you of the very first time he brought you a rose. You describe your feelings by saying, "Carl, I [indication that the feeling is yours] get really tickled [the feeling] when you remind me about that first time you brought me a rose [trigger]."

You may find it easiest to begin by describing positive feelings: "I really feel elated knowing that you were the one who nominated me for the position" or "I'm delighted that you offered to help me with the housework." As you gain success with positive descriptions, you can try negative feelings attributable to environmental factors: "It's so cloudy; I feel gloomy" or "When the wind howls through the cracks, I really get jumpy." Finally, you can move to negative descriptions resulting from what people have said or done: "Your stepping in front of me like that really annoys me" or "The tone of your voice confuses me."

PRACTICE

Describing Feelings

1. In each of the following sets of statements, place a D next to the statement or statements that describe feelings:

1. _____ a. That was a great movie!
   _____ b. I was really cheered up by the story.
   _____ c. I feel this is worth an Oscar.
   _____ d. Terrific!

2. _____ a. I feel you're a good writer.
   _____ b. Your writing brings me to tears.
   _____ c. [You pat the writer on the back] Good job.
   _____ d. Everyone likes your work.

3. ____ a. Yuck!
   ____ b. If things don't get better, I'm going to move.
   ____ c. Did you ever see such a hole!
   ____ d. I feel depressed by the dark halls.

4. ____ a. I'm not adequate as a leader of this group.
   ____ b. Damn—I goofed!
   ____ c. I feel inadequate in my efforts to lead the group.
   ____ d. I'm depressed by the effects of my leadership.

5. ____ a. I'm a winner.
   ____ b. I feel I won because I'm most qualified.
   ____ c. I did it! I won!
   ____ d. I'm ecstatic about winning that award.

ANSWERS: 1. b. (a) is expressive/evaluative; (c) is an evaluation dressed in descriptive clothing—that the word *feel* is in a statement does not mean the person is truly describing feelings. "This is worth an Oscar" is an evaluation, not a feeling; (d) is an expression.
2. b. (a) is expressive/evaluative (there's that word *feel* again); (c) is expressive; (d) is expressive/evaluative.
3. d. (a) is expressive; (b) is the result of feelings but not a description of feelings; (c) is evaluation in question form.
4. c and d. (a) is expressive/evaluative; (b) is expressive; (c) is similar to (a) except that here the feeling is described, not stated as an evaluation.
5. d. (a) is evaluative; (b) is evaluative; (c) is expressive.

2. The following is a list of nearly 200 words that can be used to describe feelings. For your convenience, they have been grouped under several broad headings. As you look at each, say "I feel . . ." and try to identify the feeling this word would describe. Which are words that are meaningful enough to you that you could use them to help make your communication of feelings more precise?

WORDS RELATED TO **ANGER**

aggravated	cruel	incensed	steaming
cranky	hostile	resentful	bitter
furious	outraged	annoyed	frenzied
irritated	angry	exasperated	infuriated
agitated	enraged	indignant	vicious

WORDS RELATED TO **HAPPINESS**

amused	fantastic	joyous	tickled
cheerful	high	thrilled	charmed
excited	soothed	calm	elated
happy	blissful	ecstatic	gratified
proud	delighted	glad	pleased
contented	giddy	jubilant	turned on

WORDS RELATED TO *HURT*

abandoned	desperate	hassled	upset
deserted	isolated	rotten	deprived
ignored	rejected	trapped	forsaken
pathetic	terrible	cheated	oppressed
snubbed	awful	dreadful	slighted
abused	dismal	scorned	wiped out

WORDS RELATED TO *BELITTLED*

betrayed	incapable	intimidated	useless
helpless	insulted	unworthy	foolish
inferior	unfit	deflated	inept
run down	defeated	inadequate	powerless
crippled	incompetent	persecuted	worn out

WORDS RELATED TO *LOVING*

affectionate	passionate	gentle	gracious
heavenly	aroused	tender	vivacious
amorous	sensitive	charming	bewitched

WORDS RELATED TO *EMBARRASSED*

anxious	humbled	silly	disgraced
doomed	ridiculous	conspicuous	overwhelmed
regretful	chagrined	jittery	thwarted
awkward	humiliated	troubled	perplexed

WORDS RELATED TO *DISGUST*

disgusted	revolted	sickened	wary
repulsed	loathsome	nauseated	obnoxious

WORDS RELATED TO *ENERGETIC*

assured	eager	lively	tough
determined	inspired	strong	confident
hardy	secure	clever	genial
robust	brave	frisky	potent
bold	firm	peppy	vigorous

WORDS RELATED TO *LONELY*

abandoned	forsaken	scorned	empty
excluded	rejected	deserted	lonely
lost	bored	jilted	snubbed
alone	ignored	slighted	isolated

WORDS RELATED TO *SURPRISED*

astounded	jarred	shocked	distracted
flustered	rattled	confused	perplexed
puzzled	bewildered	mystified	stunned
baffled	jolted	startled	astonished

WORDS RELATED TO _SAD_

blue	gloomy	pained	downcast
frustrated	moody	depressed	melancholy
miserable	dejected	low	weary
burdened	let down	troubled	dejected

WORDS RELATED TO _FEAR_

alarmed	jumpy	threatened	frightened
jittery	terrified	fearful	scared
shaken	cornered	petrified	uneasy
boxed in	nervous	troubled	bullied

WORDS RELATED TO _HELPFUL_

agreeable	helpful	compassionate	cordial
gentle	caring	obliging	supportive
amiable	neighborly	cooperative	collegial

3. Working with at least one other person, role-play typical situations (for example, Tom's roommate borrows Tom's car without asking permission; the roommate comes into the room later and, giving Tom the keys, says, "Thanks for the car") and then describe your feelings. After you have finished, have the other person or people describe their feelings in response to the same situation. Continue the exercise until each member of the group has had two or three chances to practice describing feelings.

ASSERTIVENESS

Many times in your life you will want or need to behave assertively. **Assertiveness** means standing up for what you believe in and doing so in interpersonally effective ways. It involves describing your feelings fully, giving good reasons for your belief or feelings, and suggesting the behavior or attitude you think is fair, without exaggerating for dramatic effect or attacking another individual.

Contrasting Behaviors

When people believe they are not being treated as they should be, they are likely to behave in one of three ways: _passively, aggressively,_ or _assertively._

Passive behavior   People who behave passively do not try to influence others to behave in more satisfying ways. People who are passive are reluctant to state opinions, share feelings, or assume responsibility for their actions. Thus, they often submit to the demands of others, even when doing so is inconvenient or against their best interests.

For example, when Bill uncrates the new color television set he purchased at a local department store, he notices a large, deep scratch on the left side of the cabinet. If he behaved passively, Bill would be angry about the scratch, but he would keep the set and do nothing to influence the store clerk from whom he purchased it to replace it.

Aggressive behavior   People who behave aggressively lash out at the source of their discomfort with little regard for the situation or for the feelings of those they are attacking. Unfortunately, too many people confuse aggressiveness with assertiveness. Unlike assertiveness, aggressive behavior is judgmental, dogmatic, fault-finding, and coercive.

To exemplify aggressive behavior and to extend the contrast we are making, let's return to Bill's problem. If Bill behaved aggressively, after discovering the scratch on the cabinet of his new television set, he might brashly display his anger. He might storm back to the store, loudly demand his money back, and accuse the clerk of intentionally selling him damaged merchandise. During his tirade, he might threaten the store with a lawsuit. Such aggressive behavior might or might not get Bill a new television set; it would certainly damage the interpersonal relationships he had with those to whom he spoke.

Assertive behavior   People who behave assertively state what they believe to be true for them, describe their feelings fully, give good reasons for their beliefs or feelings, suggest the behavior or attitude they think is fair, avoid exaggerating for dramatic effect, and take responsibility for their actions and feelings without personal attacks on others. If Bill behaved assertively, he would be angry about bringing home a damaged set—the feeling of anger is common to each of the response behaviors. The difference between assertive behavior and the other two response styles is not the feeling but the behavior of the person as a result of that feeling. If Bill responded assertively, he might call the store and ask to speak to the clerk from whom he had purchased the set. When the clerk answered, Bill would describe his anger that resulted from discovering a large scratch on the cabinet when he uncrated the set. He would then say that he was calling to find out what to do to return the damaged set and get a new one.

While both the aggressive and the assertive behaviors might achieve Bill's purpose of getting a new television set, the assertive behavior would achieve the result at lower emotional costs to both Bill and those with whom he talked.

In order to emphasize the contrast among the response styles, let's examine another situation in which the issue is the quality of an interpersonal relationship. Betty works in an office with both male and female employees. Whenever the boss has an especially interesting job to be done, he assigns it to a male employee whose desk is next to Betty's. The boss has never said anything to Betty or to the male employee that would indicate that the boss thinks less of Betty or her ability. Nevertheless, Betty is hurt by the boss's behavior.

If Betty behaved passively, she would say nothing to the boss. If Betty behaved aggressively, she would call her boss on his behavior by saying something like "Why the hell do you always give Tom the plums and leave me with the garbage! I'm every bit as good a worker and I'd like a little recognition!"

In contrast, if Betty behaved assertively, she would go back to the boss's office and describe his behavior and her feelings about that behavior to him. She might say, "I don't know whether you are aware of it, but during the last three weeks every time you had a really interesting job to do, you gave the job to Tom. To the best of my knowledge, you believe that Tom and I are equally competent—you've never given me any evidence to suggest that you thought less of my work. But when you 'reward' Tom with jobs that I perceive as plums and continue to offer me routine jobs, it really hurts my feelings. Do you understand my feelings about this?"

If you were Betty's boss, which of her responses would be most likely to achieve her goal of getting better assignments? Probably the assertive behavior. Which of her responses would be most likely to get her fired? Probably the aggressive behavior. Which of her behaviors would be least likely to "rock the boat"? Undoubtedly the passive behavior—but then she would continue to get the boring job assignments.

To be assertive you should (1) *identify what you are thinking or feeling* and (2) *state it in the most interpersonally sound way possible.*

You must also understand that being assertive may not achieve your goals. Every skill we have discussed in this section is designed to increase the chances of interpersonal effectiveness. But there will still be times when what you attempt won't work or may even backfire. Just as with self-disclosure and describing feelings, being assertive involves risks. For instance, in the preceding example Betty's boss might become so defensive that he fires Betty. But if being treated unfairly is a concern to Betty—and we believe it should be—then Betty is likely to accept the risk of such an undesirable outcome, knowing that if she uses the skill properly, getting fired would be very unlikely. If you are truly assertive and not aggressive, you are far more likely to achieve your goals than you would be if you behaved in some other way.

Assertiveness and Social Power

Why are some people less likely to assert themselves? For many the answer is that they do not believe they have the social power necessary to affect the outcome positively. What is social power? **Social power** is a potential for changing attitudes, beliefs, and behaviors of others. The presence of power does not ensure change, but the absence of power makes it nearly impossible for people to be willing to assert themselves.

The analysis of social power that seems to make the most sense in understanding assertiveness is French and Raven's analysis, which discusses *coercive, reward, legitimate, expert,* and *referent* power.[1] Our discussion will focus on how the tendency to grant power to others may prevent you from acting assertively.

Coercive power   **Coercive power** involves actual or threatened force. The use of coercion can be physical or psychological. The elements of physical coercion are size, strength, and possession of weapons; the elements of psychological coercion are threat, withdrawal of affection, and tone of voice.

Whether or not a person exercises these elements, if we perceive the person as being able to exercise them, then we grant that person power.

Many people are unassertive because they are intimidated by a person. You may be familiar with this old vaudeville routine: "Where does a gorilla sit when he comes into a room?" "Anywhere he wants to!" But many people feel so intimidated by aggressive people that they grant coercive power to others even when the others are not trying to be coercive.

Reward power   The giving of money, other tangible goods, or affection constitutes **reward power**. Reward power works when the person being rewarded sees the reward as large or important enough to compensate for the pain of the action called for. For instance, you may know you will be rewarded with a good grade if you write a good paper. If a good grade is important to you or if you regard a B or an A as sufficient reward for the time and effort you have to put in, the reward might motivate you. For reward power to work, a person must believe that one who promises rewards has the power to give them. If your boss promises you consideration for promotion if you do a particular job well, you may not do it well because you doubt your boss really has the power to grant you a promotion at this time.

Some people are unassertive because they fear that what they say may get in the way of their receiving a reward. For instance, if Jack's boss is giving him more to do than what Jack thinks is fair, Jack may be reluctant to assert his position because his boss may decide not to reward him in the future. Many people let others run over them because they think that giving in will help them get a reward they seek.

Legitimate power   Influence that comes from being elected, selected, or holding a position is **legitimate power**. The rationale for bestowing legitimate power is the belief that people in certain positions have the responsibility of attempting to exert influence. Thus, people give power to presidents, senators, and members of Congress because they were elected; to teachers, cabinet members, and committee chairpersons because they were appointed; and to older members of a family, parents, or oldest children because of tradition or cultural norms.

Legitimate power is highly valued in our society, yet some people are excessively intimidated by position. That a person is a senator, a teacher, or a parent does not mean that that person is infallible. Some people bestow more power on such an individual than the person deserves or wants. We have all heard of people accepting unfair actions of officials or currying favor from those who have legitimate power. Both of these behaviors are thought to be negative because they ask people to reduce their own self-worth. Legitimate power *is* legitimate—but only in the areas related to the position.

Expert power   **Expert power** derives from having knowledge in a specific field. Expert power is influential when you admit that another person holds information that you need. Your instructors have the potential for expert power in your classes because they have knowledge and expertise you need; coaches have the potential for expert power because they have knowledge that players seek.

Appreciating the usefulness as well as the limitations of expert power is important. A coach who knows the best moves for the court will not necessarily be able to offer, say, the best financial advice.

Some people are unassertive because they downplay their own expertise in whatever subject is being considered. It's unlikely that a student would challenge a professor on a matter in which the professor is far more knowledgeable than the student. On the other hand, to grant the professor expert power over you on any subject being considered just because the person is your professor is foolhardy. We are far too often blinded by the perception of expert power. For instance, when buying clothing, people are often intimidated by a salesperson just because that person is selling a particular line of clothes. Salespeople are not usually assigned because they are masters of information; they are assigned because they are persuasive. As salespeople work with a certain line of goods, they may develop true expert power. But no one should be intimidated by the fear of being shown up by another person's knowledge. Whether buying a coat, having the car repaired, or having the furnace fixed, a customer must have the right to ask questions about what is happening and why.

Referent power   The potential to influence others through image, charisma, or personality is known as **referent power**. Many of us will listen to a person for no reason other than that we like that person or have a certain respect for the person's judgment. Many times it is in our best interests to grant this kind of power. We seldom have the time and energy to solve every issue that comes before us. If your best friend recommends a movie he saw or a restaurant she went to, you may well decide to attend that movie or eat at that restaurant because the person is a friend.

But on many important issues our reliance on the power of personality is misplaced. Too often we vote for someone only because "there's something about him" that we like; too often we do things that may not be in our best interest because someone said we should. We are often unassertive because we do not think highly enough of our own judgment to trust it—we rely too much on the word of others.

Whether it is because of coercive power, reward power, legitimate power, expert power, referent power, or some combination of these, we sometimes give up our right to be heard, and that is a mistake.

- -

PRACTICE

Asserting Yourself

1. For each of the following situations write a passive or aggressive response and then contrast it with a more appropriate assertive response.

▶ You come back to your dorm, apartment, or house to type a paper that is due tomorrow, and you find someone else using your typewriter.

PASSIVE OR AGGRESSIVE RESPONSE:

ASSERTIVE RESPONSE:

▶ You're working at a store part-time. You want to rush home as soon as your hours are up because you have a big test tomorrow. When you are ready to leave, your boss says to you, "I'd like you to work overtime, if you would—Martin's supposed to replace you, but he just called and can't get here for at least an hour."

PASSIVE OR AGGRESSIVE RESPONSE:

ASSERTIVE RESPONSE:

▶ During a phone call to your parents, who live in another state, your mother says, "We're expecting you to go with us when we visit your uncle on Saturday." You were planning to spend Saturday working on your résumé for an interview next week.

PASSIVE OR AGGRESSIVE RESPONSE:

ASSERTIVE RESPONSE:

▶ You and your friend made a date to go dancing, an activity you really enjoy. When you meet, your friend says, "If it's all the same to you, I thought we'd go to a movie instead."

PASSIVE OR AGGRESSIVE RESPONSE:

ASSERTIVE RESPONSE:

2. Decide whether each of the statements below is an attempt to influence based on reward power (R), coercive power (C), legitimate power (L), referent power (Rf), or expert power (E).

_____ a. You will wear your hair the way I tell you to wear your hair because I'm your mother.
_____ b. After studying the effects of radiation for eight years, I have concluded that . . .
_____ c. As long as you do what I say, no one will get hurt.
_____ d. Sara, I'd be so proud of you if you make the dean's list.
_____ e. If you'll drop my books at the library, I'll clean the room.
_____ f. Trust me—I can do it.

ANSWERS: **a.** L; **b.** E; **c.** C; **d.** R; **e.** R; **f.** Rf.

CREDITING IDEAS AND FEELINGS

In a term paper you give credit to those from whom you have taken words verbatim or paraphrased, thus giving credit to the original source and avoiding plagiarism. In interpersonal communication you credit for two similar reasons: you credit to confirm generalizations, and you credit your own feelings to differentiate them from the feelings of others.

Crediting Others

As we have mentioned many times before, interpersonal communication involves building and maintaining relationships. People get along better with others when they believe that they are recognized as individuals—when others recognize their personal worth. Yet we may, at times, chip away at the very relationships we are trying to build or to maintain. **Crediting** means verbally identifying the person whose ideas you are using. One important application of crediting is to credit others. Consider the following illustration. Bart and Mike are discussing ways of making money, and Mike suggests buying a valuable item at discount and then selling raffle tickets. Bart expresses his interest in the idea. The next day at a meeting of the entire fund-raising committee, Bart says, "What about buying a television at discount and selling raffle tickets? We could probably make a couple of hundred dollars!" The group responds immediately with such comments as "Great idea!" and "Let's do it!" At this point what is Mike, the originator of the idea, likely to be feeling? If he says, "That was my idea," the group may think less of him for quibbling over whose idea it was. If he says nothing, he is likely to feel resentful toward Bart. In this instance it was Bart's *responsibility* to give credit to Mike for originating the idea.

Is this important? Of course it is. Think of the times you were hurt because an idea of yours was not credited. Giving credit to others is an essential skill of interpersonal communication. Had Bart said, "Mike had a great idea—what about buying a television at discount and selling raffle tickets?" the group's reactions would probably have been the same, but Mike would have felt much better because his idea would have been properly credited.

Crediting Self—Owning Feelings

But crediting your own ideas and feelings is as important as giving credit to others. When you talk, others assume your statements represent your ideas or feelings. Although people are willing to divulge most of their thoughts, they are often unwilling to take credit for their personal feelings. Instead of owning their feelings, they wrap them in impersonal or generalized language or attribute them to unknown or universal sources. Crediting self, or owning feelings, means making "I" statements to identify yourself as the source of a particular idea or feeling. Consider the following paired statements:

▶   "The Cowboys are a great team."
     "I believe the Cowboys are a great team."

▶ "Nobody likes to be laughed at."
"I don't like to be laughed at."

Each of these examples contrasts a generalized or impersonal opinion with an "I" statement. An "I" statement can be any statement that has a first person pronoun such as "I," "my," "me," or "mine." For purposes of accuracy of information and helping the listener to understand fully the nature of the message, it is essential to own feelings by making "I" statements. Why are people so reluctant to do so? Saying "Everybody knows the Cowboys have the best team" means that if listeners doubt the statement they are bucking the collective evaluation of millions of Americans. Of course, not everybody knows the Cowboys are best. In this instance the statement really means that one person holds the belief. Yet because people may think that their feelings or beliefs will not carry much power, they may feel the need to use unknown or universal sources for those ideas or beliefs. Similarly, people use collective statements such as "everybody agrees" and "anyone with any sense knows" to escape responsibility for their own feelings and thoughts. It seems far more difficult for a person to say, "I don't like Herb" than it is to say, "No one likes Herb."

To avoid misunderstandings you need to develop the skill of making "I" statements. People have a right to their opinions and to their own feelings. If what you are saying is truly your opinion or an expression of how *you* really feel, then let others know, and be adult enough to take responsibility for what you believe or feel. If you don't, you may alienate others who would understand your opinions or feelings even though they differ with you.

- -

PRACTICE

Crediting

1. Do you credit the statements of others? Of yourself? Under what circumstances?

2. Write down five opinions, beliefs, or feelings. Check to make sure each is phrased as an "I" statement. If not, correct each one; for example, "Nobody likes a sore loser" should become "I don't like a sore loser."

ASKING FOR CRITICISM

One way of improving your communication is by identifying and correcting mistakes you make. But how do you know when you have made a mistake? Since monitoring your own communication behavior is very difficult, you need to ask others for their reactions to you and your behavior. Good communication includes knowing when and how to ask for constructive criticism.

You can get some information you need from others by being very sensitive to their nonverbal cues. If you tell a joke and someone laughs, that laughter is a sign of your effectiveness; if you lean close to people to tell them something and they pull back, their pulling back is a sign that you have bad breath.

When you can't read nonverbal cues, or when you don't know what people are thinking, you may have to ask for criticism. Yet people are often reluctant to ask for constructive criticism for the very obvious reason that criticism can be threatening. People become defensive when they think they are being criticized. For instance, when a friend shies away from your garlic breath, you may see that as a put-down of you as a person, and it may make you angry. People have a vested interest in themselves, and they are protective of that self.

Let's consider a plan for getting needed constructive criticism.

1. *Ask for criticism so you will avoid surprises.* If you take the initiative in asking for criticism, you get yourself ready psychologically to deal with the criticism.
2. *Think of criticism as being in your best interest.* No one likes to be criticized, but it is often through valid criticism that we learn and grow. When you get appraisal that is negative—even when you expected it to be positive—you should see it not as destructive to you personally but as a statement that reveals something about yourself that you did not know.
3. *Outline the kind of criticism you are seeking.* Rather than asking very general questions about ideas, feelings, or behavior, phrase your questions specifically. If you say, "Marge, is there anything you don't like about my ideas?" Marge is likely to consider this a loaded question. If you say instead, "Marge, do you think I've given enough emphasis to the marketing possibilities?" you will encourage Marge to speak to the specifics.
4. *Ask for criticism only when you really want an honest response.* If you ask a friend, "How do you like this coat?" but you really only want the friend to agree with your appraisal, you are not being honest. Once others realize that your request for appraisal is not really honest, that all you really want to hear is a compliment, valuable appraisal will not be forthcoming.

5. *Try to avoid contradiction between your verbal and your nonverbal cues.* If you say, "How do you like my paper?" but your voice tone indicates that you do not really want to know, the other person may be reluctant to be honest with you.
6. *Give reinforcement to those who take your requests for criticism as honest requests.* If you ask your friends how they like your ideas for the ad campaign and get the response "The idea seems a little too understated" and you get annoyed and say, "Well, if you can do any better you can take over," your friends will learn not to give you criticism even when you ask for it. Instead, reward the person for the criticism. Perhaps you could say, "Thanks for the opinion—I'd like to hear what led you to that conclusion." In this way you encourage honest appraisal.
7. *Make sure you understand what you heard.* Don't jump to conclusions about the meaning of the criticism. When a person says something about your behavior, ideas, or feelings, make sure you understand exactly what is meant. In the last chapter we discussed the skills of questioning and paraphrasing—skills you should use to make sure that you have the right understanding.

Asking for criticism does not require that you always act on every comment. You may decide against making a change in what you've said or done for other good reasons. But asking for criticism makes possible a conscious, rational choice about whether or not you will change your behavior.

PRACTICE

Criticism

1. Write down one to three specific attitudes or behaviors of yours that you would like to have criticized. For instance:

▶ Does the way I dress make me look younger than I am?

▶ Do you think I talk too much at meetings?

▶ Did my analysis of Paul's plan help the discussion?

2. Ask a close friend for criticism on one or more of the attitudes or behaviors you have listed. Note how you react to the criticism.

PITFALLS TO AVOID

We've looked at several of the skills that will help you communicate ideas and feelings more effectively. Let's conclude this chapter with a brief look at three common problems related to communicating ideas and feelings: *transfer stations, information overload,* and *hidden agenda.*

Transfer Stations

Communication is likely to be most effective when it is person to person. If, for any reason, you find yourself using transfer stations, you are likely to be setting up a problem.

A **transfer station** is nothing more than an intervening stage of communication. If Tom tells Susan to tell Charley to call him, Susan is a transfer station. You've probably played the game called "gossip" (or "telephone"), in which one person whispers a statement to another, who, in turn, whispers what he thinks he heard to another, who whispers what she thinks

Adults like to fool themselves that "telephone" is a game for kids. Yet how much time do you spend passing along secondhand information? And how often do you discuss rumors or gossip that turns out to be inaccurate?

she heard to the next person and so on until it has gone through five, six, seven, or more transfer stations. By the time it reaches the last person, the message may be so garbled that it is unintelligible.

Why is the transfer station doomed to failure? First, because of the very nature of the system. Let's consider an example. Dora, the originator of a message, may have all the information needed to communicate her idea. When she encodes the idea into language, she has already simplified, limited, and perhaps interpreted the original idea. Glen, who represents the first transfer station, does not have the benefit of the entire background for the idea. All he has is the words Dora used. Glen may not be able to remember all the words; he may not understand all the words; he may let semantic noise interfere with his understanding. Nevertheless, he communicates what he now *perceives* as the message to Pauline, who communicates what she perceives. As the message moves on down the line, each transfer station affords another opportunity for selection and interpretation. If there are enough transfer stations (and it does not take many), the message may be totally lost.

For as long as human beings have used speech, unscrupulous persons have used the technique of transfer stations to spread rumors. *Rumors* are statements that are passed from person to person and usually embellished along the way, becoming bigger, bolder, bloodier all the time. (It is interesting that messages with many facts are not only distorted in transmission but also shortened. Messages that are storylike usually get expanded—certainly they are distorted, but instead of becoming shorter, they often become longer.)

You can avoid the problems of transfer stations by giving information directly to those who need it. If you are caught in the middle of chain-link communication, you will need to work very hard at checking the accuracy of your ideas. Do not pass a message until you have made sure you have it right.

Information Overload

There is a limit to the amount of information that human beings can process at any given time. If we are hit with more than we can handle, much of it will just be lost. Sometimes, in the interests of accuracy or objectivity, we pack so much into such a short period of time that we lose nearly everything. This is called **information overload**.

Giving directions is a good example to use to show how much or how little most of us are able to process. Very few people can listen just once to a recipe, the route to a certain place, or the rules of a game and really understand. In general, the more new information you attempt to communicate, the more careful you must be.

Hidden Agenda

A **hidden agenda** is a reason or motive for behavior that is undisclosed to others. For instance, if the account exec called Sanders in to talk about the Morris account but really wanted to find out why Sanders had seemed so depressed lately, the discovery of the reason for the depression would be the exec's hidden agenda that controls his behavior. Or if Carla called Susan to ask her over to study for the econ test when all Carla was really interested in was Susan's notes for the days Carla had missed class, that would be Carla's hidden agenda.

At best—the Sanders example—hidden agenda seems like an easier way of dealing with a difficult issue; at worst—the Carla example—hidden agenda is gross manipulation.

Interpersonal communication is supposed to be open and honest. When people start trying to achieve their goals in indirect ways that are designed to keep the other person from knowing what is happening or why, a potential for barriers between the people exists.

Some people go so far as to use the hidden agenda as a strategy to play psychological games with others. A *game* is nothing more than one person's attempting to manipulate another person's behavior until the manipulator gets some payoff, usually a predictable behavior. Glen knows that Judy gets angry when he smokes in the bedroom, so he lights up in the bedroom and acts amazed when Judy loses her temper. Rachel knows that Steve is likely to become very uncomfortable with a discussion of his former girlfriend, Doris. So in his presence Rachel in an innocent tone asks, "Say, has anyone seen Doris lately?" In both cases the person's hidden agenda was to create a painful experience. If the behavior gets the desired response, the person "wins." It is this win–lose element that makes such statements games.

Are hidden agendas always detrimental to communication? Usually they are, if not always. Although, as a matter of tact or propriety (or lack of nerve), you may sometimes stipulate one agenda when in reality you support another one, the behavior is still manipulative. If Heather suspects June of taking home company material (paper, paper clips, pencils) for her personal use, she may call June into the office to talk about a report and try to get at the subject of misappropriating indirectly. In this instance the hidden agenda may appear to be beneficial to Heather, but when the real subject is revealed, the attempt to keep it below the surface may become a bigger issue than the theft. When hidden agendas are discovered, the fragile bond of trust is often frayed or perhaps even broken, and once trust is gone, the chance for good working relations is gone.

Despite the often painful thought of approaching a difficult problem directly, it is usually superior to using a hidden agenda. If Heather suspects June of taking office supplies—or if she has seen her do it directly—she is better off saying, "June, I called you in here today because I believe you may be taking office supplies home for your personal use and I'd like to talk to you about this issue." Dealing with the issue may prove difficult, but at least the difficulty will be the issue itself and not something else.

SUMMARY

In this chapter we looked at communicating ideas and feelings. Self-disclosure—revealing information about yourself that is unknown to others—is considered the major skill for helping others to know you better. Describing feelings is essential to self-disclosure. Describing feelings helps teach people how to treat us. Although expressing feelings is good psychologically for the person doing the expressing, describing feelings is a more interpersonally sound way of handling feelings.

Assertiveness is the skill of stating your ideas and feelings openly in interpersonally effective ways. Assertiveness is possible when people believe that they have power over their fate. Social power may be coercive, reward, legitimate, expert, and referent. People lacking in assertiveness are often overly intimidated by people whom they grant various kinds of social power. Passive people are often unhappy as a result of not stating what they think and feel; aggressive people get their ideas and feelings heard but may create more problems for themselves because of their aggressiveness.

Crediting clarifies the source of ideas and contributes to the good feelings of the people being credited. Asking for criticism is a necessary skill for providing the kinds of information on which you can base decisions about your communication effectiveness. Although criticism can be threatening, you can ask for it in a way that will ensure your getting what you need without it making you defensive.

Some potential problems of transmitting information from person to person stem from the use of transfer stations, information overload, and the hidden agenda.

SUGGESTED READINGS

Pearce, W. Barnett, and Stewart M. Sharp. "Self-disclosing Communication." *Journal of Communication*, vol. 23 (December 1973), pp. 409–425. This article not only presents an excellent overview of the subject but also contains a good review of the research.

Rosenfeld, Lawrence R. "Self-Disclosure Avoidance: Why I Am Afraid to Tell You Who I Am." *Communication Monographs* 46 (March 1979): 63–74. Contrasts male and female disclosing behavior.

Tavris, Carol. *Anger: The Misunderstood Emotion.* New York: Simon & Schuster, 1982. Tavris draws on a great deal of recent research to show that most information about anger and dealing with anger is inaccurate. She points out that as a mature person you can determine the way to handle anger that is best for both you and those around you. Provides a detailed rationale for much of the analysis of dealing with feelings in this chapter.

Wallen, John L. "Developing Effective Interpersonal Communication." In R. Wayne Pace, Brent D. Peterson, and Terrence R. Radcliffe, eds., *Communicating Interpersonally—A Reader*. Columbus, Ohio: Charles E. Merrill, 1973. This article has a particularly good section on describing feelings.

BUILDING AND **M**AINTAINING **R**ELATIONSHIPS

8

OBJECTIVES

After you have read this chapter, you should be able to:

1 Explain the role of communication in the life cycle of a relationship

2 Use four different methods of starting conversations

3 Identify negative characteristics of withdrawal, surrender, and aggression

4 List guidelines for discussion in managing conflict

5 Negotiate conflict

6 Arbitrate conflict

7 Prepare a Johari window

One of the major goals of your interpersonal communication is to help you start, build, and maintain good ongoing relationships with others. Good relationships are built on *mutually satisfying* interactions with others. In this chapter we will look at the role of communication in the life cycle of relationships, the use of communication skills to manage conflict in relationships, and methods of analyzing communication effectiveness in relationships.

COMMUNICATION IN THE LIFE CYCLE OF RELATIONSHIPS

Although no two relationships develop in exactly the same manner, scholars who have studied a variety of relationships have noted that relationships follow a life cycle—people meet, they get to know each other, and, if the relationship does not stabilize, they drift apart. We all have relationships in various phases of the life cycle. In every phase of the life cycle of relationships, communication plays a major part.

Getting Acquainted

The meeting or "getting to know you" phase of a relationship is composed of initial attraction, introduction strategies, and nonthreatening communication interactions.

Attraction   An old song lamented that "she lived on the morning side of the mountain, and he lived on the twilight side of the hill." The song points out that two people may be just right for each other, but if they never meet it hardly matters whether they are or not. The point is obvious but well taken—people's lives must intersect in some way, or they will never begin a relationship. Attending college, working with a company, worshiping at a church or synagogue, or belonging to a club puts you in a context that helps you meet people. Yet whether you are in a course with 25 other students or a business environment with 300, you may be attracted to only a small number of people out of that total.

Although people are initially drawn toward those whom they perceive as physically attractive, physical attraction is only a door to developing a relationship. Whether you work to develop the relationship is likely to depend on social interests, work interests, background commonalities, attitude and value similarities, and personality fit. The more common interests people have, the more they are attracted to each other.

Introduction options   No matter how attractive you find another person, the relationship begins when you meet the person. Yet one of the most difficult times for many people is the initial interaction with someone who, although attractive, is a complete stranger. Whether we are talking about male-female encounters, same-sex encounters, or business encounters, what happens in the first few minutes of an initial conversation will have a profound effect on the nature of the relationship that develops from it. How do people strike up conversations with strangers? The following are several of the most common communication strategies for meeting people and striking up conversations.

In a society that rewards the establishment—though not necessarily the maintaining—of relationships, countless businesses thrive on providing planned opportunities for singles to meet. It's important to remember that many meaningful relationships can start with a chance meeting; the secret is to remain open to such possibilities.

1. *Formal or informal introduction.* The most straightforward way to meet another person is to introduce yourself. It takes courage, but when you find yourself in a group of strangers, the best way of getting started may be to walk up to a person and say, "Hi, my name is Gordon. What's yours?" If at least one other person knows you, that person may take the pressure off you by doing the introducing. For instance, your host might say, "Doris, I'd like you to meet my friend Gordon. Gordon, Doris is Susan's sister."

2. *Reference to context.* When you are already in the company of another person (sitting next to the person at a dinner or standing next to a person in a line), one of the safest ways of starting a conversation is to refer to some aspect of context. Perhaps the oldest and most effective comment is a reference to the weather or climatic conditions: "This is great weather for a game," or "Doesn't it seem stuffy in here?" Other contextual references include statements like "They've really decorated this place beautifully" or "I wonder how they are able to keep such a beautiful garden in this climate."

3. *Reference to yourself.* Another way to make contact is to say something about yourself: "I really like theme parties; do you?" or "I live right down the hall; do you live in the building?"

4. *Reference to the other person.* An equally effective approach is to ask a question of the other person, such as "I don't believe I've seen you

A chance meeting in a coffee shop may begin a long-term relationship.

before—have you been working here long?" or "The Phillipses have sure done a lovely job of remodeling this home. Did you ever see it before the renovation?"

Communication with acquaintances   Once a conversation is begun, the early stages of a relationship are marked by three levels of communication. Each of these is relatively nonthreatening to those involved.

The first level of communication is called phatic communication. *Phatic communication* is the ritualized and formalistic communication that we use to recognize others. It is identified by such statements as "What's happening?" "What do you say?" "How're you doing?" With these we look for little more than acknowledgment—we do not expect people to stop and give us long replies. Phatic communication is for meeting social expectations; it is used to acknowledge recognition and leaves the door open for more meaningful types of communication at other times in other places.

A slightly deeper level of communication is gossip. *Gossip* is communication among people about other people. Statements like "I hear Bill just got a really great job" or "Would you believe that Mary Simmons and Tom Johnson are going together? They never seemed to hit it off too well in the past" are typical of this level of communication.

Gossip occurs during all phases of a relationship, but it is common in the early phase since it is considered safe. You can gossip for a long time with another person without really saying anything about yourself or without learning anything about the other person except that the person enjoys talking. Gossip can be a pleasant way to pass the time of day with people whom you know but with whom you have no desire or need for a deeper relationship, or it can be a safe way to explore the bases for attraction. Gossip can, of course, be malicious; more often than not, however, gossip is a way of interacting amicably with others without getting personally involved. This is why conversations at parties are largely gossip.

The third level of communication in a developing relationship is idea exchange. In *idea-exchange communication* people share information that contains facts, opinions, and beliefs and that occasionally reflects values. This is a common type of communication between friends and acquaintances. At the office Dan may talk with Walt about sports, Martha may talk with Louise about new cars, and Pete may talk with Jack about landscaping. In more serious circumstances Jan may talk with Gloria about the U.S. role in the Middle East and Dave may talk with Sonya about abortion. Although the discussions of foreign policy and abortion are "deeper" than conversation about sports or cars, both sets of conversations are on the idea-exchange level. On this level you learn what the other person is thinking; through such conversations you can reassess your initial attraction and you can decide whether or not you would like to have the relationship grow.

Phatic, gossip, and idea-exchange communication typify early stages of relationships and meet many social needs. These types of communication are also appropriate for acquaintance relationships, since they are characterized by relatively low amounts of risk and self-disclosure. Moreover, they provide conversations on which the decision to move a relationship to the next level can be based.

Developing Friendships

Friends are people we like and who like us. Friends seek each other out because they enjoy one another's company. Friends may go out of their way to help one another; they are concerned for each other's welfare.

Deep friendships take time to develop, but the support and honesty that can blossom in such relationships is priceless.

During the early stages of relationships, people explore to determine the kinds of satisfaction they get from being together. They seek information about each other and put together images based on this information. For example, Tom, who is exploring his relationship with Nancy, takes Nancy to a museum, a place where he enjoys spending time. If Nancy doesn't seem to care about the exhibits, or if she can't intelligently discuss what they see, Tom may not pursue the relationship with Nancy as far as he would have if the experience had been more satisfying.

Exploring for deeper relationships occurs in both opposite- and same-sex relationships. For instance, Mark may seek to develop a friendship with Derek because they both like to play racquetball. But if Derek can't get enough free time to play with Mark, or if Derek is too poor or too good a player to make an enjoyable game, the racquetball friendship will not develop.

Communication in friendships　Although friends engage in phatic communication, gossip, and the sharing of nonthreatening ideas, friends will also engage in the sharing of more serious ideas and will begin to share feelings about important matters. It is through the sharing of feelings and self-disclosure that you come to know and understand another person. Although it is unrealistic to expect to share feelings with a great many others and may be undesirable to do so, the achievement of a feelings-sharing level of communication with a few people is a highly beneficial communication goal.

Deep Friendships and Intimate Relationships

Intimate relationships are built on trust and require a deep level of commitment. Friendships can evolve into intimate relationships in which people find satisfaction with each other on many levels. Intimates act reciprocally to meet each other's needs. The level of trust between them is quite high.

Deep friendships require *commitment*. Deep friendships are noted for the extent to which a person gives up other relationships in order to devote more time and energy to the primary relationship. During this stage individuals spend long periods of time together. The early days of a deep friendship are often euphoric. Especially in romantic relationships, people may develop their own language, pet names for each other, in-jokes, and the like.

As deep relationships mature, people are likely to seek formal ratification of their commitment. In a male-female relationship this stage is most often marked by marriage. In other relationships it could be marked by signing a contract, forming a partnership, or participating in any other act that is appropriate to that particular relationship.

Although deep friends and intimates continue to engage in phatic communication, gossip, and sharing ideas, their relationships are characterized by the degree to which feelings are shared and deep self-disclosure occurs.

As you may have noticed, the different kinds of communication that occur during the development of a relationship follow a continuum from impersonal-superficial to personal-deep. People may have countless acquaintance relationships and many context-specific friendships, but they are likely to have only one or two truly intimate friends at any one time. Why? Because such relationships are time-consuming and require a level of mutual trust that is hard to attain.

Stabilizing Relationships

When two people develop a relationship, whether as acquaintances, friends, or deep friends, they try to stabilize that relationship. Some people find that they maintain the same acquaintances, friends, and deep friendships throughout much of their lives. Yet the stability of relationships, especially intimate ones, is under constant pressure. And just as a relationship can *build*, so can it *deteriorate*. When the energy that was used to build a relationship is withdrawn, a relationship will deteriorate.

Deterioration of Relationships

The deterioration phase of relationships has at least three stages. The first sign of a weakening relationship is *reduction of tolerance*. When people become less tolerant of others they begin to lose interest in their opinions and feelings. They change their orientation from *we* to *I*. "Touchy" subjects begin to limit the amount of sharing of personal feelings and ideas. The relationship begins to show much less open discussion, and people begin to have more unresolved conflicts.

As deterioration progresses, they begin to *drift apart*. Their communication changes from deep sharing of ideas and feelings to small talk, gossip, and other kinds of "safe" communication. No longer are the people interested in exchanging significant ideas. Soon they may begin to avoid each other. They seek out other company to share the interests and activities that are important to them. Hostility need not be present; in fact, this stage is likely to be marked by indifference.

The ultimate outcome of a deteriorating relationship is an *ending*. If the relationship had no signs of formal commitment, the people simply stop seeing each other. Formal commitments end in divorce or the formal breaking of the contract.

Movement through the stages of deterioration can be very quick. People can easily miss the signs of deterioration.

PRACTICE

Analyzing Your Relationships

1. Make a list of the five people to whom you are closest. Can you remember the first time you met them? How did this initial meeting affect the early phases of your relationship?

2. Consider a person with whom you have a close interpersonal relationship. Does the foregoing discussion help to explain the success of this relationship?

3. With a close friend, discuss the similarities and differences in your perceptions of your behavior. What accounts for any differences that might exist?

Our culture promotes the myth that a relationship begun in bliss will remain so. How many movies end with the young couple walking into the sunset? How many present role models for the more difficult task of maintaining and developing a relationship?

MANAGING CONFLICTS IN RELATIONSHIPS

Will your relationships grow, be strengthened, and stabilize, or will they wither and ultimately die? The answer depends a great deal on how you manage conflict within them. **Conflict** is the clash of opposing attitudes, ideas, behaviors, goals, and needs. Although many people view conflict as bad (and, to be sure, conflict situations are likely to make us anxious and uneasy), conflict is sometimes useful in that it forces people to make choices and to test the relative merits of their attitudes, behaviors, needs, and goals.

Conflicts include clashes over ideas ("Charley was the first one to talk." "No, it was Mark" or "Your mother is a battle-ax." "What do you mean, a 'battle-ax'?"); over values ("Bringing home pencils and pens from work is not stealing." "Of course it is" or "The idea that you have to be married to have sex is completely outdated." "No, it isn't"); and, perhaps the most difficult to deal with, over ego involvement ("Listen, I've been a football fan for thirty years, I ought to know what good defense is." "Well, you may be a fan, but that doesn't make you an expert").

Patterns of Dealing with Conflict

People engage in many behaviors to cope with or manage their conflicts. Some are positive and some are negative. These many ways may be discussed under five major patterns. Let's consider each in turn.

Withdrawal   One of the most common—and certainly one of the easiest—ways to deal with conflict is to withdraw. **Withdrawal** is physical or psychological removal from the situation.

Physical withdrawal is, of course, easiest to identify. Dorie and Tom are in conflict over Tom's smoking. When Dorie says, "Tom, I thought you told me that whether you stopped smoking completely or not, you weren't going to smoke around the house. Now here you are lighting up!" Tom may withdraw physically, saying, "I don't want to talk about it" as he goes to his basement workshop.

Psychological withdrawal may be more difficult to detect but every bit as common. Using the same example, when Dorie speaks to Tom about his smoking, Tom sits quietly in his chair looking at Dorie, but while she is speaking, he is thinking about the poker game he will be going to the next evening.

Both of these common withdrawal behaviors are negative. Why? Because they neither eliminate nor attempt to manage the nature of the conflict. For instance, when Tom withdraws physically, Dorie may follow him to the basement, where the conflict will be resumed; if not, the conflict will undoubtedly surface later—probably in an intensified manner—when

Dorie and Tom try to cope with another issue. When Tom ignores Dorie's comments, Dorie may force Tom to cope with the smoking issue or she may go along with Tom's ignoring her but harbor a resentment that will surface later.

There appear to be two types of situations where withdrawal may work. The first is when the withdrawal is temporary disengagement used for the purpose of letting the heat of the conflict cool down. When Bill and Margaret begin to argue over having Bill's mother-in-law for Thanksgiving dinner, Margaret feels herself get angry about what her mother-in-law had said to her recently about the way she and Bill were raising their daughter. Margaret says, "Hold it a minute, let me make a pot of coffee. We can both relax a bit and then we'll talk about this some more." A few minutes later she returns, temper intact and ready to approach the conflict more objectively. Margaret's action is not true withdrawal; it is not meant as a means of avoiding confrontation. It provides a cooling-off period that will probably benefit both of them. The second case where withdrawal may work is when a conflict occurs between people who communicate infrequently. Jack and Mark work in the same office. At two office gatherings they have gotten into arguments about whether the company really cares about its employees.

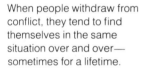

When people withdraw from conflict, they tend to find themselves in the same situation over and over— sometimes for a lifetime.

At the next office gathering Mark avoids sitting near Jack. Withdrawal is a negative pattern only when it is a person's major way of managing conflict.

Surrender　**Surrender** means giving in immediately to avoid conflict. Some people are so afraid of being in conflict that they will do anything to avoid it. For instance, Jeff and Marian are discussing their vacation plans. Jeff would like just the two of them to go somewhere together, but Marian has talked with two of their friends who are vacationing the same week about going together. After Jeff mentions that he'd like the two of them to go alone, Marian says, "But I think it would be fun to go with another couple, don't you?" Jeff replies, "OK, whatever you want." In this example Jeff really wants the two of them to go alone, but rather than describe his feelings or give reasons for his position, he gives in to avoid conflict.

　　Surrender is negative for at least two reasons. (1) Decisions should be made on merits and not to avoid conflict. If one person gives in, there is no evaluation of the decision—no one knows what would really be best. (2) Surrender can infuriate the other person. When Marian tells Jeff her thoughts, she would probably like Jeff to see her way as the best. But if Jeff just surrenders, Marian will perceive Jeff not as liking her plan but as martyring himself. His unwillingness to present his reasons could cause even more conflict.

Aggression　The use of physical or psychological coercion to get one's way is **aggression**. Through aggression people attempt to force others to accept their ideas. Through aggression a person may "win," but it seldom does anything positive for a relationship. Aggression is an emotional reaction to conflict. Thought is short-circuited, and the person lashes out physically or verbally. Aggression never deals with the merits of the issue—only who is bigger, can talk louder, or is nastier.

　　In each of the above patterns, conflict is escalated or obscured. In none is it managed.

Persuasion　Persuasion is the attempt to change either the attitude or the behavior of another person. At times during a conflict one person might try to persuade the other that a particular action is the right one. Doris and Jack are considering buying a car. Doris says, "Don't we need room?" Jack, her husband, might reply, "Enough to get us into the car together, but I don't see why we need more than that." At this point, Doris and Jack's conflict comes into focus. Now Doris might say, "Jack, remember the other day when you were cussing out our present car because it doesn't have much back-seat room? We carry a lot of stuff. I do food shopping, you're always carrying equipment for men at the lodge, and there are lots of times when we invite another couple to go somewhere with us." Statements like this one are attempts at resolving the conflict through persuasion.

　　When persuasion is open and reasonable, it can be a positive means of resolving conflict. But persuasion can degenerate into manipulation. Although persuasive efforts may fuel a conflict, if that persuasion has a solid logical base, it is at least possible that the persuasion will resolve the conflict.

Discussion **Discussion** is verbal problem solving. It involves weighing and considering the pros and cons of the issues in conflict. Discussion is the most desirable means of dealing with conflict in a relationship; nevertheless, it is often difficult to accomplish.

Problem-solving might follow the formal method of defining the problem, analyzing the problem, suggesting possible solutions, selecting the solution that best fits the analysis, and working to implement the decision. For instance, if Jeff and Marian were discussing, they might focus on the problem of how they should spend their vacation. They would seek to identify the goals they hoped to meet. They would suggest places to go and the possibilities of going there with or without others. They would consider how each possibility would meet their goals. Then they would select the place and whether to go with their friends. We consider the details of discussion further in Chapter 10. Now let's turn to guidelines for discussion in conflict.

GUIDELINES FOR DISCUSSION IN CONFLICT MANAGEMENT

You can use the following guidelines for discussion in developing a constructive program of conflict management.

1. *Try to recognize the signs of conflict.* Too often people slip into conflicts without even knowing it. When that happens, all too often one or both people start engaging in one of the negative means of coping with conflict without thinking about it. On the other hand, if both parties are aware of a conflict, or if one says something like "I think we have a conflict here," then they can take steps to begin rational discussion.

   Keep in mind that you need not fear conflict. It is often the fear of conflict that brings about such negative responses as withdrawal and surrender. Conflicts are going to occur. But when conflict is recognized and approached properly, it can be a constructive force.

2. *Try to center discussion on the specific topic on which the conflict occurs.* We have already pointed out that conflicts often start on content levels. If you can keep the focus of the discussion on those content levels, the chances of the conflict growing out of proportion are lessened. For instance, if you find yourself in a conflict over a fact, try to disengage until a source for verifying the fact can be found or until some guideline for selecting from among competing sources can be determined. Likewise, when the conflict is over an interpretation of a fact, an

inference drawn, or a definition, collect supporting material that is related directly to the issue—in short, keep the conflict confined to the issue at hand.

Some authorities refer to content conflict as "simple" conflict. Because facts can be looked up, inferences tested, definitions verified, and competing goals weighed and evaluated, the conflict can be confined to the specific issues and resolved rationally. Nevertheless, with many conflicts competing value systems will be revealed, and these will confound the conflict management.

3. *Try to keep an open mind about views that differ from your own.* Open-mindedness is flexibility in the way a person processes information. Rather than seeing concepts in absolute terms, an open-minded person is willing to tolerate other sides and examine other information. Unfortunately, conflict often brings about dogmatic responses. A dogmatic person clutches tenaciously to his or her value system and judges every event on the basis of how it fits into that value system. Highly dogmatic people take a narrow perspective of the way the world operates, are rigid in their thinking, and believe *only* those people who are in positions of strong authority. For example, suppose a Baptist and a Catholic are discussing a topic with religious ramifications. If both are open-minded, they can discuss the issues reasonably well. Even though they may be committed to certain beliefs or attitudes that grow from their value systems, they are aware of the common ground that exists between what they believe in and what they reject. In their discussion they seek a middle ground between their positions in order to resolve the question. If the two people become dogmatic, however, they focus on their differences. They view the controversy in terms of black and white and never see the shades of gray between their two positions. As a result, management of their conflict is nearly impossible, and their conflict escalates.

Your goal in conflict management should be to open your mind as much as possible, so that you can look for the common ground on which some agreement can be built. The open-minded or less-dogmatic approach compares and evaluates issues related to belief systems and accepts or rejects them according to merit, not values. Thus, the open-minded person looks for evidence and draws conclusions on the basis of the weight of that evidence.

4. *Try to cooperate rather than compete.* At the onset of a conflict, people are likely to think in terms of *winning*. Yet competitiveness leads to ego involvement. The cooperative attitude is one in which people try to find mutual benefits.

How do you go about bringing a person who is thinking competitively into a cooperative state so the conflict can be considered rationally? First, do not start talking about the issues at hand until you can convince the other person that you wish to resolve the conflict in a mutually satisfactory way; second, avoid statements that would escalate the potential conflict or result in defensive behavior. Some of the following wordings may be useful in demonstrating your resolve to be cooperative and in preventing the conflict from escalating:

"I know you feel very strongly about what you believe is right. Before we consider whether your plan is the best one, perhaps we could consider what we want to accomplish with the plan."

"I know I sometimes get a little hotheaded in conflict situations, and I'm going to try to look at this problem as objectively as I can, but I may need all your help."

"You have good reasons for your belief, and I believe I have too. Perhaps if we share our reasons and then consider the consequences of each of them, we can make a decision that we'll find satisfying."

Developing a cooperative atmosphere takes practice. But you can learn to recognize when you or the other person start to become ego involved. At that time, mentally step back and ask yourself to problem solve.

5. *Try to prearrange a conflict management procedure.* Many of the difficulties of conflict management arise because people do not have any procedure to turn to for coping with conflict. Just as people who have made plans for what they will do in case of a fire, a flood, or a tornado often weather the particular disaster in much better shape than those who have not, so do people weather conflict better if they have a plan for conflict management.

One person must recognize when conflict is escalating. It is for that person to remind the other of the prearranged procedure. For instance, Jack and Gail have agreed to list advantages and disadvantages for a particular action before the conflict heats up; then when such a conflict occurs, the prearranged procedure will take precedence over any action. Sometimes the time involved in going through the prearranged steps is enough to get people past that explosive moment when they are likely to say or do something they would like to take back later. Such prearrangement may not be practical at all times. But when people anticipate a great deal of conflict with a given issue, such prearrangements might be a necessity.

Two elements to build into a prearranged plan are negotiation and arbitration. **Negotiation** means managing conflicts through trade-offs. Conflict often results when two actions are proposed but only one can be accomplished. You cannot go to a baseball game and a concert at the same time; you cannot eat at a Chinese restaurant and an Italian restaurant at the same time. Even after people have considered every aspect of the conflict rationally, they may still truly believe that their way is the best; then perhaps they should negotiate.

With some simple problems negotiation is easily accomplished. For instance, the proposal "I'll tell you what, Joan; I'll go to the concert with you tonight if you'll go to the ballgame with me this weekend" will probably achieve the desired results. Since in this case there need not be an either/or approach, both activities can be accomplished at different times.

For negotiaton to work, the activities, goals, or ideas must be of fairly equal importance. The suggestion "Joe, if you'll let me make the decision on where to eat tonight, I'll go along with you on whatever movie you want to see" has a good chance of working. On the other hand, "Alice, if you will let me decide on the kind of car to buy, I'll let you decide on where to eat" does not stand a chance. Obviously, selecting a car is a far more important decision than picking a restaurant, a movie, or any other one-night activity. A person attempting such a negotiation is not acting in good faith. Finding situations that are indeed parallel may be difficult, but when they can be found, they make an excellent base for negotiation.

When negotiation fails, you may wish to seek arbitration. **Arbitration** requires the presence of an impartial person who, after hearing both sides, will weigh and evaluate the alternatives and make a decision for you. Labor unions and management sometimes use arbitration. It may work for you.

For interpersonal conflicts, arbitration will work if you can agree on an arbitrator who, in turn, will agree to make the decision for you. It is important that the arbitrator be a person whose judgment you both trust. The arbitrator also should in some way be competent to make a decision on the issue. Your lawyer may act as arbitrator for you over whether to sue about a car accident. Your financial counselor may arbitrate a conflict over whether to invest in a high-risk stock or a high-dividend stock.

Too often we seek to pull in a close friend or a relative to arbitrate. Not only do these people often lack the expertise needed for the particular issue but, also and more important, friends or relatives are not independent, impartial agents. They may be close to both parties or may have a vested interest in the outcome. Calling on such people puts them in a no-win situation (somebody may be upset by their decision) or, at best, makes them feel very uncomfortable in the role.

If you do agree to arbitration, the verbal contract between you and the other person should include a clause saying that whatever decision is made, both of you will willingly and happily comply. Remember, you will have gone to a third person because the two of you were unable to come to a conclusion; if you are unwilling to abide by the decision, whichever way it goes, then you should not agree to arbitration in the first place.

In some circumstances the impartial third person will act as a **facilitator** rather than as an arbitrator. The difference is that instead of making the decision for you, the third party will help the two of you (or you alone, in the case of an intrapersonal decision) use a problem-solving method to make your own decision. Psychologists, psychiatrists, marriage counselors, and other clinicians are skilled in facilitating decision making. A good facilitator not only sees to it that you are following the steps of problem solving but also helps you weigh and evaluate the variables.

6. *Discuss conflict-resolution failures.* The ideal is to resolve every conflict as it comes up ("Never let the sun set on your anger"). However, there will be times when no matter how hard both people try, they will not be able to resolve the conflict. If the person is an intimate friend or relative—if the relationship is especially important to you—after the heat of the conflict dies down, you should take steps to analyze the failure of the conflict resolution. You should consider questions like "Where did things go wrong?" "Did one or both of us become competitive? Defensive?" "Did we fail to implement our problem-solving method adequately?" "Were the vested interests in the outcome too great?" You will often find that attempts failed because one or both of you need to work on basic communication skills such as paraphrasing, describing feelings, and the like.

The chapters in the Decision-Making Groups section consider these and other skills that can work as a part of a conflict management program.

- -

PRACTICE

Managing Conflict

1. Describe a conflict situation that arose between you and a friend.

2. Identify the kind of conflict it was.

3. Did you and your friend manage the conflict by withdrawing, by surrendering, with aggression, or by discussing?

4. What was the outcome of the conflict?

5. If the outcome was negative, sketch a method of managing the conflict that would have been more productive for you.

ANALYZING COMMUNICATION IN RELATIONSHIPS

Although the old adage "If it works don't fix it" has a lot of merit, many relationships that have potential strength and endurance deteriorate and dissolve because people don't stop to analyze where the relationship is going right and where it is going wrong. The following theoretical materials provide a useful rationale for analyzing your relationships and understanding their link to communication.

Interpersonal Needs

According to the theory of interpersonal needs, whether or not a relationship can be started, built, or maintained depends on how well each person meets the interpersonal needs of the other. William Schutz has identified three interpersonal needs that people have: affection, inclusion, and control.[1] His analysis demonstrates how interpersonal communication contributes to meeting these basic interpersonal needs.

Affection   **Affection** is a fond or tender feeling for another person. Schutz says people differ in how much they need to express affection toward others and in how much they need to receive affection from others. People you know probably run the gamut of showing and expressing affection both verbally and nonverbally. At one end of the spectrum are the "underpersonal" individuals. These people avoid close ties, seldom show tenderness toward others, and shy away from those who show or who want to show affection to them. At the other end of the spectrum are the "overpersonal" individuals. These people lavish affection on everyone, think of all others as their close friends, confide in people they have just met, and need affection from others—they need to be praised, held, and so on. "Personal" people are those who can express and receive affection easily; they get a joy out of their relationships with others.

Inclusion   The need to be in the company of other people is the need for **inclusion**. Schutz says that people differ in how much they seek the company of others and in how much they need others to seek their company. At one extreme are the "undersocial" persons, who prefer to go through life alone. Although occasionally seeking company or enjoying being included with some others if specifically invited, these people do not need a great deal of social interaction to feel satisfied. At the other extreme are the "oversocial" persons, who need constant companionship and feel tense when they must be alone. If a party is happening, they are there; if there is no party, they start one. Their doors are always open—everyone is welcome, and they expect others to welcome them. Most of us are not either of these extreme types. Rather, we are sometimes comfortable being alone and at other times need and enjoy interaction with others.

Control   The need for **control** is the need to exercise power over others. According to Schutz, people vary in their needs to control the behavior of others and in their need to be controlled by others. At one extreme are persons who need no control. They seem to shun responsibility and do not want to be in charge of anything. The "abdicrats," as Schutz calls them, are extremely submissive and are unlikely to make decisions or accept responsibility. At the other extreme of the need for control are persons who must be in charge. "Autocrats" need to dominate others at all times and are anxious if they cannot. They usurp the responsibility of those who have the authority to control a situation, and they try to determine every decision. Most of us fall between these extremes and could be called the "democrats." At certain times we need to lead; at other times we feel free to follow the lead of others. Democrats can stand behind their ideas, but they can be comfortable submitting to others at least some of the time.

Through verbal and nonverbal communication behavior, people display clues to the level of their immediate interpersonal needs. Thus, as you interact with others you can detect whether their needs for affection, inclusion, and control seem compatible with yours. Relationships develop and deteriorate in part because of compatability and incompatibility of interpersonal needs. Thus, how you display your own interpersonal needs when you interact with others helps determine the effectiveness of your relationships.

Schutz's theory of interpersonal needs is useful because it explains a great deal of interpersonal behavior.[2] Research on this model has been generally supportive of its major theses.[3] In analyzing any relationship it is useful to see whether you are able to meet or coexist with the other person's needs.

Exchange Theory

Thibaut and Kelley, who originated exchange theory, believed that social relationships and interactions between people can be understood in terms of the exchange of rewards and costs incurred by each member of a relationship or interaction.[4] **Rewards** are outcomes that are valued by their receiver. Some common rewards are good feelings, prestige, economic gain, and fulfillment of emotional needs. **Costs** are outcomes that the receiver does not wish to incur. Costs include time, energy, and anxiety. For instance, Jill may be willing to spend time talking with Jan if she anticipates a good feeling as a result; she may not be willing to spend that time if she expects to be depressed at the end of the conversation.

According to Thibaut and Kelley, people seek interaction situations in which their behaviors will yield a high reward and a low cost outcome. If Jill runs into Sarah on campus, several communication options are available to Jill: She can ignore Sarah; she can smile; she can say, "Hi!" in passing; or she can attempt to start up a conversation. What Jill does will depend in part on her appraisal of the *cost-reward analysis* of the outcome of the interaction. For instance, if Jill had been thinking about giving Sarah a call to arrange a game of tennis, she will probably take the time now to attempt to seek that outcome—she will be willing to pay the cost of taking time and using energy in hopes of receiving a suitable reward, a tennis date. If Jill and Sarah do talk, the duration of the interchange will continue until one or both realize that the interaction has achieved the reward or is falling below the satisfactory level. For Jill, this might mean until a tennis game is set. For Sarah, this might mean something else. Thibaut and Kelley suggest that the most desirable ratio between cost and reward varies from person to person and within one person from time to time.

If, over an extended period of time, people's *net rewards* (reward minus cost) in a relationship are below a certain level, they will experience that relationship as unsatisfactory or unpleasant. But if their net rewards are higher than the level they set as satisfactory, they will experience a pleasant and satisfying relationship or interaction. Moreover, if people have a number of relationships they see as giving them a good cost-reward ratio, the satisfaction level they set will be high, and they are not likely to be satisfied with low-outcome relationships. Thus, if Joan has four or five men she gets along well with, she is not likely to put up with Charley, who irritates her. On the other hand, the person who does not have many positive interactions will be satisfied with relationships and interactions that the person with wider choice would find unattractive. If Joan felt that Charley was the only man who could provide the benefits she sought, she would be inclined to put up with his irritating habits.

While the ratio of rewards to costs determines how satisfactory a relationship or an interaction might be to those involved, it does not determine how long a given relationship or interaction will last. Although it seems logical to leave a relationship or an interaction in which costs exceed rewards, circumstances are sometimes such that people will stay in a relationship that is plainly unsatisfactory.

The explanation for these situations that Thibaut and Kelley offer involves what they call the *comparison level of alternatives*. They explain that the decision to continue in a relationship may depend on what alternatives or other choices a person perceives as available elsewhere. Thus, durability of a relationship also depends on possible alternatives. If the satisfaction level a person is experiencing drops below the level that person can attain elsewhere, the person will leave the relationship or interaction in order to engage in the next best alternative. If, however, a person is not satisfied with the net rewards, that person may continue in the relationship or interaction because no viable alternative exists. The experience, as unsatisfactory as it may seem, is the best this person believes can be attained *at that time*.

Like Schutz's interpersonal needs theory, Thibaut and Kelley's exchange theory is helpful in understanding important aspects of relationship development. Yet critics of this theory point out an important limitation of this explanation. Exchange theory suggests that people *consciously* and *deliberately* weigh the costs and rewards associated with any relationship or interaction. Based on this analysis, according to the theory, people *rationally* choose to continue or terminate relationships. Thus, the theory assumes that people behave rationally from an economic standpoint.[5] But although we may behave rationally in most situations, there are times when rational models cannot account for our behavior. Still, it is useful to examine your relationships from a cost-reward perspective. Especially if the relationship is stagnating, you may be able to see areas where costs are seen as greater than rewards. If so, you may be able to change some aspects of the relationship before it is too late.

Self-Disclosure and Feedback in Relational Development

A good, growing relationship is likely to be one in which there is a mutually satisfying blend of self-disclosure and feedback between the two persons. How can you tell whether you and another are sharing enough to keep the relationship growing? As the basis for a worthwhile discussion, we suggest drawing and discussing Johari windows.

The Johari window (named after its two originators, Joe Luft and Harry Ingham) is a tool that you can use to examine the relationship between self-disclosure and feedback. The window is divided into four sections or panes as shown in Figure 8.1.

The first quadrant is called the "open" pane of the window. The open pane is used to represent everything about people that is known and freely shared with others. It also shows others' observations of them or their behavior that they are aware of. For instance, most people are willing to discuss where they live, the kinds of cars they drive, the activities they enjoy, and countless other items of information. Moreover, most people are aware of certain of their mannerisms that others observe. People may be well aware that they get red when they are embarrassed or that they wrinkle their nose when they are not sure of something. If you were preparing a Johari window that represented your relationship with another person, you would include in the open pane all the items of information that you would be free to share with that other person.

The second quadrant of the window is the hidden self or "secret" pane. This pane is used to represent all those things people know about themselves that they do not normally share with others, for whatever reason. This information may run the gamut from where Tim keeps his pencils or which green vegetables he does not like to deep secrets that seem very threatening to him. If you were preparing a Johari window that represented your relationship with another person, you would include in the secret pane all the items of information that you are unwilling to share with that other person. Secret information moves into the open part of the window only when you change your attitude about revealing that specific information. If, for example, Angela was engaged at one time but the information is something that she usually does not let people know, it would be in the secret

FIGURE 8 · 1

Adapted from *Group Processes: An Introduction to Group Dynamics* by Joseph Luft. By permission Mayfield Publishing Company. Copyright © 1963, 1970 by Joseph Luft.

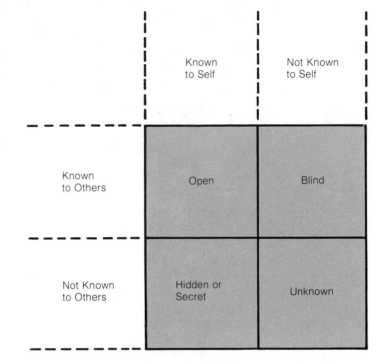

	Known to Self	Not Known to Self
Known to Others	Open	Blind
Not Known to Others	Hidden or Secret	Unknown

part of her window. If, for some reason, she decided to disclose this information to you, it would move into and enlarge the open part of the Johari window that she might draw to represent her relationship with you.

The third quadrant of the window is called the "blind" area. The blind pane is used to represent information others know about people that those people are themselves unaware of. Most people have blind spots—behaviors that are observed by others but are unknown to the people who do them. If Charley snores when he sleeps, if he always wrinkles up his nose when he does not like something, or if he gets a gleam in his eye when he sees a girl he would like to get to know, these may well be nonverbal behaviors that he is blind to. Information in the blind area of the window moves to the open area through feedback from others. If you were preparing a Johari window that represented your relationship with another person, the size of the blind pane would include your guess as to the amount of information the other person holds about you that either the person is reluctant to share or that you are unwilling to hear. For instance, if Ken is Charley's roommate at the dorm, he may not tell Charley that he has bad breath. If he does tell Charley directly or indirectly through some nonverbal response, Charley may not choose to "hear" what Ken tells him. In both cases, the blind spot continues. On the other hand, if Charley is receptive to such feedback, the blind pane gets smaller and the open pane enlarges.

The fourth and last quadrant of the window is called the "unknown." It represents aspects of a given person that are not known to anyone—not to the people themselves or to others. If, for instance, you have never tried hang gliding, neither you nor anyone else knows how you might react and behave at the point of takeoff—you might chicken out, or you might follow through, do it well, and love every minute of flight. Once you had tried, your feelings and abilities would be known by you and probably at least a few others.

Thus, as you can see, with each bit of self-disclosure or feedback the sizes and shapes of the various panes of the window change. For any relationship you have with another person you can construct a window that represents the ratio of openness to closedness. Let us look at four different representations and consider what they mean.

Figure 8.2 shows a relationship in which the open area is very small. The people are not sharing much information about themselves and are blind to what other people know or think about them. This window might

FIGURE 8 · 2

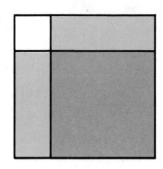

FIGURE 8 · 3

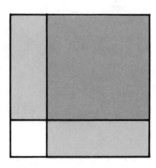

FIGURE 8 · 4

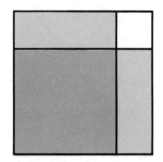

FIGURE 8 · 5

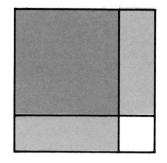

represent your relationship with another person during the first stages of getting to know that person; it is also typical of people who keep to themselves and do not want, desire, or need to interact on more than a superficial level with others.

Figure 8.3 shows a relationship in which people are willing to share their thoughts and feelings but get or are receptive to very little feedback from others. Such people may perceive themselves to be very open in their communication. Yet their communication is limited by their unwillingness to learn or lack of interest in learning about what others observe.

Figure 8.4 shows a relationship in which people seek out and are very receptive to feedback but are quite reluctant to share much of themselves. They want to hear what others have observed, but they are not willing or are afraid to disclose their observations and feelings.

Figure 8.5 shows a relationship in which people both seek out and are very receptive to feedback and are willing to share information and feelings they have. This is the kind of window we would expect to see depicting a close relationship of friends or intimates. Even though Figure 8.5 is the best model of communication for friends and intimates, the other windows depict many of our communication relationships. Although people need not share every idea or feeling with others and people need not be receptive to every reaction to them, having a relatively large "open" pane is helpful for good interpersonal communication.

PRACTICE

Analyzing Relationships

1. Consider a person with whom you have a close interpersonal relationship. Analyze it on the basis of (1) meeting interpersonal needs and (2) its costs versus its rewards.

2. On a scale of 1 to 5 (1 = low, 5 = high) how would you rate yourself on the following?
   a. Need to show affection
   b. Need to receive affection from others
   c. Need to be included with others (in bull sessions, informal gatherings, parties)
   d. Willingness to include others (in leisure-time activities)
   e. Need to be in charge of situations
   f. Willingness to allow others to be in charge of situations
   Ask a close friend to rate you on these same six criteria.

3. Try this with a close friend. Each of you draws a window that represents your perception of your relationship with the other. Then each of you draws a window that represents what you perceive to be the other's relationship with you. Share the windows. How do they compare? If there are differences in the representations, talk with your friend about them.

SUMMARY

An effect of, if not the primary reason for, interpersonal communication is developing relationships. Although at times we seem to fall into and drift out of relationships without rhyme or reason, there are identifiable elements underlying the success or failure of a relationship. A good relationship is any mutually satisfying level of interaction with another person.

People are inclined to view their relationships in the social categories of acquaintances, friends, and deep friends or intimates. Communication in relationships will occur on the phatic level, the gossip level, the idea-exchange level, and the feelings-sharing level. Although phatic communication and gossip are most associated with acquaintances, they both occur in all social categories. Feelings-sharing communication, the highest level, is likely to occur only with close friends and intimates.

Relationships may develop from acquaintances to deep friendships or intimate relationships. If the relationship does not stabilize at its highest level, it is likely to deteriorate. The stages of deterioration are reduction of tolerance, drifting, and, finally, an ending.

One cause of deteriorating relationships is failure to manage conflict successfully. Conflict is a clash of opposing ideas or feelings. Conflicts may be content conflicts over facts, interpretations of facts, definitions, or choices; they may be value conflicts over competing value systems that are brought to bear on the issues; or they may be ego conflicts that personalize the nature of the conflict. Conflicts become more complicated as they escalate to value and ego conflict.

People cope with conflicts in a variety of ways. Negative behaviors include withdrawal, surrender, and aggression. Positive behaviors include persuasion and discussion. Guidelines for managing conflict include recognizing signs of conflict, keeping discussion centered on the topic on which conflict occurs, keeping an open mind, cooperating rather than competing, and prearranging a management procedure.

Many different theories have been proposed to help analyze relationships. Schutz sees relationships in terms of ability to meet the interpersonal needs of affection, inclusion, and control. Thibaut and Kelley see relationships as functions of exchange analysis—the cost-reward ratio of energy, time, and money invested weighed against satisfaction gained. Luft and Ingham developed the Johari window as a tool for examining the ratio of openness to closedness in a relationship.

SUGGESTED READINGS

Berscheid, Ellen, and Elaine Walster, *Interpersonal Attraction.* Reading, Mass.: Addison-Wesley, 1969. Highly readable, exhaustive review of interpersonal attraction in short paperback form.

Deaux, Kay, and Larence S. Wrightsman. *Social Psychology in the 80's.* 4th ed. Monterey, Calif.: Brooks/Cole, 1984. An excellent social psychology book with a chapter on relationships.

Duck, Steve, and Robin Gilmour, eds. *Personal Relationships.* New York: Academic Press, 1981. An excellent short work that surveys some of the best research available in family and friendship relationships.

Hocker, Joyce L. and Wilmot, William W. *Interpersonal Conflict.* 2d ed. Dubuque, Iowa: William C. Brown, 1985. An excellent analysis of the nature of conflict, styles of coping with conflict, and methods of managing conflict.

Knapp, Mark L. *Interpersonal Communication and Human Relationships.* Boston: Allyn & Bacon, 1984. Some very good explanations of how relationships build, stabilize, and deteriorate.

Penman, Robert. *Communication Processes and Relationships.* New York: Academic Press, 1980. Includes discussion of the role of communication in relationships.

Watzlawick, Paul, Janet H. Beavin, and Don D. Jackson. *Pragmatics of Human Communication.* New York: W. W. Norton, 1967. A classic study of relational communication.

INTERVIEWING

OBJECTIVES

After you have read this chapter, you should be able to:

1 Prepare open, closed, primary, secondary, neutral, and leading questions

2 Conduct an information interview

3 Outline the procedure used by job interviewers

4 Write a résumé

5 Participate in a job interview

A common and useful communication format is the interview. **Interviewing** is a form of interaction based primarily on the asking and answering of questions. An interview may be for appraisal (making value judgments that may lead to hiring, promotion, reward, or firing), for counseling (helping people to examine and perhaps solve their problems), for persuasion (influencing people to buy a product), or for gaining information and job interviewing, the primary subjects of this chapter. Unlike most of your interpersonal communication, interviewing can be planned ahead.

In this chapter we consider the phrasing of questions, information interviews, and procedures for job interviews.

QUESTIONS IN INTERVIEWING

An interview differs from other forms of interpersonal communication in its reliance on the asking and answering of questions. Although we deal here specifically with questions in the interview situation, a knowledge of good question construction can be applied to any interpersonal encounter. Questions may be phrased as open or closed, primary or secondary, leading or neutral.

Open or Closed Questions

Open questions are broad based questions that ask the interviewee to provide whatever information he or she wishes to answer the questions; **closed questions** are those that ask for "yes" or "no" answers or specific information, such as "January 12, 1982." Open questions range from those with virtually no restrictions, like "Will you tell me about yourself?" to those that give some direction, like "Will you tell me about your preparation for this job?" Why do interviewers ask open questions? Mostly to encourage the person to talk, allowing the interviewer an opportunity to listen and to observe. Through the open question the interviewer finds out about the person's perspectives, values, and goals. Open questions take time to answer, and interviewers can lose their organization if they are not careful.

Closed questions range from those that can be answered "yes" or "no," such as "Have you had a course in marketing?" to those that require a short answer, such as "How many restaurants have you worked in?" By asking closed questions, interviewers can control the interview; moreover, they can get large amounts of information in a short time. But the closed question seldom enables the interviewer to know why a person gave a certain response, and it is not likely to yield much voluntary information.

Which type of question should you use? The answer depends on what kind of material you are seeking and how much time you have for the interview. Both kinds of questions are used in most information and employment interviews.

Neutral or Leading Questions

Neutral questions are those in which the person being interviewed is free to give an answer without direction from the interviewer; **leading questions** are those in which the interviewer suggests the expected or desired answer. A neutral question would be "How do you feel about your new job?" There is nothing about the wording of the question that gives the respondent any indication of how the question should be answered. Except in very rare instances your questions in information and employment interviews should be neutral.

Leading questions, on the other hand, are phrased in a way that suggests a preferred answer. "You don't like the new job, do you?" is a leading question. In the majority of interviewing situations, leading questions are inappropriate. They make the person being interviewed defensive by trying to force the person in one direction.

Primary or Secondary Questions

Primary questions are those you plan ahead of time; **secondary questions** follow up on the answers. Primary questions serve as the main points for your interview outline. Primary questions may be open or closed, depending on the kind of information you want; moreover, primary questions may be neutral or leading. When you plan your interview, you'll want to include enough primary questions and to ask them in an order that will reveal all the information you want.

Secondary questions may be planned ahead if you can anticipate the interviewee's possible answers. More often than not, however, secondary questions are composed as the interview goes along. To come up with good secondary questions you must pay close attention to what the interviewee is saying. Some secondary questions encourage the person to continue ("And then?" "Is there more?"), some probe into what the person has said ("What does 'frequently' mean?" "What were you thinking at the time?"), and some plumb the feelings of the person ("How did it feel to get the prize?" "Were you worried when you didn't find her?").

The major reason for secondary questions is to motivate a person to elaborate on an answer that appears inadequate. Following up is necessary because interviewees may purposely try to be evasive, incomplete, or vague or may not really understand how much detail you are looking for.

Your effectiveness with follow-up questions may depend on your interpersonal skill in asking them. Since asking probing questions can alienate the interviewee (especially when the questions are perceived as threatening), such in-depth probes work best after you have gained the confidence of the interviewee and when the questions are asked within the atmosphere of a positive interpersonal climate.

PRACTICE

Identifying and Phrasing Questions

1. Indicate which of the following are (O) open questions and which are (C) closed questions. If the question is open, write an example of a closed question seeking similar information; if the question is closed, write an open question. Make sure that all your write-in questions are neutral rather than leading.

___O___ a. What makes you think that Parker will be appointed?
___C___ b. How many steps are there in getting a book into print?
___C___ c. Will you try out for cheerleaders?
___O___ d. What is your opinion about guidelines for promotion?
___O___ e. How do you think the school should make its budgetary decisions?

a.

b.

c.

d.

e.

ANSWERS: a. O; b. C; c. C; d. O; e. O.

2. Change these leading questions to neutral questions:
   a. Doesn't it depress you to see so many patients who never get well?
   b. After what Angeline did, I bet you are really out to get her, aren't you?
   c. Wouldn't you be upset about going to Toronto if you were traded?
   d. Aren't you really excited about your promotion?
   e. After the way he acted, I'll bet you're really going to chew him out the next time you see him, aren't you?

3. You are interviewing your professor for an article for the school paper. To the question "What motivated you to choose college teaching as a career?" the professor answers, "It seemed to me like a really good job." Write three well-phrased follow-up questions you would be likely to ask.

A.

B.

C.

INTERVIEWING FOR INFORMATION

Interviewing can be a valuable method for getting information on nearly any topic. Students can use the interview to get information for papers, lawyers interview witnesses to get facts to build their cases, doctors interview patients to get medical histories before making diagnoses, and reporters interview sources to get facts for their stories. A good interviewing plan involves clearly defining the purpose of the interview, selecting the best person to interview, researching the subject area or person to be interviewed, determining a procedure, and conducting the interview.

Defining the Purpose of the Interview

Too often interviewers go into an information interview without a really clear purpose for the interview. Your purpose is clear when you can write it down in one complete sentence. Without such a clear purpose it is all too likely that your list of questions will have no direction. As a result, you are likely to come out with information that does not fit well together.

Suppose you are thinking about getting information about the food service in your dormitory. The following are possible specific purposes for your interview:

1. To get a personal sketch of the person responsible for planning meals
2. To determine the major elements a dietitian must take into account in order to plan dormitory meals
3. To determine how a dietitian can run a cost-effective program that provides good nutrition at a reasonable price

Selecting the Best Person

Somewhere on campus or in the larger community there are people who have or can get the information you want. How do you find out whom you should interview? If you are pursuing the second purpose, to determine the major elements a dietitian must take into account in order to plan dormitory meals, one of the employees can tell you who is in charge of the dining hall. Or you can phone your student center and ask who is in charge of food service. When you have decided whom you should interview, make an appointment. You cannot walk into an office and expect the prospective interviewee to drop everything on the spur of the moment.

Researching the Subject Area or Person to Be Interviewed

Before going into the interview, get information on the topic. If, for instance, you are going to interview the dietitian who makes out menus and orders the food, you should already know something about the job of dietitian and something about the problems of ordering and preparing institutional food. Interviewees are more likely to talk with you if you appear informed; moreover, familiarity with the subject will enable you to ask better questions. If, for some reason, you go into an interview uninformed, then at least approach the interviewee with enthusiasm and apparent interest in the subject.

You should also be forthright in your reasons for scheduling the interview. Whether your interview is part of a class project, for a newspaper article on campus food, or for some other reason, say so.

Planning Carefully

Good interviewing results from careful planning. A good plan begins with good questions. Write down all the questions you can think of, revise them until you have worded them clearly and concisely, and put them in the order that seems most appropriate. Your questions should be a mix of open and closed questions and should be neutral rather than leading. Moreover, you will need to be alert to the need for follow-up questions.

When you list your questions, leave enough space between them to fill in answers as completely as possible. Leave just as much space for answers to the secondary questions you decide to ask. Some interviewers try to play the entire interview by ear. However, even the most skilled interviewer needs some preplanned questions to ensure that important areas will be covered. The order and type of questions depend somewhat on what you are hoping to achieve in the interview. How many primary questions should you have planned? The answer, of course, depends on how much time you have for the interview. If you have thirty minutes, about ten questions would be a reasonable number. Why ten? For a thirty-minute interview that would give about three minutes per question. Remember, for some of your questions you will need one or more follow-ups to get the information you want. If most of your questions are closed, then you can have more; if nearly all of your questions are open, maybe you'd want fewer than ten. You never know how a person will respond. Some people are so talkative and informative that in response to your first question they answer every question you were planning to ask and in great detail; other people will answer all questions in a few words.

In the opening stages you should, of course, start by thanking the person for taking time to talk with you. Try to develop a good rapport between you and your respondent. Start by asking some questions that can be answered easily and that will show your respect for the person you are interviewing. In an interview with the head dietitian, you might start with such questions as "How did you get interested in nutrition?" or "I imagine working out menus can be a very challenging job in these times of high food costs—is this true?" When the person nods or says "yes," you can then ask about some of the biggest challenges he or she faces. The goal is to get the interviewee to feel at ease and to talk freely. Since the most important consideration at this initial stage is to create a positive communication climate, keep the questions easy to answer, nonthreatening, and encouraging.

The body of the interview includes the major questions you have prepared to ask in order to achieve your purpose. A good plan is to group questions so that the easy-to-answer questions come first and the hard-hitting questions that require careful thinking come later. For instance, the question "What do you do to try to resolve student complaints?" should be near the end of the interview. You may not ask all the questions you planned to, but you don't want to end the interview until you have the important information you intended to get.

As you draw to the end of your planned questions, again thank the person for taking time to talk with you. If you are going to publish the substance of the interview, it is courtesy to offer to let the person see a copy of the article, or at least to tell the person exactly when it will be published. Under some circumstances you may want to show the person a draft of your reporting of the interview before it goes into print. If a person does wish to see what you are planning to write, get a draft to that person well before deadline to give him or her the opportunity to read it and to give you the opportunity to deal with any suggestions. Although this practice is not followed by many interviewers, it may help to build and maintain your own credibility.

The following example gives you an idea of the method of setting up a question schedule. If you were planning to interview the dietitian, you might prepare the following question schedule:

BACKGROUND:
- What kind of background and training do you need for the job?
- How did you get interested in nutrition?
- Have you worked as a dietitian for long?
- Have you held any other food-related positions?

RESPONSIBILITIES:
- What are the responsibilities of your job besides meal planning?
- How far in advance are meals planned?
- What factors are taken into account when you are planning the meals for a given period?
- Do you have a free hand, or are there constraints placed upon you?

PROCEDURES:
- Is there any set formula for how often you put a particular item on the menu?
- Do you take individual differences into account?

- How do you determine whether you will give choices for the entrée?
- What do you do to try to answer student complaints?
- How do your prices compare with meals at a commercial cafeteria?

Conducting the Interview

By applying the interpersonal skills we have discussed in this unit, you'll find that you can turn your careful planning into an excellent interview.

First, of course, you will want to be courteous during the interview. The person who is taking time to talk with you is getting nothing for it. Be patient at all times. And encourage the person to speak freely. Most of all, respect what the person says regardless of what you may think of the answers.

Second, listen very carefully. At key places in the interview you should paraphrase what the person has said. You remember that a *paraphrase* is a sentence that states in your own words the idea or feeling you got from what the person has told you.

Third, keep the interview moving. You do not want to rush the person, but when the allotted time is ending, you should call attention to that fact and be prepared to conclude.

The success of an interview can depend as much on the interviewer as the interviewee. Demonstrating interest and enthusiasm (rather than reticence and cool objectivity) will result in a more rewarding interview, not to mention a more pleasant experience for both parties.

Fourth, make sure that your nonverbal reactions—your facial expressions and your gestures—are in keeping with the tone you want to communicate. Maintain good eye contact with the person. Use supportiveness skills. Nod to show understanding, and smile occasionally to maintain the friendliness of the interview. How you look and act is likely to determine whether the person will warm up to you and give you a good interview.

PRACTICE

Interviewing

1. Determine a topic on which you might wish to conduct an information interview. Determine whom you would interview. Then devise a list of questions for this interview. Remember to ask open as well as closed questions. Check to make sure most questions are neutral rather than leading. Group the questions under major headings. Make sure you have some questions that are appropriate for opening the interview. Write the finished product on paper for posting. Share your work with the class.

2. Conduct an in-class interview with a classmate on a subject of her or his expertise.

3. Conduct an interview outside of class and submit a written report or deliver a speech based upon the interview. Use the material you prepared for the first exercise as a basis for this interview.

EMPLOYMENT INTERVIEWING

Although there is some question about the interview as a valid tool for personnel selection, applicants for nearly every position in nearly any field will go through an interview. At its worst, an interview can be a waste of time for everyone; at its best, an interview can reveal vital information about an applicant. A skillfully conducted interview can help interviewers determine the applicants' specific abilities, ambition, energy, ability to communicate, knowledge and intelligence, and integrity. Moreover, it can help the interviewees show their strengths in these same areas.

Assuming the validity of the interview in the selection process, let's consider some of the procedures and methods that an interviewer uses in conducting an interview and that an interviewee uses in taking part in one.

Responsibilities of the Interviewer

As an interviewer you are the link between a job applicant and the company. Much of the applicant's impression of the company will be made on the basis of her or his impression of you. You should know what kinds of information applicants want to know about your company. In addition to the obvious desire for salary information, applicants may also seek information about opportunity for advancement, influence of personal ideas on company policy, company attitudes toward personal life and life style, and so forth. Moreover, you have nearly the sole responsibility for determining whether this person will be considered for the position available or whether this person will be kept in the running for possible company employment.

Sometimes a job interview requires you to meet with a group or committee. In such cases don't be intimidated by the size of the group ("I was outnumbered!"). Ask relevant questions of each member; show your interest in what they enjoy about their job. Being able to overcome shyness and create a friendly atmosphere may have a stronger influence on the group than your ability to have the "right" answers.

Procedure

You are likely to get the most from a highly to moderately structured interview. In the unstructured interview the interviewer tends to talk more and to make decisions based on less valid data than in the structured interview.[1] Especially if you are screening a large number of applicants, you want to make sure that all interviewees have been asked the same questions and that the questions cover a variety of subjects.

Before the interview starts, you should be familiar with all available data about the applicant—application form, résumé, letters of recommendation, test scores, if any are available. These written data will help determine some of the questions you will want to ask.

The Interview

Like a good speech, an interview has an opening, a body, and a conclusion.

The opening of the interview   Open by greeting applicants warmly. Call them by name, and introduce yourself so that they can use your name. A warm handshake also helps get things off to a good start. Be open with applicants. If you are going to either take notes or record the interviews, let the applicants know why you are doing so.

A major concern is whether you should begin with "warm-up" questions to help establish rapport or whether you should move right into the question schedule. A good interviewer senses the nature of the situation and tries to use a method that is most likely to encourage applicants to talk and provide adequate answers. Although warm-up questions may be helpful, most applicants are ready to get down to business immediately. As a result, many warm-up questions may be misinterpreted. Applicants may wonder about the motivation for such questions, and the questions may make them even more nervous. Unless you have good reason for proceeding differently, the best advice seems to be to move into the question schedule right away in as warm and friendly a manner as you can.

The body of the interview   The body of the interview consists of the questions you are planning to ask. Let's begin with some guidelines for presenting yourself and your questions.

1. *Be careful of your own presentation.* Talk loudly enough to be heard. Try to be spontaneous. The interviewees are not going to respond well to obviously memorized questions fired in machine-gun fashion. Be sensitive to your own nonverbal communication. The interviewees are going to be looking for signs of disapproval—any inadvertent looks or unusual

changes in quality or rhythm of your speech may give a false impression. Remember that you can load a question by giving it a particular tone of voice, so be especially careful.

2. *Do not waste time.* You have available a wide variety of information about the candidates. Ask questions about things you already know only if you have some special reason for doing so. For instance, if applicants indicate employment with a particular organization but do not give any detailed account of responsibilities, questions relating to that employment period would be appropriate.

3. *Avoid trick or loaded questions.* Applicants are always leery of questions that may be designed to make them look bad. Moreover, if candidates believe that you are trying to trick them, the suspicion may promote a competitive rather than a positive atmosphere. Anything that serves to limit the applicant's responsiveness will harm the interview.

4. *Do not ask questions that violate fair employment practice legislation.* In 1964 Congress created the Equal Employment Opportunity Commission (EEOC). In subsequent years EEOC has written guidelines that spell out very carefully the kinds of questions that are lawful and unlawful. Questions directed to a woman about her plans for marriage or having children are not only irrelevant but illegal. Actually, any questions about marital status, family, physical characteristics, age, education, criminal record, or social security are illegal if this information is not deemed a bona fide occupational qualification.

5. *Give the applicant an opportunity to ask questions.* Usually, near the end of the interview you will want to take time to see whether the applicant has any questions.

Now let's look at some of the specific questions that interviewers usually ask. This list is a combination of questions from a variety of sources and is only representative, not exhaustive. It sets no limitations on your own creativity but is intended to suggest the kinds of questions you may wish to ask. You might use this as a starter list or as a checklist for your own wording of questions. Notice that some questions are open-ended and some are closed but none is a "yes" or "no" question.

SCHOOL:
- How did you select the school you attended?
- How did you determine your major?
- What extracurricular activities did you engage in at school?
- In what ways does your transcript reflect your ability?
- How were you able to help with your college expenses?

PERSONAL:
- What are your hobbies?
- How do you work under pressure?
- At what age did you begin supporting yourself?
- What causes you to lose your temper?

- What are your major strengths? Weaknesses?
- What do you do to stay in good physical condition?
- What kind of reading do you like to do?
- Who has had the greatest influence on your life?
- What have you done that shows your creativity?

POSITION

- What kind of position are you looking for?
- What do you know about the company?
- Under what circumstances will you be willing to relocate?
- Why do you think you would like to work for us?
- What do you hope to accomplish?
- What qualifications do you have that make you feel you would be beneficial to us?
- How do you feel about traveling?
- What part of the country would you like to settle in?
- With what kind of people do you enjoy interacting?
- What do you regard as an equitable salary for a person with your qualifications?
- What new skills would you like to learn?
- What are your professional goals?
- How would you proceed if you were in charge of hiring?
- What are your most important criteria for determining whether you will accept a position?

The closing of the interview   Toward the end of the interview, you should always tell the applicants what will happen next. Tell them about the procedures for making the decision. Who has the authority? When will the decision be made? How will applicants be notified? These are some of the questions you certainly should answer. Then close the interview in a courteous, neutral manner. You should neither build false hopes nor seem to discourage the applicants.

Responsibilities of the Job Applicant

Interviews are an important part of the process of seeking employment. Even for part-time and temporary jobs, you will benefit if you approach the interviewing process seriously and systematically. There is no point in applying for positions that are obviously outside your area of expertise. It may seem a good idea to get interviewing experience, but you are wasting your time and the interviewer's time if you apply for a position you have no intention of taking or a position for which you are not qualified.

When you are granted an employment interview, remember that all you have to sell is yourself and your qualifications. You want to show yourself in the best possible light. You should be concerned about your appearance; if you want a particular job, you should dress in a way that is acceptable to the person or organization that may—or may not—hire you. You should be fully prepared for the interview. Two important responsibilities that you must meet before the interview itself are the cover letter and the résumé.

Cover letter

The *cover letter* is a short, well-written letter that you send in application for a position. Address the letter to the person with the authority to hire. You are trying to capture the reader's interest in you, the applicant. Try to write it in a way that tells the reader that it is not a form letter. Elements of the letter should include where you found out about the position, your main qualifications (a summary of a few key points), how you fit the requirements for the job, items of special interest about you that would raise the reader's interest in your potential for the job, and a request for an interview. You will also include a résumé.

Résumé

While there is no universal format for résumé writing, there is agreement on what should be included. In writing your résumé, you should consider including personal information, professional objectives, education, experience, activities and interests, background, and references. In addition, you should consider several guidelines for construction: ample margins, proper spacing, and a good system of indentation. Also, be honest in your appraisals. The résumé should be no more than three pages long, preferably one or two. Figure 9.1 is a sample résumé of a person who has just graduated from college.

Specific Guidelines

Some of the information you might want to include is mandatory, that is, it is the kind of material that recruiters in the nation's largest corporations look for.[2] These items appear with asterisks. The remaining items

FIGURE 9 · 1

Joyce M. Turner

Present Address:
2326 Tower Ave.
Cincinnati, Ohio 45220
(513) 861-2497

Permanent Address:
914 Market St.
Columbus, Ohio 43217
(614) 662-5931

**PROFESSIONAL
OBJECTIVE**

A challenging position in sales or public relations with a medium-sized corporation. Geographical preference for the Midwest.

EDUCATION
1981-85

University of Cincinnati, Cincinnati, Ohio Candidate for B.A. degree in June, 1985. Major in Communication with minor in Business (Marketing). Overall grade point average of 3.3

EXPERIENCE
1984-85

Sales. Shillito-Rikes Department Store. Full-time during summer and Christmas vacation; part-time during school year. Experience in clothing, appliances, and jewelry.

1985

Internship. WLW-TV. Received 3 credit hours for working 10 hours per week Spring quarter. Worked with sales force selling commercial time.

ACTIVITIES

Forensics. Represented the University of Cincinnati at five individual events tournaments over a two-year period. Won first place in extemporaneous speaking at Ohio Forensic Championships in 1985.

President, Women in Communication, an organization for women who aspire toward careers in communication.

INTERESTS

Sports (tennis and racquetball); travel

REFERENCES

On request

are optional, which means that some personnel directors, but not the majority, are interested in such information.

PERSONAL
- *Address(es)—present and permanent
- *Telephone number(s)
- Height
- Weight
- Marital status
- Military status
- Security clearance
- Dependents
- Health
- Citizenship
- Religion

PROFESSIONAL
- *Immediate objective

EDUCATION (reverse chronological order)
- *Name of school
- *Location
- *Degree and date
- *Major
- *Honors
- *Scholarships
- Other strengths
- Leadership roles
- Class standing
- Grade point average
- Special skills
- Professional or academic activities
- Societies
- Foreign language proficiency
- Source of financing

EXPERIENCE (indicate company name, location, time period, responsibilities, and accomplishments)
- *Employment in field in which you are seeking a job
- *Self-employment
- *Part-time employment—summer or school year
- *Military service
- *Volunteer work

ACTIVITIES
- *Employment-related activities
- Other activities
- Hobbies

REFERENCES
- Names and addresses

Getting ready for the interview   It is a good idea to give yourself a practice session. Try to anticipate some of the questions you will be asked and think carefully about your answers. You need not write out and practice answers, but before the actual interview, you should have anticipated key questions, and you should have thought about such subjects as salary expectations, contributions to the company, and special skills.

The interview   You are likely to give the best possible impression in your interview if you do these things:

1. *Do your homework.* Know about the company's services, products, ownership, and financial health. Knowing about a company shows your interest in that company and will usually impress the interviewer.
2. *Be prompt.* The interview is the company's only clue to your work behavior. If you are late for such an important event, the interviewer may well conclude that you are likely to be late for work. Give yourself plenty of time in travel to cover any possible traffic problems, and so forth.
3. *Be alert and look at the interviewer.* Remember that your nonverbal communication tells a lot about you. Company representatives are likely to consider eye contact and posture as clues to your self-confidence.
4. *Give yourself time to think.* If the interviewer asks you a question that you had not anticipated, give yourself time to think before you answer. It is better to pause and think than to give a hasty answer that may cost you the job. If you do not understand the question, paraphrase it before you attempt to answer.
5. *Ask questions about the type of work you will be doing.* The interview is your chance to find out if you would enjoy working for this company. You might ask the interviewer to describe a typical work day for the person who will get the job. If the interview is conducted at the company offices, you might ask to see where you would be working.
6. *Avoid engaging in long discussions on salary.* On your résumé you have probably indicated a range of salary expectations. if the company representative tries to pin you down, ask, "What do you normally pay someone with my experience and education for this level of position?" Such a question allows you to get an idea of what the salary will be without committing yourself to a figure first.
7. *Avoid harping on benefits.* Detailed questions about benefits are more appropriate after the company has made you an offer.

As a further guide for your behavior, you will want to make sure that you don't do anything that will label you as "an undesirable applicant." In short, the undesirable applicant[3]

1. Is caught lying
2. Shows lack of interest
3. Is belligerent, rude, or impolite

4. Lacks sincerity
5. Is evasive
6. Is concerned only about salary
7. Is unable to concentrate
8. Is indecisive
9. Is late
10. Is unable to express himself or herself clearly
11. Wants to start in an executive position
12. Oversells his or her case

PRACTICE

*Employment
Interviewing*

1. What do you see as your major interviewing strengths? Weaknesses?

2. Prepare a cover letter and a résumé for a position such as you might apply for after graduation.

3. Select a partner in class and interview each other for particular jobs for which your résumés were prepared. Try to follow the guidelines for employment interviewing that were discussed in this section.

SUMMARY

You are most likely to use interviewing as a means of getting information from an expert for a paper, an article, or a speech. You are most likely to be interviewed when you are looking for a job. In either event, interviewing skills are important to you.

The key skill of interviewing is using questions effectively. Open questions allow for flexible response; closed questions are answered "yes" or "no" or with a few words. Primary questions stimulate response; secondary questions follow up the primary questions. Neutral questions allow the respondent free choice; leading questions require the person to answer in a particular way.

When you are interviewing for information, you will want to define the purpose of the interview, select the best person to interview, determine a framework for the interview, conduct the interview according to the framework, and interpret the results.

When you are interviewing prospective applicants for a job, you will need to structure your interview carefully to get maximum information about each candidate. Before the interview starts, make sure that you are familiar with the data from the applicant's application form, résumé, letters of recommendation, and test scores that may be available. Be careful of your presentation, do not waste time, avoid loaded questions, do not ask questions that violate fair employment practice legislation, and give the applicant an opportunity to ask questions. At the end of the interview, tell the applicant what will happen next in the process.

When you are being interviewed for a job, you will want to learn about the company and prepare an appropriate cover letter and résumé. For the interview itself, you will want to be prompt, be alert and look directly at the interviewer, give yourself time to think before answering difficult questions, and ask intelligent questions about the work.

SUGGESTED READINGS

Biagi, Shirley. *Interviews That Work: A Practical Guide for Journalists*. Belmont, Calif.: Wadsworth Publishing Co., 1986. An excellent short work that focuses on information interviewing.

Bostwick, Burdette E. *Résumé Writing*, 3rd ed. New York: John Wiley and Sons, 1985 (paperback). A short book devoted entirely to writing résumés and cover letters.

Downs, Cal W., G. Paul Smeyak, and Ernest Martin. *Professional Interviewing*. New York: Harper & Row, 1980. This book is quite comprehensive and gives information related to all types of interviewing. Covers general principles of interviewing and specific guidelines for various types of interviews.

Goodale, James G. *The Fine Art of Interviewing*. Englewood Cliffs, N.J.: Prentice-Hall, 1982. A much shorter book that focuses on business interviews from the interviewer's perspective. Some excellent material on asking questions that comply with EEOC guidelines.

Pettus, Theodore T. *One on One: Win the Interview, Win the Job*. New York: Random House, 1981. A guide for a person going on a business interview. Written to motivate a person to prepare well for the interview.

Stewart, Charles J., and William B. Cash. *Interviewing: Principles and Practices*. 4th ed. Dubuque, Iowa: Wm. C. Brown, 1985. A comprehensive college textbook.

PART FOUR

▶ Ours is a government by committee—small groups of people working together to reach decisions. Indeed, reliance on the group process as an instrument of decision making extends into nearly every facet of our lives. But as informal conversation moves to the structure of small-group communication, the group itself presents a new set of variables we need to consider.

DECISION-MAKING GROUP COMMUNICATION

Self-Analysis

Decision-making groups are small units whose members interact face to face while working toward a common goal. Group-member roles are characterized by a combination of leadership and participation, each person accomplishing various task and maintenance functions. Task functions contribute to getting the job done; maintenance functions help people feel good about what they are doing.

Most of the interpersonal skills included in the first part of this book are fundamental to effective decision-making group work. In this analysis (and in this part of the book) we will focus on those skills that are particularly relevant to group decision making.

What has been your experience in groups? Have you expected someone else to somehow find the means for making the decision or solving the problem? For each of the statements listed below, circle the number that best indicates how you see your behavior. The numbers 1 and 2 represent the negative behavior; the numbers 4 and 5 represent the positive behavior. The number 3 represents a position between the extremes; it may also say you are not sure of your behavior.

| I believe that participating in groups like committees is a waste of time. | 1 2 3 4 5 | I enjoy participating in group discussions like committees. |
| I seldom do any research or think very deeply about the problem to be discussed beforehand. | 1 2 3 4 5 | I prepare well beforehand for group discussions. |

I assume that during discussion the issues necessary to solve the problem will emerge.	1	2	3	4	5	I analyze a problem to determine the questions that need to be asked in order to solve the problem.
I tend to contribute in a group discussion only if I am called upon.	1	2	3	4	5	I contribute freely and openly in groups.
I am not usually the one who provides key information for the group.	1	2	3	4	5	My contributions are very helpful in the group's effort to accomplish its task.
I seldom pay attention to whether material presented is relevant.	1	2	3	4	5	I help the group consider whether material presented is relevant.
I am not very good at helping develop or maintain a good discussion climate.	1	2	3	4	5	I am good at saying things that help the group work well together.
I prefer to let others lead a group.	1	2	3	4	5	I try to provide leadership for the group.
When I am a leader I do not usually prepare a suggested outline for group procedure.	1	2	3	4	5	When I am a leader I provide the members of the group with a carefully thought-out suggested procedure.
No matter what the group decides to do, I do what I think is right.	1	2	3	4	5	I abide by the group decision even when it is not one I would make on my own.

First, consider your analysis. Is the number you circle indicative of where you would like to be in that category? If not, in a different color of ink or pencil circle the number that represents your goal for this term. If you would like verification of your self-analysis, have a friend or fellow worker complete this same analysis for you.

Then select one of the areas in which your goals are farthest from your current behavior. Write a communication improvement contract similar to the sample contract in Appendix C.

10 ▷ PARTICIPATING IN DECISION-MAKING GROUPS

OBJECTIVES

After you have read this chapter, you should be able to:

1. Write questions of fact, value, and policy

2. Outline an organization for a discussion of a question of fact, value, or policy

3. Brainstorm for possible solutions

4. Solve a problem using the problem-solving method

5. Contrast task roles with maintenance roles

6. Identify negative roles

Probably no communication institution has been satirized more than the group. The saying "A camel is a horse designed by a committee" expresses a widely held opinion of group experience. Yet when we consider our family life, our business or work life, and our social life, we become aware of the tremendous investment of our time in group communication. In each of these settings groups function as decision-making bodies. Given our reliance on groups in decision making, we should focus on what we can do to make our group work more effective.

A **decision-making group** is a small, cohesive unit whose members interact face to face while working toward a common goal. Summaries of group research list many elements that effective groups have in common. In this chapter we will look at the responsibilities of effective group participation.

PREPARING FOR DISCUSSION

Whether your group is meeting for a one-shot effort or on an on-going basis, you need to be prepared: Never go into a group decision-making session without having done your homework!

Once you are a member of a group, you have a commitment to that group. If you don't want to discuss the issue before the group, don't agree to be on the committee. If you have agreed to take part, you have an obligation, a responsibility to work. Many people like to meet with a group and "bat around ideas." But your responsibility involves both getting ready to discuss and the actual discussion itself. Instead of taking a "Well, here I am; what do we do now?" attitude, you need to take an active part.

Preparing for discussion involves identifying the problem, outlining the issues, and researching the problem. These three aspects involve both individual and group preparation.

Identifying the Problem for Discussion

Groups are formed either to consider all issues that relate to a specific topic (a social committee, a personnel committee, or a public relations committee would be formed for this reason) or to consider a specific issue (such as the year's social calendar, criteria for granting promotions, a long-range plan for university growth). Much of the wheel-spinning that takes place during the early stages of group discussion results from members not understanding their specific goal. It is the duty of the person, agency, or parent group that forms a particular work group to give the group a clear goal. For instance, a group may be formed for the purpose of "determining the nature of the curriculum" or "preparing a guideline for hiring at a new plant." If the goal is not this clear, it is up to the group leader or representative to find out exactly why the group was formed and what its goals are. If the group is free to determine its goal, then the group should move immediately to get the goal down on paper; until everyone in the group agrees on their goal, they will never agree on how to achieve it.

Regardless of the clarity of the charge, the group may still want to reword or in some way modify it. A group should consider several criteria before finalizing the wording of its statement of purpose.

1. *Is the problem phrased as a question?* The group discussion format is one of inquiry. A group begins from the assumption that answers are not yet known. Although some decision-making groups serve merely as rubber-stamping agencies, the ideal is for the group to have the freedom of choice. Phrasing the group's purpose as a question furthers the spirit of inquiry.

2. *Does the question contain only one central idea?* The question "Should the college abolish its foreign language and its social studies requirements?" is poorly phrased because it contains two distinct problems. Either one would make a good discussion, but they cannot both be discussed at once.

3. *Is the wording of the question clear to all group members?* Sometimes a topic question contains a word that is so ambiguous that the group may waste time quibbling over its meaning. For instance, a group that

Do you think the members of this group will be able to arrive at a decision easily? Why or why not? If you were a part of the group, would you feel comfortable suggesting changes in the physical environment?

is examining a department's curriculum might suggest the following question:

> What should the department do about courses that aren't getting the job done?

Although the question is well intentioned and participants may have at least some idea about their goal, such vague wording as "getting the job done" can lead to trouble in the discussion. Instead of waiting until trouble arises, reword questions so they are specific *before* the group begins to get into discussion of the material. Notice how this revision of the preceding question make its intent much more clear:

> What should the department do about courses that receive low scores on student evaluations?

4. *Does the question encourage objective discussion?* The phrasing of a question may drastically affect a group's decisions. Consider the following: "Should our ridiculous set of college requirements be revised?" What kind of objective discussion is likely to occur when right from the start the group has agreed that requirements are ridiculous? With such wording the scales are tilted before the group even gets into the issues involved. The phrasing of the question should not indicate which way the question will be decided.

5. *Is the question appropriate for group discussion?* A group should consider only those questions that are most appropriate for group discussion. One of the most common criticisms of the group process is that it tends to waste time on tasks best dealt with by individuals. How can you tell whether your group should be discussing the question? Victor Vroom and his associates[1] have suggested guidelines for evaluating the appropriateness of a question for group discussion. Among the most important considerations are whether a high-quality decision is necessary and whether acceptance by members of the group is necessary to put the decision into practice. A high-quality decision is one that is well documented. High-quality decisions are usually too much for one person to handle: Gathering the data alone may require hours of work by every member of the group. Moreover, since vigorous testing is necessary at *every* stage of the decision-making process, a group is more likely to ask the right questions. Likewise, individuals within the organization are the ones who must carry out the decision. If group members are involved in the decision, they will be motivated to see that the decision does not fail.

If one person has the necessary information and authority to make a good decision, if a solution that has worked well in the past can be applied to this situation, or if time is limited and an immediate action is necessary, it may be appropriate for an individual to make the decision. For example, in government, business, or industry the dissemination of information may be restricted to persons at higher levels. Under these circumstances an individual must make the decision alone. Likewise, since we make many decisions on the basis of what has worked in the past, if a situation seems to be much like another one in which a particular decision was successful, a similar decision might be adopted without the participation of group members. Finally, the right timing may be vital to the success or failure of any venture, and the leader or manager may have to act quickly when the opportunity occurs.

6. *Can the question be identified easily as one of fact, value, or policy?* How you organize your discussion will depend on the kind of question. Later we will discuss organization. For now, let's consider the three types of questions.

Questions of fact concern the truth or falsity of an assertion. Implied in such questions is the possibility of determining the facts by way of direct observed, spoken, or recorded evidence. For instance, "Is Smith guilty of robbing the warehouse?" is a question of fact. Smith either committed the crime or he did not.

Questions of value concern subjective judgments of quality. They are characterized by the inclusion of some evaluative word such as *good, reliable, effective, worthy*. The purpose of questions of value is to compare a subject with one or more members of the same class. "What was the best movie last year?" is a question of value. Although we can set up criteria for "best" and measure our choice against those criteria, there is no way to verify our findings. The answer is still a matter of judgment, not fact. Although questions of value are widely discussed in social groups, they are not as likely to be the ultimate goal of work groups.

Questions of policy judge whether or not a future action should be taken. The question is phrased to invite a solution or to test a tentative solution to a problem or a felt need. "What should we do to lower the crime rate?" seeks a solution that would best solve the problem of the increase in crime. "Should the university give equal amounts of money to men's and women's athletics?" provides a tentative solution to the problem of how to achieve equity in the financial support of athletics. The inclusion of the word *should* in all questions of policy makes them the easiest to recognize and the easiest to phrase of all discussion questions. Most issues facing work groups are questions of policy.

Outlining the Issues of Discussion Questions

Before discussion of content begins, the group should outline the issues of the discussion question. An **issue** is a key question that must be considered in order to arrive at the best decision. Although issues for no two discussion questions can be outlined exactly alike, general issues can be identified that will serve as a foundation for the specific outlining of each type of discussion question. Since each of the three major types of questions—fact, value, and policy—requires the consideration of different issues, we'll consider each separately.

Outlining the issues for a question of fact   Most questions of fact are resolved by discussing the issues of definition, classification, and justification. Sometimes the task is to discover the characteristics of the classification; sometimes the task is to select a choice from among various classifications. The outline for a discussion of a question of fact will include at least the following issues:

1. What are the meanings of each of the key terms?
2. What information satisfies the definition and/or determines classifications?
3. What extenuating circumstances, if any, affect the decision?

For purposes of illustration, let's consider outlines for two slightly different questions of fact. The first is a question of classification; the second is a question of descriptive judgment, the kind of question of fact considered in courts of law.

What are the goals of the Republican Party?

1. What do we mean by a party's *goals*? (Defining key terms)
2. What data determine each of these separate goals? (Determining each classification)
3. What circumstances, if any, affect or override any of the apparent goals? (Determining extenuating circumstances)

Is Jones guilty of murdering Smith?

1. What is meant by *murdering*? (Defining key terms)
2. Did Jones cause the death of Smith? (Determining whether Jones committed the act)
3. Can Jones's actions be defined as "murder"? (Determining whether information fits the classification)
4. What, if any, extenuating circumstances affect the decision?

Outlining the issues for a question of value   The judgment of comparative value requires finding standards or criteria from which to work. An outline of a question of value will include at least the following issues:

1. What are the criteria on which the judgment will be made?
2. What are the facts surrounding the object(s) or person(s) being evaluated?
3. How do facts relate to the criteria?
4. What, if any, extenuating circumstances affect the evaluation?

For purposes of illustration, let's consider an outline of the following question of value:

Is Professor X an effective teacher?

1. What are the criteria for establishing teaching effectiveness? (Criteria)
2. What are the facts about Professor X's teaching? (Determining facts)
3. Do the facts show that Professor X's teaching meets enough of the criteria to be called effective? (Matching facts with criteria)
4. Are there any extenuating circumstances that affect the evaluation?

Outlining the issues for a question of policy   Because questions of policy deal with courses of action, they involve determining the nature of the problem and finding an acceptable solution. Most questions you will work with in decision-making discussions are likely to be questions of policy. The outline for a question of policy includes at least the following issues:

1. What is the nature of the problem?
   a. What is the size of the problem?
   b. What are the symptoms of the problem?
   c. What are the causes of the problem?
2. What criteria should be used to test the solutions? (Specifically, what checklist of items must the solutions meet in order to solve this problem beneficially and practicably?)
   a. Does the plan eliminate the symptoms?
   b. Does the plan eliminate the causes?
   c. Is the plan capable of being implemented soon with present resources?
3. What are the possible solutions?
4. What is the best solution?
   a. How does each solution meet the criteria?
   b. Which solution best meets the criteria?

For purposes of illustration, let's outline the issues that would form the foundation of a discussion of one question of policy. Only a few of the possible questions are shown under each issue.

What should be done to equalize athletic opportunities for women on campus?

1. What has happened on campus that signifies the presence of a problem for women? (Nature of the problem)
   a. Have significant numbers of women been affected?
   b. Do women have less opportunity to compete in athletics than men?

      c. Has the University behaved in ways that have adversely affected women's opportunities?

  2. By what means should we test whether a proposed solution solves the problem? (Criteria)

      a. Does the proposed solution cope with each of the problems uncovered?

      b. Can the proposed solution be implemented without creating new and perhaps worse problems?

  3. What can be done to equalize opportunities? (Possible solutions)

      a. Can more scholarships be allocated to women?

      b. Can time allocated to women's use of university facilities be increased to a level comparable with men's use?

  4. Which proposal (or combination) would work the best? (Best solution)

      a. Will increasing women's scholarships solve the problems without creating worse problems?

      b. Can women's time for use be increased without creating worse problems?

Will Your Discussion Follow the Outline?

How closely a group follows the outline of issues depends on the quality of leadership in the group. A well-prepared leader will have suggested an outline of issues and put it in your hands before the meeting. Such an outline is called an **agenda**. As a participant it is your obligation to help the group form a tentative outline of issues if the leader has not or if controversies arise about the suggested outline.

During discussion very few groups ever work linearly through all the suggested issues. More likely the group will move on and off the subject, forward and backward, and sometimes in circles. But if the group has decided on a plan, then at least they will know what has to be accomplished before they are finished.

Since most questions you will discuss are likely to deal with policy questions, let's consider two pitfalls to group procedure:

1. *Trying to discuss possible solutions before the nature of the problem is discussed.* It seems to be human nature for groups to focus on possible solutions. For instance, if your question is "What should the marketing department do to save money?" early in the discussion someone might say, "The problem is easy enough to solve—let's cut back on the supplies budget." Because such statements are relevant to the question, the group tendency is to go along with discussion of such prematurely offered solutions right away. Since a solution must *solve* the problem at hand, the nature of the problem must be discussed first.

With some questions the nature of the problem can be identified in a few short minutes; with others, determining the nature of the problem may take hours, days, or even weeks to identify. The penalty for avoiding discussion of the problem is often the failure of the solution that is decided upon.

2. *Agreeing with the first solution offered.* Most questions of policy have many possible solutions. Unless you are considering a "yes" or "no" question, your group should identify several potential solutions.

One way to identify potential solutions is to *brainstorm* for ideas. Brainstorming is a free-association procedure; that is, it involves stating ideas as they come to mind, in random order, until you have compiled a long list. In a good ten- to fifteen-minute brainstorming session you may think of several solutions by yourself. Depending on the nature of the topic, a group may come up with a list of ten, twenty, or more possible solutions in a relatively short time.

Brainstorming works best when the group doesn't evaluate each solution as it is mentioned. If people feel free to make suggestions—however bizarre they may sound—they will feel much freer to think creatively than if they fear that each idea will be evaluated on the spot.

Later, each solution will be measured against the criteria. The solution that meets the most criteria or the one that meets several criteria best should be selected.

PRACTICE

Identifying Goals and Outlining Subquestions

1. Label the following questions (F) fact, (V) value, or (P) policy.

_____ a. Is Ohio State the largest single-campus university in the United States?

_____ b. Should the United States support any government that seeks to remain free of communism?

_____ c. Which minicomputer costs the least to own and operate?

_____ d. Is Sparky Anderson the best manager in the American League?

_____ e. Should tuition be increased at Miller University next year?

ANSWERS: **a.** F; **b.** P; **c.** F; **d.** V; **e.** P.

2. Think of the last group with which you worked. Did the group agree on an outline before it got into content? If not, how did it proceed? What effect did leaving out steps have on the discussion? On the quality of the solution?

3. Outline the subquestions for a discussion of the following question: What should be the role of the student in determining college requirements? Share your outline with other class members.

RESEARCHING

The better the information, the better the quality of the group decision. It is up to you to prepare fully. Getting prepared includes the following:

1. *Read circulated information carefully before the meeting.* In some groups the information necessary for decision making may be given to you before the meeting. But the whole point of starting a meeting with well-prepared members is short-circuited if you and other members of the group don't do the reading beforehand.

2. *Think about relevant personal experience.* There's a chance that the topic being discussed is one that you have thought about or worked with before. For instance, if your group is considering how to arrange available parking space so that it is equally distributed to administrators, faculty, and students, your own parking experiences may be useful to the group. Nevertheless, personal experience is seldom enough for your total preparation.

3. *Survey library sources.* For many of the questions you will be considering you will need solid, documented materials. Suppose you are considering changing college requirements. What are the requirements at similar colleges and universities? Your library should have catalogues from other schools that you can check. Or suppose you are considering instituting a class on television literacy. Your library has various magazines and journals that will have articles related to the issue. For any number of topics being considered you may need to do library research to be prepared. The three most basic research tools are the library's card catalogue, which indexes all the books and materials held by the library; the *Readers' Guide to Periodical Literature*, an index of some 150 popular magazines and journals; and the *Magazine Index*, an index of topics covered during the last five years in more than 250 magazines.

These and other library sources are discussed in detail in Chapter 12. Your reference librarian can suggest various books, articles, government publications, newspapers, and other sources that contain useful data.

4. *Poll public opinion.* For some topics a public opinion poll is appropriate. For instance, for the question of campus parking you may be able to take advantage of the experience and opinions of current students. What do they think of the present system? What would they like to see done? Prepare a few well-worded questions, go to the parking lots, and ask your questions. If a personal survey is not practicable, put your survey questionnaire under the windshield wiper of every car. Ask each driver to answer the questions and leave the results at the entry gate or drop them in the campus mail. You need data to work with, and a survey is one good way of getting information. Of course, you need to make sure that you have polled a large enough group and that you have sampled different segments of the larger group before you attempt to draw any significant conclusions from your poll.

5. *Interview for information.* An effective but often overlooked means of preparation is the personal interview. One interview with the right person may be all that is needed for your subject, or you may have to interview several people. Recall that we discussed interviewing for information in Chapter 9.

PRACTICE

Finding Information

1. Your work group should select a topic area for discussion, such as one of the following:

   ■ A revision of your college's requirements
   ■ The extent of drug abuse on campus
   ■ Meeting the needs of commuter students
   ■ Reducing crime on campus

2. Each member of the group should bring in at least *one* item of relevant information from three of the following: personal experience, observation, written sources, public opinion polls, interviewing.

MEETING ROLE REQUIREMENTS

Productive group participation fills task or maintenance roles. **Task roles** include the work a group must do to accomplish its goal; **maintenance roles** include the group behaviors that keep the group working together smoothly. As we proceed you will notice that many of the roles correlate with interpersonal skills that we discussed in the last section of this book. Of course, not all roles played in a group are positive. By accident or, occasionally, by design, people say and do things that hurt the group's ability to work together.

Group members often perceive the most important role in the group as that of the leader. The leader is designated by outside authority, is appointed or elected by the group, or takes over leadership responsibilities in the group for a given period of time. The leader's role is to exert influence toward attaining group goals and maintaining group interpersonal needs. The role of leader is not one role but a combination of many task and maintenance roles. Leadership is not solely the province of the leader. Nearly every role played contributes to the leadership of a group, but the leader may well be the one who plays certain task or maintenance roles most competently. Because leadership is so important to any group, we will reserve the entire next chapter for discussion of this vital role.

Task Roles

In effective groups people will present information and opinions, ask for information and opinions, analyze information, create ideas, help keep the group on the topic, and record the group's key decisions. Since some of these roles may be new to you, we will assign each a name. Then as you get into your group work you can better determine whether or not these tasks have been accomplished; moreover you can practice the various roles.

Information giver   Your most important task in a group is to provide information and opinions. About 50 percent of group time is spent presenting information and opinions; without these the group will not have the material on which to base its decisions. Although everyone in a group is likely to have some information and opinions to present, there are usually one or more persons who have really done their homework. In some groups a designated resource person or consultant is called in solely to fulfill the information-giving role; in most groups it is up to the individuals themselves to come well prepared.

Being a really valuable information giver requires solid preparation. You should not only have sound information but also be prepared to draw conclusions from information that others have presented. Discussants must pool information to provide a basis for conclusions about the topic question. You can give your opinions, too. But unlike social sessions, in which opinions substitute for data, in decision-making discussions your opinions are based on previously tested information.

Your information will be most useful if you can present it objectively. First, *try to report data without associating yourself with it.* If you reported that crime has risen 33 percent in the past five years, don't feel that because you presented the data that you must defend it. A good way to present controversial information is illustrated by the following statement: "According to *U.S. News and World Report*, crime has risen 33 percent in the past five years. That seems very high to me. Did anyone else find either any substantiating or any contradictory data?" Presenting data in this way tells the group that you want discussion of the data and that, whether it is substantiated or disproven, you have no personal association with it. Contrast that statement with the following one: "I think crime is going up at a fantastic rate. Why, I found that crime has gone up 33 percent in the past five years, and we just can't put up with that kind of thing." This speaker is taking a position with the data. Since anyone who questions the data or the conclusions is going to have to contend with the speaker, there's a good chance that the discussion that follows will not be objective.

Second, *try to encourage differing viewpoints.* Suppose that after extensive reading you became convinced of one point of view. If in the discussion you spoke only to support your position and you took issue with every bit of contrary material, you would not be responding objectively. You should present material objectively whether it supports or opposes your tentative claims. If the group draws a conclusion that corresponds to your tentative conclusion, fine: All views have had the opportunity to be presented. If the group draws the opposite conclusion, you are not put in a defensive position. By being objective, you may find that during the discussion your views will change many times. Remember, if the best answer to the topic question could be found without discussion, the discussion would not be necessary.

Information seeker   Information seeking is just the opposite of information giving. In this case, instead of your presenting information, you are asking others whether they have information.

Information seeking takes several forms. The most obvious and most important is asking for information when the information the group has is insufficient for drawing a conclusion. For instance, a group that is discussing whether to raise fees will need to know how raising fees is likely to affect membership. At a given point in discussion, then, a person may ask whether anyone has relevant information. If not, the group will make note that this information is needed before a decision can be made on this point. Sometimes people ask for information about where in the decision-making process the group is at the moment, whether or not they are in agreement, and what they should be doing next. Although it is very important to have information to present, it is also important to know when more information is needed.

Analyzer Analyzers know the problem-solving method inside out. Analyzers know when the group has skipped a point, has passed over a point too lightly, or has not taken a look at matters they need to. They help the group penetrate to the core of the problem they are working on. In addition, analyzers examine the reasoning of various participants.

Analyzing is usually accomplished by asking questions about and probing into the contributions of others. As information is presented, everyone in the group is obligated to determine whether the information is accurate, typical, consistent, and otherwise valid. Suppose that in a discussion on reducing crime a person mentioned that, according to *U.S. News & World Report*, crime had risen 33 percent in the past five years; the group should not leave this statement until they have explored it fully. What was the specific source of data? On what were the data based? To what time period do the data refer? Is this consistent with other material? Is any countermaterial available? The purpose of these questions is not to debate the data but to test them. If these data are partly true, questionable, or relevant only to certain kinds of crime, a different conclusion or set of conclusions would be appropriate.

The analyzer may offer statements like these: "Tom, you're generalizing from only one instance. Can you give us some others?" or "Wait a minute; after symptoms, we have to take a look at causes," or "I think we're passing over Jones too lightly. There are still criteria we haven't used to measure him by," or "What did we say the base numbers were?" or "Have we decided how many people this really affects?" or "What functions does this person serve?"

Idea person The idea person is an individual with imagination who thinks originally, rattles off alternative ideas, and often comes up with an idea that serves as the basis for the ultimate decision. Although everyone in the group may bring information, usually only one or two people seem truly inventive. When others seem unable to see past tried-and-true solutions, the idea person invents a new one; when others think they have exhausted the possibilities, idea people come up with still another; and when others seem up against a stone wall, idea people find a way out. As we might expect, not all of these ideas may be "world beaters." The creative mind is constantly mining ideas, but from among all that come, only a few are golden. Nevertheless, a good idea person is indispensible.

Expediter Expediters help the group stay on the subject. Invariably in group discussion some remarks will lead the group away from the issue they are discussing. Although some digressions are necessary to get background, to enlarge the scope of the discussion, or even to give people an opportunity to get something off their chest, even these momentary digressions can lead to tangents that take the group far afield of their assignment. Because tangents are sometimes more fun than the task itself, the group may discuss it as if it were important to the group decision. When the group has strayed, expediters help lead it back to its agenda. A person who is expediting will make statements like "Say, I'm enjoying this, but I can't quite see what it has to do with whether permissiveness is really a cause," or "Let's see, aren't we still trying to find out whether these are the only criteria that we should be considering?" or "I've got the feeling that this is important to the point we're on now, but I can't quite get hold of the relationship—am I off base?" or "Say, time is getting away from us and we've only considered two possible solutions. Aren't there some more?"

Recorder   People's perceptions and memories differ. In a one-hour group discussion about 9,000 words will be spoken. Unless special effort is made to record the group procedure and decisions, much of the value of a one-hour discussion can be lost.

The record of a formal group meeting is called the "minutes." Minutes include major motions, key debates, and conclusions agreed upon by the group. The recorder types the minutes and circulates them to group members prior to the next meeting. The minutes then become a public record of the group's activities.

A good record of group proceedings is necessary for the following reasons:

1. To provide a formal statement of the group's accomplishments. Statements such as "In the early portion of discussion the group decided to limit its analysis to activity in the southeastern states where declines in sales have been noted" summarize what took place and apprise every group member of the decision. If some controversy arises later, the group can be reminded of the decision.
2. To provide a record of all intermediate decisions that led to and supplied a basis for the major decisions. Unless a group can record the information that leads to the major decisions, the group's process is open to question. Parent groups or other organizations cannot rely on blind faith that the group has made a comprehensive analysis of the question. A record of decisions shows others what was done.
3. To protect against misunderstanding and misperception by individual members. As time goes by, people recall less and less of what was said unless they are reminded of it. At the end of a day's meeting, you may be able to summarize key decisions and key information; three weeks later, however, the substance of a meeting is likely to be a blur. You may alter the wording of key points or even transpose information. A precise record shows the exact wording of what the group agreed on.
4. To act as a running account of group process. An accurate record is also important to the group during discussion. It helps group members

find out where the group is, whether the discussion fits the group goal, on what foundation new information is being built. Good discussion is and should be a slow process, but anything that can be done to make the process more efficient without detracting from the necessary spontaneity should be encouraged. A written account keeps what is happening in front of the group and avoids ambiguity.

Group recording can be accomplished in several ways. The size of the group, the complexity of the issues, and the resources available can help you determine which method to use.

■ *Audiovisual recording.* Audiovisual recording appears to be the ideal method of record keeping because every word is preserved. However, your group may find the method totally impractical because someone will have to listen to the entire tape and record points that were made. Second, the listener may discover that at certain key places the group did not arrive at any decision. In this case, the group would have to reconsider those particular points. And third, unless the group "performs," it is likely that some key thoughts will be lost along the way. Audiovisual recording makes an excellent backup for the group, but it is not likely to be the best means of recording decisions.

■ *Leader record keeping.* Record keeping by the leader is the most common method in decision-making groups. In many groups, the leader has an informal responsibility to report the findings of the group. Because the leader's role is less likely to be one of information giver or opinion giver, he or she can more easily focus on such roles as summarizing, drawing conclusions, and testing the wording of conclusions. The leader can keep a running record and check for consensus in wording or content. However, because the leader holds a high-status position, group members may not be willing to press the leader into stating key decisions that are reached. Furthermore, the leader may interpret the group's meaning rather than recording the exact wording of a group's decision. Thus, group members should always ask the leader to read what has been written before proceeding to the next point.

■ *Delegated recording.* Since it is difficult for people heavily involved in the discussion to keep an accurate record, your group may want a recorder who is not a part of the group. For in-class exercises one person per group should be assigned the recorder role to learn the skill—a skill that is as important as any other skill within the group.

As a recorder, you should have a copy of the agenda or the procedure that the group has agreed to. Although the group may stray from the written plan, you will still have some idea of what is going to happen or what should be happening, and your note-taking will be made easier. Briefly note key information as it is presented. It is a good idea to make note of what each person says. When a key question is answered, record the answer in full and underline or star it. Read it back to the group so that the group recognizes when it has arrived at a key decision and so it can double-check wording. Record too much rather than too little—it is much easier to cut out material than it is to add information that you find difficult to remember. After the meeting, type up and duplicate the notes and circulate them to group members before the next meeting.

Doyle and Strauss[2] recommend that the recorder write notes on large sheets of paper taped to a wall or a chalkboard so that members of the group can see exactly what is happening at all times. The same goal can be accomplished by a person sitting with the group and taking notes. Every person has the right to ask the recorder to read the last decision made or to read back a summary of information.

As with any other skill, good recording takes a great deal of practice. You will find that when a person gets good at the job, the entire group prospers.

Maintenance Roles

Whereas task roles help the group with the content of discussion, maintenance roles help the group work together smoothly as a unit. In effective decision-making groups people will support each other, relieve tensions, control conflict, and give everyone a chance to talk.

Supporter People participating in groups are likely to feel better about their participation when their thoughts and feelings are recognized. Although we expect that nearly everyone will be supportive, sometimes peo-

ple get so wrapped up in their own ideas that they may neglect to reward the positive comments that are made.

The supporter responds nonverbally or verbally whenever a good point is made. Supporters give such nonverbal cues as a smile, a nod, or a vigorous head shake and make statements like "Good point, Mel," "I really like that idea, Susan," "It's obvious you've really done your homework, Peg," and "That's one of the best ideas we've had today, Al."

Tension reliever   Folklore has it that "all work and no play makes Jack a dull boy." When group members really get working on their tasks, they sometimes get so involved and try to work so hard that they begin to wear themselves down. Nerves get frayed, vision becomes cloudy, and the machinery of progress grinds to a halt. The tension reliever recognizes when the process is boring or when the group is getting tired. This person has an uncanny sixth sense for when to tell a joke, when to take off on a digression, when to get the group to loosen up a little before returning to the task. In some situations a single well-placed one-liner will get a laugh, break the monotony, and jolt the group out of their lethargy. At other times the group can be saved only with a real break—sometimes a minute or so will suffice; at other times five, ten, or even fifteen minutes will be necessary. Tension relieving adds nothing to the content of the discussion, but it does improve the spirits of the participants immeasurably. Of all the roles, this one is the most difficult to play consciously. When people have to try to be tension relievers, they are likely to fail. Although not every group has a person who fills the bill completely, most groups include at least one person who can meet it well enough to be helpful. Even if a group can accomplish its task without a tension reliever, it certainly is not as much fun. You will know, recognize, and be thankful for the person playing this role well.

Harmonizer   It is a rare group that can expect to accomplish its task without some conflict. Harmonizers are responsible for reducing and reconciling misunderstandings, disagreements, and conflicts. They are skilled at encouraging objectivity and are especially good mediators for hostile, aggressively competing opponents. A group cannot avoid some conflict, but if there is someone to harmonize, conflict can be handled constructively. Harmonizers make such statements as "Bill, I don't think you're giving Mary a chance to make her point," or "Tom, Jack, hold it a second. I know you're on opposite sides of this, but let's see where you might have some agreement," or "Lynne, I get the feeling that something Todd said really bugged you. Is that right?" or "Hold it, everybody, we're really coming up with some good stuff; let's not lose our momentum by getting emotional."

All group members can contribute to the harmonizing function by trying to engage in behaviors that are *cooperative* rather than *competitive*. Cooperative behaviors help a group integrate their resources toward a common task; competitive behaviors foster a win–lose strategy among the group—that is, if one person wins, it must be at the other person's expense. Conflicts that develop from these behaviors will be largely negative and difficult to deal with. Cooperative and competitive behaviors may be illustrated by comparing the behavior of people completing a jigsaw puzzle to that of people playing poker. In solving a jigsaw puzzle each person cooperates with the others; in a poker game each individual works at the expense of the others. Let's look at five contrasting sets of competitive and cooperative behaviors:

COMPETITIVE BEHAVIORS THAT WILL RESULT IN NEGATIVE CONFLICT	COOPERATIVE BEHAVIORS THAT WILL REDUCE CONFLICT OR RESULT IN POSITIVE OR USEFUL CONFLICT
1. Purposefully pursuing your own goals	1. Purposefully pursuing goals held in common
2. Maintaining secrecy	2. Maintaining openness
3. Disguising or misrepresenting your own needs, plans, and goals	3. Accurately representing your own needs, plans, and goals
4. Being unpredictable—using an element of surprise	4. Being predictable—using behavior consistent with past experience
5. Threatening and bluffing	5. Avoiding threats or bluffing

Suppose Tom wants to make sure the group will be finished by 3 P.M. so he can get to another meeting. If Tom doesn't reveal his reason for rushing, this hidden agenda results in secrecy instead of openness. If Tom considers information in light of the hidden agenda, we have an example of purposeful pursuit of individual goals as well as disguise and misrepresentation. Tom's hidden agenda may be so overpowering that it alters his ordinary behavior. To get his way, he may threaten or bluff. On the other hand, if at the beginning of the meeting Tom said, "I've got another meeting at 3 P.M.; let's try to get finished by then. If we can't, either you can continue without me or we can meet again at another time," he would be establishing a base for a cooperative approach. If each of the participants were to follow his lead, it is much more likely that their behavior would be positive and that their conflict management would be much better.

Gatekeeper   Gatekeepers help keep communication channels open. In a group of seven people all seven should have something to contribute. To ensure balanced contributing, those who tend to dominate need to be held in check and those who tend to be shy need to be encouraged. A gatekeeper is the one who sees that Jane is on the edge of her chair, ready to talk, but just cannot seem to get in, or that Don is rambling a bit and needs to be directed, or that Tom's need to talk so frequently is making Cesar withdraw from the conversation, or that Betty has just lost the thread of discussion. Gatekeepers assume responsibility for helping interaction.

Gatekeepers make statements like "Joan, I see you've got something to say here . . ." or "You've made a really good point, Todd; I wonder whether we could get some reaction on it," or "Bill and Marge, it sounds like you're getting into a dialogue here; let's see what other ideas we have."

Negative Roles

The following are the four most common negative roles that group discussants should try to avoid.

Aggressor   Aggressors work for their own status by criticizing almost everything or blaming others when things get rough. The main purpose of aggressors seems to be to deflate the ego or status of others. One way of dealing with aggressors is to confront them. Ask them whether they are aware of what they are doing and of the effect it is having on the group.

Joker   The behavior of jokers is characterized by clowning, mimicking, or generally disrupting by making a joke of everything. Jokers, too, are usually trying to call attention to themselves. The group needs to get the jokers to consider the problem seriously; otherwise, they will be a constant irritant to other members. One way to proceed is to encourage them when tensions need to be released but ignore them when there is serious work to be done.

Withdrawer   Withdrawers refuse to be a part of the group. Withdrawers are mental dropouts. Sometimes they are withdrawing from something that was said; sometimes they are just showing their indifference. Try to draw them out with questions. Find out what they are especially good at and rely on them when their skill is required. Sometimes complimenting will bring them out.

Monopolizer   People who need to talk all the time are called monopolizers. Usually they are trying to make the impression that they are well read, knowledgeable, and of value to the group. They should, of course, be encouraged when their comments are helpful. However, when they are talking too much or when their comments are not helpful, the leader needs to interrupt them or draw others into the discussion.

Normal Group Behavior

You may be wondering about how all of these fit together in a "normal" group. One of the leading researchers in group interaction processes, Robert Bales, has noted that (1) 40 to 60 percent of discussion time is spent on giving and asking for information and opinion, (2) 8 to 15 percent of discussion time is spent on disagreement, tension, or unfriendliness (behavior that we have discussed as negative functions), but (3) 16 to 26 percent of discussion time is characterized by agreement or friendliness—behavior that we have discussed as positive maintenance functions.[3] Two norms we can use as a guidelines are, therefore, that approximately half of all discussion time is concerned with information sharing and that group agreement far outweighs group disagreement.

PRACTICE

Group Process

1. Identify the roles that are represented in the following examples as (a) Information or Opinion Giver; (b) Information Seeker; (c) Analyzer; (d) Idea Person; (e) Expediter; (f) Supporter; (g) Tension Reliever; (h) Harmonizer; or (i) Gatekeeper.

_____ a. Millie, I get the feeling that you have something you wanted to say here.

_____ b. The last couple of comments have been on potential causes of the problem, but I don't think we really finished with the scope of the problem. If we've really identified the scope, perhaps we could draw a conclusion and then move on to causes.

_____ c. Tony, that was a good point. I think you've really put the problem in a perspective.

_____ d. Paul and Gwen, I know you see this issue from totally different positions. I wonder whether we might not profit by seeing whether there are any points of agreement; then we can consider differences.

_____ e. Well, according to the latest statistics cited in the *Enquirer*, unemployment in the state has gone back up from 7.2 to 7.9 percent.

_____ f. Sarah, you've given us some good statistics—can we determine whether or not this is really an upward trend or just a seasonal factor?

ANSWERS: a. i; b. e; c. f; d. h; e. a; f. c

2. Each group has ten to fifteen minutes to arrive at a solution to the following dilemma:

▶ Five people are boating: the father, a 55-year-old heart specialist reputed to be the best in the state; his 36-year-old wife, a dermatologist; their 8-year-old child; their neighbor, a 43-year-old industrial salesman for a major corporation; and his wife, a 35-year-old former model who appears in television commercials. If the boat started to sink and only one of the five could be saved, who should it be?

After discussion, the group should determine (1) what roles were operating in the groups during the discussion, (2) who were performing those roles, and (3) what factors helped or hurt the problem-solving process.

SUMMARY

Effective groups begin with a well-worded topic for discussion. Topics should be phrased as a question, should contain only one idea, should be clearly worded, should encourage objective discussion, should be appropriate for group discussion, and should be easily identified as a question of fact, value, or policy.

Next, your group should outline the issues that it will need to consider. Issues differ depending on whether the question is one of fact, value, or policy.

As an effective group participant, you have many responsibilities. The first is to be prepared. Whether you need only to think about the problem or whether you need to carry out some research, you should have some solid material to take into the discussion with you.

The measure of your value in the group discussion will be in your participation. You may perform one or more of the task roles of information giver or seeker, analyzer, expediter, idea person, and recorder; you may perform one or more of the maintenance roles of supporter, tension reliever, harmonizer, or gatekeeper. You will want to try to avoid the negative roles of aggressor, joker, withdrawer, or monopolizer.

SUGGESTED READINGS

Bormann, Ernest G. *Discussion and Group Methods: Theory and Practice.* 2nd ed. New York: Harper & Row, 1975. This is a comprehensive textbook on the subject of group discussion.

Brilhart, John K. *Effective Group Discussion.* 4th ed. Dubuque, Iowa: Wm. C. Brown, 1982. This paperback is a very popular textbook.

Verderber, Rudolph F. *Working Together.* Belmont, Calif.: Wadsworth, 1982. Gives a complete discussion of analyzing and resolving various types of discussion questions.

11 ▷ LEADERSHIP IN GROUPS

OBJECTIVES

After you have read this chapter you should be able to:

1 List and explain characteristics of leadership

2 Differentiate between task and maintenance leadership

3 Prepare for leadership

4 List and explain seven leadership responsibilities

Leadership means many things to many people. To some it is an inherent, almost divine complex of traits that sets one person apart from his or her peers. To others it is the luck of being in the right place at the right time. Yet within most of us is some deep feeling that whatever leadership is, we have what it takes. Although we may say publicly that we wouldn't take the job of leader for all the tea in China, in private we may see ourselves as the only logical candidates for the job.

There is absolutely nothing wrong with thinking you are the best person for the job. However, leadership is not something that can be thought of lightly. Our goal in this chapter is to show what it means to be the leader of a work group, how to proceed if you want to try for leadership, and what you are responsible for doing in the group after you get the job. Although much of this discussion is applicable to all leadership situations, we will focus on the question of leadership in the decision-making group context.

WHAT IS LEADERSHIP?

The definition of leadership varies from source to source, yet common to most definitions are the ideas of influence and accomplishment. Leadership means being in charge—exerting influence—and leadership means reaching a goal. Let's explore these two ideas.

1. *Leadership means exerting influence.* **Influence** is the ability to bring about changes in the attitudes and actions of others. Influence can be indirect (unconscious) or direct (purposeful). Many times we influence without being aware of it. If you have a new hairstyle, or are wearing a new suit, or have purchased a flashy new car, you may well influence someone who sees you to try your hairstyle or to buy a similar suit or car. In a group, a leader can influence members indirectly by serving as a role model. In this chapter, we will look at what you can do consciously to help guide your group through the decision-making process.

   We should also mention that the exercise of influence is different from the exercise of raw power. When you exercise raw power, you force a person or a group to submit, perhaps against their will; when you influence others you show them why an idea, a decision, or a means of achieving a goal is superior in such a way that members of the group will seek to follow those ideas of their own free will. Members will continue to be influenced as long as they are convinced that what they have agreed to is right or is in their individual best interest or in the best interest of the group.

2. *Leadership results in reaching a goal.* In the context of task or problem-solving discussion this means accomplishing the task or arriving at the best solution available at that time.

   In an organizational setting a leader is usually appointed or elected. In a decision-making group setting, however, the struggle for leadership often proceeds without benefit of election or appointment. In fact, those involved may not perceive that a struggle takes place. In settings in which one individual has high needs to control and the others have high needs to be controlled, leadership will be established with no struggle at all. In most decision-making group settings, however, leadership is shared, switches back and forth, or develops into power struggles in which people exercise their need to lead.

LEADERSHIP TRAITS

What kind of person is most likely to be the leader of a group? Are there such things as leadership traits that, if discovered within a person, will predict his or her success as a leader? Although researchers have, at times, downplayed the presence of verifiable leadership traits, during the last decade there have been renewed research efforts in this direction.[1] Paul J. Patinka[2] is but one researcher who has substantiated Shaw's claim that there is enough consistency among individual traits and leadership measures to draw generalizations.[3]

What conclusions have been drawn? Leaders exemplify traits related to ability, sociability, motivation, and communication skills to a greater degree than do nonleaders. In group studies, with regard to ability, leaders exceed average group members in intelligence, scholarship, insight, and verbal facility. Leaders exceed group members in such aspects of sociability as dependability, activity, cooperativeness, and popularity. In the area of motivation, leaders exceed group members in initiative, persistence, and enthusiasm. And leaders exceed average group members in the various communication skills we focus on in this text. This does not mean that people with superior intelligence, those who are most liked, those with the greatest enthusiasm, or those who communicate best will necessarily be the leaders. However, we believe it does mean that people are unlikely to be leaders if they do not exhibit at least some of these traits to a greater degree than do those they are attempting to lead.

Do you perceive yourself as having any or many of these traits? If you see these traits in yourself, then you are a potential leader. Since several individuals in almost any grouping of people have the potential for leadership, which one ends up actually leading others depends on many things other than possession of these traits.

LEADERSHIP STYLES

A person's collection of behaviors is called **style**. A casual examination of groups in operation will reveal a variety of leadership styles. Some leaders give orders directly; others look to the group to decide what to do. Some leaders appear to play no part in what happens in the group; others seem to be in control of every move. Some leaders constantly seek the opinions of group members; other leaders do not seem to care what individuals think. Each person will tend to lead a group with a style that reflects his or her own personality, needs, and inclination. Although people have a right to be themselves, an analysis of operating groups shows that how groups work and feel about the work they have done depends on the style of leadership.

What are the major leadership styles? Most recent studies look at leadership styles as task-oriented (sometimes called authoritarian) or person-oriented (sometimes called democratic).

The task leader exercises more direct control over the group. Task leaders will determine the statement of the question. They will make the analysis of procedure and state how the group will proceed to arrive at the decision. They are likely to outline specific tasks for each group member and suggest the roles they desire members to play.

The person-oriented or maintenance leader may *suggest* phrasings of the question, *suggest* procedure, and *suggest* tasks or roles for individuals. Yet in every facet of the discussion the maintenance leader encourages group participation to determine what actually will be done. Everyone feels free to offer suggestions to modify the leader's suggestions. What the group eventually does is determined by the group itself. Maintenance leaders will listen, encourage, facilitate, clarify, and support. In the final analysis, it is the *group* that decides.

Which is best? If we go back to the definition of leadership as exerting influence to reach a goal, we can see that by definition an effective style is one in which the leader takes some active role in the discussion in order to influence its outcome. If this is true, then why isn't the task style the ultimate form for leadership? Although there are situations when task leadership may, in fact, be the most desirable style, there are situations in which maintenance style is more effective.

Choosing a Leadership Style

The approach that has received the greatest explanation and has been researched in greatest depth is Fiedler's *contingency model* of leadership effectiveness.[4] Fiedler's work provides at least two benefits in the study of leadership behavior. First, it clarifies the variables that interact; second, it gives guidance in determining whether a task style or a maintenance style is most likely to be effective. Fiedler sees a leader style as one that fulfills either the task or the maintenance function within a group.

Let us consider the variables that interact: leader–member relations, task structure, and position power. *Leader–member relations* are the interpersonal relations the leader has with members of the group. What kind of working relationship exists? Is there mutual trust? Will followers be loyal to the leader? Do the leader and the members like working with each other?

Fiedler discusses *task structure* in terms of four dimensions: (1) goal clarity (how sharply the goal is defined), (2) goal-path multiplicity (the extent to which there are other ways to accomplish the task), (3) decision verifiability (the extent to which accomplishments can be evaluated by objective, logical, or feedback means), and (4) decision specificity (whether the task has only one correct outcome versus several equally good outcomes). The more clear, the more easily verifiable, the more specific, and the fewer paths of accomplishment, the more favorable the task structure is to the leader.

Position power may be analyzed along the lines of social power we considered in our discussion of assertiveness. The leader can be judged to be in a low-power or a high-power position. The higher the power position, the more favorable the situation is to the leader. Through these three dimensions, then, we can determine the favorableness of the leader situation.

This leads us to the second benefit of Fiedler's work: help in determining when a given style is most appropriate. Fiedler's approach states that whether a task-oriented leader or a maintenance-oriented leader will be more effective is contingent on the interaction among leader–member relations, task structure, and position power.

The sense of Fiedler's work is that a person's style is predetermined and somewhat inflexible; therefore, instead of a leader changing styles for different situations, Fiedler suggests changing leaders. Some leaders, however, do learn to adapt.

Now let us see how Fiedler puts these variables together. Figure 11.1 summarizes his framework. Situations 1 through 3 represent relatively favorable conditions in which a task orientation is likely to be quite effective. Notice that 1 through 3 represent good leader–member relations. The task is structured in two of the three, and in the remaining unstructured task the leader is in a high-power position.

In situations 4 through 7, three of the situations have leader–member relations that are relatively poor. In the remaining situation, in which leader–member relations are good (situation 4), the task is unstructured and leader position power is weak. In the situations that are relatively unfavorable to the leader, a maintenance-style leader will have greater opportunity for success. Yet in situation 8, the least favorable, a task leader is likely to have the greatest success even though everything points toward failure. It seems that in this case everything is so bad that only a task-style leader could possibly achieve success.

We have already pointed out that the model does not take into account the potential for a leader to be both task-oriented and maintenance-oriented. Regardless of your basic orientation, you can learn to adapt to either approach. You can then use the Fiedler model to help determine when you should approach a situation from a strong task orientation and when you should adopt a strong maintenance orientation. The question is not which style is best, but rather, which style will work best

FIGURE 11 · 1

Summary of Fiedler's Contingency Model

Situation	Leader–member relations	Task structure	Position power	Appropriate leader style	Favorableness of situation to leader
1	Good	High	Strong	Task	Favorable
2	Good	High	Weak	Task	Favorable
3	Good	Low	Strong	Task	Favorable
4	Good	Low	Weak	Maintenance	Less favorable
5	Fair to poor	High	Strong	Maintenance	Less favorable
6	Fair to poor	High	Weak	Maintenance	Less favorable
7	Fair to poor	Low	Strong	Maintenance	Less favorable
8	Fair to poor	Low	Weak	Task	Unfavorable

Adapted from Fred E. Fiedler, *A Theory of Leadership Effectiveness* (New York: McGraw-Hill, 1967), p. 34. By permission.

under the circumstances. As Fiedler's and other research suggests, one style will not work under all circumstances. Our advice is that you examine your style very closely. What is your natural inclination? How has it worked in the past? What can you do that will allow you to work in a situation that requires a different style?

PRACTICE

Assessing Your Leadership Style

1. What is your leadership style? What are the strengths and weaknesses of that style?

2. Under which leadership style do you work best? Why?

RESPONSIBILITIES OF THE LEADER

Now that we have defined leadership and looked at its various components, we want to focus on individual responsibilities in exercising leadership in decision-making groups. We will start with suggestions for leadership preparation. Then we will present a step-by-step list of leadership behaviors from the beginning to the end of a group's meeting.

Preparing to Lead

Most of us consider it normal for a person to be appointed or elected to act as leader. We may fail to realize that regardless of whether someone is designated as leader, a "real leader" emerges from the group. The designated leader may become the real leader. Sometimes the designated leader and one or more others share leadership. But sometimes a different person emerges as the real leader of the group. Whether you are the designated leader or not, you have the opportunity to share leadership or be recognized as the real leader.

What characteristics or behaviors will you need to exhibit to earn the right of leadership? Here are some guidelines.

1. *You must have knowledge related to the particular group tasks.* Context determines who will lead far more than any particular leadership traits you may believe you have. You must grasp enough of the content of the task to recognize which members are contributing effectively and which are not.
2. *You must work harder than anyone else in the group.* Leadership is often a question of setting an example. When a group sees a person who is willing to do more than his or her fair share for the good of the group, they are likely to support the person. Of course, such effort often takes a lot of personal sacrifice, but the person seeking to lead must be willing to pay the price.
3. *You must be personally committed to the group goals and needs.* It is quite possible that in any given group for any given situation there may be several who can perform as leaders. To gain and maintain leadership takes great commitment to the particular task. When you lose commitment, your leadership may wane and may be transferred to others whose enthusiasm is more attuned to a new set of conditions.
4. *You must be willing to be decisive at key moments in the discussion.* When leaders are unsure of themselves, their groups may ramble aimlessly. When leaders are unskilled at making decisions, their groups can become frustrated and short-tempered. When decisions are not made by the designated leader, one or more other persons must assume

leadership. Sometimes leaders must make decisions that will be resented; sometimes they must decide between competing ideas about courses of action, and any decisions leaders make may cause conflict. Nevertheless, people who are unwilling or unable to be decisive are not going to maintain leadership for long.

5. *You must interact freely.* People will not support leaders who remain silent most of the time. Now this does not mean that you should always dominate the discussion—but no one can know how you think, how you feel, or what insights you have unless you are willing to share your ideas in discussion. Too often people sit back silently, thinking, "If only they would call on me for leadership, I would do a really good job." Groups do not want unknown quantities. Perhaps by talking you run the risk of showing your lack of qualifications for leadership, but it is better to find out during the early stages of group work whether you can talk sensibly and influence others before you try to gain leadership.

6. *You must develop skill in maintenance functions as well as skill in task functions.* Leaders must make others in their groups feel good, they must be able to contribute to group cohesiveness, and they must be able to give credit where it is due. Although a group often has both a task leader and a maintenance leader, the overall leader is equally as likely as if not more likely than others to be the one who shows maintenance skills.

If you want to lead, these are some of the behaviors you must show. However, becoming a leader and carrying out leadership are two different things. Many people reach the top of the leadership pole only to slide slowly to oblivion. Perhaps the key question you must ask yourself when it becomes obvious that you are the leader is "How am I going to proceed with my leadership?"

Leading the Group

The material in this section can be considered a checklist for procedure. It is put together as a step-by-step procedure to refer to when you are leading a decision-making group meeting.

Gathering a group of optimum size   Conventional wisdom dictates that "bigger is better." When people examine major problems facing society, they almost always create groups with large numbers of people. But large groups are seldom effective as decision-making bodies; many people cannot or will not contribute, cohesiveness is nearly impossible to develop, and the decision is seldom a product of the group's collective thought.

What is the ideal size of a decision-making group? Most research finds that although optimum size depends on the nature of the task, five-person groups are considered ideal by many.[5] Why five? Groups with fewer than five members almost universally complain that they are too small and that there are not enough people for specialization. To be effective, a group needs certain skills. When the group contains only three or four members, chances are small that these skills will be present. Moreover, if one member of a group of three does not feel like contributing, you no longer have much of a group.

Nevertheless, for small tasks the three-person group often works well. It's easier to get three people together than five or more. And if the task is relatively simple or within the expertise of the individuals, the three-person group may be a good choice.

When a group numbers more than seven or eight, reticent members are even less likely to contribute. As the group grows larger, two, three, or four people may become the central spokespersons, with others playing more passive roles.[6]

Just as there are conditions under which the three-person group may be the best, so there are circumstances where a group of ten, eighteen, or even thirty may be appropriate. A larger group is better when the plan calls for several smaller decision-making groups. For instance, if a university committee of twenty-six is formed to consider the question of what the university's participation, if any, should be in the process of selecting and using cable television, the large group might subdivide into three groups. One group might deal with the issues of responding to cable company bids, another might examine the programming potential of the university, and the third might determine contractual matters.

In a group of any size, an odd number is better than an even number. Why? Although voting is not the best way of reaching a decision, if a group finds it necessary to resolve an issue on which it cannot achieve consensus, the odd number will prevent tie votes.

Will the size of this group inhibit its ability to reach agreement? What does the shape of the table tell you about the type of meeting?

Preparing the meeting place   An effective leader creates an environment that promotes group interaction. As leader, you are in charge of such physical matters as heat, light, and seating. Make sure the temperature of the room is comfortable. Make sure that lighting is adequate, and, most important, make sure the seating arrangements will promote spirited interaction.

By far the most important consideration is the seating. Too often, seating is too formal or too informal for the best interaction. Too formal would be a board of directors seating style. Imagine the long polished oak table with the chairperson at the head, the leading lieutenants at right and left, and the rest of the people down the line, as illustrated in Figure 11.2a.

FIGURE 11 · 2

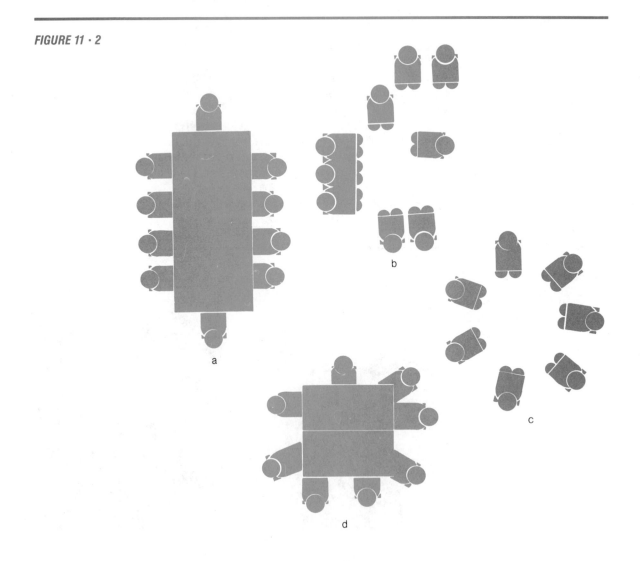

a

b

c

d

Seating is an indication of status. Thus, how the seating is arranged can facilitate or inhibit real and total interaction. In the board of directors seating style, a boss and subordinate pattern emerges. People are unlikely to speak until they are asked to do so. Moreover, no one has a good view of all the people present.

On the other hand, an excessively informal setting may also inhibit interaction. In an informal arrangement, people just sit where they can be most comfortable. In Figure 11.2b, three people sitting on the couch form their own little group; the two seated next to each other form another group. Two members have placed themselves out of the main flow. The group interaction will be casual, but it may not be the most effective.

The ideal arrangement is the circle, represented by Figure 11.2c. Here everyone can see everyone else. At least in terms of seating position, everyone has equal status. If the meeting place does not have a round table, you may be better off without a table or with an arrangement of tables that make a square, as in Figure 11.2d, which approximates the circle arrangement.

The advantages of the circle are that sight lines are better and motivation to speak is higher. At an oblong table, for example, those at the ends will be perceived as having higher status—they will be treated as

This group has chosen an informal setting; the absence of a table and the circular seating pattern reflect a shared philosophy. Although a leader may be chosen, the message of the environment is that each member has an equal say on the matters discussed.

leaders. Those sitting on the corners will tend to speak less than those on the ends or in the middle.

The physical dimension lays the groundwork for the psychological dimension, the climate for discussion. From the beginning, it is important for the group to establish a climate that allows each person to participate. Anything that suggests that only one person is to be listened to or that some persons have ideas that are generally unworthy will hurt the group's efforts to achieve a balance of participation. People will not participate if they fear personal attack or if they feel unable to protect themselves from the attacks of others. If people believe that their ideas will be belittled, ridiculed, or discounted or that no one will intervene to allow their ideas to be heard, the chance for total interaction is destroyed.

As a group deliberates, certain individuals will earn higher status than others. In a particular subject area, for instance, one person may be acknowledged as having better information, greater insight, or more logical perspective. As a result, that person's comments will carry more weight in that area. But an effective group provides a climate where everyone has equal opportunity to earn higher status.

Planning the agenda   An agenda is an outline of the topics that need to be covered at a meeting. In a problem-solving discussion the agenda should include a suggested procedure for handling the problem. In essence, it is an outline of the issues discussed in the last chapter. The following would be a satisfactory agenda if you were leading a group discussing the question, "What should be done to integrate the campus commuter into the social, political, and extracurricular aspects of student life?"

1. How many students commute?
2. Why aren't commuters involved in social, political and extracurricular activities?
3. What criteria should be used to test possible solutions to the problem?
4. What are some of the possible solutions to the problem?
5. What one solution or combination of solutions will work best to solve the problem?

You may prepare the agenda yourself or in consultation with the group. When possible, the agenda should be in the hands of the group several days before the meeting. How much preparation any individual member will make is based on many factors, but unless the group has an agenda beforehand, members will not have an opportunity for careful preparation. Too often, when no agenda is planned, the group discussion is a haphazard affair, often frustrating and usually unsatisfying.

Working to develop a cohesive unit   **Cohesiveness** means sticking together, pulling for each other, and being caught up in the task. Remember the three musketeers, who were all for one and one for all? They are the prototype of a cohesive group.

What determines the potential for group cohesiveness? At least three qualities seem particularly important. First is the *attractiveness of the group's purpose*. Members identify with each other when the group's goals are particularly appealing. Social or fraternal groups, for example, build cohesiveness out of devotion to service or brotherhood. In a decision-making group, attractiveness is likely to be related to how important the task is to members. Suppose a department forms a committee to consider how its curriculum can be made more responsive to student needs. The cohesiveness of the members of that committee will depend, at least in part, on the importance they attribute to this issue.

A second important quality necessary for cohesiveness is *similarity of the needs and interests of members*. Groups may be characterized as homogeneous or heterogeneous. A homogeneous group is one in which members have a great deal in common. For example, a group of five women of the same age who are all strong feminists would be homogeneous. A heterogeneous group is one in which various ages, knowledge, attitudes, and interests are represented. A homogeneous group is likely to achieve cohesiveness more quickly than a heterogeneous group because the members are more likely to identify with each other's needs and interests from the start.

If a department has three divisions (communication, theater, and speech therapy, for example), a committee of faculty or students drawn from all three divisions may have more difficulty developing cohesiveness than a committee of faculty or students drawn from only one of the divisions.

On the other hand, the committee drawn from three divisions is likely to be more cohesive than a committee drawn from separate departments in a college. A group needs some heterogeneity to ensure differing viewpoints and experiences. But a group that is extremely heterogeneous runs the risk of failing to achieve necessary cohesiveness.

A third important quality is *reinforcement of interpersonal needs*. As we noted in Chapter 8, William Schutz has identified affection (showing affection to others and receiving affection from others), inclusion (including others in activities and being included by others in their activities), and control (having a role in determining what will happen) as major interpersonal needs. Group cohesiveness seems directly related to the belief of individual members that they are liked, included, and respected. As people decide they like each other, that they want to be around each other, and that their opinions will be respected, they begin to work more effectively as a unit.

Cohesiveness is difficult to develop in a one-meeting group. It is and should be characteristic of ongoing groups. It is usually generated after initial meetings and should be well established during or before the group reaches its most productive stages.

Helping the group form appropriate norms **Norms** are the guidelines for behavior that are established or are perceived to be established for conducting group business and are the most powerful determiners of behavior in groups. In this section we will explore how norms develop, how they affect member behavior, and how you can help your group form appropriate norms.

Norms begin to be established at the onset of a group's deliberations. They grow, change, and solidify as people get to know one another better.

Norms for a group may be formally spelled out in a group's operating guidelines (such as in parliamentary procedures for organizational meetings), they may be adapted from proven social guidelines (such as "Don't talk about yourself in a decision-making group meeting"), or they may simply develop within a particular context. For instance, without any conscious decision, group members may avoid using common four-letter words during the meeting. When business has ended, conversation may become more earthy.

Although formally stated norms may be known to you from the beginning, most group norms are learned through experience with a specific group, and because norms may vary from one group to the next, we have to relearn them. Two particularly important areas of norm development are group interaction and group procedure. In one group it may be all right to interrupt any speaker at any time; in another no one may speak until he or she is recognized. Thus, Martha, who is used to raising her hand to be recognized at the business meetings of her social organization, may find herself unable to speak in a group meeting where the participants break in whenever they have a chance. In one group it may be all right for someone to openly express anger or hostility toward a person or an idea; in another group, anger and hostility are never allowed to surface. In one group, member status may determine who speaks first, longest, or most often, while in another group, member status may have no effect on interaction.

Similarly, in one group, it may be accepted that people will come and go as they please; in another group business does not start until everyone is present, and the group stops its work when someone has to leave. In one group, members may socialize for a few minutes, exchanging greetings or inquiring about family or activities; in another group, members may move directly to the task at hand. In one group, members may sit in a definite predetermined spatial arrangement; in another group, members may sit where they feel most comfortable.

Norms help a group develop cohesiveness. As members conform to stated or implied guidelines of behavior, they find themselves relating to each other more effectively. One of the initial hurdles group members must surmount is *primary tension*—the anxieties of getting to know each other. As group members test out verbal and nonverbal behavior to see what will be accepted, they begin to become more comfortable with each other, primary tension is lessened, and the group is able to concentrate on its task.

As the group proceeds, you should be very conscious of what norms seem to be in operation and whether or not those norms are helping the group's work. If you believe that certain norms are detrimental or destructive, you will need to make your position and the reasons for that position known. If you do not, those norms can become established. Once norms are established and reinforced, they are very difficult to change.

Norms can be detrimental or destructive. Suppose that at the beginning of the first meeting a few members of the group tell jokes and generally have a good time. If such behavior is allowed or encouraged, then cutting up, making light of the task, and joke telling become a group norm. As a result, the group may get so engaged in these behaviors that the task is delayed, set aside, or perhaps even forgotten. Participants may describe their experience by saying, "We don't do much, but it's fun." Others may be very concerned about such behavior, but if it goes on for several meetings, it will be very hard to change. As a result of the norms that are developed, the group is likely to waste a great deal of time. In fact, the group may not be able to make the kinds of decisions that were expected.

What happens when norms are violated? People who do not go along with developing norms may be ignored, their words may be discounted, and they may even be punished by the group. For instance, in the fun-loving group described above, if Janet is appointed to the committee after it has held several meetings, and if she tries to get the committee down to business early in the meeting, Janet is very likely to be ignored. It is even more likely that the group will look on Janet as a company person or a spoilsport, and her words will be greeted with a certain amount of contempt or hostility. The more cohesive a group becomes, the more pronounced will be the pressure to adhere to group norms.

The group's leader should be instrumental in helping the group develop its norms. Before the group ever meets, you can make a mental assessment of group goals and determine the kinds of norms that are most appropriate for that group to achieve its goals. Then, as the group begins its work, you can behave according to norms you think will be of value and make statements that will be in keeping with those norms. If you act as a role model, others may pick up your cues and conform; the likelihood that conformity will occur depends on many variables, including your perceived status within the group. If the group seems to be establishing norms that are contrary to what you think is appropriate, you can speak early in the group's deliberations to tell why certain behaviors are important to the group's productivity. You may not, of course, be able to establish the norms you think are best, but if you make an effort, and if that effort is seen as constructive, there is a good chance that you will be at least partially successful.

Introducing the topic and establishing procedures   At the beginning of the group's first meeting, you need to introduce the topic and establish procedures. In a newly formed group, commitment may be low for some members, expectations may be minimal, and the general attitude may be skeptical. People may be thinking, "We know that many group sessions are a waste of time, and we will take a wait-and-see attitude." A good leader will start the group by drawing a verbal contract and motivating members to live up to it. The leader will answer questions such as "Why are we here?" "Who got us together?" "What is our mission?" "To whom are we responsible?" "What kinds of responsibilities will each group member have?" "What rules or guidelines for behavior will the group follow?" and "How much will each member be expected to do?" Some of these questions will already have been discussed with individuals, but the first meeting gives the leader a chance to put everything together.

Keeping communication channels open   The leader is primarily responsible for gatekeeping, directing the flow of discussion. It is in this area that leadership skill is most tested. Let's examine carefully four of the most important elements of this responsibility.

Give everyone an equal opportunity to speak. Decisions are valid only when they represent the thinking of the entire group. However, in discussions some people are more likely or more willing to express themselves than others. For instance, if a typical eight-person group is left to its own devices, two or three people may tend to speak as much as the other five or six together; furthermore, one or two members may contribute little, if anything. At the beginning of a discussion you must assume that every member of the group has something to contribute. You may have to hold in check those who tend to dominate, and you may have to work to get reluctant members into the discussion.

Accomplishing this ideal balance is a real test of leadership. If ordinarily reluctant talkers are embarrassed by a member of the group, they may become even more reluctant to participate. Likewise, if talkative yet valuable members of the group are constantly restrained, they may lose value.

You may have to clear the road for shy speakers. For instance, when Mary gives visual or verbal clues of her desire to speak, you may have to say something like, "Just a second, Jim, I think Mary has something she wants to say here." You may be able to phrase a question so that it stimulates a response. Try to ask a question that requires an opinion rather than a fact. For instance, "Mary, what do you think of the validity of this approach to combating crime?" is much better than "Mary, do you have anything to say here?" Not only is it specific, but also it requires more than a "yes" or "no" answer. Furthermore, such an opinion question will not embarrass Mary if she has no factual material to contribute. Tactful handling of shy or reluctant persons can pay big dividends. You may get some information that could not have been brought out in any other way; moreover, when people contribute a few times, it builds up their confidence, which in turn makes it easier for them to respond later when they have more to say. Of course, there are times when some members do not have anything worth saying because they are simply not prepared. Under such circumstances it is best for you to leave them alone.

You must also use tact with overzealous speakers. Jim, the talkative person, may be talkative because he has done his homework—he may have more information than any other member of the group. If you turn him off, the group may suffer immensely. After he has finished talking, try statements such as, "Jim, that's a very valuable bit of material; let's see whether we can get some reactions from other members of the group on this issue." Notice that a statement of this kind does not stop him; it suggests that he should hold off for a while. Difficult participants to deal with are those who must be heard regardless of whether they have anything to say. If subtle reminders are ineffective with these individuals, you may have to say, "Jim, I know you want to talk, but you're just not giving anyone else a chance. Would you wait until we've heard everyone else on this point?" Of course, the person who may be the most difficult of all to control is the leader. Leaders often engage in little dialogues with each member of the group. They sometimes exercise so much control that participants believe that they can talk only in response to the leader.

There are three common patterns of group communication (see Figure 11.3, in which the lines represent the flow of discussion among the eight participants). Discussion A represents a leader-dominated group. The lack of interaction often leads to a rigid, formal, and usually poor discussion. Discussion B represents a more spontaneous group. Since three

FIGURE 11 · 3

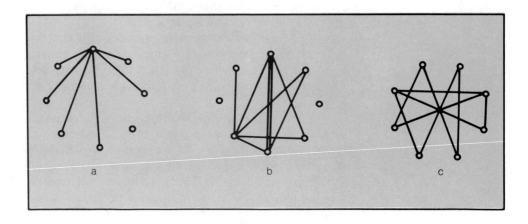

people dominate and a few are not heard, however, conclusions will not represent group thinking. Discussion C represents something close to the ideal pattern. It illustrates a great deal of spontaneity, a total group representation, and—theoretically, at least—the greatest possibility for reliable conclusions.

Ask appropriate questions. Although the members of any group bring a variety of skills, information, and degrees of motivation to the group, they do not always operate at peak efficiency without help from the leader. Perhaps one of the most effective tools of leadership is the ability to question appropriately. This skill requires knowing when to ask questions and knowing what kinds of questions to ask.

By and large, the leader should refrain from questions that can be answered "yes" or "no." To ask group members whether they are satisfied with a point that was just made will not lead very far, for after the "yes" or "no" answer you must either ask another question to draw the people out or change the subject. The two most effective types of questions are those that call for supporting information and the completely open-ended question that gives members complete freedom of response. For instance, rather than asking John whether he has had any professors who were particularly good lecturers, you could ask, "John, what are some of the characteristics that made your favorite lecturers particularly effective?"

When to ask questions is particularly important. Although we could list fifteen to twenty circumstances, let's focus on four purposes of questioning:

1. *To focus discussion.* Individual statements usually have a point; the statements themselves relate to a larger point being made; and the general discussion relates to an issue or to an agenda item. You can use questions to determine speakers' points or to determine the relationship

of the points to the issue or agenda item; for instance, "Are you saying that the instances of marijuana leading to hard-drug use don't indicate a direct causal relationship?" Or, to what has just been said, "How does that information relate to the point that Mary just made?" Or, to ask about an issue or an agenda item, "In what way does this information relate to whether or not marijuana is a health hazard?"

2. *To probe for information.* Many statements need to be developed, supported, or in some way dealt with. Yet often members of a group apparently ignore or accept a point without probing it. When the point seems important, the leader should do something with it. For instance, on a question of source, you can say, "Where did you get that information, Jack?" Or, to develop a point, "That seems pretty important; what do we have that corroborates the point?" Or, to test the strength of a point, "Does that statement represent the thinking of the group?" Or, to generate discussion, "That point sounds rather controversial—should we accept the point as stated?"

3. *To initiate discussion.* During a discussion there are times when lines of development are apparently ignored, when the group seems ready to agree before sufficient testing has taken place. At these times, it is up to the leader to suggest a starting point for further discussion. For instance, "OK, we seem to have a pretty good grasp of the nature of the problem, but we haven't looked at any causes yet. What are some of the causes?"

4. *To deal with interpersonal problems that develop.* Sometimes the leader can help members ventilate very personal feelings. For instance, "Ted, I've heard you make some strong statements on this point. Would you care to share them with us?" At times, a group may attack a person instead of the information that is being presented. Here you can say, "I know Charley presented the point, but let's look at the merits of the information presented. Do we have any information that runs counter to this point?"

Questions by themselves are not going to make a discussion. In fact, some questions can hurt the discussion that is taking place. The effective leader uses questions sparingly but decisively.

Summarize frequently. Often a group talks for a considerable period, then takes a vote on how the members feel about the subject. A good problem-solving discussion group should move in an orderly manner toward intermediate conclusions represented by summary statements seeking group consensus. For instance, on the question "What should be done to lower the crime rate on campus?" the group would have to reach consensus on each of the following questions:

1. What is the problem?
2. What are the symptoms of the problem? (Draw intermediate conclusions; ask whether the group agrees.)
3. What are the causes? (Draw intermediate conclusion on each cause

separately or after all causes have been considered; ask whether group agrees.)

4. What criteria should be used to test the solutions?
5. What is one criterion? (Draw conclusions about each criterion.)
6. What are some of the possible conclusions? (Determine whether all possible solutions have been brought up.)
7. What is the best solution?
8. How does each of the solutions meet the criteria? (Discuss each and draw conclusions about each; ask whether group agrees.)
9. Which solution best meets the criteria? (The conclusion to this final question concludes the discussion; ask whether all agree.)

During the discussion the group might draw six, eight, ten, or even fifteen conclusions before it is able to arrive at the answer to the topic question. The point is that the group should not arrive at the final conclusion until each of the subordinate questions is answered to the satisfaction of the entire group.

It is up to the leader to point up these conclusions by summarizing what has been said and seeking consensus on a conclusion. Everyone in the group should realize when the group has really arrived at some decision. If left to its own devices, a group will discuss a point for a while, then move on to another before a conclusion is drawn. The leader must sense when enough has been said to reach a consensus. Then the leader must phrase the conclusion, subject it to testing, and move on to another area. You should become familiar with phrases that can be used during the discussion.

▶ "I think most of us are stating the same points. Are we really in agreement that . . ." (State conclusion.)

▶ "We've been discussing this for a while and I think I sense an agreement. Let me state it, and then we'll see whether it does summarize group feeling." (State the conclusion.)

▶ "Now we're getting into another area. Let's make sure that we are really agreed on the point we've just finished." (State the conclusion.)

▶ "Are we ready to summarize our feelings on this point?" (State the conclusion.)

Maintain necessary control. A leader must maintain control of the discussion. Remember, absence of leadership leads to chaos. Group members need to feel that someone is in charge. If the group has a set of formal rules, be sure that the rules are followed (at times bending is necessary, but total breaking does not help the group). As leader, remember that some members will be playing negative roles in the discussion; do not let them spoil the outcome. You are in charge; you are responsible. You have authority, and you will need to exercise it on occasion for the benefit of the group. If John is about to talk for the fortieth time, it is up to you to harness him. If Jack and Mary are constantly sparring with each other, it is up to you to harmonize their differences. If something internal or external threatens the work of the group, it is up to you to deal with it. Also, when the group has solved its problem, end the discussion smoothly. Some discussion groups meet by time instead of by problem. That you are scheduled to discuss for an hour does not mean that you cannot stop in 45 minutes if you have done the job.

Helping the group achieve consensus   If a decision is not a product of group thought and group interaction, the advantages of group decision making are lost. When a leader has too much authority, a group runs the risk of having its decisions made by decree. For example, after the group discussion, the leader tells the group what its decision will be. If leaders have enough power, are very persuasive, or are very manipulative, they can get the group to approve a decision. This method, called rubber-stamping, often destroys group decision making and group morale.

Group members often feel more pleased about the process and more committed to the group decisions when such decisions are reached democratically, through group interaction. Democratic decision making may be reached by consensus. **Consensus** means total group agreement. After the group has discussed a point for a while, the leader poses a question that is phrased to capture the essence of the group's position. For example, after a group has been discussing departmental problems for a while, the leader might ask, "Are we in agreement that lack of direction is frustrating the efforts of department members?" If everyone agrees, the decision is reached by consensus.

If the group does not agree, the group continues to discuss the point until a statement can be made that incorporates differing viewpoints without compromising the principles behind the viewpoints. But it takes the participation of most group members to arrive at a statement that represents the group position.

If consensus still cannot be reached, the group usually takes a vote. Let us say that after considerable discussion on determining a major cause of department frustration, it becomes obvious that no single statement can be made that will be satisfactory to all. The group should then take a vote. If the vote is six to one or five to two in a seven-person group, the decision has been given solid support. If it is a four-to-three decision, there may be some questions about later group support of that decision. Nevertheless, on some issues, at some times, the principle of majority rule is the only choice open.

If you see that only a few members are getting a chance to talk or are making an effort to talk, it is up to you to bring the other members of the group into the discussion. Even if that person only confirms his or her agreement with what is said, at least the group is getting the person's position.

EVALUATING GROUP COMMUNICATION

Groups can be evaluated on the quality of the decision, the quality of individual participation, and the quality of leadership.

The Decision

The questionnaire in Appendix B-3 gives you an opportunity to look at the group *decision*. Since the group's goal is to arrive at a decision, a decision-based questionnaire will consider the end product of group communication. This questionnaire calls for you to consider three major questions:

1. *Did the group arrive at a decision?* That a group meets to discuss does not necessarily mean that it will arrive at a decision. As foolish as it may seem, some groups thrash away for hours only to adjourn without having arrived at a decision. Of course, some groups discuss such serious problems that a decision cannot be reached without several meetings, but in this case we are not talking about a group that plans to meet later to consider the issue further; we mean the group that "finishes" without arriving at some decision. Not arriving at a decision results in frustration and disillusionment.

2. *What action is taken as a result of the discussion?* Problem-solving discussion implies implementation. If the group has "finished" without considering means for putting the decision into action, then there is reason to question the practicality of the decision.

3. *Was the group consensus a good one?* This may be the most difficult question to answer. Of course, whether a decision is good or bad is a value judgment. We suggest applying six criteria for such an evaluation:

   ■ Was quality information presented to serve as a base or foundation for the decision?
   ■ Were the data discussed fully?
   ■ Did interim conclusions relate to information presented, or were they stated as opinions that had no relation to content?
   ■ Did a given conclusion seem to be the product of consensus, or was it determined by the persuasive or authoritarian power of the leader?
   ■ Was the final decision measured against some set of criteria or objectives?
   ■ Did the group agree to support the decision?

Individual Members

Although a group will have difficulty without good leadership, it may not be able to function at all without members who are willing and able to meet the task and maintenance functions of the group. The questionnaire in Appendix B-4 incorporates each of the elements considered in the participation chapter and provides a simple checklist that can be kept for each individual.

Leadership

Although some group discussions are leaderless, no discussion should be without leadership. If there is an appointed leader—and most groups have one—you can focus on that individual. If the group is truly leaderless, then you must consider attempts at leadership by the various members or focus on the apparent leader who emerges from the group. Appendix B-5 is a simple checklist for evaluating group leadership.

- -

PRACTICE

Analyzing Group Communication

Each group is given or selects a task that requires some research. Each group is then given approximately 30 to 40 minutes of class time for discussion. While group A is discussing, members of group B should observe and, after the discussion, analyze the proceedings. For practice in using the various questionnaires, some of the observers could be asked to do a decision analysis (Appendix B-3), some could be asked to do an individual member analysis (Appendix B-4), and some could be asked to do a leadership analysis (Appendix B-5). After the discussions, the observers could share their observations with the group. In the next class period, group B would discuss and group A would observe and critique. Sample questions:

- What should be done to improve parking (advising, registration) on campus?
- What should be done to increase the participation of minorities in college or university teaching (governance, administration)?

SUMMARY

Leadership is exerting influence to accomplish a goal. Although leaders may show greater degrees of ability, sociability, motivation, and communication effectiveness than others in the group, the presence of such traits does not guarantee that you will lead effectively.

How well you lead may depend on your style and how you put it into operation. Some leaders adopt the task style, focusing on what needs to be done and how to do it; others adopt the maintenance style, focusing on interpersonal relationships of group members. As Fiedler's work has shown, how a leader performs is contingent on the interaction of task structure, leader–member relations, and position power. From Fiedler we can get a better understanding of the interacting variables and guidance for our attempts to adopt a task or a maintenance approach to leadership.

In order to lead a group well you must gather a group of optimum size, prepare the meeting place, work to develop a cohesive unit, help the group form appropriate norms, prepare an agenda, introduce the topic and establish procedures, keep communication channels open, summarize frequently, maintain necessary control, and help the group reach consensus.

SUGGESTED READINGS

Hare, A. Paul. *Handbook of Small Group Research*. 2nd ed. New York: Free Press, 1976. This may be the single most complete survey of small-group research available. The extensive bibliography includes every important work on leadership published prior to 1976.

Hunt, James G., and Lars L. Larson, eds. *Crosscurrents in Leadership*. Carbondale: Southern Illinois University Press, 1979. An excellent collection of readings that outlines the status of leadership research and clarifies what we can document about leadership.

Lawson, John D. *When You Preside.* 5th ed. Danville, Illinois: The Interstate Printers & Publishers, Inc., 1980. Written as a handbook for leaders of a variety of types of groups. A great deal of good, practical information.

Shaw, Marvin E. *Group Dynamics: The Psychology of Small Group Behavior.* 3rd ed. New York: McGraw-Hill, 1981. An excellent section summarizing group research.

Stech, Ernest L. *Leadership Communication.* Chicago: Nelson-Hall, 1983. Good discussion of task-oriented and person-oriented leadership.

PART FIVE

Winston Churchill, Franklin D. Roosevelt, and Martin Luther King, Jr., are but three speakers whose words made history.

Whether our words will make history or not, we will often be called upon, by choice or by necessity, to speak our ideas in public. This unit considers the variables that affect public speaking.

PUBLIC SPEAKING

Self-Analysis

Many people dream of influencing others' attitudes and behavior. But when you go from the safety of personal and group communication to expressing your ideas in front of considerably larger audiences, a great deal of pressure is placed on your communication ability. In public speaking your message must be well prepared, you must speak without verbal feedback, and you must do it alone.

Yet of all the communication settings, effectiveness in public speaking may be the most important. As a member of many types of action groups, you have the power and the opportunity to make a difference. But if you cannot or will not speak out on issues, you, your organization, and perhaps society may suffer for your failure. Your ideas count—you need to make the most of them!

For each of the paired statements in the following public speaking analysis, circle the number that best indicates how you see your behavior. The numbers 1 and 2 represent the negative behavior; the numbers 4 and 5 represent the positive behavior. The number 3 represents the midpoint between the extremes. It may also say you are not sure of your behavior.

When I am asked to speak, I never seem to know what to talk about.	1 2 3 4 5	When I am asked to speak, I am able to select a topic with confidence.
In my preparation I seldom consider whether I have developed ideas to meet audience needs.	1 2 3 4 5	In my preparation I am careful to be sure that I have developed ideas to meet audience needs.

In my preparation I seldom consider the order of my ideas.	1 2 3 4 5	In my preparation I work to organize material to follow some consistent pattern.
When I speak, audiences show signs of restlessness and inattention.	1 2 3 4 5	When I speak, audiences are alert and listen attentively.
When I speak, the "right words" never seem to come to me.	1 2 3 4 5	When I speak, I sense that my audience perceives my language as clear and vivid.
I tend to avoid looking directly at members of my audience when I speak.	1 2 3 4 5	I look directly at members of my audience when I speak.
My public-speaking voice tends to remain on the same levels of pitch, speed, and loudness.	1 2 3 4 5	My public-speaking voice shows variation in pitch, speed, and loudness.
When I speak, I never know what to do with my hands; I feel and look awkward.	1 2 3 4 5	When I speak, my bodily actions help to supplement or reinforce my ideas; I feel and look involved.
When I have finished, I seldom feel that I have made an impact on my audience.	1 2 3 4 5	When I have finished, I usually feel I have achieved my speech objective.
I have considerable fear about speaking in public.	1 2 3 4 5	I have confidence in my ability to speak in public.

First, consider your analysis. Is the number you circled indicative of where you would like to be in that category? If not, in different color of ink or pencil, circle the number that represents your goal for this term. If you would like verification of your self-analysis, have a friend or a work partner complete the same analysis for you.

Then select one of the areas in which your goals are farthest from your current behavior. Write a communication improvement contract similar to the sample contract in Appendix C.

12 SELECTING TOPICS AND FINDING MATERIAL

OBJECTIVES

After you have read this chapter, you should be able to:

1 Use brainstorming to select a topic

2 Write a speech goal that meets tests

3 Analyze your audience

4 Analyze your occasion

5 Find sources for a speech

Benjamin Franklin once said "An empty bag cannot stand up-right." The content of the speech is of utmost importance—without it, your speech will fold like Franklin's empty bag. Without something of value to say, there is no reason for speaking. Every effort should be made to find and develop the best material possible. Determining your content involves five steps: selecting a topic, writing a specific speech goal, analyzing your audience, analyzing the occasion, and locating the material you can use to meet your goal. Although we discuss each step separately, they overlap and are often accomplished in a different order.

SELECTING A TOPIC

Sometimes an organization inviting you to speak suggests a specific topic; at other times, however, and especially in the classroom, topic selection is up to you. Selecting a topic is for some people the most difficult part of the preparation process. We often hear, "Oh, I'm sure I can give a good speech—if only I could find a topic!" Yet finding a good topic should be quite easy if you choose from topics you know about and topics that interest you. Your main areas of interest probably include your school major (or prospective profession), your hobbies (or spare-time activities), or current events or social issues that concern you. Let's see how you can identify good topics from these areas.

To generate a list of topics, I suggest you use a form of *brainstorming*. As we discussed in the group communication section, brainstorming is an uncritical, nonevaluative process of generating ideas, much like the old word-association process. For example, in response to the word *music* you might brainstorm "rock," "new wave," "dance," "electronic," "amplifiers." When you start with a word or an idea related to a subject you know about and are interested in, you can often list 20, 30, or even 50 other related words.

Start by dividing a sheet of paper into three columns. Label column 1 "Major" or "Vocation;" label column 2 "Hobby" or "Activity;" and label column 3 "Current Events" or "Social Issues." Then select a word to head each column, and, one column at a time, brainstorm from each word. If, for instance, in column 2, "Hobby," you write "pocket billiards," you might brainstorm such related words as "cue," "English," "games," "tables," and "equipment." After you have worked for at least five minutes on a column, turn to the next column. Although you may not finish all three columns in one sitting, do not go on to the next step of speech preparation until you have listed at least 20 items in each column.

When you believe your list under each column is complete, read the entries and check the three or four words or phrases that "ring a bell," that sound most compelling to you. Brainstorming allows you to take advantage of a basic common-sense principle—just as it is easier to select the correct answer to a multiple-choice question than it is to think of the answer to the same question without the choices, so too is it easier to select a topic from a list than to come up with a topic out of the blue. Instead of asking yourself, "What should I talk about?" ask yourself, "What are the one, two, or three best topics that I have listed under each heading?"

If the words or phrases you select still seem too general, start a new brainstorming list with one of these topics. When you have checked two or three topics from each of the three columns, you will have six to nine good topics, enough for all your speeches this term!

PRACTICE

Brainstorming for Topics

1. Fill in the blanks under the three headings (such as "art history" under *vocation or major*, "chess" under *hobby or activity*, and "energy" under *current event or issue*). Then brainstorm a list of 20 to 40 words in each column.

Vocation or Major	Hobby or Activity	Current Event or Issue
_____	_____	_____

1.

2.

3.

	Vocation or Major	Hobby or Activity	Current Event or Issue
4.			
5.			
6.			

2. Check the three topics in each column that are most striking or important to you.

WRITING A SPEECH GOAL

Each of the words you checked in the brainstorming exercise identifies a topic for your speech. You continue the preparation process by turning that topic into a speech goal.

Your speech goal (sometimes called a specific purpose or a speech objective) is a single sentence that states what you want your audience to do as a result of the speech. For a speech on the topic of diamonds you might state your goal as "I would like the audience to know the four major criteria for evaluating a diamond." For a speech on United Appeal you might state your goal as "I would like the audience to donate money to United Appeal." In the first example what you want the audience to do is to know the criteria; in the second example what you want your audience to do is to donate money.

Your speech goal serves as a basis for your thesis statement. Whereas the goal is a sentence that states what you want your audience to do, the thesis statement is a sentence that outlines the specific elements that were forecast in the goal statement. Although the speech goal "I would like the audience to know the four major criteria for evaluating a diamond" clearly states what you want the audience to do (know the criteria), it does not tell what those criteria are. The thesis statement for such a speech would be "Diamonds are evaluated on the basis of carat (weight), color, clarity, and cutting." Likewise, for the speech goal, "I would like my audience to donate money to United Appeal," a thesis statement would be "You should donate to United Appeal because it covers a wide variety of charities with one gift, it spends a very low percentage on overhead, and it allows you to designate your dollars to specific agencies if you so desire."

With any topic a number of speech goals are possible, and any speech goal may be explained with many different thesis statements. Let us illustrate this relationship among subject area (heading of brainstorming list), topic (word or phrase you have checked), speech goal, and thesis statement with two additional examples:

SUBJECT AREA
Home decoration

TOPIC
Macramé hangers

SPEECH GOAL
I would like the audience to know how macramé hangers may be used.

THESIS STATEMENT
Macramé hangers may be used in the home to enhance the beauty of your plants, to help conserve space in a small room, and to decorate.

SUBJECT AREA
Theater

TOPIC
A Chorus Line

SPEECH GOAL

I would like the audience to attend the school's production of *A Chorus Line.*

THESIS STATEMENT

A Chorus Line is a Tony Award–winning show that has excellent music and vibrant dance numbers and presents a memorable insight into the characters.

Now let's consider a step-by-step procedure for writing the speech goal and the corresponding thesis statement:

1. *Keep writing until your tentative speech goal is a complete sentence that states the specific response or behavior you want from your audience.* Suppose you want to talk about capital punishment. The subject itself is just the start of a complete speech goal. "Methods of capital punishment" indicates the aspect of the topic you want to consider. "Three methods of capital punishment" limits what you will say to a specific number. "I would like the audience to know three methods of capital punishment practiced in the United States" is a complete-sentence statement of a speech goal.

2. *Write out three or more different wordings of the goal.* Even if you like your first sentence, write at least two additional ones. You may find that the second, third, or fourth turns out to be the clearest statement of your goal.

3. *Do not write the goal as a question or as an imperative.* "Is capital punishment inhumane?" is a good question for discussion, but it is not a good speech goal, because it does not show direction. Likewise, "Capital punishment—man's inhumanity to man" may be a clever title, but it, too, fails as a speech goal for much the same reason: it does not give clear enough direction.

4. *Write the goal so that it contains only one idea.* "I would like the audience to understand the three methods of capital punishment practiced in the United States and to see that all three are inhumane" includes two distinct ideas; either can be used, but not both. Make a decision. Do you want to talk about methods? Then the goal "I would like the audience to understand the three methods of capital punishment practiced in the United States" is the better statement. Do you want to talk about morality? Then the goal "I would like the audience to believe that the methods of capital punishment practiced in the United States are inhumane" is the better statement.

5. *Revise the infinitive or the infinitive phrase until it indicates the specific audience reaction desired.* If you regard your idea as noncontroversial, universally accepted, or an expression of observation, then your intent is basically informative, and the infinitive will be "to understand" or "to show." If, however, your idea is controversial, a statement of belief, or a

call to action, then your intent is persuasive, and that intent will be shown with such infinitives as "to believe" or "to petition."

6. *When you have sufficient information, write a thesis statement that explains the speech goal.* You may not be able to complete this step until you begin research for your speech. For instance, you may know that you want "to have the audience believe that capital punishment should be abolished," but you may not yet have enough material to fill in the specifics. After you have studied the subject, you will be able to write a thesis statement like this one: "Capital punishment should be abolished because it does not deter crime, because it is not just, and because it is an inhumane form of punishment."

As you write a number of goal statements, you may notice that almost all of them can be grouped under two major headings: speeches that are concerned with understanding information and speeches that involve belief or action. Since one common way of assigning classroom speeches is by the kind of the response you want an audience to give, assignments discussed later are grouped under the headings of "Informative Speaking" and "Persuasive Speaking."

PRACTICE

Writing Your Speech Goal and Thesis Statement

1. For one of the topics you listed earlier, write three well-worded speech goals.

2. For the speech goal that you plan to use for your first speech, try to write a complete thesis statement. If you don't have enough information, come back to this step later.

ANALYZING YOUR AUDIENCE

Audience analysis is the study of audience knowledge, interests, and attitudes. You will use the results of your audience analysis to guide you in selecting supporting material, organizing the speech, and presenting it.

Gathering Data

Since you can't give a prospective audience a comprehensive examination, an aptitude test, or an opinion poll, you must get the information in some other way. If you already know many of the listeners, you can gather data from your previous observation and experience. For instance, you can analyze a fraternal organization, a church group, or your speech class in this way.

If you don't know anything about the listeners, you can ask the chairperson or group contact to provide data about them for you. If you cannot get any data, you will have to guess on the basis of such things as the kind of people most likely to attend your speech, the location of the meeting place, and the sponsor of the speech. Perhaps you will have time before you speak to observe the audience and talk with a few of its members.

Types of Data

To draw conclusions about your audience you will need the following data:

AGE
What is the average age? What is the age range?

SEX
Is the audience all or predominantly male? Female? Or are the sexes of the group reasonably evenly balanced?

OCCUPATION

Are the members of the audience all of one occupation, such as nurses? Bankers? Drill press operators? Are the members of the audience all of one group, such as professionals? Educators? Skilled laborers?

INCOME

Is average income high? Low? Average? Is range of income narrow? Wide?

RACE, RELIGION, NATIONALITY

Is the audience primarily of one race, religion, or nationality? Or is the audience mixed?

GEOGRAPHIC UNIQUENESS

Are the people from one state? City? Region?

GROUP AFFILIATION

Is the audience made up of members of one group, such as a gardening club? Professional organization? Political group?

Processing Data

From your data you will determine how the members of the audience are alike and how they differ. The ways that they are alike or different will help you predict audience knowledge, interests, and attitudes.

The following three groups of questions give you a good working framework for such an analysis. As you gain experience, you may change the wording of these questions or add other questions.

1. *What are my predictions of my listeners' knowledge of this topic?* Are my listeners likely to have enough information to allow them to understand my speech? For some subjects special knowledge is necessary; for others some basic level of information may be needed for your speech to make sense (an explanation of calculus requires understanding certain mathematical information).

   Will the speech provide new information to most of my listeners? If your listeners already know what you plan to tell them, you will need to reconsider your goal.

   What kinds of development material will best meet their level of knowledge? Audiences are most receptive to material they can understand.

2. *What are my predictions of my listeners' interest in this topic?* Do my listeners already have an immediate interest? If not, can I relate my topic to their interest? It is a rare topic that creates an automatic interest; most topics require some creativity to make them interesting.

   What kinds of material are most likely to arouse or to maintain their interest? Audiences are most receptive to material they find interesting.

3. *What are my predictions of my listeners' attitude toward this topic?* Will my listeners be sympathetic? Apathetic? Hostile? Knowing, or at least attempting to determine, audience attitude beforehand should help you determine procedure.

   If sympathetic, how can I present my material to take advantage of their favorable attitude?

   If hostile, how can I present my material to lessen, or at least not arouse, their hostility?

PRACTICE

Analyzing Your Audience

1. Complete the following questions about your classroom audience:

   a. The age range is from _____ to _____. The average age is about _____.

   b. In the class there are _____ males and _____ females.

   c. My estimate of the income level of the class is _____ below average, _____ average, _____ above average.

   d. The class is basically _____ the same race, _____ a mixture of races.

   e. The class is basically _____ urban or _____ rural.

2. Write your speech goal.

3. Based on this information, answer the following questions.

   a. The class's knowledge of the subject will be

   b. The class's interest in the subject will be

c. The class's attitude toward the subject will be

d. As a result, I will have to make sure that I

ANALYZING THE OCCASION

While you are analyzing your audience, you will also want to analyze the occasion and the effect it will have on both speech preparation and presentation. Your analysis should include the following three questions:

1. *When will the speech be given?* The question of *when* includes whether the speech is part of some special occasion, at what time of day it occurs, and where on the program it occurs.

    Some speeches commemorate a special occasion, such as Labor Day, the anniversary of the founding of an organization, or Martin Luther King's birthday. In such cases the occasion itself will affect the content of the speech.

    The time of day the speech is presented provides a different set of problems. For instance, a speech given just before a meal presents a different problem from a speech given after a meal. Before a meal the audience may be anxious, short of patience, and hungry; an audience that hears you after a meal may be lethargic, mellow, and, at times, on the verge of sleep.

    Equally important is where your speech occurs on the program. If you are the featured speaker, you have an obvious advantage: You are the focal point of audience attention. In the classroom yours is one of many speeches. Your place on the schedule may affect how you are received. In your classroom speech you will be guaranteed enough speaking time, but going first or last will still make a difference. If you go first, you may have to be prepared to meet the distraction of a few class members strolling in late; if you speak last, you must counter the tendency of the audience to be a bit weary from listening to several speeches in a row.

2. *Where will the speech be given?* The room in which you are scheduled to speak will affect your presentation. If you are fortunate, your classroom will be large enough to seat the class comfortably. But classrooms vary in size, cleanliness, seating arrangements, and the like. You have to meet the demands of any situation.

   Outside of the school setting you may encounter even greater variations. You should study any place in which you are scheduled to speak before you make final speech plans. If possible, visit the place and see it for yourself. In most instances you will have some kind of speaking stand, but you can never count on it. You must be prepared for the situation as it exists.

3. *What facilities are necessary to give the speech?* For some speeches you may need a microphone, a chalkboard, an overhead projector, or a slide projector and screen. If the person who has contacted you to speak has any control over the setting, make sure you explain what you need. But always have alternative plans in case what you asked for does not arrive.

The standard accoutrements at a traditional auditorium—formal podium and fixed microphone—can be considered as obstacles or aids to your speech; your attitude will depend on whether you have anticipated the surroundings and planned for all possibilities.

PRACTICE

*Analyzing the
Occasion*

Draw conclusions about the effect occasion will have on your speech; base your conclusions on the three questions just discussed. What is the most important factor to take into account in preparing to adapt to that occasion?

FINDING YOUR MATERIAL: WHERE TO LOOK

Effective speakers know where to look for the best material available on their topics. Such speakers start with their own experiences and work outward to other sources.

Your Own Knowledge

If you have chosen to speak on a topic you already know something about, you may already have material you can use for your speeches. For instance, athletes have special knowledge about their sports, coin collectors about coins, detective-fiction buffs about mystery novels, "do-it-yourselfers" about house and garden, musicians about music and instruments, farmers about animals or crops and equipment, and camp counselors about camping. For most of your speeches, then, *you* should be your first, and perhaps your best, source of information. Your firsthand knowledge will contribute to the development of unique, imaginative, and original speeches.

You will be able to prepare the first speech assignment in this book with material based on your personal knowledge and experience alone. Yet even when you use other sources your knowledge and experience will still be an important part of your preparation.

Observation

You can get good, specific information for many topics through careful observation. If, for instance, you are planning to talk about how newspapers are printed, you can learn a lot about the printing operation by taking a tour of your local newspaper printing plant and observing the process in action. If you are planning to talk about the effectiveness of your city council, you can attend a couple of meetings and observe the council in action. If you want to talk about urban renewal in your downtown area, you can go downtown and look around. Observation adds a personal dimension to your speeches that can make them more informative as well as more interesting.

Interviewing

Interviewing helps you get material directly from people who have firsthand information. Let's review the steps of a good interview. Start by listing people who are likely to have the kind of information you need. For a speech on newspapers you may want to interview one of the reporters or even one of the editors; for a speech on the city council you may want to interview a member of the council. Will people take the time to talk with you? You will be surprised by how cooperative people can be if you approach them correctly. When you have decided whom you want to interview, call well in advance to make an appointment.

When you have selected the person, prepare a good list of questions. If you have questions prepared beforehand, you can maximize the time available and you will not waste the time of people who are willing to talk with you. For information about preparing questions, refer back to the discussion in Chapter 9.

A variation of the interview is the survey. A survey is a list of one or more questions that can be asked of a great number of people. For such diverse topics as student reaction to a particular course, the local football team's chances in an upcoming game, or how well the council is governing the city you can get your information through a survey.

Sometimes a survey can be taken on a single question. For instance, you could write

> The College of Arts and Sciences is considering requiring all its students to take the three-hour course Fundamentals of Effective Speaking for graduation. Please indicate your reaction to this proposal:
>
> _____ I agree
> _____ I disagree
> _____ No opinion

A survey can, of course, be considerably longer. But the shorter the survey, the more likely you are to get a large number of responses. You will want to make sure that you have polled a large enough group and that you have sampled different segments of the larger group before you attempt to draw any significant conclusions from your poll.

Research

For many of your speeches, the best material will come from what you read. Effective speakers are also effective researchers.

Books   Books are especially good sources for major topics on which large amounts of material are available. Whether your library is large or small, well equipped or poorly equipped, it is likely to have at least one or two books on any subject you choose, but you must know how to find what you need. Your library's *card catalog* lists all the books your library holds by title, author, and subject.

To be a good researcher you have to be creative in determining the headings you will use to find the books that might be useful to you. Suppose you are researching the topic "minimum cash income." You may find little or nothing under that heading in the card catalog. With a few minutes of creative thinking, however, you should be able to come up with such additional headings as "economic assistance—domestic," "guaranteed income," "income," "negative income tax," "poverty," "war on poverty," "welfare," and so forth. You will often have to turn to alternative headings to discover the extent of your library's listings.

Periodicals   Periodicals are publications that appear at fixed periods: weekly, biweekly, monthly, quarterly, or yearly. Material you get from weekly, biweekly, and monthly magazines is more current than that which you find in books. The *Readers' Guide to Periodical Literature* is an index of articles in some 150 popular magazines and journals, such as *Business Week, Ebony, Newsweek, Reader's Digest,* and *Vital Speeches.* The *Magazine Index* is a microfilm machine index of nearly 350 magazines with articles from the last five years. Each month the *Magazine Index* features a number of "Hot Topics" in an accompanying looseleaf binder. The *Humanities Index* and the *Social Sciences Index* will lead you to articles in scholarly journals, such as the *American Journal of Sociology,* the *Economist, Modern Language Quarterly,* and *Philosophical Review.*

A magazine is likely to be your best source when the focus of the topic you are considering is less than two years old. Since it usually takes one to three years for current topics to appear in books and encyclopedias, it may be a waste of time to search the card catalog or encyclopedias for information. Occasionally a book is rushed into print within six months of an event, but such speed is rare—and the worth of such a hastily prepared work is questionable. A magazine is also your best source when the topic is so limited in scope that it is unlikely to provide enough material for a book or when you are looking for a very specific aspect of a particular topic.

Magazine indexes are published each year and in monthly and quarterly supplements for the current year. In order to find appropriate articles about your topic, you need to determine when the events occurred or when the topic was actively discussed. If you are preparing a speech on what it was like to be a television writer during the McCarthy era, you should begin your research in the index for 1953, the height of the McCarthy era, and work forward and backward from there until the supply of articles dries up. If you are preparing a speech on the effects of the Arab oil embargo of the early 1970s, you would begin with 1973.

Encyclopedias   Most libraries have a recent edition of *Encyclopaedia Britannica, Encyclopedia Americana,* or *World Book Encyclopedia.* An encyclopedia can be a good starting point for research. Encyclopedias give an excellent overview of many subjects and they also provide bibliographies. But because the material is usually very general and may be years out of date, you should never limit your research to an encyclopedia.

Statistical sources   Statistical sources are books that present statistical information on a wide variety of subjects. When you need facts about population, continents, heads of state, weather, or similar subjects, you should refer to one of the many single-volume sources that report such data. Two of the most popular sources in this category are the *World Almanac and Book of Facts* and the *Statistical Abstract.*

Biographical sources   When you need accounts of a person's life, from thumbnail sketches to reasonably complete essays, you can turn to one of the many biographical sources available. In addition to full-length books and encyclopedia entries, you can consult such books as *Who's Who* (a collection of sketches of noted British subjects) and *Who's Who in America* (a similar collection of sketches of American citizens) or *Dictionary of National Biography* and *Dictionary of American Biography* (compilations of rather complete essays about prominent British subjects and American citizens, respectively).

Newspapers   Despite the relatively poor quality of reporting in many of our daily newspapers, newspaper articles can be good sources of facts and of interpretations of contemporary problems. You should approach newspaper research in much the same way as you approach magazine research: to gather information on subjects that were current at a particular time.

Your library probably holds both an index of your nearest major daily and the *New York Times Index.* Consult your reference librarian for a detailed account of other bibliographies, indexes, and special resources your library may have. Do not hesitate to ask library staff for help; helping library patrons is a major professional responsibility, and, with very few exceptions, librarians will gladly offer their assistance. Furthermore, you will not learn how to use all of your library's resources without the help of its staff.

PRACTICE

Sources
      For one of your three speech goals you wrote earlier, list three sources that would provide information. Don't forget to consider personal knowledge and observation.

_____

FINDING YOUR MATERIAL: WHAT TO LOOK FOR

Knowing where to look will help you only if you know what to look for. To develop your topic creatively, you should look for material that is interesting and that supports your points. The following kinds of materials can be used as found, can be modified, or can be completely reworked to provide the most creative development of your speeches.

Examples and Illustrations

Examples are single instances that show or prove a point; **illustrations** are more detailed examples. Most examples you find will be real. "Advertisers must give the source of the tests of their products" is a real example supporting the statement "Television commercials are required to be true." Yet examples may also be fictitious or hypothetical. The fable of the turtle beating the hare is a fictitious example to support the statement "Slow and steady wins the race." The statement "If you put a sheet of glass in a pool and removed it one hour later, a fish probably wouldn't attempt to go beyond the line where the glass was" would be a hypothetical example to prove the point that fish are easily conditioned. Fictitious and hypothetical examples may be very interesting, but they provide less support than real examples.

Anecdotes and Narratives

Anecdotes are brief, often amusing stories; **narratives** are tales, accounts, or lengthier stories. Remember the last time one of your professors said, "That reminds me of a story"? Probably more people listened to the story than to any other part of the lecture. Inclusion of anecdotes and narratives will pay dividends in audience attention as well as in audience understanding. For instance, if you were making a point about the influence of television on behavior, you might relate the following story:

▶ When we went next door to hear our neighbor's new stereo set, he put on a record, sat down squarely in front of the machine, and stared at it intently. Finally, I asked him what in the world he was looking at. Grinning sheepishly, he tried to settle back in his armchair. "I'm so doggone used to looking at television," he explained, "I just can't listen any other way!"

Comparisons and Contrasts

Probably the very best ways of giving meaning to new ideas are through comparison and contrast. **Comparisons**, of course, are forms of material that show similarities; **contrasts** show differences. Literal comparisons show similarities of real things: "It costs about as much as a luxury automobile"; "It's about the size of a chestnut." Figurative comparisons express one thing in terms normally denoting another: "He's as fast as greased lightning." Metaphors, figures of speech in which a word or phrase denotes one kind of object or idea used in place of another ("Advertising is the sparkplug that makes our system work"), and similes, figures of speech in which a thing or idea is likened to another ("He walks like an elephant"), are both forms of comparisons. "Unlike last year, when most of our advertising money went to newspaper ads, this year we're spending most of our money on radio and television" illustrates the contrast. Because comparisons and contrasts talk about unknowns in terms of the familiar, they are excellent forms of explanation.

Statistics

Numerical facts, or **statistics**, such as "7 out of every 10 people voted in the last election" or "the cost of living rose 13.5 percent in 1979," enable you to pack a great deal of information into a small package. When statistics are well used, they can be most impressive; when they are poorly used, they may be boring and, in some instances, downright deceiving. How can you use statistics effectively?

1. *Make sure you know when your statistics were true.* In 1971 only 12 out of 435 members of Congress, or 2.7 percent, were women. If you wanted to make a point about the number of women in Congress today, you would want the most recent figures.
2. *Use statistics comparatively whenever possible.* For instance, to say that this year industry offered the nation's supermarkets about 5,200 new products does not take on meaning until you say that 5,200 products equals the total number on their shelves the year before. In your com-

parisons be careful not to present a misleading picture. If we say that during the last six months Company A doubled its sales while its nearest competitor, Company B, improved by only 40 percent, the implication would be misleading if we did not indicate the size of the base; Company B could have more sales even though its improvement was only 40 percent.

3. *Do not overdo statistics.* Although statistics may be an excellent way of presenting a great deal of material quickly, be careful not to overdo them. A few pertinent numbers are far more effective than a battery of percentages.

Quotable Explanations and Opinions

When you find an explanation or an opinion that seems to be just what you are looking for, you may quote it directly in your speech. Because we want to see *your* creative processes at work, your speech should not be composed merely of a long string of quotations. Nevertheless, a well-selected quotation might be the perfect thing in one or two key places. If you keep quotations relatively short and few in number, they can and should serve you well. If you use a direct quotation, you should give credit to the source: The undocumented use of any quotation or close paraphrase is plagiarism.

Visual Aids

A form of speech development **visual aids** allow the audience to see as well as to hear about the material. So far, all of the material that we have asked you to look for is verbal. But in a speech, ideas may be supported visually as well as verbally. Since various studies indicate that specific information is remembered best when it is presented both verbally *and* visually, you should look for visual representations of information in your reading. When you find a good graph, chart, sketch, or drawing that depicts specific information visually, you should consider using those visual representations in your speech. In addition, you can create visual materials for your speech that will serve the same purposes.

Since visual aids are especially important in showing how things work, are made, done, or used, we have presented a detailed discussion of types and uses of visual aids in Chapter 15 on pages 339–342.

Recording Material

Any kind of material you plan to keep on file should be recorded on note cards. Try to keep each item on a separate 3 × 5 or 4 × 6 card. Although it may seem convenient to record materials from one source on a single sheet of paper (or to photocopy source material), sorting and arranging material is much easier when each item is recorded separately. On each card indicate the name of the source; the name of the author, if one is given; and the page number from which it was taken. You will not necessarily need this material, but should you decide to quote directly or to reexamine a point, you will know where it came from. Figure 12.1 illustrates a useful note card form.

PRACTICE

Supporting Material

1. Develop one of the following three statements with any *three* of the following types of development: an example, an illustration, an anecdote or a narrative, a comparison, statistics, or a quotable explanation or opinion.

   Women are careful (careless) drivers.

   _____ has a very good _____ team this year.

   _____ should win an Academy Award.

2. Complete two note cards for one of your speech goals.

FIGURE 12 · 1

Topic: Emphysema--scope of disease

"When combined with bronchitis, emphysema kills an estimated 35,000 people in the United States each year and contributes to the deaths of 30,000 more."

"Clues to the Cause of Emphysema"
Newsweek, April 14, 1980, p. 111

SUMMARY

The first step of effective preparation is to determine your content. Select a topic that you are interested in and that you know something about.

Then phrase a clear speech goal and a clear thesis statement. Keep writing until your tentative speech goal is a complete sentence. Write out at least three different wordings of the goal; instead of writing it as a question or as an imperative, describe the goal so that it contains only one idea. Use an infinitive or infinitive phrase that indicates the specific audience reaction desired.

You will then want to analyze your audience and the occasion to decide how to shape and direct your content. Audience analysis is the study of audience knowledge, interests, and attitudes. You will want to gather specific data about your audience to determine how members of the audience are alike and how they differ. While you are analyzing your audience, you will also want to consider when the speech will be given, where the speech will be given, and what facilities are necessary to give the speech.

Finally, you will need to find material for your speech. To find material you will need to explore your own knowledge, observe, interview, and do research. As you read various sources you will look for examples and illustrations, anecdotes and narratives, comparisons and contrasts, statistics, quotable explanations and opinions, and visual materials.

SUGGESTED READINGS

Hennessy, Bernard. *Public Opinion.* 5th ed. Monterey, Calif.: Brooks/Cole, 1985. Several excellent sections on conducting polls and administering questionnaires.

Rubin, Rebecca B., Alan M. Rubin, and Linda J. Piele. *Communication Research: Strategies and Sources.* Belmont, Calif.: Wadsworth, 1986. A comprehensive analysis of research sources.

13 ORGANIZING SPEECH MATERIAL

OBJECTIVES

After you have read this chapter, you should be able to:

1   Prepare the body of your speech

2   Determine the best order for your speech

3   Select an appropriate introduction

4   Select an appropriate conclusion

5   Outline your speech

As Tom read over the material he had collected for his speech, he felt overwhelmed with facts, figures, and opinions. "I'll never get this together," he thought. Twice more he went through everything he had. Then, as if someone had opened the shades to let light into a dark room, he said, "Wow, I see how it all fits together!" Tom had come to grips with a primary need in speech preparation. Now he *saw* an organization.

After you have written a clear, well-worded speech goal and a thesis statement and you have gathered the best material you can find, you must organize the speech. A body of material can be organized in many different ways. Your objective is to find or create the way that makes the most sense out of your material and will best achieve your goal.

Start by outlining the material. You can use the outline—a short, complete-sentence representation of the speech—to test the logic, development, and overall strength of the structure before you prepare wording or practice the delivery. In this chapter we discuss the development of each part of the outline: the body, the introduction, and the conclusion. We conclude the chapter by examining a complete outline and discussing the tests you should make before presenting the speech.

PREPARING THE BODY OF THE SPEECH

Many students assume that since the introduction is the first part of the speech to be heard by the audience, they should begin outlining with the introduction. If you think about it, however, you will realize that it is very hard to work on an introduction until you have considered the material you will be introducing. Unless you have a very good idea of what will be in the speech, you should probably outline the body first.

To outline the body you select and state the main points, determine the best order, and then select and develop the examples, quotations, and other elements that explain or support the main points.

Selecting and Stating Main Points

Main points are the key building blocks of your speech. You expect your audience to remember the main points, if nothing else about the speech. Since main points are so important, they should be carefully selected and worded.

If your speech goal is well written, the main-point ideas will already be stated or suggested. For instance, what would be the main points for a speech with the goal "I want my audience to know the four most important considerations for planting roses"? Each main point would be one of the four considerations. If the thesis statement is well written at this stage of preparation, selection and statement of main points are even easier. If the thesis statement is "Roses should be planted in an area that receives morning sun, that is close to a supply of water, that contains well-drained soil, and that is away from trees and shrubs," writing out the main points will be no problem whatsoever. Written in outline form, the main points would be as follows:

    I. Roses should be planted in an area that receives four to six hours of morning sun.
    II. Roses should be planted close to a supply of water.
    III. Roses should be planted in an area with good, well-drained soil.
    IV. Roses should be planted in an area away from other trees and shrubs.

Once you have selected the main points, you need to state them in complete sentences that are specific, vivid, and parallel in structure. *Specific* main points tell exactly what you mean. *Vivid* main points arouse interest. *Parallel* main points follow the same structural pattern, often using the same introductory words for each main point. To illustrate main points that are clear, vivid, and parallel, let us examine three contrasting ways of stating the same main points:

SPEECH GOAL

I want the audience to understand the insights our clothes give us into our society.

THESIS STATEMENT

Our clothing gives insight into the casual approach, youthful look, similarity in men's and women's roles, and lack of visual distinction between rich and poor in our society.

SET 1	SET 2	SET 3
I. Casual	I. They are casual.	I. Our clothes indicate our casual look.
II. Youthful	II. They are youthful.	II. Our clothes indicate our emphasis on youthfulness.
III. Similarities	III. There is a similarity in men's and women's roles.	III. Our clothes indicate the similarity in men's and women's roles.
IV. Little distinction.	IV. There is little distinction between rich and poor.	IV. Our clothes indicate the lack of visual distinction between the rich and the poor.

The labels in the first column indicate the subject areas only. Although the words *casual, youthful, similarities,* and *little distinction* relate to the purpose and indicate the subject areas of the thesis statement, how they are related is unknown. Although these labels might be useful as idea triggers on notecards, they won't work at this stage of preparation. In the second set, the complete-sentence main points are clearer than the labels. Nevertheless, the use of *they* and *there* along with the verb *to be* makes the statements vague.

Notice the significant improvement in the third set. The main points not only include each of the classifications but also explain the relationships of the categories to the goal sentence. In addition, starting each with "Our clothes indicate" makes the main points parallel. If the listeners remember only the main points of set 3, they will know exactly what our clothes tell us about our society.

As you begin to phrase prospective main points, you may find your list growing to five, seven, or even ten points that seem to be main ideas. Since every main point must be developed in some detail, it is usually impractical to have more than two to five main points. If you have more than five, you need to rework your speech goal to limit the number of points or you need to group similar ideas under a single heading.

Determining Best Order

Main points are more easily understood and remembered by an audience if they follow some identifiable order. For most speeches that you give—whether in or out of class—a *time order,* a *space order,* a *topic order,* or *problem-solution order* will meet your needs. In Chapter 16 we consider basic orders appropriate to persuasive speeches.

Time order   **Time order** follows a chronological sequence of ideas or events. It tells the audience that there is a particular importance to the sequence as well as to the content of those main points. This kind of order often evolves when you are explaining how to do something, how to make something, how something works, or how something happened. In the following example notice how the order of main points is as important to the logic of the speech as the wording of the main points.

SPEECH GOAL
I want the audience to be able to picture the three layers that make up the earth's atmosphere.

THESIS STATEMENT
Antiquing a table can be accomplished by following the four steps of cleaning the table, painting on the base coat, applying the antique finish, and shellacking.

I. Clean the table thoroughly.
II. Paint the base coat right over the old surface.
III. Apply the antique finish with a stiff brush, sponge, or piece of textured material.
IV. Apply two coats of shellac to harden the finish.

Space order   **Space order** follows a spatial relationship of main points. Space order is likely to be used in descriptive, informative speeches. If your intent is to explain a scene, place, person, or object in terms of its parts, a space order will allow you to put emphasis on the description, function, or arrangement of those parts. Because we remember best when we see a logical pattern to the development, you should proceed from top to bottom, left to right, inside to outside, or in any constant direction that the audience can picture. In the following example notice how the order proceeds spatially.

SPEECH GOAL
I want the audience to be able to picture the three layers that comprise the earth's atmosphere.

THESIS STATEMENT
The earth's atmosphere comprises the troposphere, the stratosphere, and the ionosphere.

I. The troposphere is the inner layer of the atmosphere.
II. The stratosphere is the middle layer of the atmosphere.
III. The ionosphere is the succession of layers that constitute the outer regions of the atmosphere.

Topic order   **Topic order** is an arbitrary order of main points that develop the speech purpose. Points may go from general to specific, least important to most important, or in some other logical order at your discretion. If all the topics are of equal weight, their order is unimportant; if topics vary in weight and in importance to the audience, how you order them may influence your audience's understanding or acceptance of them. In the following example each of the main points is a topic—a presidential role.

SPEECH GOAL
I want the audience to understand the major roles of the presidency.

THESIS STATEMENT
The president is chief of foreign relations, commander in chief of the armed forces, head of his party, and head of the executive branch.

I. The president is the chief of foreign relations.
II. The president is commander in chief of the armed forces.
III. The president is the head of his party.
IV. The president is the head of the executive branch.

Problem-solution order   **Problem-solution order** is a form of organization in which the main points are written to show (1) that there is a problem that requires a change in attitude or behavior (or both), (2) that the solution you are presenting will solve the problem, and (3) that the solution you are presenting is the best way to solve that problem. Since the problem-solution order is used when you want to prove to the audience that a different solution is needed to remedy a major problem, the organization will work best for a persuasive speech. Notice how the three points of the problem-solution order are presented in the following example.

SPEECH GOAL

I want the audience to believe that a minimum annual cash income should be guaranteed to families with incomes below $7,500.

THESIS STATEMENT

A minimum annual cash income should be guaranteed to families with an income below $7,500 because nearly 20 percent of the people in the United States live on incomes below the poverty level of $7,500, because such a guaranteed income would eliminate poverty, and because such an income is better than welfare.

I. Nearly 20 percent of the people in the United States are living on incomes below the poverty level of $7,500.
II. A guaranteed cash income would eliminate the problem of poverty for those people.
III. A guaranteed cash income is a much better solution than the present welfare system.

Summary of Guidelines

Let's summarize the guidelines for stating main points that have just been discussed. To serve as a visual example, let us reproduce an outline of main points we discussed earlier:

SPEECH GOAL

I want the audience to understand the insights our clothes give us into our society.

THESIS STATEMENT

Our clothing gives insight into the casual approach, youthful look, similarity in men's and women's roles, and lack of visual distinction between rich and poor in our society.

I. Our clothes indicate our casual look.
II. Our clothes indicate our emphasis on youthfulness.

III. Our clothes indicate the similarity in men's and women's roles.
IV. Our clothes indicate the lack of visual distinction between the rich and the poor.

1. State each main point as a complete sentence. Notice that each of the four main points is a complete sentence.
2. State each main point in a way that develops the key words in the speech goal. If the speech goal speaks of "several insights," then each main point is an insight; if the speech goal speaks of the "steps" involved, then each main point should be a step. If you have written the thesis statement correctly, you will already have part of the wording for each main point.
3. State each main point as specifically and concisely as possible. For example, saying, "Our clothes indicate our emphasis on youthfulness" is more concise than saying, "The clothes in our society indicate the emphasis most of us are likely to place on trying to look as youthful as we can."
4. State main points in parallel language whenever possible. Since the first main point begins "Our clothes indicate . . .," each of the other main points also begins "Our clothes indicate . . . ."
5. Limit the number of main points to a maximum of five. If you have more than five points, you are likely to find that two or more of the points can be placed under a broader heading.
6. Organize the main points so they follow a time order, a space order, a topic order, or a problem-solution order. In the preceding example, the main points follow a topic order.

Taken collectively, your main points outline the structure of your speech. Whether your audience understands, believes, or appreciates what you have to say will usually depend upon the nature of your development of those main points.

Selecting and Outlining Supporting Material

In the last chapter you learned that examples and illustrations, anecdotes and narratives, comparisons, statistics, and quotations were the materials to look for. Now you must select the most relevant of those materials and decide how you will use them to develop each of the main points.

First, write down each main point and under it state the information that you believe develops that main point. For example, for the first main point of a speech with the goal "I want the audience to know the criteria for evaluating diamonds," you might write the following:

I. Carat is the weight of a diamond.
Recently standardized.
Used to be weighed against the seed of the carob.

Now the weight is a standard 200 milligrams.
Weight is also shown in points.
How much a diamond costs depends on its size.
But the price doesn't go up in even increments—it multiplies: a
½ carat costs $1,000; a 1 carat, $3,000.
The reason involves the amount of rock that has to be mined.

Once you have put down the items of information that make the point, you work to subordinate material so that the relationships between and among ideas are shown. You accomplish this organization by using a consistent set of symbols and by indenting some ideas more than others. Organization of the statements about diamonds might evolve into the following outline form:

I. Carat is the weight of the diamond.
   A. Diamond weight has only recently been standardized.
      1. Originally, merchants measured weight of diamonds against the seed of the carob.
      2. Now the carat has been standardized as 200 milligrams.
   B. As diamond weights increase, the costs multiply.
      1. A ½-carat stone will cost about $1,000.
      2. A 1-carat stone will cost about $3,000.

For each of the subpoints you should have various examples, illustrations, anecdotes, and other material to use in the speech itself. Put down enough material on paper so that you can test both the quality and the quantity of your material.

Rules of Outlining

What rules should you use to guide your writing of the development of the speech? The following five rules will help you test your thinking and produce a better speech. Over the years we have seen ample proof of the generalization that there is a direct relationship between quality of outline and quality of speech content.

1. *Use a standard set of symbols.* Main points are usually indicated by Roman numerals, major subdivisions by capital letters, minor subheadings by Arabic numerals, and further subdivisions by small letters. Although greater breakdown can be shown, an outline will rarely be subdivided further. Thus an outline for a speech with two main points might look like this:

   I.
     A.
       1.
       2.

B.

II.

    A.

    B.

       1.

          a.

          b.

       2.

2. *Use complete sentences for major headings and major subdivisions.* By using complete sentences you are able to see (1) whether each main point really develops the thesis of your speech goal and (2) whether the wording really makes the point you want to make. Although a phrase or key-word outline is best when the outline is to be used as a speaker's notes, for the planning stage—the blueprint of the speech—complete sentences are best. Unless you write key ideas out in full, you will have difficulty guaranteeing accomplishment of the next two rules.

3. *Each main point and major subdivision should contain a single idea.* By following this rule you will assure yourself that development will be relevant to the point. Let us examine a correct and an incorrect example of this rule:

> INCORRECT
> I. The park is beautiful and easy to get to.
>
> CORRECT
> I. The park is beautiful.
> II. The park is easy to get to.

Trying to develop the incorrect example will lead to confusion, for the development cannot relate to both ideas at once. If your outline follows the correct procedure, you will be able to line up your supporting material with confidence that the audience will see and understand the relationship.

4. *Minor points should relate to or support major points.* This principle is called *subordination.* Consider the following example.

> I. Proper equipment is necessary for successful play.
>   A. Good gym shoes are needed for maneuverability.
>   B. Padded gloves will help protect your hands.
>   C. A lively ball provides sufficient bounce.
>   D. And a good attitude doesn't hurt.

Notice that the main point deals with equipment. A, B, and C (shoes, gloves, and ball) relate to the main point. But D, attitude, is not equipment, and should appear somewhere else, if at all.

5. *Main points should be limited to a maximum of five.* A speech will usually contain from two to five main points. Regardless of the length of time available, audiences will have difficulty really assimilating a speech with

more than five points. When a speech seems to have more than five points, you can usually group points under headings in such a way that the number will be five or less. Audiences will remember two main points with four divisions each more easily than they will remember eight main points.

6. *The total words in the outline should equal no more than one-third to one-half of the total number anticipated in the speech.* An outline is a skeleton of the speech and should be a representation of it—not a manuscript with letters and numbers. One way of testing the length of an outline is by computing the total number of words that you could speak during the time limit and then limiting your outline to one-third of that total. Since approximate figures are all that are needed, you can assume that your speaking rate is about average—160 words per minute. Thus, for a two- to three-minute speech, which would include roughly 320 to 480 words, the outline should be limited to 110 to 160 words. The outline for an eight- to ten-minute speech, which will contain roughly 1,200 to 1,500 words, should be limited to 400 to 500 words.

PREPARING THE INTRODUCTION

At this stage of preparation, the body of the speech is ready for practice. Now you must concern yourself with the strategy of getting your audience to listen to the entire speech. You must prepare a good introduction.

Goals of the Speech Introduction

Although your audience is captive (few of them will get up and leave), their physical presence does not guarantee that they will listen. A good introduction will (1) get initial attention, (2) create a bond of goodwill between you and your audience, and (3) lead into the content of your speech. Let us look at each of these goals separately.

Getting attention   Many audiences are like the one you face in class: a group of people who, though they may not throw tomatoes, have little motivation for giving undivided attention. They hope they will like your speech, but if they do not, they can always daydream their way through. Your first goal, therefore, is to create an opening that will win your listeners' undivided attention. You may get attention by pounding on the stand, by shouting "Listen!" or by telling a joke, but the attention will be short lived if it doesn't lead well into the body of the speech. The attention getter should be an opening sentence (or more, depending on the length of the speech) that gets attention *directed* to the body of the speech.

Creating a bond of goodwill　If your audience has heard you before, they may be looking forward to hearing you again. On the other hand, they may not know you at all. Or they may even view you as a potential threat, as a person who will tell them things they do not want to hear, who will make them feel uncomfortable, or who will make them work. If they are going to invest time listening to you, they have to be assured that you are OK. To meet this second goal your opening must make the audience feel good about listening to you. Goodwill may be established with a separate statement, but in most speeches it is conveyed through the sincerity of your voice and your apparent concern for the audience as people. Creating goodwill is less important in an informative speech than in a persuasive speech, where it is vital.

Leading into the speech　The introduction must focus the audience's attention on the goal of the speech. In most speeches you tell your listeners what you are going to talk about. For instance, in an informative speech on cooking, after your attention getter you may say directly, "In this speech I'll show you the five steps in creating a gourmet's delight." In a persuasive speech, you may proceed more indirectly and keep the audience in suspense until their attention is firmly established. We will discuss indirect approaches when we consider alternate organizations in the section on persuasive speaking.

　　You lead into most speeches by stating your thesis statement as a forecast of your main points; thus, the thesis statement is written as the last

point of your outline of the speech introduction. (See Figure 13.1.) If there is some strategic reason for *not* stating the thesis statement, you will still write it on the outline, but you will put it in parentheses. This means that your speech has a thesis statement but that you have a reason for not stating it in the introduction.

How long should the introduction be? Introductions may range from less than 7 percent to nearly 50 percent of the speech. Yours should be long enough to put the audience in the frame of mind that will encourage them to hear you out—of course, the shorter the speech, the shorter the introduction.

Types of Introductions

Ways to begin a speech are limited only by your imagination. Let's look at some representative approaches that will work for short and long speeches.

Startling statement   Especially in a short speech, the kind you will be giving in your first few assignments, you must get your listeners' attention and focus on the topic quickly. One excellent way to do this is to make a startling statement that will penetrate various competing thoughts and get directly to the listener's mind. The following example illustrates the attention-getting effect.

▶   If I pointed a pistol at you, you would be justifiably scared. But at least you would know the danger to your life. Yet every day we let people fire away at us with messages that are dangerous to our pocketbooks and our minds, and we seldom say a word. I'm talking about televison advertisers.

Question   Asking a question is another way to get your listeners thinking about an idea. Like the startling statement, this opening is also adaptable to the short speech. Whether the question method works will depend on how the audience perceives it. The question has to have enough importance to be meaningful to the audience. Notice how a student began her speech on counterfeiting with a series of short questions:

▶   What would you do with this ten-dollar bill if I gave it to you? Take your friend to a movie? Treat yourself to a pizza and drinks? Well, if you did either of these things, you could get in big trouble—this bill is counterfeit!

Anecdote, narrative, or illustration   Nearly everyone enjoys a good story, so an introduction that includes story material will get audience attention. Keep in mind that a good opening must also lead into the speech. If your story does both, you probably have an unbeatable opening. If your story is

FIGURE 13 · 1

OUTLINE	ANALYSIS
SPEECH GOAL: I want the audience to understand two categories of risk factors influencing heart disease.	Written at the top of the page, the speech goal is used to remind the speaker of the goal and to test the relevance of the outline's points. The word "introduction" sets this section apart as a separate unit. The introduction gets attention and often, by stating the thesis of the speech, leads into the body.

INTRODUCTION

I. According to the American Heart Association heart disease is still the leading cause of death in the U.S.

II. Researchers have noted a consistent association between certain behaviors and the development of blood vessel disease.

Thesis: Heart disease is an acquired disease in which cultural and environmental risk factors have an overwhelming effect.

	The word "body" sets this section apart as a separate unit. Main point I reflects a topical relationship of main ideas. It is stated as a complete substantive sentence. The main point could be developed in many ways. These subdivisions further elaborate on the definition and quantify its extent.

BODY

I. The cultural factors (uncontrolled) include sex, heredity, and age.
  A. Heart disease affects males more often than females.
  B. Heart disease in a father or uncle before age 60 is a significant factor in tendency to inherit disease.
  C. Heart disease occurs in the middle years.

II. Environmental factors (controlled) include blood fat, obesity, smoking, stress, high blood pressure, and lack of exercise.
  A. Blood fat, cholesterol, and triglycerides are correlated with hardening of the arteries.
  B. Obesity increases the workload of the heart.
  C. Smoking damages the lining of the arteries and robs cells of oxygen.
  D. Stress heightens heart failure.
  E. High blood pressure increases wear and tear on the arteries.
  F. Lack of exercise causes muscles to work harder, putting extra load on heart.

Main point II continues the topical relationship. Notice that each main point considers one major idea. Ordinarily, subordination is shown by the following sets of symbols: major points—I, II, III, etc.; subdivisions— A, B, C, etc.; subdivisions of subdivisions—1, 2, 3, etc. Words and phrases are often substituted for complete sentences after the first two stages of subordination.

The substance of the outline should be tested by asking:
1. Is the speech goal a clear, concise statement?
2. Are the main points stated as clear, substantive sentences?
3. Do the main points develop the speech goal directly?
4. Does each main point consider only one idea?
5. Do the various subpoints really support or develop the division they are subordinate to?

CONCLUSION

The modification or elimination of cardiac risk factors is the practical means toward prevention of heart disease.

The word "conclusion" sets this apart as a separate unit. The content of the conclusion may take any form that ties the speech together and leaves a lasting impression.

not related to the subject, save it for another occasion. Since most good stories take time to tell, they are usually more appropriate for longer speeches; however, you can occasionally come across a short one that is just right for your speech. How do you like this opening to a speech on making money on antiques?

▶ At a recent auction bidding was particularly brisk on an old hand-blown whiskey bottle, and finally a collector on my left was the successful taker at $50. When the purchase was handed over to him, an aged but sharp-eyed farmer standing nearby leaned over and took a good look at the bottle. "My God," he gasped to his friend. "It's empty!" To that farmer an empty bottle wasn't worth much. But in today's world anything that's empty might be worth a fortune, if it's old enough. Today I want to talk with you about what might be lying around your basement or attic that's worth real money—a branch of antiques called "collectables."

Personal reference   Although any good opening relates to the audience, the personal reference is directed solely to that end. In addition to getting attention, a personal reference can be especially good for building goodwill between you and your audience. A personal reference opening like this one on exercising may be suitable for any length of speech.

▶ Say, were you panting when you got to the top of those four flights of stairs this morning? I'll bet there were a few of you who vowed you're never going to take a class on the top floor of this building again. But did you ever stop to think that maybe the problem isn't that this class is on the top floor? It just might be that you are not getting enough exercise.

Quotation   A particularly vivid or thought-provoking quotation makes an excellent introduction to a speech of any length. You'll need to use your imagination to develop the quotation so that it yields maximum benefits.

▶ Shakespeare wrote: "If music be the food of love, play on." A modern-day poet might write: "If music be the food of love and money, write on." And that's exactly what a lot of people are doing. Pop music is big business—one of the biggest. And the people who write the songs are budding millionaires.

Selecting Your Introduction

How do you know whether the introduction you have prepared is the best for your speech? You cannot tell unless you have something to compare it with. Try working on three or four different introductions; then pick the one you like best.

For instance, if you were giving a speech on computer technology, you might prepare the following three introductions:

▶ In 1946 it took an entire room filled with vacuum tubes to power the ENIAC Computer. Today the capacity of that entire room filled with vacuum tubes can be duplicated in one single chip—a technological advancement that has revolutionized the computer industry and made it possible to get more and more sophisticated computers into smaller packages. Today I'd like to talk with you about the next round of innovation in computer technology.

▶ During the last ten years all of us have marveled at the innovations that have brought highly sophisticated computers into a price range that makes a computer network possible for even the smallest of businesses. What could possibly be in store for the future? Well, the fact is, "You ain't seen nothing yet." Today I'd like to talk with you about the next round of innovation in computer technology.

▶ In just a little more than a decade the computer has gone from a high-priced machine affordable by only the largest of companies to a common part of every business. We get our groceries checked out by computer at our local food market, all our purchases are recorded by computer at any clothing store, and the kid who cuts your grass is likely to have your account on computer at home! But as amazing as the recent past has been, future potential is unlimited. Today I'd like to talk with you about the next round of innovation in computer technology.

Which introduction do you prefer?

Although each has been discussed individually, the various types of introductions may be used either alone or in combination, depending upon the time you have available and the attitude of your audience. The introduction won't make your speech an instant success, but it can get an audience to look at you and listen to you. That is about as much as you have a right to ask of an audience during the first minute of your speech.

PRACTICE

Speech Introductions

For the topic that you are planning to use for your first speech, prepare three separate introductions that would be appropriate for your classroom audience. Which is the best one? Why?

PREPARING THE CONCLUSION

So now you have a body of the speech and a way to start it. But before you decide you have licked this organization problem, you had better think a little about how you are going to end the speech. Too many speakers either end their speeches so abruptly that the audience is startled or ramble on aimlessly until they exhaust both the topic and the audience. A poor conclusion—or no conclusion at all—can destroy much of the impact of an otherwise very effective speech. Even the best conclusion cannot do much for a poor speech, but it can heighten the effect of a good speech.

Goals of the Conclusion

What is a conclusion supposed to do, and how can you do it? A conclusion has two major goals: (1) wrapping the speech up in a way that reminds the audience of what you have said and (2) hitting home in such a way that the audience will remember your words or consider your appeal. Look at it this way. You may have talked for five minutes or fifty-five minutes, but when you get near the end you have only one last chance to put the focus where you want it. Even though the conclusion will be a relatively short part of the speech—seldom more than 5 percent—it is worth the time to make it good.

Types of Conclusions

Now let's look at several of the most common types of conclusions.

Summary   By far the easiest way to end a speech is by summarizing the main points. Thus, the shortest appropriate ending for a speech on the warning signals of cancer would be "So remember, if you experience a sudden weight loss, lack of energy, or blood in your urine or bowels, then you should see a doctor immediately." Such an ending restates the main points, the ideas that are, after all, the key ideas of the speech.

Because the conclusion may be important for heightening the emotional impact of the speech, even when you are using a summary you may want to add something to it to give it greater impact. The following are several ways of adding to or taking the place of the summary.

Illustration or personal experience   Since one of the goals of the conclusion is to leave your subject on a high point, the illustration or personal experience is often an excellent way to end. Edward Crutchfield ends his speech "Profitable Banking in the 1980s" with a personal experience that shows that bankers must be ready to meet competition that can come from any direction.

▶ I played a little football once for Davidson—a small men's college about 20 miles north of Charlotte. One particularly memorable game for me was one in which I was blindsided on an off-tackle trap. Even though that was 17 years ago, I can still recall the sound of crackling bones ringing in my years. Well, 17 years and 3 operations later my back is fine. But, I learned something important about competition that day. Don't always assume that your competition is straight in front of you. It's easy enough to be blindsided by a competitor who comes at you from a very different direction.[1]

Humorous statement   Humor can be used effectively at the beginning, the middle, or the end of a speech. Usually a humorous conclusion will leave a good impression of you with an audience. And if an audience feels good about you, they may adopt your message.

The following conclusion of Ruth Bryant's speech on application of economic principles illustrates the power of humor:

▶ There was a joke going around Moscow last year. It seems that in the big May Day parade, the final vehicle, following all of those rockets and tanks, was a truck carrying three solemn-looking, middle-aged men. Chairman Brezhnev turned to one of his aides and asked what in the world those men were in the parade for.

"Those men are *economists*, Comrade," the aide replied. "Their destructive capability is enormous!"

Amen to that, and thank you for letting me get some of that destructive capability out of my system.[2]

Appeal to action   The appeal is a common way of ending a persuasive speech. The appeal describes the behavior you want your audience to follow after they have heard the arguments.

Notice how Reginald Jones uses figurative language to develop his direct appeal for restoration of technological leadership:

▶ Our economy, like Gulliver in Jonathan Swift's masterpiece, is a giant potential source of strength when freed to serve the nation. But thousands of Lilliputian disincentives and regulations—no one perhaps in itself disabling—are weakening the ability of the business community to serve.

Let's untie Gulliver. The world community will be better served by a United States that has domestic and international vitality than by a weakened giant.[3]

Emotional appeal   No conclusion is more impressive than one that drives home the most important point(s) with real emotional impact. Consider the powerful way General Douglas MacArthur finished his speech when he ended his military career:

▶ But I still remember the refrain of one of the most popular barrack ballads of that day, which proclaimed most proudly that—
    "Old soldiers never die; they just fade away."
    And like the old soldier of that ballad, I now close my military career and just fade away—an old soldier who tried to do his duty as God gave him the light to see that duty.
    Goodby.[4]

Selecting Your Conclusion

As with introductions, it is difficult to tell whether a conclusion you have prepared is effective unless you have something to compare it with. Try out several conclusions for your speech; then choose the best one.

PRACTICE

Speech Conclusions

For the topic you are planning to use for your first speech, prepare three different conclusions you could use. Which is the best one? Why?

THE COMPLETE OUTLINE

Throughout your preparation process you have been building your speech outline. Does a speaker really need to write such an outline? Most of us do. Of course, some speakers do not prepare outlines; they have learned, through trial and error, alternate means of planning speeches and testing structure that work for them. Some accomplish the entire process in their heads and never put a word on paper—but they are few indeed. As a beginner, you can save yourself a lot of trouble if you learn to outline ideas.

Then you will *know* the speech has a solid, logical structure and that the speech really meets its goal.

The outline shown in Figure 13.1 illustrates the principles in practice. In the analysis we emphasize each of the rules we have considered.

PRACTICE

Speech Outline

Complete an outline for your first speech assignment. Test the outline to make sure that it conforms to the assignment. If you wish, include a title for your speech.

SUMMARY

After determining content, the next step of effective speech preparation is to organize the material. First, work on the body of the speech—the main points and development that accomplish the speech goal. After you have the material organized into main points, you can work on an introduction that gains attention and leads into the body of the speech and a conclusion that ties the speech together and ends it on a high note. You can then test the logic and development of the speech through analysis of the speech outline.

SUGGESTED READINGS

Amato, Phillip, and Donald Ecroyd. *Organizational Patterns and Strategies in Speech Communication.* Skokie, Ill.: National Textbook Company, 1975. This book focuses on speech organization.

Gibson, James. *Speech Organization: A Programmed Approach.* San Francisco; Rinehart Press, 1971. The programmed approach enables you to check your understanding of organization systematically.

14 *S*PEECH *P*RESENTATION

OBJECTIVES

After reading this chapter, you should be able to:

1 Test the wording of your speech for clarity, vividness, emphasis, and appropriateness

2 Present your speech with enthusiasm, good eye contact, and spontaneity

3 Practice your speech effectively

4 Prepare useful notecards

5 Cope with nervousness

6 Evaluate a speech objectively

At this stage of speech preparation your emphasis switches from what you plan to say to how you plan to say it. Speech presentation involves both wording and delivery. In this chapter we consider guidelines for wording and delivery, how to practice your speech for maximum effect, and how to cope with speech nervousness.

WORDING YOUR SPEECH

If you were preparing a paper, a newspaper article, or a magazine story, you would write out drafts of the work, criticize what you had written, and rewrite until you were satisfied. "Writing out" a speech in a similar way may help you. However, good writing and good speaking are not necessarily the same; good speech is measured not by the eye but by the ear.

Written and oral language are not totally different, but if you compare tapes of what people say with sections of books and magazines, you will find that oral language has more personal pronouns; more contractions; shorter sentences, on average; more simple sentences; greater use of one- and two-syllable words; and many more common or familiar words.

In this section we consider what criteria you can use to measure whether the words you use in practice will result in an effective oral style. To help achieve an oral style adapted to a specific audience, you need to test your language for clarity, vividness, emphasis, and appropriateness.

Clarity

Speaking clearly means using words that are understood instantly by your audience. **Clarity** eliminates ambiguity and confusion. Suppose a teacher recommended a student to a prospective employer by saying, "He does pretty well on tests, he gets his other stuff done in pretty good order, and he talks in class—no complaints." If you were the prospective employer, would you know much about that student's work? Suppose instead the teacher said, "He gets B grades or better on tests, he completes all his homework and turns it in on time, and his class discussion shows his understanding of basic theory—he's a pleasure to have in class." The second phrasing gives a much clearer picture of the student's behavior.

Clear language uses words that are precise, specific and concrete, and simple. Since we discussed precision and specific/concrete words in Chapter 3, we will just summarize them briefly here.

Precision   Words are **precise** when they create a meaning in the minds of your audience that is like the meaning you intended. Thus, when you are thinking of a large body of running water, you say "river"; when you are thinking of a small body of running water, you say "stream" or "creek."

Specific/concrete words   **Specific/concrete** words call up a single image. The more choice you give a listener, the more likely the listener will have an image different from the one you intended. To be specific and concrete we say "books, paper, and pencils" instead of "things"; "two maples, an oak, and four evergreens" instead of "trees"; and "an '85 Honda" instead of "a foreign car."

Simple words   In addition to precise and specific/concrete words, you will also want to select simple words. When handling complex ideas, students sometimes go overboard and use words that seem pompous, affected, or stilted. When you have a choice, select the simplest, most familiar precise word. The following list makes the point. Use

- *building* instead of *edifice*
- *clothing* instead of *apparel*
- *bury* instead of *inter*
- *engagement* instead of *betrothal*
- *begin* instead of *commence*
- *avoid* instead of *eschew*
- *wedding* instead of *nuptials*
- *predict* instead of *presage*
- *beauty* instead of *pulchritude*
- *home* instead of *residence*
- *view* instead of *vista*

Vividness

In addition to speaking clearly, effective public speakers also speak vividly. Vivid language paints meaning in living color. **Vivid** means full of life, vigorous, bright, intense. If your language is vivid, your audience will picture your meanings in striking detail. A baseball announcer might portray a center fielder's catch by saying, "Jackson made a great catch." This is an evaluation that states the announcer's opinion but creates no images. Saying, "Jackson made a great one-hand catch against the wall" would be more vivid. "Jackson, racing with his back to the infield, leaped and made a one-hand stab just as he crashed into the center field wall" is even more vivid, because the words *racing, leaped, stab,* and *crashed* paint an intense verbal picture of the action.

Speakers through the ages have experimented with various language techniques to enhance the vividness of their speeches. Two of the most frequently used techniques are similes and metaphors, concepts that we introduced in an earlier chapter.

A *simile* is a direct comparison of dissimilar things. Similes usually contain the words *like* and *as*. Many common clichés we use are similes. We may say "He runs like a turtle" or "She's slow as molasses" to make a

point about lack of speed. We say "He swims like a rock" or "She's built like a pencil" to dramatize a negative description. Similes are vivid when the base for the direct comparison is imaginative or different: "Trucks are like monstrous boxcars that eat highways for breakfast" is a vivid simile.

A *metaphor* is a comparison that draws a direct identification between objects being compared. Problem cars are called "lemons"; a team's infield may be a "sieve." In a speech delivered in Fulton, Missouri in 1946, Winston Churchill spoke of an "iron curtain" that had descended upon Europe. This metaphor to describe Russian-dominated countries as those "behind the iron curtain" is just as vivid today as it was when Churchill first coined the expression.

Vivid speech begins with vivid thought. You must have a striking mental picture before you can communicate one to your audience. If you cannot feel the bite of the wind and the sting of the nearly freezing rain, if you cannot hear the thick, juicy sirloin strip steaks sizzling on the grill, if you cannot feel the empty yet exhilarating feeling as the jet climbs from takeoff, you will not be able to describe these sensations vividly. The more imaginatively you can think about your ideas, the more likely you can state them vividly.

Emphasis

A third important element of style is **emphasis**. In a 500-word speech, all 500 words are not of equal importance. We neither expect nor necessarily want an audience to remember every word spoken. Still, if you leave it up to listeners to decide which words are most important, they may select the wrong ones. You are the speaker; you should know what you want to emphasize. How can you do it? Although you can emphasize with your voice and body, in this section we want to consider how you can emphasize with wording by means of proportion, repetition, and transition.

Emphasizing through proportion   **Proportion** means spending more time on one point than on another. If a speaker spends five minutes on the president's role as head of the executive branch and only two minutes each on his roles as head of his party and commander in chief of the armed forces, the audience would assume that his role as head of the executive branch was the most important.

Emphasizing through repetition   If you say, "There are 500 steps, that's 500," a listener will probably perceive the repetition as an indication that the point must have greater importance and should, therefore, be remembered. Repetition is widely used because it is relatively easy to practice and quite effective. If you want the audience to remember your exact word, then you can repeat it once or twice: "The number is 572638, that's 5, 7, 2, 6, 3, 8," or "A ring-shaped coral island almost or completely surrounding a lagoon is called an atoll—the word is *atoll*."

If you want the audience to remember an idea but not necessarily the specific language, you will probably restate it rather than repeating it. Whereas **repetition** is the exact use of the same words, **restatement** is echoing the same idea but in different words: for instance, "The population is 975,439—that's roughly one million people" or "The test will be comprised of about four essay questions; that is, all the questions on the test will be the kind that require you to discuss in some detail."

Emphasizing through transition   **Transitions** are the words, phrases, and sentences that show idea relationships. Transitions summarize, clarify, forecast, and, in almost every instance, emphasize.

Our language contains a number of words that show idea relationships. Words like "also," "likewise," and "moreover" forecast additional material; words like "therefore," "all in all," and "in short" bring ideas together to show results; words like "but," "however," and "on the other hand" indicate changes in direction; and words like "in other words," "for example," and "that is to say" explain or exemplify. The following list shows transitional words and their uses.

TRANSITIONS	USES
also and likewise again in addition moreover	You will use these words to add material.
therefore and so so finally all in all on the whole in short	You will use these expressions to add up consequences, to summarize, or to show results.
but however yet on the other hand still although while no doubt	You will use these expressions to indicate changes in direction, concessions, or a return to a previous position.
because for	You will use these words to indicate reasons for a statement.
then since as	You will use these words to show causal or time relationships.
in other words in fact for example that is to say more specifically	You will use these expressions to explain, exemplify, or limit.

Moreover, you can make statements that call special attention to words and ideas. Such special-attention statements act like a tour guide leading the audience through the speech. At the start of the body of the speech, you might say, "This speech will have three major parts." After a main heading in a process speech, you might say, "Now that we see what the ingredients are, let's move on to the second step; stripping the surface."

In addition to acting like a tour guide, special-attention transitions can announce the importance of a particular word or idea. You might say, "Now I come to the most important idea in the speech," or "If you haven't remembered anything so far, make sure you remember this," or "But maybe I should say this again, because it is so important." These examples represent only a few of the possible expressions that interrupt the flow of ideas and interject subjective keys, clues, and directions to stimulate audience memory or understanding.

Appropriateness

The final aspect of an effective oral style is appropriateness. **Appropriateness** means using language that adapts to the needs, interests, knowledge, and attitudes of the audience. Appropriate language cements the bond of trust between speaker and audience. In most situations the more personal you can make your language, the more appropriate it will be.

Using personal pronouns　Often by merely speaking in terms of "you," "us," "we," and "our," you will give the audience a verbal clue to your interest in them. In a speech on football defenses, instead of saying, "When *an individual* goes to a football game, *he* often wonders why defensive players change their position just before the ball is snapped," why not try "When *you* go to a football game, *you* may often wonder why players change their position just before the ball is snapped." Although this pronoun change may seem to be a very small point, it may make the difference between audience attention and audience indifference.

Asking rhetorical questions　Although public speaking is not direct conversation with your audience, you can create the impression of direct conversation by asking rhetorical questions. **Rhetorical questions** are questions phrased to encourage a mental response rather than an actual audience response. Rhetorical questions encourage mental participation; once audiences start participating, they become more involved with the content of the speech. For instance, one more change in the football example we used above would increase the audience adaptation. Instead of saying, "When you go to a football game, you may often wonder why players change their position just before the ball is snapped," you might ask "When you go to a football game, have you ever asked, 'I wonder why Kessel moved to the other side of the line before the snap' or 'I wonder why Jones started to rush the passer and then all of a sudden stepped back'?"

Sharing common experience　If you think your audience has had experiences like yours, share them in the speech. Talking about common experiences will allow your audience to identify more with you. If you were talking to a group of Girl or Boy Scouts, to drive home the point that really important tasks require hours of hard work, you might say, "Remember the hours you put in working on your first merit badge? Remember wondering whether you'd ever get the darned thing finished? And do you remember how good it felt to know that the time you put in really paid off?" (Notice how this example incorporates common experience along with personal pronouns and rhetorical questions to heighten the adaptation.) When members of an audience identify with you as a speaker, they will pay more attention to what you have to say.

Speaking hypothetically   Although you cannot involve the audience directly with every topic, you can relate to them by speaking hypothetically. If you were talking to a garden club about chartering an airplane for a group vacation, you might use the following hypothetical discussion:

▶   Let's say that for your club trip this month you wanted to go to the Tulip Festival in Holland, Michigan. Now, you could drive, but 500 miles is a long way to drive. You could fly, but individual passage from here to Holland, Michigan, would be pretty expensive, plus you'd have to make two intermediate stops. Now, if you chartered an airplane, you could fly directly to Holland for a lot less.

Even though the example is only hypothetical, for purposes of audience adaptation it would work quite well.

PRACTICE

Clarity, Vividness, Emphasis, and Appropriateness

1. Revise each of the following sentences to make them clearer and/or more vivid:

- The game was fun.
- The dinner was tasty.
- He talks mean.
- The class is yucky.

2. Divide into groups of three (this may be combined with the previous exercise). A talks with B, and C observes. During the discussion C should try to keep track of the way ideas are expressed—note vivid versus trite or common, clear versus unclear. After five minutes of discussion, the observers share their comments. Then switch speakers and observer.

3. Divide into groups of three. Each person prepares a one-minute statement containing at least *five* facts on the topic. In the presentation the speakers should practice proportion, repetition,

and transition to emphasize the five facts. After the presentation the two listeners indicate the order of importance of the facts. Each person should be given one or two opportunities to speak.

4. What methods could you use to relate the following ideas to your class? Share methods with other members of your group.

- People are afraid to report venereal disease to authorities.
- Pitching horseshoes is fun.
- The average American watches a lot of television.
- The Amazon basin is a dense jungle.

PRACTICING THE DELIVERY

When Demosthenes, the famous Athenian orator, was asked, "What is the single most important element of speaking?" he answered, "Delivery." And, of course, you've often heard people say, "It's not what you say but how you say it that counts."

Why do people place such emphasis on the importance of delivery? Primarily because delivery is the source of our contact with the speaker's mind. Delivery is what we see and what we hear. Think of delivery as a window through which we see a speech: When it is cracked, clouded over, or dirty, it obscures the content, organization, and language of the speech; when it is clean, it allows us to appreciate every aspect of the speech more fully. Although delivery cannot improve the ideas of a speech, it can help to make the most of those ideas.

Delivery is the use of voice and body to communicate the message of the speech. Your delivery will be evaluated by an audience on conversational quality, the effective use of voice, and bodily action.

Conversational Quality

Conversational quality means that good speech delivery should *sound* like conversation to an audience. Although speeches and conversation are different, using the best characteristics of conversation in your speeches will give listeners the feeling that you are conversing with them. A good conversational quality is achieved with enthusiasm, eye contact, and spontaneity.

Enthusiasm   Good conversationalists and good public speakers are enthusiastic about what they have to say. A review of speech research shows that by far the most important element of effective speaking is speaker enthusiasm. A speaker who looks and sounds enthusiastic will be listened to, and that speaker's ideas will be remembered. If you really want to communicate, if you really care about your topic and your audience, your voice will show your enthusiasm, and your audience will listen.

If you are an outgoing person who displays feelings openly, you may find it easy to sound enthusiastic in your speech. If you are rather reserved, your audience may not pick up the more subtle signs of your enthusiasm as readily. You may have to work to intensify your feelings about what you are doing so that the emotions can be communicated. How can you do this?

First, select a topic that really excites you. The outgoing person might be able to show enthusiasm about an uninspiring topic—the reserved person cannot. Second, get involved in the material. Try to develop vivid mental pictures of what you are trying to say. Mental activity will lead to physical activity. Third, remind yourself that your speech will benefit the audience. If you can convince yourself that your audience really ought to listen, you will raise your level of enthusiasm.

Eye contact   Good conversationalists and good public speakers look at their listeners while they talk. Good eye contact helps audiences concentrate. We expect speakers to look at us while they are talking. If they do not, we are unlikely to continue to pay attention to them either in conversation or in public speeches.

In addition to holding audience attention, good eye contact also increases audience confidence in the speaker. It is perceived as a sign of speaker sincerity.

Good **eye contact** involves looking at individuals and small groups in all parts of your audience throughout your speech. So long as you are looking at people and not at the ceiling, the floor, or out the window, everyone in the audience will perceive you as having good eye contact. But don't spend all your time looking front and center. The people at the ends of the aisles and those in the back of the room are every bit as important as those right in front of you.

Spontaneity   Good conversationalists and good public speakers talk spontaneously. A **spontaneous** speech is one that is fresh. Remember how painful it was to listen to class members reciting bits of prose or poetry they had memorized? Since the people were struggling so hard to remember the words, they were not communicating any sense of meaning. The words sounded memorized, not spontaneous. Although good actors can make lines they have spoken literally thousands of times sound spontaneous, most public speakers cannot. Avoid memorizing a speech word for word; instead, allow some variation in your wording each time you practice or give a speech.

Voice, Articulation, and Bodily Action

Just as our words communicate, so does the sound of our voice. The meanings expressed by the way we sound (called *paralanguage*) may tell our audience what we intended and may contribute to the meanings of our words. However, *how* we sound may interfere with sharing meaning and may at times even contradict our words.

Our voice has all the capabilities of a musical instrument. The major characteristics of pitch, volume, rate, and quality of voice work together to give us the variety, expressiveness, and precision in meaning that assist communication.

Pitch   **Pitch** refers to the highness or lowness of your voice. Your voice is produced in the larynx by the vibration of your vocal folds. In order to feel this vibration, put your hand on your throat at the top of the Adam's apple and say "ah." Now, just as the pitch of a violin string is changed by making it tighter or looser, so the pitch of your voice is changed by the tightening and loosening of the vocal folds.

Fortunately, most people speak at a pitch that is about right for them. A few persons do have pitch problems. If you have questions about your pitch level, ask your professor about it. If you are one of the few people with a pitch problem, your professor can refer you to a speech therapist for corrective work. Since for most of us our normal pitch is satisfactory, the question is whether we are making the best use of our pitch range.

Volume   The loudness of the tone you make is its **volume**. You increase volume by contracting your abdominal muscles, thus giving greater force to the air you expel when you breathe.

To feel how these muscles work, place your hands on your sides with your fingers extended over the stomach. Say "ah" in a normal voice. Now say "ah" as loud as you can. If you are making proper use of your muscles, you should feel the stomach contraction increase as you increase volume. If you feel little or no muscle contraction, you are probably trying to gain volume from the wrong source, and such a practice can then result in tiredness, harshness, and lack of sufficient volume to be heard in a large room.

Each person, regardless of size, can make his or her voice louder. If you have trouble talking loudly enough to be heard in a large classroom, work on increasing pressure on exhalation from the abdominal area.

Rate   Our **rate** of speech is the speed at which we talk. Although most of us talk between 140 and 180 words per minute, the best rate is a highly individual matter. The test of rate is whether an audience can understand what you are saying. Usually even very fast talking is acceptable if words are well articulated and if there is sufficient vocal variety and emphasis. If your instructor believes you talk too fast or too slowly, he or she will tell you and suggest ways you can improve.

Quality   The tone, timbre, or sound of your voice is its **quality**. The best vocal quality is a clear, pleasant-to-listen-to voice. Problems of quality are nasality (too much resonance in the nose on vowel sounds), breathiness (too much escaping of air during phonation), harshness (too much tension in throat and chest), and hoarseness (a raspy sound to the voice). If your voice seems to have too great a degree of one of these undesirable qualities, consult your professor. Although you can make some improvement on your own, improvement requires a great deal of work and rather extensive knowledge of vocal anatomy and physiology. Severe problems of vocal quality should be referred to a speech therapist.

Vocal variety and emphasis   These involve your use of the voice to help listeners understand *your* meaning. By **variety**, we mean contrasts: higher or lower pitch, louder or softer, faster or slower. These variations give the voice the dimension that makes it easier or harder for an audience to pay attention and to understand. Take the simple sentence "I am not going to the movie." The entire meaning of the sentence depends upon how you say it. If you emphasize "not," the sentence means you are answering the question of *whether* you are going; if you emphasize "movie," the sentence means you are answering the question of *where* you are going. If you were to speak the sentence in a monotone with all words at the same pitch, the same volume, and the same rate (speed), the listener could not be sure what question you were answering. The more variety and emphasis, the more meaning is communicated.

If you want to check your variety and emphasis, get someone to listen as you read short passages aloud. Ask the person to tell you which words were higher in pitch, or louder, or slower. When you find that you can give a speech in such a way that the person recognizes which words you were trying to emphasize, you will be showing improvement in using vocal variety to clarify meaning.

Articulation   **Articulation** is the shaping of speech sounds into recognizable oral symbols that go together to produce a word. Many speakers suffer from minor articulation problems of adding a sound where none appears (ath*a*lete for athlete), leaving out a sound where one occurs (li*b*ary for li*br*ary), transposing sounds (rev*a*lent for re*lev*ant), and distorting sounds (tru*f* for tru*th*). Although some people have consistent articulation problems that require speech therapy (substituting *th* for *s* consistently in speech), most of us are guilty of carelessness that is easily corrected.

Articulation is often confused with *pronunciation*, the form and accent of various syllables of a word. In the word "statistics," articulation refers to the shaping of the ten sounds (*s, t, a, t, i, s, t, i, k, s*); pronunciation refers to the grouping and accenting of the sounds (*sta tis' tiks*). If you are unsure of how to pronounce a word you are going to use in your speech, look it up in a dictionary.

Although true articulatory problems (distortion, omission, substitution, or addition of sounds) need to be corrected by a speech therapist, the kinds of articulatory problems shown by most college students can be improved during a single term. The two most common faults for most students are slurring sounds (running sounds and words together) and leaving off word endings. Spoken English will always contain some running together of sounds. For instance everyone says "tha-table" for "that table." It is just too difficult to make two "t" sounds in a row. But many of us slur sounds and drop word endings to excess. "Who ya goin' ta see?" for "Who are you going to see?" illustrates both these errors. If you have a mild case of "sluritis," caused by not taking the time to form sounds clearly, you can make considerable improvement by taking 10 to 15 minutes three days a week to read passages aloud, trying to *overaccentuate* each of the sounds. Some teachers advocate "chewing" your words, that is, making sure that you move your lips, jaw, and tongue very carefully for each sound you make. As with most other problems of delivery, you must work conscientiously several days a week for months to bring about significant improvement.

Since constant mispronunciation and misarticulation labels a person as ignorant or careless (or both), you will want to try to correct mistakes that you make. Figure 14.1 indicates many common problem words that students are likely to mispronounce or misarticulate in their speeches.

FIGURE 14 · 1   PROBLEM WORDS

Word	Correct	Incorrect
arctic	*arc' tic*	*ar' tic*
athlete	*ath' lete*	*ath' a lete*
family	*fam' a ly*	*fam' ly*
February	*Feb' ru ary*	*Feb' yu ary*
get	*get*	*git*
larynx	*ler' inks*	*lar' nix*
library	*ly' brer y*	*ly' ber y*
particular	*par tik' yu ler*	*par tik' ler*
picture	*pic' ture*	*pitch' er*
recognize	*rek' ig nize*	*rek' a nize*
relevant	*rel' e vant*	*rev' e lant*
theater	*thee' a ter*	*thee ay' ter*
truth	*truth*	*truf*
with	*with*	*wit* or *wid*

Bodily Action

Your nonverbal communication, or bodily action, says the same kinds of things in a speech as it does in normal interpersonal or group communication. It is true that when you get in front of an audience, you may tend to freeze up—that is, to limit your normal nonverbal action—and occasionally the speaking situation may bring out nervous mannerisms that are not so noticeable in your daily speaking. However, if you are thinking actively about what you are saying, your bodily action will probably be appropriate. If you use either too much or too little bodily action, your instructor can give you some pointers for limiting or accenting your normal behavior. Although you may find minor errors, you should not be concerned unless your bodily action calls attention to itself—then you should determine ways of controlling or changing the behavior.

During practice sessions you may try various methods to monitor or alter your bodily action. If you have access to video tape, you will have an excellent means of monitoring your bodily action. You may want to practice in front of a mirror to see how you look to others when you speak. (Although some speakers swear by this method, others find it a traumatic experience.) Perhaps the best is to get a willing listener to critique your bodily action and help you improve. Once you have identified the behavior you want to change, you can tell your helper what to look for. For instance, you might say, "Raise your hand every time I begin to rock back and forth." By getting specific feedback when the behavior occurs, you can make immediate adjustment.

PRACTICE

Voice and Bodily Action

1. Indicate what you regard as your major problem of voice and articulation (such as speaking in a monotone or slurring words). Outline a plan for working on the problem.

2. Divide into groups of three to six. Each person should have at least two minutes to tell a personal experience. The other members of the group should observe for any problems in vocal variety and emphasis, articulation, and bodily action.

Methods of Delivery

How you proceed at this point in your preparation depends on your method of delivery. Speeches may be delivered impromptu, by manuscript, by memorization, or extemporaneously.

An *impromptu* speech is done on the spur of the moment, without previous specific preparation. Although nearly all of our conversation is impromptu, most people prefer to prepare their thoughts well ahead of the time they face an audience. Regardless of how good you are at daily communication, you would be foolhardy to leave your preparation and analysis for formal speeches to chance. Audiences expect to hear a speech that was well thought out beforehand.

A common and often misused mode of delivery is the *manuscript* speech. Because the speech is written out in full and then read aloud, the wording can be planned very carefully. Although presidents and other heads of state have good reason to resort to the manuscript (even the slightest mistake in sentence construction could cause a national outcry), most speakers have little need to prepare a manuscript. Often their only excuse is the false sense of security that the written speech provides. The major disadvantages of manuscript speeches, as you can attest from your listening experience, are that they are not likely to be very spontaneous, very stimulating, or very interesting. Poor manuscript speaking results from a natural tendency to write a speech without any audience adaptation within it. Because of these difficulties, you should usually avoid manuscript speaking, except as a special assignment.

A *memorized* speech is merely a manuscript committed to memory. In addition to the opportunity to polish the wording, memorization allows the speaker to look at the audience while speaking. Unfortunately for beginning speakers, memorization has the same disadvantages as the manuscript. Few individuals are able to memorize so well that their speech sounds spontaneous. Since a speech that sounds memorized affects an audience adversely, you should also avoid memorization for your first speech assignment.

Most speeches you will give, in class and out, will be delivered extemporaneously. In ordinary conversation extemporaneous is often used synonymously with impromptu. In a public-speaking context, though, an *extemporaneous* speech is prepared and practiced, but the exact wording is determined at the time of utterance. Why should most of your speeches be given extemporaneously? Extemporaneous speaking gives a lot more control to the speech than does impromptu speaking, but it maintains the spontaneity. It allows for far greater spontaneity and opportunity for audience adaptation than the full manuscript or memorized speech, but it is fully prepared. Most experienced speakers prefer the extemporaneous method for most of their speeches. Now let's consider how a speech can be carefully prepared without being memorized.

Rehearsing the Speech

Novice speakers often believe that preparation is complete once the outline has been finished. Nothing could be further from the truth. If you are scheduled to speak at 9 A.M. Monday and you have not finished the outline for the speech until 8:45 A.M. Monday, the speech is not likely to be as good as it could have been had you allowed yourself sufficient practice time. You should try to complete your outline at least two days before the speech is due. This will give you time to practice your speech. Practice gives you a chance to revise, evaluate, mull over, and consider all aspects of the speech.

A good rehearsal period involves going through the speech, analyzing what you did, and then going through the speech again.

FIRST PRACTICE

1. Read through your outline once or twice to get ideas in mind. Then put the outline out of sight.
2. Stand up and face your imaginary audience. You want to make the practice as similar to the speech situation as possible. If you are practicing in your room, pretend that the chairs, lamps, books, and other objects in your view are people.
3. Write down the time that you begin.
4. Begin the speech. Keep going until you have finished the ideas.
5. Write down the time you finish. Compute the length of the speech for this first practice.

ANALYSIS

Look at your outline again. Then begin the analysis. Did you leave out any key ideas? Did you talk too long on any one point and not long enough on another? Did you really clarify each of your points? Did you try to adapt to your anticipated audience?

SECOND PRACTICE

Go through the entire process again. If you can get a friend or relative to listen to later practices, so much the better.

After you have completed one full rehearsal period consisting of two sessions of practices and criticism, put the speech away for a while. Although you may need to go through the speech three, four, or even ten times, there is no value in going through all the sessions consecutively. You may find that a practice session right before you go to bed will be very helpful; while you are sleeping, your subconscious will continue to work on the speech. As a result, you are likely to find tremendous improvement in mastery of the speech at the first practice session the next day.

Using Notes in the Speech

Should you use notes in practice or during the speech itself? The answer depends on what you mean by notes and how you plan to use them. It is best to avoid using notes at all for the first short speech assignments. Then, when assignments get longer, you will be more likely to use notes properly and not as a crutch. Of course, there is no harm in experimenting with notes to see what effect they will have on your delivery.

Appropriate notes are composed of key words or phrases that help trigger your memory. Notes will be most useful to you when they consist of the fewest words possible written in lettering large enough to be seen instantly at a distance. Many speakers condense their written preparatory outline into a brief word or phrase outline. A typical set of notes made from the preparatory outline illustrated in Figure 13.1 is shown in Figure 14.2.

For a speech in the five- to ten-minute category, a single 3 × 5 notecard should be enough. When your speech contains a particularly good quotation or a complicated set of statistics, you may want to write them out in detail on separate 3 × 5 cards.

During practice sessions you should use notes the way you plan to use them in the speech. Either set them on the speaker's stand or hold

---

FIGURE 14 · 2

Notes

Risk factors in heart disease
Cultural (uncontrolled)
    Males more than females
    Male relative indicates tendency
    Disease in middle years
Environmental (controlled)
    Blood fat and arteries
    Obesity workload
    Smoking: lining, oxygen
    Stress and failure
    Blood pressure, wear and tear
    Exercise and work

them in one hand and refer to them only when you have to. Speakers often find that the act of making a note card is so effective in helping cement ideas in the mind that during practice, or later during the speech itself, they do not need to use the notes at all.

In any event you should practice the speech until you gain a complete understanding of meaning and order of ideas—do not try to memorize the words. When people memorize, they repeat the speech until they have mastered the wording; when people stress the learning of ideas, they practice the speech a little differently each time. For instance, practice 1 may have this wording: "A handball court is a large rectangular box 20 feet wide, 40 feet long, and 20 feet high"; practice 2 may be phrased this way: "A handball court is 20 by 40 by 20—a lot like a large rectangular box." In both practices the ideas are the same but the wording is different. When you are not tied to a particular phrasing, you can adapt to audience reaction at time of delivery; moreover, because each experience builds on the last, the speech itself is often better than any wording used during practice.

- -

PRACTICE

Rehearsal

Make a diary of your rehearsal program for your first speech. How many times did you practice? At what point did you feel you had a mastery of substance? How long was each of your practice periods?

COPING WITH NERVOUSNESS

According to their study, R. H. Bruskin Associates found that when people were asked to pick items from a list of things that frightened them, 40.6 percent said they were frightened by speaking in public—more than anything else on the list, including heights, insects, flying, sickness, and death![1] Yet you must learn to cope with nervousness, *because speaking is important.* Through speaking we show others what we are thinking. Each of us has vital information to share: We may have the data needed to solve a problem; we may have a procedure that will save countless dollars; we may have insights that will influence the way people see an issue. Think of the tremendous loss to business, governmental, educational, professional, and fraternal groups because fear prevents people from being heard!

Let's start with the assumption that you are indeed nervous—you may be scared to death. Now what? Experience has proven that people (and this includes you) can learn to cope with these fears. Consider the following points:

1. *You are in good company.* Not only do 40 percent of the population regard public speaking as the thing they fear most, but many experienced speakers confess to nervousness when they speak. Now, you may say, "Don't give me that line—you can't tell me that [fill in the blank with the name of some person you know] is nervous when he [or she] speaks in public!" Ask the person. He or she will tell you. Even famous speakers like Abraham Lincoln and Franklin D. Roosevelt were nervous before speaking. The difference in nervousness among people is a matter of degree. Some people tremble, perspire, and experience shortness of breath and increased heartbeat. As they go through their speech, they worry about themselves and lose all contact with the audience, they jump back and forth from point to point, and on occasion they forget what they had planned to say. Some people's anxiety is so great that they cannot eat or sleep before a speech, and some people avoid speaking at any cost. The question is not whether you are nervous but how you will deal with the nervousness. Good speakers learn to channel their nervousness.

2. *Despite nervousness, you can make it through a speech.* Very few people are so bothered that they are literally unable to function. You may not

Sometimes you are so nervous that your audience feels like the enemy.

enjoy the experience—but you can do it. In fact, it would be disappointing if you were not nervous. Why? Because you must be a little nervous to do your best. Of course, this does not mean that you should be blind with fear, but a bit of nervousness gets the adrenalin flowing—and that brings you to speaking readiness.

3. *Your listeners aren't nearly as likely to recognize your fear as you might think.* Inexperienced speakers find their fear increases because they perceive their audiences as recognizing their nervousness. This recognition makes the speaker more self-conscious, more nervous. The fact is that people, even speech instructors, will greatly underrate the amount of stage fright they believe a person has.[2] Recently a young woman reported that she broke out in hives before each speech. She was flabbergasted when other students said to her, "You seem so calm when you speak." Once you realize that your audience does not really recognize the fear that you as the speaker believe is so noticeable, you will no longer experience the acceleration of nervousness.

4. *The more experience you get in speaking, the better you become at coping with nervousness.* As you gain experience, you learn to think about the audience and the message and not about yourself. Moreover, you come to realize that audiences, your classmates especially, are very supportive, especially in informative speech situations. After all, most people are in the audience because they want to hear you. As time goes on you will come to find that having a group of people listening to *you alone* is a very satisfying experience.

Now let's consider what you can do about your nervousness. Coping with nervousness begins during the preparation process and extends to the time you actually begin the speech.

The very best behavior for controlling nervousness is to pick a topic you know something about and are interested in. Public speakers cannot allow themselves to be content with a topic they don't care about. An unsatisfactory topic lays the groundwork for a psychological mind set that almost guarantees nervousness at the time of the speech. By the same token, having a topic that you know about and are truly interested in lays the groundwork for a satisfying speech experience. In Chapter 12 we emphasized how to ensure that you had the best topic possible. Heed that advice and you will be well on the way to reducing nervousness.

During the preparation period you can also be "psyching yourself up" for the speech. If you have a good topic, and if you are well prepared, your audience is going to profit from listening to you. That's right—even though this is only a class and not a professional speaking experience, the audience is going to be glad they have heard you. Now, before you say, "Come on, who are you trying to kid!" think of speeches you have heard. When someone had really good ideas, weren't you impressed? Of course you were. The fact is that some of the speeches you hear in class are some of the best and most valuable speeches you are ever going to hear. Students learn to put time and effort into their speeches, and many of their speeches turn out to be quite good. If you work at it, your class will look forward to listening to you.

Perhaps the most important time for you is shortly before you give your speech. Research indicates that it is during the period right before you walk up to give your speech and the time when you have your initial contact with the audience that your fear is most likely to be at its greatest.[3]

When speeches are being scheduled, you may be able to control when you speak. Are you better off "getting it over with," that is, being the first person to speak that day? If so, you can usually volunteer to go first. But regardless of when you speak, don't spend your time thinking about yourself or your speech. At the moment the class begins, you have done all you can to be prepared. This is the time to get your mind on something else. Try to listen to each of the speeches that comes before yours. Get involved with what each speaker is saying. Then when your turn comes, you will be as relaxed as possible.

As you walk to the speaker's stand, remind yourself that you have good ideas, that you are well prepared, and that your audience is going to want to hear what you have to say. Even if you make mistakes, the audience will profit from your speech.

When you reach the stand, pause a few seconds before you start. Take a deep breath; this may help get your breathing in order. Try to get movement into your speech during the first few sentences. Sometimes a few gestures or a step one way or another is enough to break some of the tension.

PUBLIC-SPEAKING EVALUATION

Public speeches are fair game. Perhaps more than any other form of communication, a speech is evaluated instantly by nearly everyone who hears it. If evaluation is to help a speaker, some form of analysis is necessary. In this section we want to outline the key elements that should be considered in determining a speech's value. Our goal is not only to determine whether a speech was "good" or "bad" but also to determine what made the speech more or less effective in achieving its behavioral goal.

When is a speaker a success? On the surface, a speaker is successful when he or she is able (1) to achieve the behavioral objective sought or (2) to bring the audience significantly closer to that objective. If what a speaker says motivates you to go see a particular movie or convinces you that Congress should pass handgun control laws or helps you understand how the pyramids were built, then the speech has been successful. Yet sometimes the speaker reaches a measure of success even when the desired behavior is not achieved. If none of the members of the audience were planning to go see the particular movie but after hearing what you had to say some were willing to consider going, or if most members of the audience were hostile to any form of gun control legislation but now they are willing to weigh the arguments, or if the majority of the audience had no idea how the pyramids were built but now they have some comprehension, then you will have achieved some measure of success.

Is a successful speaker a good speaker? Success is the goal of any speaker. But success alone does not make a good speaker. Hitler was successful; Senator Joseph McCarthy was successful; nearly every demagogue of history can thank speaking skill for at least part of his or her success. As we know, speakers can always increase their chances of success by lying to their listeners, by distorting, by relying on emotion to inflame the passions, or by other unethical means. But unethical speakers cannot be called good speakers. Public speakers in the public forum have a great responsibility; those who cannot or will not bear that responsibility achieve their success only through trickery and cannot or should not be acclaimed.

What criteria can you apply in your evaluation? First, how well did the speaker adapt to the occasion? If a speaker faces 5,000 people in the university field house but the public address system is bad and the seating arrangements unfavorable, the speaker will have little chance of success even though the majority of the audience are advocates of the speaker's ideas.

A successful speaker generally views the audience as a friend—and, usually, friendliness soon results.

Second, how well did the speaker adapt to the audience? The age, sex, occupation, religion, socioeconomic level, attitudes, interests, and knowledge of the audience all affect how that audience will view the speaker's ideas. For instance, although an audience of auto dealers is not likely to be receptive to Ralph Nader's ideas on methods of controlling air pollution, it is likely to be receptive to those of Lee Iacocca.

Third, and most important, how good were the content, the organization, and the presentation of the speech? Since we have covered each of these elements of the speech in detail earlier, let's now turn to the evaluation questionnaire (Appendix B-6).

PRACTICE

Speech Evaluation

Use the material presented in Appendix B-6 to evaluate a speech.

SUMMARY

Effective speakers adapt their language to the audience. Speech language must be clear, vivid, emphatic, and appropriate to the audience.

Effective speeches are well delivered. Good delivery requires enthusiasm, good eye contact, and spontaneity and is achieved through voice and bodily action. Methods of delivery are impromptu, manuscript, memorization, and extemporaneous speaking. Between the time the outline has been completed and the time the speech is to be given, you will want to practice the speech several times, weighing what you did and how you did it after each practice.

Speech nervousness is a common experience and may be eased, if not entirely overcome, through careful speech preparation.

SUGGESTED READINGS

Blankenship, Jane. *A Sense of Style*. Belmont, Calif.: Dickenson, 1968. A great deal of valuable information about style in a short paperback volume.

Clevenger, Theodore, Jr. "A Synthesis of Experimental Research in Stage Fright," *Quarterly Journal of Speech* 45 (April 1959), 134–145. This article draws 11 conclusions about stage fright that are still consistent with recent data.

Fisher, Hilda. *Improving Voice and Articulation.* 3rd ed. Boston: Houghton Mifflin, 1981. Of the many good books on voice and articulation, this is one of the best.

McCroskey, James C. "Oral Communication Apprehension: A Summary of Recent Theory and Research," *Human Communication Research* 4 (1977), 78. A companion article to the Clevenger article cited above.

Newman, Edwin. *Strictly Speaking: Will America Be the Death of English?* New York: Warner, 1975 (paperback). A highly readable and popular look at contemporary problems of English usage.

15 *I*NFORMATIVE *S*PEAKING

OBJECTIVES

After you have read this chapter, you should be able to:

1   List and explain the goals of informative speaking

2   Demonstrate a process

3   Narrate an event

4   Describe an object

5   Define a concept

6   Report information

Information—it's difficult to do anything without adequate, accurate information. In spite of our most advanced technology for information dissemination and retrieval, we still get a great deal of the information we need or want through the spoken word. You listen to your radio or your television for the news of the day. You attend classroom lectures to learn psychology, economics, history, and the like. You listen to your friends, neighbors, and co-workers to find out how to get from here to there, how to bake a carrot cake, how the new computer works, and literally thousands of other topics.

Unfortunately our own abilities to process and disseminate information have not improved as fast as our technological means. As much as we talk, most of us are not nearly so good at information exchange as we could be. Yet learning to share information clearly and interestingly is not all that difficult. It does, however, require an understanding of basic principles and a plan for applying them effectively. First, we consider the goals of information exchange; then we examine the means of demonstrating, narrating, describing, defining, and reporting.

GOALS OF INFORMATION EXCHANGE

In this course you are likely to be asked to give one or more informative speeches. Although you may not be able to "teach" your classmates, you can *help* them learn the material you present. You can do this (1) by helping them become receptive to the information, (2) by helping them *understand* the material through vivid explanation and application, and (3) by helping them *retain* the material they have received. An informative speech can focus on any one or more of these three goals.

PRINCIPLES OF INFORMATIVE SPEAKING

Before we consider the specific means of sharing information, let us consider basic principles of informative speaking that will help you get an audience to listen, to understand, and to remember. In this section we present eight principles under the headings of relevance, newness, emphasis, and creativity.

Relevance of Information

Audiences are more likely to listen to information they perceive as relevant. Rather than acting like a sponge, absorbing every bit of information that comes our way, most of us act more like filters: We pay attention only to information we perceive as relevant.

The ultimate in relevance is information people perceive as vital, that is, information that is truly a matter of life and death. Just as police cadets are likely to pay attention when the subject is what to do when attacked, so will members of your audience pay attention when they think what you have to tell them is critical to them. Although very little of what you tell an audience will actually help them stay alive, you can focus on points that will improve the quality of their lives. For instance, students are likely to pay attention when they are being told what is going to be on the mid-term; men and women pay attention when they are being told what they can do to ensure fidelity of their girlfriend, boyfriend, or spouse; and college seniors will pay attention to suggestions for increasing their likelihood of getting a job.

If your speech material can promise vital information, you can and should take advantage of it. But even when what you have to say seems somewhat remote from audience experience, you can usually build some relevance if you will think creatively and take the time to work at it. A speech on Japan can focus on the importance of Japanese manufacturing to our economy; a speech on the Egyptian pyramids can be related to our interest in building techniques. Audience relevance can be shown for *any* topic. It is up to you to find that relevance and make a point of it in your speech.

One very good way of discovering relevance is to consider information as answers to questions audiences have. Suppose you were giving a speech on weather forecasting. How relevant that is to your audience will depend in part on what need the audience has for the information. Many student activities are weather dependent. Since most students have plans for such things as attending a football game, going on a picnic, taking a hike, or playing a game, the weather is relevant to them. By referring to how weather affects these activities, you would be more likely to get and to hold their attention than if you ignored those obvious ties. So in terms of your topic, what does your audience need to know? How does your information meet their needs?

Newness of Information

Audiences are more likely to listen to information they perceive as new. When people think they already know the information you are presenting, they are less likely to pay attention. It is up to you as speaker not only to find information that will be new to your audience but also to feature the newness.

But how do you know what is new to your audience of college students? Beginning speakers often overestimate an audience's amount of specific information. Your audience is likely to be comprised of some extremely intelligent and able students. Nevertheless, even intelligent people do not necessarily have a great amount of specific information about even those subjects they are familiar with. Recently a young woman speaking in class mentioned the name of Adolf Hitler and then went on to say that Hitler was a twentieth-century example of tremendous oppression. She was very surprised when many of the people in her audience gave her vague looks.

In most of your speeches, then, you will want to make sure that you take time to give the details about information that you regard as key to audience understanding of your topic.

How can you be sure of the information level of your audience? A week or so before your speech, you can circulate a questionnaire containing questions about key information related to your topic. Or you can talk to two or three people before one of the classes to get an idea of their level of knowledge. Or you can assume that most of your audience will have roughly the same level of information you have. If before you prepared for your speech you did not know the answers to several key questions covered in the speech, then you can assume that many members of your class will not either.

Even when you are talking about a topic that most of the people in your audience are familiar with, you can uncover new angles, new applications, new perspectives on the material. If you are planning to talk about football, it is likely that most people will know what the game of football is and how points are scored. But a speech on zone defenses may provide new information even to folks who think they have a pretty good grasp of football. The principle is not to change the topic but to keep thinking about the topic in different ways until you have uncovered an aspect that will be new to most of the audience.

New information is even better received when it is novel. *Novelty* is newness with a special pull, something unexpected that commands our involuntary attention. For instance, in a speech on the perils of cliff diving, an audience is likely to listen because of the novelty of the topic itself. If the topic itself is not novel, the next best thing is to take a novel approach to the material by focusing on the features that make the information unusual. A Rolls Royce grill makes a standard Volkswagen bug novel; solar heating makes a three-bedroom ranch-style house novel. Novelty is often the product of the creative mind. We consider creativity in speech making later in this chapter.

Emphasizing Ideas

Audiences are more likely to remember information that is emphasized. One way of emphasizing information in a speech is to organize the information in a way that focuses on key ideas. Good organization does not necessarily influence the total amount of information remembered. If an audience listens to two 30-minute speeches, one well organized and one disorganized, the audience is likely to remember about the same amount of information. The difference is that with the well-organized speech it is possible to influence *what* the audience will remember by emphasizing key points. Taking the time to organize well puts you in control.

The old journalistic advice, "Tell them what you're going to tell them, tell them, and tell them what you've told them," recognizes the importance of organization. The speaker who states, "In my speech I will cover three goals; the first is . . . the second is . . . and the third is . . ." will often have more success getting an audience to remember than one who does not. Likewise, such transitional statements as "Now we come to the second key point" or "Here's where we move from the third stage of development to the fourth" have proven effective in directing audience thinking.

A second way of emphasizing key information is to repeat it. Determine the two, three, four, or five most important words, ideas, or concepts in the speech and repeat them for emphasis. Sometimes you will want to repeat the words or ideas just as you said them: "The tallest building in the world is the Sears Tower in Chicago—that's the Sears Tower in Chicago." Other times you may want the audience to remember the idea but not necessarily the specific words. So instead of repeating the words, you will restate the idea: "The Sears Tower is 1454 feet high—that's roughly 1500 feet!"

Creativity

Audiences are more likely to remember information that is presented creatively. First, we will consider the nature of creativity; then we will discuss several specific ways of making your speeches more creative.

The nature of creativity   John Haefele defines creativity "as the ability to make *new* combinations."[1] A creative speech is new; it is not copied, imitated, or reproduced. In short, your speech must be a product of, but not entirely different from, the sources you used. You find material, you put it in a usable form, and then you inject your own insights, your own personality into the speech—insights and personality are the foundation of creativity.

Some people believe that creativity is possible only for a gifted personality. Actually, we all have the potential for thinking creatively—some of us just have not given ourselves a chance to try.

To be creative you must first have enough information to give you a broad base from which to work. Mark Twain is said to have been the first to speak of invention being 1 percent inspiration and 99 percent perspiration. What this means is that you must have done your homework on the topic. The more you know, the more likely you are to approach the topic creatively.

Second, and equally important, give yourself enough time for the creative process to work. Once you think you are prepared (say, when you have completed your outline), you need time, perhaps two or three days, for your mind to reflect upon the material. You may find that the morning after a few uninspiring practices you suddenly have two or three fresh ideas for lines of development. While you were sleeping, your mind was still going over the material. When you awoke, the product of unconscious or subconscious thought reached the level of consciousness. Had there been no intervening time between those unrewarding practice sessions and the actual speech delivery, your mind would not have had the time to work through the material. Sometimes we are not creative simply because we have not given our minds time to process the material we have.

Third, practice different ways of expressing important ideas. Beginning speakers are often so pleased to have found a way of expressing an idea that they are content with the first thought that comes to mind. Suppose that for a speech on computers you thought you would begin with "Years ago, even the simplest computer had to be housed in a large room; today you can hold a functioning computer in your hand. Let's examine some of the advances that have led to computer miniaturization." Now, there is probably nothing wrong with that opening, but is it the best you can do? You cannot know until you have tried other ways. Brainstorm a little. Start your speech in two, three, or even five different ways. Chances are that one or two of the ways will be far superior and much more imaginative than any of the others.

Another way to find different expressions of an idea is by being familiar with possible lines of development and by trying to take an idea along each of the possible lines. With any given set of facts you may create several lines of development. Let us say that you are to give a speech about London. You learn that London is a city of 7 million people, it rests roughly at the fifty-first parallel, its average temperature is in the mid-sixties in the summer and in the mid-forties in the winter, and it is the largest city in a nation of some 50,000 square miles. With only these four facts about London, you could still be creative. For instance, you could develop a comparative line by showing each of these in comparison with a familiar spot in the United States. You could develop a generalization line by making a statement using each of the facts as an example. Or you could develop an illustration or story line by taking one of the facts and developing a hypothetical situation. The potential is limited only by your willingness to work with the available materials.

Fourth, you must be prepared for creative inspiration whenever it comes. Have you ever noticed how ideas come to you while you are washing dishes or watching television or waiting at a stop light? Have you also noticed that when you try to recall those ideas later, many have slipped away? Many speakers, writers, and composers carry a pencil and paper with them at all times; when an idea comes, they make note of it. Not all of these inspirations are the flashes of creative genius, but some of them are at least worth exploring. If you do not make note of them, you will never know whether they were good or not.

Finally, by definition creativity suggests occasional failure. You may work for two hours on a line of development that seems remarkably creative only to discover that it is inappropriate, wrong, or just plain ridiculous. If so, you have to be willing to forget the whole thing and start again. Creativity involves risk. When it pays off, it pays off in "A" speeches, audience applause, and high regard for your work. But when it misfires, you must be willing to chalk it up to experience and start again.

Creativity in speeches   One way to show creativity in your speeches is by associating ideas. *Association* is the tendency of one thought to recall another similar to it. That means when one word, idea, or event reminds you of another, you are associating. When you walk into a room of people, you seek out familiar faces. Likewise, when you are confronted with information that you do not readily understand, your ear listens for certain familiar notes that will put the new information into perspective. Through vivid comparisons, a speaker can take advantage of this tendency on the part of the audience by associating new and difficult information with the familiar.

If you were trying to show your audience how a television picture tube works, you could build an association between the unknown of the television tube and audience knowledge. The metaphor "a television picture tube is a gun shooting beams of light" would be an excellent association between the known and the unknown. The image of a shooting gun is a familiar one. A gun shooting beams of light is easy to visualize. If you made the association striking enough, every time your audience thought of a television picture tube, they would associate it with a gun shooting beams of light. If you can establish one or more associations during your speech, you are helping to ensure audience retention of key ideas.

A second way you can show creativity in your speeches is to express ideas with *emotional impact*. Think back over your life and recall what stands out most vividly about the past. What you probably remember most readily are happenings, events, experiences, or accidents that had highly emotional impact. Was it the day you got to drive the family car for the first time? Or the time you fell off the ladder reaching a little too far when you were painting? Or your first kiss? A good speaker can create this kind of impact through vivid anecdotes, illustrations, and examples. The more vivid you make your development, the more powerful the emotional impact will be. Too much repetition can become boring, but audiences seldom tire of emotional impact.

Some speakers achieve emotional impact through startling statements. Startling statements give an audience an emotional jolt. If your professor wears a new sports coat, it may get your attention; if your professor comes to class wearing a toga, a bearskin, or a loin cloth, it would be startling.

Startling the audience is often accomplished through action. Blowing up a balloon and letting it sail around the room to illustrate propulsion is startling. Taking off one's outer clothes in class to reveal a gym suit underneath would be startling. Sometimes, however, what you do may be so startling that the audience never recovers. Although startling actions may get attention, they can disrupt a speech if they are too overpowering.

A third way you can show creativity in your speeches is to *express ideas humorously*. You do not have to be riotously funny or sprinkle your speech with jokes—in fact, both of these methods are likely to hurt the audience's attention to your information more than they will help. To be most effective, relate humor to the topic. Here is how one speaker heightened audience interest in his speech on hotel management:

▶ Frankly, I think the hotel business has been one of the most backward in the world. There's been very little change in the attitude of room clerks in the 2000 years since Joseph arrived in Bethlehem and was told they'd lost his reservation.[2]

If trying to be funny makes you self-conscious, then do not force humor into your speech. But if you think humor is one of your strengths, then make the most of it.

DEMONSTRATING

Much of our daily talk involves explaining processes—telling how to do something, how to make something, or how something works. A **demonstration** involves going through the complete process that you are explaining. You may want to demonstrate how to get more power on a forehand table-tennis shot, how to make homemade fettucine noodles, or how to purify water.

When the task is relatively simple, you may want to try a complete demonstration. If so, practice until you can do it smoothly and easily under the pressure of facing an actual audience. Remember that in the actual speech the demonstration may take longer than in practice.

For a relatively complicated process you may want to consider the modified demonstration. For a modified demonstration you complete various stages of the demonstration at home and do only part of the actual work in front of the audience. If you were going to demonstrate construction of a floral display, you would have a complete set of materials to begin the demonstration, a mock-up of the basic floral triangle, and a completed floral display. During the speech you would first talk about all the materials you need and then you would begin the demonstration of making the basic floral triangle. Rather than try to get everything together perfectly in a few seconds, you could draw from a bag or some concealed place the partially completed arrangement that illustrates the floral triangle. You would then use this in your demonstration, adding flowers as if you were planning to complete it. Then from another bag you could draw the completed arrangement that illustrates one of the possible effects you were discussing. A modified demonstration is often easier than trying to complete an entire demonstration within a short time limit.

Throughout your demonstration, speak slowly and repeat key ideas often. We learn best by doing, so if you can include audience participation, you may be even more successful. In a speech on origami, Japanese paper folding, you could explain the principles, then pass out paper and have the audience participate in making a figure. Actual participation will increase interest and ensure recall. Finally, through other visual aids you could show how these principles are used in more elaborate projects.

Although your audience may be able to visualize the process through vivid word pictures (in fact, in your impromptu explanations in ordinary conversation it is the only way you can proceed) you will probably want to make full use of visual aids for your speech. In explaining how to make or do something—perhaps more than with any other kind of informative speech—carefully prepared visual material may be essential to listener understanding.

Visual Aids

Anything that is used to appeal to the visual sense is a visual aid. Let's look at the ones we are most likely to see used in speeches.

Yourself　Sometimes, through your gestures, movement, and personal attire, you can become your own best visual aid. Through descriptive gestures you can show the size of a soccer ball, the height of a tennis net, and the shape of a lake; through your posture and movement you can show the correct stance for skiing, a butterfly swimming stroke, and methods of artificial respiration; and through your own attire you can illustrate the native dress of a foreign country, the proper outfit for a mountain climber, a cave explorer, or a scuba diver, or the uniform of a firefighter, a police officer, or a soldier.

Objects　The objects you are talking about make good visual aids if they are large enough to be seen and small enough to carry around with you. A vase, a basketball, a braided rug, or a sword is the kind of object that can be seen by the audience and manipulated by the speaker.

Models　When an object is too large to bring to the speech or too small to be seen, a model will usually prove a worthwhile substitute. If you were to talk about a turbine engine, a suspension bridge, an Egyptian pyramid, or the structure of the atom, a model might well be the best visual aid. Working models are especially eye-catching.

Chalkboard　Because every classroom has a chalkboard, you are likely to want to consider using it in your speeches. As a means of visually portraying simple information, the chalkboard is unbeatable. Unfortunately, the chalkboard is easy to misuse and to overuse. The principal misuse students and teachers make of it is to try to write too much material while they are talking. More often than not, what they write while they talk is either illegible or at least partly obscured by their body while they are writing. Furthermore, the tendency is to spend too much time talking to the board instead of to the audience.

Most people use the chalkboard in an impromptu fashion because it happens to be available. Yet good visual aids require considerable pre-planning to achieve their greatest value. Keep in mind that anything that can be done with a chalkboard can be done better with a prepared visual aid that can be used when needed.

If you still want to use the chalkboard, think about putting the material on the board before you begin, or use the board for only a few seconds at a time. If you plan to draw your visual aid on the board before you begin, get to class a little early so that you can complete your drawing before the class begins. It is not fair to your classmates to use several minutes of class time completing your visual aid. In addition, it is usually a good idea to cover what you have done in some way. If you plan to draw or to write while you are talking, practice doing that as carefully as you practice the rest of the speech. If you are right-handed, stand to the right of what you are drawing. Try to face at least part of the audience while you work. Although it seems awkward at first, your effort will allow your audience to see what you are doing while you are doing it.

Pictures, drawings, and sketches   These three forms probably account for most visual aids used in speeches in or out of the classroom. Pictures, of course, are readily available; however, you must make sure that they are large enough to be seen. The all-too-common apology "I know you can't see this picture, but . . ." is of little help to the audience.

You may want to draw your own visual aid. If you can use a compass, a straightedge, and a measure, you can draw or sketch well enough for speech purposes. A drawing need only be a representation of the key ideas. Stick figures may not be as aesthetically pleasing as professional drawings, but they work every bit as well. The important thing about this kind of visual aid is to make your lettering large enough to be seen easily by the person sitting farthest away.

Charts   A chart is a graphic representation of material that compresses a great deal of information into a usable, easily interpreted form. Word charts, maps, line graphs, bar graphs, and pie graphs are all examples. To get the most out of them, however, you should be prepared to make intelligent interpretations. Since charts do not speak for themselves, you should know how to read, test, and interpret them before you try to use them in speeches.

Films, slides, and projections　In a classroom presentation you will seldom have the opportunity to use films, slides, or projections. The scheduling of projectors, the need for darkened classrooms, and the tendency for these visual aids to dominate the speaker all combine to outweigh possible advantages of their use. Nevertheless, slides, opaque projections, and overhead projections can make even a classroom speech more exciting. If possible, use a partner to run the machinery for you while you are speaking. Make sure that each picture really relates to, supplements, or reinforces what you are saying.

Using Visual Aids

As with any other speech skill, you must practice using visual aids to get the most from them. The following are some useful guidelines for you to consider in your practice.

1. *Show visual aids only when you are talking about them.* You are competing with visual aids for attention. When you are using a visual aid to make a point, you expect audience attention to be directed to it. But if your visual aids are still in view when you are talking about something else, the audience will continue to look at them. When the visual aid is not contributing to the point you are making, keep it out of sight.
2. *Talk about the visual aid while you are showing it.* Although a picture may be worth a thousand words, you know what you want your audience

Visual aids can be helpful, but you must be careful to avoid using too many.

to see in the picture. Tell your audience what to look for; explain the various parts; and interpret figures, symbols, and percentages.

3. *Show visual aids so that everyone in the audience can see them.* If you hold the visual aid, hold it out away from your body and point it toward the various parts of the audience. If you place your visual aid on the chalkboard or easel or mount it in some way, stand to one side and point with the arm nearest the visual aid. If it is necessary to roll or fold your visual aid, bring some transparent tape to mount it to the chalkboard or wall so that it does not roll or wrinkle.

4. *Talk to your audience and not to your visual aid.* You may need to look at the visual aid occasionally, but you want to maintain eye contact with your audience as much as possible to see how they are reacting to your visual material. When people become too engrossed in their visual aids, they tend to lose audience contact entirely.

5. *Don't overdo the use of visual aids.* You can reach a point of diminishing returns with them. If one is good, two may be better; if two are good, three may be better. But somewhere along the line you will reach a point where one more visual aid is too many. Visual aids are a form of emphasis, but attempts to emphasize too many things result in no emphasis at all. Decide where visual aids would be of most value. A visual aid is an *aid* and not a substitute for good speech making.

6. *Pass objects around the class at your own risk.* People look at, read, handle, and think about whatever they hold in their hands, and while they are so occupied, they may not be listening to you. Moreover, when something is being passed around, the people who are not in possession often spend their time looking for the object, wondering why people are taking so long, and fearing that perhaps they will be forgotten. If you are going to pass things out, have enough for everyone. Then keep control of audience attention by telling them what they should be looking at and when they should be listening to you. Anytime you actually put something in your listeners' hands, you are taking a gamble—make a conscious decision whether it is worth the risk.

PRACTICE

Demonstrating

Prepare a three- to six-minute speech in which you demonstrate how something is made, how something is done, or how something works. An outline is required. Criteria for evaluation will include quality of topic, use of visual aids, and skill in organization and presentation.

1. Select a topic that lends itself to the use of visual aids.

2. Organize the process in steps. If you have more than five steps, group them so that the end product is fewer than five. Audiences will remember three points with three or four subdivisions each better than they will remember ten points. For instance, for a speech on woodwork, grouping would be done as follows.

A.	B.
I. Gather the materials	I. Plan the job
II. Draw the pattern	A. Gather materials
III. Trace the pattern on wood	B. Draw a pattern
IV. Cut out the pattern so that the tracing line can still be seen	C. Trace the pattern on wood
V. File to the pattern line	II. Cut out the pattern
VI. Sandpaper edge and surfaces	A. Saw so the tracing line can be seen
VII. Paint the object	B. File to the pattern line
VIII. Sand lightly	C. Sand edge and surface
IX. Apply a second coat of paint	III. Finish the object
X. Varnish	A. Paint
	B. Sand lightly
	C. Apply a second coat of paint
	D. Varnish

NARRATING

A **narrative** is a story, a tale, or an account. The purpose of a narrative is to relate a sequence of events in chronological order. The following statement is a narrative: *John worked all day to finish a report for the five o'clock deadline, only to find as he turned it in that he was a day early.* The primary goal of a narrative is to make a point in such a unique or interesting way that the audience will remember the point because of the way it was presented. In a speech, a narrative can present information and it can have a persuasive message, but, most of all, it should be interesting. As worded, however, the one-sentence narrative about John isn't particularly interesting and is not likely to be remembered. Still, even this short statement can be stretched to be both interesting and memorable.

Let's consider the elements of the narrative and how they can be enhanced.

1. *Usually a narrative has a point, a climax to which the details build up.* A joke has a punch line; a fable has a moral; other narratives have some

climactic ending that makes the stories interesting. The point of this one-sentence narrative is that John worked all day to finish a project that didn't have to be done until tomorrow.

2. *A narrative is developed with various supporting details.* Thus, a narrative speech can be long or short depending on the number and the development of supporting details. Supporting details give background, but most of all they build the story so that the point of the story has maximum effect. For instance, in the narrative of John's report you could introduce such details as how John got to work at 6 A.M., more than two hours earlier than usual, in order to find the time to work on the report and how John had to turn down a lunch invitation from a man he'd been trying to see for three weeks about an important issue related to company policy.

3. *A narrative is often developed with suspense in mind.* Part of the power of the narrative is to withhold the punch line until the end. If you can tease the audience, you will hold their attention. They will be trying to see whether they can anticipate what you have to say. Vocally, a slight pause before the punch line will heighten the effect: "John worked all day to finish his report for the five o'clock deadline, only to discover when he turned it in (pause) that it was one full day early!"

4. *Use dialogue whenever possible.* A story will be much more enjoyable to an audience if they can hear it unfold through dialogue. For instance, notice how our one-line story improves with this presentation: "As John burst into his boss's office with report in hand, his boss's secretary stared at him, dumbfounded. When he said breathlessly, "Here's the report, right on the dot!" she said "John, the report isn't due until tomorrow!""

5. *Develop the humor of the situation whenever possible.* Not all narratives are funny, but more often than not, narratives will have an element of humor. If what happened can be made funny, it will hold attention.

PRACTICE

Narrating

Prepare a two- to five-minute narrative. Select a personal experience that you think your audience will enjoy hearing about. Criteria for grading will include the way you develop the point of the narrative, how well you are able to hold audience attention, clarity and vividness of the experience, and delivery.

DESCRIBING

"What does it look like?" "How do the parts fit together?" Questions like these are answered by our describing what we see. A **description** is a verbal picture. At least some of the informative communicating we do every day is descriptive. But like any of the skills of informative speaking, a description must be carefully worded to be effective.

How do you describe accurately and vividly? Effective description requires at least two skills: (1) observing and (2) communicating the observation. Description is a product of alert observation. Since effective description reflects firsthand observation, you must first know what to look for, then create ways of reporting the essentials that will be accurate and vivid.

To describe you must be conscious of size, shape, weight, color, composition, age and condition, and the relationships among various parts.

Size

How large is the object? Size is described subjectively by "large" and "small" and objectively by dimensions. But a description is more likely to be meaningful if it is comparative. For instance, "The book, nine by six by three inches thick, is the same length and width as your textbook but more than twice as thick" is more descriptive than either of the following: "The book is a large one" or "The book is nine inches by six inches by three inches."

Shape

What is the object's spatial form? Shape is described in terms of common geometric forms. "Round," "triangular," "oblong," "spherical," "conical," "cylindrical," and "rectangular" are all descriptive. A complex object is best described as a series of simple shapes. Since most objects do not conform to perfect shapes, you can usually get by with approximations and with comparisons to familar objects. "The lake is round," "The lot is wedge-shaped," and "The car looks like a rectangular box" all give reasonably accurate impressions. Shape is further clarified by adjectives like "jagged," "smooth," and "indented."

Weight

How heavy is it? Weight is described subjectively as "heavy" or "light" and objectively by pounds and ounces. As with size, descriptions of weight are clarified by comparisons. Thus, "The suitcase weighed about 70 pounds; that's about twice the weight of a normally packed suitcase" is descriptive.

Color

What color is it? Color, an obvious necessity of description, is difficult to describe accurately. Although most people can visualize black and white, the primary colors (red, yellow, and blue), and their complements (green, purple, and orange), very few objects are exactly these colors. Perhaps the best way to describe a color is to couple it with a common referent. For instance, "lemon yellow," "brick red," "green as a grape," or "sky blue" give rather accurate approximations.

Composition

What is it made of? The composition of an object helps us visualize it. A ball of aluminum does not look the same as a ball of yarn. A pile of rocks gives a different impression than does a pile of straw. A brick building looks different from a steel, wood, or glass building. Sometimes you refer to what the object *seems like* rather than what it is. An object can appear metallic even if it is not made of metal. Spun glass can have a woolly texture. Nylon can be soft and smooth, as in stockings, or hard and sharp as in toothbrush bristles.

Age and Condition

How old is it? What condition is it in? Whether an object is new or old can make a difference in its appearance. Since age by itself may not be descriptive, an object is often discussed in terms of condition. Condition is difficult to describe objectively, but it can be very important to an accurate description. The value of coins, for instance, varies tremendously depending on whether they are uncirculated or whether their condition is good or only fair. A 1917 Lincoln penny in fair condition may be worth two cents, whereas an uncirculated 1960 penny may be worth ten cents. Books become ragged and tattered, buildings become run down and dilapidated, land is subject to erosion. Age and condition together often prove valuable in developing informative descriptions.

Relationship Among Parts

How does it all fit together? If the object you want to describe is complex, its parts must be fitted into their proper relationship before a mental picture emerges. Remember the story of the blind men who described an elephant in terms of what each felt? The one who felt the trunk said the elephant was like a snake; the one who felt a leg said the elephant was like a tree; and the one who felt the body said the elephant was like a wall. Not only must we visualize size, shape, weight, color, composition, age, and condition, but we must also understand how the parts fit together.

Since the ultimate test of description is to enable the audience to visualize, you should include too much detail rather than not enough. Moreover, if some particular aspect is discussed in two or three different ways, everyone might get the mental image, whereas a single description might make the image vivid to only a few.

Description is likely to be used in any speech; for practice, however, your instructor may assign a descriptive speech exercise.

PRACTICE

Describing

Prepare a two- to four-minute description. Write an outline. Criteria for evaluation will include clarity and vividness of the description. The following guidelines will help you prepare such an assignment.

1. Select an object, a structure, a place, an animal, or a person.

2. Organize the description by space order; that is, go from top to bottom, left to right, upper right corner to lower left corner, clockwise around an object, or the like.

3. Focus on clarity, vividness, emphasis, and appropriateness, the fundamental qualities of language we discussed in the chapter on speech presentation.

DEFINING

As we discussed earlier, our entire language is built on the assumption that we, as a culture, share common meanings of words. Since many of the words you want to use may not be totally understood by your audience, you need to define words when it is appropriate.

The following are the five most common methods of defining. In your speech they can be used separately or in combination. The ultimate test of the effectiveness of a **definition** is whether the receiver or receivers can understand the meaning and can use the word appropriately.

Classification and Differentiation

When you define by **classification**, you give the boundaries of the particular word and focus on the single feature that gives the word a different meaning from similar words. Most dictionary definitions are of the classification-differentiation variety. For instance, a dog may be defined as a carnivorous, domesticated mammal of the family Canidae. "Carnivorous," "mammal," and "family Canidae" limit the boundaries to dogs, jackals, foxes, and wolves. "Domesticated" differentiates dogs from the other three.

Synonym and Antonym

Synonym and antonym may be the most popular means of defining. Both enable the speaker to indicate approximate, if not exact, meaning in a single sentence; moreover, because they are analogous to comparison and contrast, they are often vivid as well as clear. **Synonyms** are words that have the same or nearly the same meanings; **antonyms** are words that have opposite meanings. Defining by synonym is defining by comparison. For instance, synonyms for "arduous" would be "hard," "laborious," and "difficult." Antonyms define by contrast. Antonyms for "arduous" would be "easy" and "simple." Synonyms are not duplicates for the word being defined, but they do give a good idea of what the word means. Of course, the synonym or antonym used must be familiar to the audience or its use defeats its purpose.

Use and Function

Another way to define is to explain the **use** or **function** of the object a particular word represents. Thus, when you say, "A plane is a hand-powered tool that is used to smooth the edges of boards" or "A scythe is a piece of steel shaped in a half circle with a handle attached that is used to cut weeds or high grass," you are defining tools by indicating their use. Since the use or function of an object may be more important than its classification, this is often an excellent method of definition.

Etymology and Historical Example

Etymology is the derivation or history of a particular word. Since words change over time, origin may reveal very little about modern meaning. In some instances, however, the history of a word reveals additional insight that will help the audience remember the meaning a little better. For instance, a *censor* originally was one of two Roman magistrates appointed to take the census and, later, to supervise public morals. The best source of word derivation is the *Oxford English Dictionary*.

Examples and Comparisons

Regardless of the way you define, you are likely to have to supplement your definitions with examples and/or comparisons to make them truly understandable. This is especially true when you are defining abstract words. Consider the word *just* in the following sentence: "You are being just in your dealings with another when you deal honorably and fairly." Although you have defined by synonym, listeners are still likely to be unsure of the meaning. If you add, "If Paul and Mary both do the same amount of work and we reward them by giving them an equal amount of money, our dealings will be just; if, on the other hand, we give Paul more money because he's a man, our dealings will be unjust." In this case you are clarifying the definition with both an example and a comparison.

PRACTICE

Defining

Prepare a two- to four-minute definition. Write an outline. Criteria for evaluation will include clarity of the definition and quality of the development of the various aspects.

1. Select a word that is abstract or complex, such as "jazz," "impressionism," or "tantalizing."

2. Organize the definition by topic order. Each part of the definition becomes a main point.

3. Use one or more of the major methods of definition (classification, synonym, function, etymology). Give at least one example or comparison to help clarify.

REPORTING

With demonstration, narration, description, and definition, we work with skills related to shaping and developing information. Informative speaking, however, often requires the use of source material beyond your experience. In this section we consider means of going beyond your own knowledge and then **reporting** that information in your speech. We look at research evaluation and citing source material.

Research Evaluation

One of the criteria you should apply to your research is whether it is comprehensive. Comprehensive means researching until you have discovered all the relevant information. Although comprehensive research on any subject could take a team of researchers weeks or more, for a class assignment we expect the speech to be comprehensive "within reason." This might be defined as using at least four different authoritative sources of information. Our advice is to look into eight or ten different sources and then focus your efforts on the best four.

If you research properly, you will have on hand more material than you can read completely. To locate and record the best material, you should develop a system of evaluation that will enable you to review the greatest amount of information in the shortest period of time. A skill that helps you with this is **skimming**. Let's define skimming by showing how it works. If you are evaluating a magazine article, spend a minute or two finding out what it covers. Does it really present information on the part of the topic you are exploring? Does it contain any documented statistics, examples, or quotable opinions? Is the author qualified to draw valid conclusions? If you are evaluating a book, read the table of contents carefully, look at the index, and skip-read pertinent chapters, asking the same questions you would for a magazine article. During this skimming period you will decide which sources should be read in full, which should be read in part, and which should be abandoned. Minutes spent in evaluation will save you hours of useless reading.

A second criterion you should apply to your research is whether the material you plan to use is accurate and objective. Determining accuracy can be a long and tedious job. In most instances accuracy can be reasonably assessed by checking the fact against the original source, if one is given, or against another article or book on the same subject. Although checking accuracy may seem a waste of time, you will be surprised at the difference in "facts" reported in two or more sources. If at least two sources say about the same thing, you can be a little more confident. Objectivity is tested much the same way. If two or more sources give different slants on the material, you will know that what is being discussed is a matter of opinion. Only after you have examined many sources are you in a position to make an objective value judgment.

Citing Source Material

A special problem of a research speech is how to cite source material. In speeches, as in any communication in which you are using ideas that are not your own, you should attempt to work the source of your material into the context of the speech. Such efforts to include sources not only will help the audience in their evaluation of the content but also will add to your credibility as a speaker. In a written report ideas taken from other sources are designated by footnotes; in a speech these notations must be included within the context of your statement of the material. In addition, since a speech using sources should reflect a depth of research, citing the various sources of information will give concrete evidence of your research. Your citation need not be a complete representation of all the bibliographical information. Here are some examples:

▶ According to an article about Margaret Thatcher in last week's *Time* magazine . . .

▶ In the latest Gallup poll cited in last week's issue of *Newsweek* . . .

▶ But to get a complete picture we have to look at the statistics. According to the *Statistical Abstract*, the level of production for the Common Market rose from . . .

▶ In a speech before the National Association of Manufacturers given just last spring, Philip Dunbar, an authority on advertising, said . . .

PRACTICE

Reporting

Prepare a four- to seven-minute speech. An outline and a bibliography are required (at least four sources). Criteria for evaluation will include the quality of the content, the use of source material in the speech, and the creativity shown in developing ideas. The speech should be informative and interesting. A question period of one to three minutes will follow (optional).

SUMMARY

Communication of information involves principles of reception, understanding, and retention. Information is more readily received and understood when it is relevant to receiver experience. Audiences are more likely to listen to information that they perceive as new, that is emphasized, and that is presented creatively.

Demonstrating involves showing how to do something, how to make something, or how something works. The effectiveness of a demonstration is improved by such visual aids as the speaker; objects; models; the chalkboard; pictures, drawings, and sketches; charts; and films, slides, and projections.

Narrating is telling a story. Usually a narrative has a point, a climax. Narratives are enhanced with suspense, humor, and dialogue.

Describing means creating a verbal picture. Describing requires skill in recognizing and portraying size, shape, weight, color, composition, age and condition, and the relationship among parts.

Defining is giving the meaning of a word or concept. Effective definition involves classification and differentiation, synonym and antonym, use and function, and etymology and historical example.

Reporting involves going beyond your own knowledge by using resource material. Reporting requires research evaluation and good citing of sources.

SUGGESTED READINGS

Braun, Jay J., and Darwyn E. Linder. *Psychology Today*. 4th ed. New York: Random House, 1979. See especially Chapter 4, "Learning," and Chapter 5, "Memory." Nearly any recent introductory psychology textbook will have chapters on how people learn.

Good, Thomas L., and Jere E. Brophy. *Educational Psychology*. 2nd ed. New York: Holt, Rinehart and Winston, 1980 (paperback). See especially the four chapters in Part 2, "Learning."

Guth, Hans P. *Words and Ideas*. 4th ed. Belmont, Calif.: Wadsworth, 1975. Although this is a book on writing, chapters on observation, personal experience, definition, tone and style, and the research report present material that can be adapted to the study of informative speaking.

Petrie, Charles. "Informative Speaking: A Summary and Bibliography of Related Research." *Speech Monographs*, vol. 30 (June 1963), pp. 79–91. This summary is still a useful source.

Verderber, Rudolph. *The Challenge of Effective Speaking*. 6th ed. Belmont, Calif.: Wadsworth, 1985. Includes student examples of each of the kinds of speeches discussed in this chapter.

16 ▶ PERSUASIVE SPEAKING

OBJECTIVES

After you have read this chapter, you should be able to:

1   Write a proposition of belief and/or action

2   Find reasons to justify the proposition

3   Find facts and opinions to support reasons

4   Organize reasons effectively

5   Phrase key ideas with emotional appeal

6   Build personal credibility

7   Deliver a speech with conviction

8   Respond to a persuasive speech

You are likely to have many chances during your life to make a statement designed to change an audience's attitude or move an audience to action. You will be giving a persuasive speech. Building a persuasive speech follows much the same steps as preparing any other speech.

WRITING A CLEAR PERSUASIVE SPEECH GOAL

How you write your speech goal may well determine the degree of success you are likely to realize. Although any random statement may influence another person's actions (merely saying "I see the new Penney's store opened in Western Woods" may "persuade" another person to go to Penney's for some clothing need), the successful persuader does not leave the effect of the message to chance. A good persuasive speech goal, often called a **proposition**, states what you want your audience to *believe* or to *do*.

PROPOSITIONS OF BELIEF
■ I want my audience to believe that the Bluebirds are the best team on the circuit.
■ I want my audience to believe that state lotteries should be outlawed.
■ I want my audience to believe that Social Security taxes should be lowered.

PROPOSITIONS OF ACTION
■ I want my audience to buy Wheat Puffs the next time they shop for breakfast cereals.
■ I want my audience to write to their congresspeople to support the Powell bill.
■ I want my audience to go to the school's production of *A Chorus Line*.

Now let's adapt the guidelines that were offered in Chapter 12 for writing a speech goal to writing persuasive speech goals.

1. *Write a tentative speech goal in a complete sentence that states the specific response or behavior you want from your audience.* "I want my audience to believe that state lotteries should be outlawed" is a complete sentence.
2. *Write several potential wordings of the goal.* Your first wording is likely to be general or abstract; write out at least two more and choose the statement that is clearest and most specific.
3. *Write the goal so that it contains only one idea.* "I want my audience to believe that state lotteries and abortion should be outlawed" contains two ideas, either of which might be suitable for a persuasive speech.
4. *Include an infinitive or infinitive phrase that shows the audience reaction desired.* For the persuasive speech you will use such statements as "to

believe," "to petition," "to buy," or some other infinitive incorporating a specific action.

5. *Consider rewording the proposition if it calls for a total change in audience attitude.* To expect a complete shift in attitude or behavior as a result of one speech is probably unrealistic. William Brigance, one of the great speech teachers of this century, used to speak of "planting the seeds of persuasion." If you present a modest proposal seeking a slight change in attitude, you may be able to get an audience to consider the value of your message. Later, when the idea begins to grow, you can ask for a greater change. For instance, if your audience believes that taxes are too high, you are unlikely to make them believe that taxes should be increased. However, you may be able to influence them to see that taxes are not really as high as they originally thought or not as high as other goods and services.

   Major attitude change is more likely to come over a period of time than from a single speech. One author encourages seeing persuasion as "a campaign" stretched over a period of time and including many speeches.[1] Because your classroom speaking allows for only one effort, you are going to have to make the most of it.

6. *Consider rewording the proposition if it seems impractical.* When an audience perceives that what you want them to do is impractical they are likely to ignore your appeal regardless of its merits. For instance if your goal is to have the class write a letter to their congressman, the act of writing that letter may seem impractical to most of the class. If on the other hand you suggest writing a short message on a postcard, *and* you can give your audience pre-addressed postcards, they are more likely to dash off a few lines if they agree with the merits of your appeal.

   Does this mean you should never ask an audience to believe something or to do something that is difficult? No. The point is that the greater the demand you place on your audience, the more prepared you must be to meet resistance.

PRACTICE

Writing Persuasive Goals

Write a persuasive speech goal. Rewrite it two or three times with slightly different wordings. Which one would be the best wording for your classroom audience? Why?

BUILDING THE BODY OF THE SPEECH WITH GOOD REASONS

The main points of a persuasive speech are usually stated as reasons, statements that tell *why* a proposition is justified. Human beings take pride in being rational. We seldom do anything without some real or imagined reason. One way of satisfying the need to be rational is to give your audience reasons.

Finding Reasons

How do you find reasons for your speech? Some reasons are so obvious you can state several by just taking a little time to think about the subject. Suppose you wanted to persuade your friends to increase their level of exercise. You might begin by asking yourself, "Why should my friends increase their level of exercise?" You might then think of the following three reasons: (1) it will help them control their weight, (2) it will help them strengthen their cardiovascular system, and (3) it will help them feel better. For most of your speeches, however, you will need to go beyond your own thoughts by using material you get from observing, interviewing, and reading. Try to find as many reasons as you can and then choose the best.

For a speech in support of the proposition that the United States should overhaul the welfare system, you might find at least six reasons:

I. The welfare system costs too much.
II. The welfare system is inequitable.
III. The walfare system does not help those who need help most.
IV. The welfare system has been grossly abused.
V. The welfare system does not encourage seeking work.
VI. The welfare system does not encourage self-support.

Once you've compiled a list of possible reasons, select the best ones (probably no more than three or four) on the basis of how well they prove the proposition, whether they can be supported, and how much impact they are likely to have on the audience.

1. *Choose the reasons that best prove the proposition.* Sometimes statements look like reasons but don't really supply much proof. For instance, "The welfare system is supported by socialists" may sound like a reason for overhauling it, but it doesn't really provide proof that the system needs overhauling.
2. *Choose reasons that can be supported.* Some reasons that sound impressive cannot be supported with facts. A reason that cannot be supported should not be used in the speech. The fourth reason in the

preceding list, "The welfare system has been grossly abused," sounds like a really good one. But if you cannot find facts to support it, you should not use it in your speech. You will be surprised at how many reasons that are mentioned in various sources have to be dropped from consideration for a speech because they cannot be supported.

3. *Choose reasons that will have an impact on the intended audience.* Suppose that for the proposition "Eat at the Sternwheeler" you have a great deal of factual evidence to support the reason "The seafood is excellent." Even though you have a good reason and good support, it would be a poor reason to use in the speech if the majority of the audience did not like seafood!

Although you cannot always be sure about the potential impact of a reason, you can make a reasonably good estimate of possible impact based on your general audience analysis. For instance, on the topic of eating out, a college audience is likely to weigh price much more than an audience of business executives.

Finding Information to Support Your Reasons

Reasons are only generalizations. Although some are self-explanatory and occasionally even persuasive without further support, most do require development before people will either accept or act upon them.

The two major kinds of evidence are fact and expert opinion. *Facts*, the best support for any reason, are statements that are verifiable. That metal is heavier than air, that World War II ended in 1945, and that Oakland won the World Series in 1972, 1973, and 1974 are all facts. If you say "It's really hot today—it's up in the nineties" and the thermometer registers 94 degrees, your support (temperature up in the nineties) is factual.

Although factual support is best, there are times when the facts are not available or when facts are inconclusive. In these situations you will have to support your conclusions further with opinion. The quality of *opinion* as evidence is dependent on whether the source, the person giving the opinion, is expert. If Tom Roth, your gas station attendant, says it is likely that there is life on other planets, his statement would not be evidence—the opinion is not expert; his expertise lies in other areas. If, on the other hand, Nancy Marshall, an esteemed space biologist, says there is a likelihood of life on other planets, her opinion is evidence—it is expert. Of course, opinions are most trustworthy when they are accompanied by factual data. If Bill Campbell, an automotive engineer, says that a low-cost electric car is feasible, his opinion is valuable, since automotive engineering is his area of expertise. If, accompanying his opinion, he shows us the advances in technology that are leading to a low-cost battery of medium size that can run for more than 200 hours without being recharged, his opinion is worth even more.

Let's illustrate by developing a proposition with fact and opinion.

Shop at Schappenhouper's food stores. Why?

A. EVIDENCE BY FACT:

If we look at prices for five basic foods—eggs, chopped meat, lettuce, potatoes, and milk—at four major markets, we find the following: eggs—Schappenhouper's, 87 cents; A, 91 cents; B, 96 cents; C, 89 cents; sirloin steak per pound— Schappenhouper's, $2.25; A . . . , and so on.

B. EVIDENCE BY OPINION:

Mrs. Goody, fraternity cook, who comparison shops every week, says, "I shop at Schappenhouper's because prices are lower for comparable foods."

At this stage your persuasive speech will have a logical structure—a clear speech goal, reasons in support of that goal, and support for the reasons.

PRACTICE

Selecting Reasons

1. Write the proposition you would use for your first persuasive speech.

2. Write at least *six* reasons in support of that proposition.

I.

II.

III.

IV.

V.

VI.

   3. Star the three or four reasons you believe are best.

CREATING THE BEST ORGANIZATION FOR THIS SPEECH

Although most persuasive speeches follow a topical organization, many different organizational frameworks may be selected.

Audience Attitude

The specific organization you select will depend on whether your audience favors your proposition and to what degree. Unless you poll the audience, you cannot be sure of their attitude. If you analyze your audience in the way described in Chapter 12, you will be able to make reasonably accurate estimates of whether your audience has no opinion, is in favor, or is opposed. Then you can select an organization that is likely to work with that attitude.

An audience that has no opinion is either uninformed or apathetic. If they are uninformed, you should use an organization that will give the necessary information first—then you can work on persuading them. If they are apathetic, all of your effort can be directed to breaking them out of their apathy.

If your audience is in favor, you can devote most of your time to bringing them to a specific action. Many times people are in favor of doing *something*, but they are not in agreement on *what* to do. Your job is to provide a specific course of action they can rally around. When you believe your audience is on your side, try to crystallize their attitudes, recommit them to a particular direction, or suggest a specific course of action that will serve as a rallying point.

An audience that is opposed will range in attitude from slightly negative to thoroughly hostile. If an audience is slightly negative, you can approach them rather directly with your plan, hoping that the weight of argument will swing them to your side. If they are hostile, you will usually have to approach the topic indirectly and work hard to develop common ground; perhaps you will have to be content with planting the seeds of persuasion and not expecting much at the moment.

Organizational Methods

The following organizational methods may prove useful to adopt as stated, or they may suggest an organization that you believe will work for your audience given the material you have to work with. For purposes of illustrating persuasive organizational patterns, we will use the same proposition and the same (or similar) arguments. With some topics and some material one form is likely to be better—the forms are not entirely interchangeable. Nevertheless, by using essentially the same arguments, you can contrast the forms and better understand their use.

Statement-of-reasons method   When you believe your listeners have no opinion on the subject, are apathetic, or are perhaps only mildly in favor or opposed, the straightforward topical **statement of reasons** may be your best organization. With this pattern each reason is presented as a complete statement justification for the proposition:

PROPOSITION
I want my audience to vote in favor of the school tax levy on the November ballot.
   I. Income will enable the schools to restore vital programs.
  II. Income will enable the schools to give teachers the raises they need to keep up with the cost of living.
 III. The actual cost to each member of the community will be very small.

Problem-solution method   The **problem-solution** pattern provides a framework for clarifying the nature of the problem and for illustrating why the new proposal is the best one. There are usually three main points of a problem-solution speech: (1) there is a problem that requires action; (2) the proposal will solve the problem; and (3) the proposal is the best solution to the problem. This pattern may be best for an audience that has no opinion or is mildly pro or con. Now let's see how a problem-solution organization would look for the school tax levy proposition:

> PROPOSITION
> I want my audience to vote in favor of the school tax levy on the November ballot.
> I. The shortage of money is resulting in serious problems for public education.
> II. The proposed increase is large enough to solve those problems.
> III. For now, a tax levy is the best method of solving the schools' problems.

Comparative-advantages method The **comparative-advantages** pattern focuses on the superiority of your newly proposed course of action. With this pattern you are not trying to solve a grave problem as much as you are suggesting a better alternative. This pattern can work for any audience attitude except hostility. A comparative-advantages approach to the school tax levy proposition would look like this:

> PROPOSITION
> I want my audience to vote in favor of the school tax levy on the November ballot.
> I. Income from a tax levy will enable schools to raise the standards of their programs.
> II. Income from a tax levy will enable schools to hire better teachers.
> III. Income from a tax levy will enable schools to better the educational environment.

Criteria-satisfaction method When you are dealing with audiences that are opposed to your ideas, you need a pattern of organization that will not aggravate the hostility. The **criteria-satisfaction** pattern is one of two patterns that are particularly effective with hostile audiences. The pattern focuses on developing a "yes" response before you introduce the proposition and reasons. A criteria-satisfaction organization for the school tax levy proposition would look like this:

> PROPOSITION
> I want my audience to vote in favor of the school tax levy on the November ballot.
> I. We all want good schools.
>   A. Good schools have programs that prepare our youth to function in society.
>   B. Good schools are those with the best teachers available.

II. Passage of the school tax levy will guarantee good schools.
  A. Passage will enable us to increase the quality of vital programs.
  B. Passage will enable us to hire and to keep the best teachers.

Negative method   The **negative** pattern, the other method that is particularly effective for hostile audiences, focuses on the shortcomings of all of the solutions except the one offered in the proposition. To persuade a hostile audience to vote for a tax levy, you might use this organizational pattern:

PROPOSITION
I want my audience to vote in favor of the school tax levy on the November ballot.
  I. Saving money by reducing services and programs will not help the schools.
  II. The federal government will not increase its help to the schools.
  III. The state government will not increase its help to the schools.
  IV. All we have left is to pass the tax levy.

WORDING MAIN POINTS AND KEY IDEAS WITH EMOTIONAL APPEAL

The driving force of motivation will be your wording of key ideas. You should look for ways to word your ideas to increase their emotional impact. Because effectiveness of emotion seems to depend so much on related factors such as audience mood, attitude, and wording, emotional language is best used as a supplement to good reasons. Good speech development seems to be logical-emotional. Instead of looking for additional material that will arouse an emotion, look for good, logical reasons that, *if properly phrased and developed*, will arouse emotions.

Suppose you are trying to get your audience to support a more humane treatment of elderly people. One of your reasons might be that "elderly people are often alienated from society." If you have material to support that reason, you can then ask yourself, "How can I phrase the material in a way that will motivate the audience to actually *feel* the impact of that material?"

You could respond with the following:

Currently, elderly people are alienated from society. A high percentage live in nursing homes, live on small fixed incomes, and exist out of the mainstream of society.

This states the facts but provides little motivation. Contrast the following statement of the same material:

> Currently, elderly people are alienated from the society that they worked their entire lives to support. What happens to elderly people in America? They become the forgotten segment of society. They are often relegated to "old people's homes" so that they can live out their lives and die without being "a bother" to their sons and daughters. Because they must exist on relatively small fixed incomes, they are confined to a life that for many means separation from the very society they helped to create.

With just the addition of an audience question and some restatement of the point, the same material takes on considerably more emotional strength.

Perhaps your greatest opportunities for emotional appeal occur in the introduction and conclusion to your speech. Betsy Burke's speech on euthanasia illustrates excellent use of emotional appeal in both her introduction and her conclusion.[2] She began her speech as follows:

> Let's pretend for a moment. Suppose that on the upper right-hand corner of your desk there is a button. You have the power by pushing that button, to quickly and painlessly end the life of one you love: your brother, sister, or father. This loved one has terminal cancer and will be confined to a hospital for his remaining days. Would you push the button now? His condition worsens. He is in constant pain and he is hooked up to a life-support machine. He first requests, but as the pain increases he pleads for you to help. Now would you push that button? Each day you watch him deteriorate until he reaches a point where he cannot talk, he cannot see, he cannot hear—he is only alive by that machine. Now would you push that button?

After giving reasons for changing our laws, she ended her speech as follows:

> I ask again, how long could you take walking into that hospital room and looking at your brother or father in a coma, knowing he would rather be allowed to die a natural death than to be kept alive in such a degrading manner? I've crossed that doorstep—I've gone into that hospital room, and let me tell you, it's hell. I think it's time we reconsider our laws concerning euthanasia. Don't you?

What do you do to create wording that has the emotional impact shown in these last few examples?

1. *Get in touch with your own feelings about the ideas.* If you are involved enough in a topic to give a persuasive speech, then it is likely that you

have some strong feelings about the people, conditions, or situations that relate to that topic. What are they? Are your feelings ones of sadness? Happiness? Guilt? Anger? Caring? Grief? If you feel sadness, anger, and grief about elderly people, you may see pictures of nursing homes, old people with blank looks on their faces huddled together in wheelchairs in front of televisions, and so forth.

Then you can practice describing your feelings and your mental pictures of those feelings. Your first practices are likely to be clumsy— maybe even laughable. As you work with your descriptions, however, you will find yourself speaking more and more vividly and with more genuine feeling.

2. *Create a common ground.* In a persuasive speech you are trying to establish the feeling that both you the speaker and the audience are operating from the same value system and sharing many of the same experiences. In short, you are in this together. The response you seek from the audience is "We agree, or have so much in common, on so many various points that we can reach agreement on a single point of difference." In trying to get support for their latest programs politicians often try to show that they have the same background, the same set of values, beliefs, and attitudes, the same overall way of looking at things as the audience, so that a point of difference does not represent a difference in philosophy.

3. *Develop a "yes" response.* Psychologists have found that when people get in the habit of saying "yes," they are likely to continue to say "yes." If you can phrase questions that establish areas of agreement early in your speech, the audience will be more likely to listen to you and perhaps to agree with your proposition. The criteria-satisfaction method of organization is built on the "yes" response. For instance, if you ask your audience, "Do you like to have a good time? To get your money's worth? To put your money into a worthy cause? To support your community if you will profit from the support?" and then ask, "Will you support Playhouse-in-the-Park?" you are using the "yes" response method.

4. *Suggest agreement.* Suggestion involves planting an idea in the mind of the listener without developing it. It is an idea stated in such a way that its acceptance is sought without analysis or consideration.

A prevalent use of suggestion in speech making is the directive. Such expressions as "I think we will all agree," "As we all know," and "Now we come to a most important consideration" are forms of suggestion that will help you direct audience thinking.

5. *Avoid vague, general words that carry no emotional impact.* In writing the outline make sure that every main point and major subdivision is stated with emotional appeal in mind. Saying the atmosphere is "interesting" creates no mental image and therefore is not nearly as impressive as saying the atmosphere is "mysterious," "sensuous," or "robust."

6. *Avoid pedantic statements of fact.* For instance, you may decide to use the information that "one out of every eight children suffers some birth

defect." As impressive as that statement appears to be, you will realize far more emotional involvement with a short case history or specific example. People do not see or feel statistics.

USING YOUR CREDIBILITY ADVANTAGEOUSLY

Persuasion is more likely to be achieved when the audience likes, trusts, and has confidence in the speaker. The Greeks had a word for this concept—they called it *ethos*. But whether we call it ethos, image, charisma, or the word we prefer—**credibility**—the effect is the same. Almost all studies confirm that speaker credibility has a major effect on audience belief and attitude.[3]

Why are people so willing to take the word of someone else on any issue? Since it is impossible to know all there is to know about everything (and even if it were possible, few of us would be willing to spend the time and effort), we seek shortcuts in our decision making. We rely on the judgment of others. We think, why take the time to learn about the new highway or all the restaurants in town or all the candidates' records when someone we trust tells us how to behave? Every one of us listens to people we trust in order to take shortcuts in our decision making. Is this reliance based solely on blind faith? No, the presence (or our perception of the presence) of certain qualities will make that person a *high-credibility* source for us.

Characteristics of Credibility

Although sources differ in their listings of characteristics of credibility, most of them include competence, intention, character, and personality.

Competence   The qualification or capability of a source determine **competence**. Students are often attracted to competent professors. Although all professors are supposed to know what they are talking about, some are better able to convince their students. One way professors demonstrate competence is by saying things in a way that convinces us they know far more than what they are telling us. For instance, when a student asks a question, the competent professor is able to present more detail, an example, a story, or a list of additional reading material on the subject. Another way is by compiling a good record of accuracy of detail. If what a person has told us in the past is true, we will tend to believe what that person tells us now.

Intention   **Intention** refers to a person's apparent motives. Since you know that clothing salespeople are trying to sell you the garments they help you try on, when they say "This is perfect for you," you may question their intentions. On the other hand, if a bystander looks over at you and exclaims, "Wow, you really look good in that!" you are likely to accept the statement as true because the bystander has no reason to make such a statement if it were not true. The more positively you view the intentions of the person, the more credible his or her words will seem to you.

Character   The whole of a person's mental and ethical traits is that person's **character**. We are more likely to trust and believe in a person whom we perceive as honest, industrious, trustworthy, dependable, strong, and steadfast. We will often overlook what are otherwise regarded as shortcomings if a person shows character.

Personality   **Personality** is the total of a person's behavioral and emotional tendencies. In short, it is the impression a person makes on us. Sometimes we have a strong "gut reaction" about a person based solely on a first impression. In response to such aspects of personality as enthusiasm, friendliness, warmth, a ready smile, and a caring attitude—or lack of any of these—we may take a natural liking or disliking to a person.

Building Your Credibility

The characteristics of credibility may not be known to the audience before the speech begins, but you may be able to show their presence as the speech goes on. You can demonstrate competence by letting the audience know that you have experienced what you are talking about or that you have made an exhaustive study. In a speech on police public relations you might say, "I had read about police public relations, but I wanted to see for myself, so I spent several days talking with police officers, watching how they worked, and riding around in squad cars." Intention can be shown by emphasizing the benefits to be gained from your ideas. Although personality and character are more reflections of what you are, in your speech you can be friendly, caring, sincere, honest, and trustworthy.

Credibility is not something that you can gain overnight or turn off or on at your whim. Still, by being ready to speak on time, approaching the assignment with a positive attitude, showing complete preparation for each speech, giving thoughtful evaluation of others' speeches, and demonstrating sound thinking, you can build your credibility with your classmates and your professor during the term.

Perhaps one of the best ways of building your credibility is by behaving in ways that are ethical. **Ethics** are the standards of moral conduct that determine our behavior. Ethics include both how we ourselves act and how we expect others to act. How we treat those who fail to meet our standards says a great deal about the importance we give to ethics. Although ethical codes are personal, society has a code of ethics that operates on at least the verbal level within that society.

How you handle ethical questions says a great deal about you as a person. What is your code of ethics? The following four guidelines reflect the standards of hundreds of students that I have seen in my classes during the last few years. I believe that these four make an excellent starting point for a set of personal ethical standards.

1. *Lying is unethical.* Of all the attitudes about ethics, this is the one most universally held. When people know they are being lied to, they will usually reject the ideas of the speaker; if they find out later, they often look for ways to punish the speaker who lied to them.
2. *Name calling is unethical.* Again, there seems to be almost universal agreement on this guideline. Even though many people name-call in their interpersonal communication, they regard name calling by public speakers unethical.
3. *Grossly exaggerating or distorting facts is unethical.* Although some people seem willing to accept a little exaggeration as a normal product of human nature, when the exaggeration is defined as "gross" or "distorted," most people consider the exaggeration the same as lying. Because the line between some exaggeration and gross exaggeration or distortion is often so difficult to distinguish, many people see *any* exaggeration as unethical.
4. *Condemning people or ideas without divulging the source of the information is unethical.* Where ideas originate is often as important as the ideas themselves. Although a statement may be true regardless of whether a source is given, people want more than the speaker's word

when a statement is damning. If you are going to discuss the wrong-doing of a person or the stupidity of an idea by relying on the words or ideas of others, you must be prepared to share the sources of those words or ideas.

These four are but a starting point in the construction of your ethical standard. Effective speaking should be ethical speaking.

PRACTICE

Credibility

1. Write your speech proposition.

2. Gather data that you can use in your speech to establish, build, or maintain your credibility.
   a. What indications are there that you are competent to speak on this topic?
   b. What evidence can you collect to show that your intentions are for the audience's benefit?
   c. What do you see as your three main character strengths?
   d. What do you see as your three main personality strengths?

3. Indicate three things you can do in this speech to demonstrate your credibility to the audience.

DELIVERING THE SPEECH CONVINCINGLY

Effective delivery for persuasive speeches is no different from effective delivery for an informative speech. Still, because delivery is so important, let us focus on one of its key aspects especially relevant to persuasion: The effective persuader shows conviction about the subject. Some people show conviction through considerable animation. Others show conviction through quiet intensity. However it is shown, though, the audience must perceive it to be convinced. If you have a strong conviction about the subject, let your voice and bodily action show it.

RESPONDING TO PERSUASION

Many times when you want to speak, it is not to originate an idea or plan but to respond to an idea or plan offered by someone else. To make the best use of your persuasive potential, you must have or develop some confidence in your ability to refute.

By definition, **refutation** is the process of proving that a statement is false or erroneous—or, at least, doubtful. Someone says, "Chris Evert-Lloyd will win the match," and you say, "No, she isn't even entering the tournament." Someone says, "We need more governmental control of basic industry," and you say, "No, according to Milton Friedman, that's about the last thing we need." What you say in reply is refutation. The following discussion is concerned with what can be refuted and how refutation is prepared and presented.

What to Refute

Refutation begins with anticipation of what the opposition will say. For any controversial issue you should know the material on both sides—if you have an idea of how an opponent will proceed, you will be in a much better position to reply. If the opponent talks for very long, you should probably take some notes; you do not want to run the risk of being accused of distorting what your opponent really said. You can base your refutation on amount of support, quality of support, or reasoning.

If the opposition's case is built on assertion with little or no evidence to support the assertion, you can refute the argument on that basis.

A better method is to attack the quality of the material. If sheer amount of evidence were the most important criterion in proving a point, the person with the most material would always win. However, there is often no direct relationship between amount of material and quality of proof. A statement by a judge who has studied the rights of individual citizens to privacy would be worth far more than several opinions on the rights of privacy from athletes, musicians, or politicians who have not studied the subject.

Testing Evidence

For every bit of evidence that is presented, you should ask the following:

1. *Is the evidence fact or opinion?* As we said earlier, fact is usually worth more than opinion, and expert opinion is worth more than inexpert opinion.

2. *Where does the evidence come from?* This question involves both the people who offered the opinions or compiled the facts and the book, journal, or source where they were reported. Just as some people's opinions are more reliable than others, some printed sources are more reliable than others. That something appeared in print does not make it true. If data come from a poor source, an unreliable source, or a biased source, no reliable conclusion can be drawn from them, and you should refute the argument on the basis of dubious quality.

3. *Is the evidence recent?* Products, ideas, and statistics often are obsolete as soon as they are produced. You must ask when the particular evidence was true. Five-year-old evidence may not be true today. Furthermore, an article in last week's news magazine may be using five-year-old evidence in the story.

4. *Is the evidence relevant?* You may find that the evidence has little to do with the point being presented. This question of relevancy may well lead you into the reasoning process itself.

Reasoning from the evidence   Although attacks on evidence are sometimes effective means of refutation, the form of refutation that is most telling and most difficult to reply to is the attack on the reasoning from the evidence. Each argument presented in a persuasive speech is composed of at least three elements: (1) evidence or data from which a conclusion is drawn, (2) the conclusion itself, and (3) a stated or implied link that takes speakers from their evidence to the conclusions they have drawn. Analysis of reasoning focuses on that stated or implied link. Because the link is more often implied than stated, you must learn to phrase it before you can proceed to attack the argument. For instance, your opponent may say:

> Our point is that once a government agency begins uncontrolled gathering of information, abuses—serious invasions of privacy—are inevitable. According to X the Army's efforts at gathering information have led to the following abuses: . . . . According to Y the FBI's efforts at gathering information have led to the following abuses: . . . . According to Z the Census Bureau's efforts at gathering information have led to these abuses: . . . .

Since in this argument the conclusion is clearly stated as a reason and the evidence is documented and appears above reproach, you would have to determine the reasoning link so you could determine whether or not the conclusion really followed from the evidence. In the preceding example the speaker is reasoning that if abuses resulted from information-gathering efforts in each of three governmental agencies analyzed, then it is reasonable to conclude that similar abuses would follow from information-gathering efforts of any or all government agencies.

Once you have the reasoning link stated rather than implied, you can begin to apply the proper tests to the reasoning. Perhaps the best way to approach the problem of phrasing the reasoning link is to ask, "How could the relationship between evidence and conclusion be stated so that the conclusion does follow from the evidence?" Then, to begin testing the soundness of the link, you can ask, "What circumstances would need to be present to prevent the conclusion from coming about even if the evidence is true?"

Our goal here is not to explain every kind of reasoning link that can be established but to consider the major forms that will work for you in the great majority of circumstances.

1. *Reasoning by generalization.* You are reasoning by **generalization** when your conclusion states that what is true in some instances is true in all instances. Generalization links are the basis for polls and predictions. Take, for example, the fact "Tom, Jack, and Bill studied and got A's" and the conclusion based on it, "Anyone who studies will get an A." The reasoning link can be stated, "What is true in these representative instances will be true in all instances." To test this kind of argument you should ask, "Were enough instances cited? Were the instances typical? Were the instances representative?" If the answer to any of these questions is "no," you have the basis for refutation of the reasoning.

2. *Reasoning by causation.* You are reasoning by **causation** when your conclusion is a result of a single circumstance or set of circumstances. Causation links are one of the most prevalent types of arguments you will discover. An example would be as follows: *evidence:* "We've had a very dry spring"; *conclusion:* "The wheat crop will be lower than usual." The reasoning link can be stated: "The lack of sufficient rain *causes* a poor crop. To test this kind of argument you should ask, "Are the data (is the evidence) alone important enough to bring about the particular conclusion? If we eliminate the data, would we eliminate the effect?" If the answer to one of these questions is "no," then you have the basis for refutation of the reasoning by causation. "Do some other data that accompany the cited data cause the effect?" If so, you have the basis for refutation.

3. *Reasoning by analogy.* You are reasoning by **analogy** when your conclusion is the result of a comparison with a similar set of circumstances. Although reasoning by analogy is very popular, it is regarded as the weakest form of reasoning. The analogy link is often stated, "What is true or will work in one set of circumstances is true or will work in a comparable set of circumstances." An example would be as follows: *evidence:* "A state lottery has proved very effective in New Jersey"; *conclusion:* "A state lottery will prove effective in Ohio." The reasoning link can be stated, "If something works in New Jersey, it will work in Ohio, because Ohio and New Jersey are so similar." To test this kind of argument you should ask, "Are the subjects really comparable? Are the subjects being compared really similar in all important ways?" If the answer to these questions is "no," you have the basis for refutation of the reasoning. "Are

any of the ways that the subjects are dissimilar important to the conclusion?" If so, then the reasoning is not sound.

4. *Reasoning by definition.* You are reasoning by **definition** when your conclusion is a definition or a descriptive generalization that follows from agreed-upon criteria. Again, this is a very popular form of reasoning. An example would be as follows: *evidence:* "She takes charge; she uses good judgment; her goals are in the best interests of the group"; *conclusion:* "She is a good leader." The reasoning link could be stated, "Taking charge, showing good judgment, and considering the best interests of the group are the characteristics most often associated with good leadership." To test this kind of argument you should ask, "Are the characteristics mentioned the most important ones in determining the definition? Are those characteristics best labeled with the stated term?" If the answer to these is "no," you have the basis for refutation of the reasoning. "Is an important aspect of the definition omitted in the statement of the characteristics?" If so, then the reasoning is not sound.

5. *Reasoning by sign.* You are reasoning by **sign** when your conclusion is based on the presence of observable data that usually or always accompany other unobservable data. If, for example, Martha breaks out in hives, the presence of that condition (breaking out in hives) is usually or always associated with another variable (an allergy reaction), and we can predict the existence of the other unobserved variable. Signs are often confused with causes, but signs are indications, not causes. Hives are a sign of an allergy reaction. Hives occur when a person is having such a reaction, but the hives do not *cause* the reaction. To test this kind of argument you would ask: "Do the data cited always or usually indicate the conclusion drawn? Are sufficient signs present?" If not, you have the basis for refutation of the reasoning.

How to Refute

Although you do not have as long to consider exactly what you are going to say, your refutation must be organized nearly as well as your planned speeches. If you will think of refutation as units of argument, each of which is organized by following four definite steps, you will learn to prepare and to present refutation effectively:

1. State the argument you are going to refute clearly and concisely. (Or, as an advocate replying to refutation, state the argument you are going to rebuild.)
2. State what you will prove; you must tell your listeners how you plan to proceed so they will be able to follow your thinking.
3. Present the proof completely with documentation.

4. Draw a conclusion; do not rely on the audience to draw the proper conclusion for you. Never go on to another argument before you have drawn your conclusion.

In the following abbreviated statement, notice how the four steps of refutation (stating the argument, stating what you will prove, presenting proof, and drawing a conclusion) are incorporated. For purposes of analysis, each of the four steps is enumerated:

> (1) Ms. Horan has said that buying insurance provides a systematic, compulsory savings. (2) Her assumption is that "systematic, compulsory savings" is a benefit of buying insurance while you are young. But I believe that just the opposite is true—I believe that there are at least two serious disadvantages resulting from this. (3) First, the system is so compulsory that if you miss a payment you stand to lose your entire savings and all benefits. Most insurance contracts include a clause giving you a 30-day grace period, after which the policy is canceled . . . [evidence]. Second, if you need money desperately, you have to take a loan on your policy. The end result of such a loan is that you have to pay interest in order to borrow your own money . . . [evidence]. (4) From this analysis I think you can see that the "systematic, compulsory saving" is more a disadvantage than an advantage for people who are trying to save money.

PRACTICE

Suggested Speech Assignments

1. *Speech of Conviction.* Prepare a three- to six-minute speech of conviction. An outline is required. The speech should have a short introduction that leads into the proposition. By the end of the speech (probably by the end of the introduction), the audience should be aware of the specific behavioral objective— the proposition. The major portion of the speech should be on the statement and development of two to five *good reasons*. Development should both prove the truth of the reasons through facts and/or expert opinion and indicate the relevance of the reasons to the audience. A brief conclusion should summarize the reasons or in some way reemphasize the importance of the proposition.

2. *Speech to Actuate.* Prepare a four- to seven-minute persuasive speech on a topic designed to bring your audience to action. An outline is required. In addition to clarity of purpose and soundness of rationale, criteria for evaluation will include your ability to satisfy audience needs, your ability to phrase your ideas in a way that will motivate, and your ability to organize the speech to adapt to audience attitude.

3. *Speech Replying to a Persuasive Speech.* Working with a classmate, select a debatable proposition and clear the wording with your professor. Phrase the proposition so that the first speaker is in favor of the proposal. The first speaker will present a three- to six-minute speech of conviction. This first speech should be prepared as a speech of reasons. The second speaker presents a three- to six-minute speech of refutation. The second speaker should spend the entire time in direct refutation of the reasons presented. This assignment gives an opportunity to cover a speech of conviction and a speech of refutation in one assignment.

SUMMARY

Directions for preparing a persuasive speech are similar to directions for preparing an informative speech.

First, write a clear persuasive speech goal, or proposition, stating what you want your audience to believe or do.

Second, build the body of the speech with good reasons, statements that answer *why* a proposition is justified. Support reasons with facts and opinion.

Third, create the best organization for the speech. Your organizational choices are statement-of-reasons method, problem-solution method, comparative-advantages method, criteria-satisfaction method, or negative method.

Fourth, word your main points and key ideas with emotional appeal. To get the most out of your speech you need to get in touch with your own feelings about the ideas; create a common ground; develop a "yes" response; suggest agreement; replace vague, general words with words that call up a specific image; and avoid pedantic statements of fact.

Fifth, use your credibility advantageously. Credibility is built on speaker competence, intention, character, and personality. One of the most important ways of building credibility is to behave in an ethical manner.

Finally, deliver the speech convincingly. Good delivery is especially important in persuasive speaking.

In addition to giving a persuasive speech, you also need to know how to reply to persuasion. An effective speaker knows what to refute and how to refute.

SUGGESTED READINGS

Kahane, Howard. *Logic and Contemporary Rhetoric.* 5th ed. Belmont, Calif.: Wadsworth, 1986 (paperback). This excellent source gives some outstanding pointers on the use and development of logical argument and places considerable emphasis on identifying and eliminating the fallacies of reasoning.

Larson, Charles U. *Persuasion: Reception and Responsibility.* 4th ed. Belmont, Calif.: Wadsworth, 1986. A solid textbook that places more emphasis on the receiver of the persuasive message than on the persuader.

Packard, Vance O. *The Hidden Persuaders.* New York: Pocket Books, 1975 (paperback). This popular book, first published in the 1950s, still makes for excellent reading about the problems and excesses of persuasion.

Smith, Mary John. *Persuasion and Human Interaction.* Belmont, Calif.: Wadsworth, 1982. An excellent review and critique of theories of persuasion.

*A*PPENDICES

APPENDIX A / SAMPLES AND ANALYSES

1 Interpersonal Conversation and Analysis

2 Informative Speech and Analysis

3 Persuasive Speech and Analysis

APPENDIX B / ANALYSIS CHECKLISTS

1 Interpersonal Communication Analysis—Form A

2 Interpersonal Communication Analysis—Form B

3 Group Communication Analysis—Form A, Decision

4 Group Communication Analysis—Form B, Individual

5 Leadership Analysis

6 Speech Evaluation

APPENDIX C / THE COMMUNICATION CONTRACT

SAMPLES AND ANALYSES

- -

Samples can be useful means for studying the principles of any speech communication format. Each of the following is a sample that was presented by students much like yourself to meet a communication assignment. The first is an interpersonal conversation; the second is an informative speech; the third is a persuasive speech. Each contains enough examples of successful applications of principles to make them worth analysis. Your goal is not to copy what others have done but to read and analyze in order to better test the value of what you are planning to do.

In each case my suggestion is to read the sample and make your own judgments about which parts are good, bad, or indifferent. After you have made your analysis, read the critique and compare it with your own.

1. INTERPERSONAL CONVERSATION AND ANALYSIS

Dating   Sheila and Susan talk about the advantages and disadvantages of dating exclusively within one's own religion. Read the conversation aloud in its entirety. After you have considered its merits, read it again, this time noting the analysis in the left hand column.

ANALYSIS	CONVERSATION
Susan introduces the subject with a question.	SUSAN: How are you and Bill getting along these days?
Sheila's answer is neither as specific nor as concrete as it could have been.	SHEILA: Not too well. I think you could say our relationship is coming to an end. The feelings just aren't there, and so many problems have been building up.
Susan responds with a *perception check* wording; she's responding	SUSAN: I get the impression from the expression on your face that

---

Conversation presented in Interpersonal Communication class, University of Cincinnati. Reprinted by permission of Sheila Slone and Susan Lautman.

both to Sheila's spoken words and to what she is implying. A *feelings paraphrase* wording would be better: "From the way you're talking, I get the impression that you're very sad about the outcome of the relationship."

you're having problems. Is there one specific problem?

Sheila says, "It really does make a difference," but she doesn't go on to say what the difference is. We would expect Susan to ask about the difference.

SHEILA: Well, there are a lot, but one that I didn't think would make such a difference at the beginning of the relationship that's made a difference now is the fact that we're from different religions. I'm Jewish and he isn't, and at first I never thought it would affect me, but it does make a difference.

Susan assumes she understands. She needs a question or a content paraphrase here. Instead, she changes the emphasis to her own experience. Now apparently the conversation will focus on Susan and an implied contrast in upbringing.

SUSAN: I think I was kind of lucky, well, lucky in the long run. When I was in high school, my parents wouldn't allow me to go out with anybody who wasn't Jewish. I really resented that at first, but now I'm kind of glad since I'm thinking about the future now. And as my parents said, you don't know what could come out of a high-school relationship.

Although Sheila's paraphrase is satisfactory, the wording could be even more specific: "It seems like you were a little upset at first, but now that you're older you have a better understanding of your parents' position."

SHEILA: It seems like you were a little upset at first, but now you're pretty happy with the whole situation.

Susan's response has a slightly superior ring to it. Note the implications of the word *predicament*. Susan needs to empathize with Sheila more directly.

SUSAN: Yes, now that I look around, I'm not in the predicament that you are of having to get out of a relationship for something that's not what you want.

Sheila's reaction is to defend her parents' policy. Then she makes a statement about the value of independence.

Notice that even though the statements are at odds, Sheila and Susan seem to be maintaining a good climate.

Sheila says "feel," but she's not really describing feelings.

SHEILA: I can see what you mean, but I'm also happy that my parents didn't restrict me because I think I would have felt a lot of pressure just to always . . . I wouldn't have had a choice of whom to go out with, and I wouldn't have felt very independent. But I feel I have to make my own choices. As long as I know what I want, I feel it's all right.

Susan begins a response to the subject of the last sentence: choices. But then she returns to her parents' policy. Good, clear statement of position.

SUSAN: That was my problem—having to pick and choose. My parents would say, "Oh, is he Jewish?" "I don't know, should I ask him?" They wanted me to say, "Are you Jewish? Oh, you're not? Well, you can't go out with me, then."

Sheila's acknowledgment of Susan's feelings is in the right direction, but her wording appears a bit half-hearted. She needs a good paraphrase of feelings. In the midst of her response, she switches to a description of her feelings. The rest of the sentence is well-worded. She needs a clearer division between her response to Susan and her description of feelings.

SHEILA: I can see how you feel—that's a tough situation, but I see now that I feel pretty frustrated because I want to date people who are Jewish, but I'm not going to go around picking on them saying this one is and this one isn't. It's too hard to do that. You can't turn your feelings on and off. You have to be interested in someone. So I get pretty frustrated a lot of times.

This is probably one of the best responses in the dialogue. Although it is cast in question form, it is still a good attempt at seeking clarification of Sheila's feelings.

SUSAN: Are you saying that you are kind of glad that your parents didn't restrict you in that manner, or are you saying that you're glad they didn't but wish they had?

SHEILA: I guess I'm glad they didn't, but maybe it would have been better if they had. I would have been more conscious about it.

ANALYSIS	CONVERSATION
Notice the use of the word *feel* when *believe* or *think* would be more appropriate.	SUSAN: In the long run, I feel it's best to start early to get an idea in your mind of what you really want to do. I never thought a relationship in high school would go anywhere, but the man I'm dating, it's been four years already. That's a long time.
A nicely phrased personal feedback statement—a nice compliment.	SHEILA: You seem happy together. I saw you the other day and that's really nice. I wish I could find some-body that . . .
	SUSAN: I saw you start shrugging Bill off and just ignoring him.
Sheila again describes her feelings quite well.	SHEILA: Yes, that's a hard situation. I get pretty depressed about it, too. I just never thought religion could make such a big difference. But it means a lot to me, and that's why it makes such a difference.
Here's one of the few times when Susan focuses her attention on Sheila. Good question.	SUSAN: What are you planning on telling him?
Sheila states her plans and continues to describe her feelings.	SHEILA: Well, I guess I'll just say that it won't work out. It depresses me to think about that, too.
Susan gives advice that is meant to be supportive of Sheila's predicament.	SUSAN: You should really try to go easy—don't let it upset you too much. It's what you want, right?
	SHEILA: I guess so. I'll have to try to do the best I can.

In trying to help Sheila deal with her problem, Susan probably spent too much time talking about her own background and situation. Although some of her remarks show that she heard what Sheila was saying, some of her comments did not deal directly with Sheila's problem. Since the dialogue began as a response to Sheila's problem, Sheila's attempts at directing conversation to her problem are in order.

Both speakers made satisfactory attempts at paraphrasing and describing feelings; however, there were no good examples of perception checking. Still, the conversation was friendly (nonverbal responses were very supportive, but you can't see that on paper), and no major barriers developed.

2. INFORMATIVE SPEECH AND ANALYSIS

In Search of Noah's Ark

ANALYSIS

SPEECH

The speech opens with a good historical narrative designed to get the attention of the class.

Notice the use of rhetorical questions to lead into the speech goal.

In this case the speech goal is stated at the end of the speech introduction and leads into the body of the speech. If you are going to state or paraphrase your speech goal, this is the place to do it.

In 1916 during the first World War, in the Russian-occupied sector of eastern Turkey, a Russian airman, W. Roskavitsky, swore that while flying over one of the slopes of Mount Ararat he saw a large vessel. This amazing report was taken all the way to the Czar, who himself organized an expedition to climb Mount Ararat, and this expedition brought back the description of just such a large vessel half-submerged in the glacial lake. The Czar's commission believed that they had found Noah's Ark. Could this be? Is it possible that Noah's Ark is real? In this speech, I'd like to examine with you some of the historical documentation supporting the statement that an ark, vessel, or boat is on top of Mount Ararat—and that the vessel is in fact Noah's Ark.

Here the body of the speech begins. The first main point—that

First, and probably most familiar to us, of this historical evidence is

Speech given in Fundamentals of Speech class, Miami University. Printed by permission of Thomas Grossmann.

historical writings suggest the presence of a real Ark—is implied rather than stated directly. Although you should probably state each main point clearly, in this speech the method fits well with the historical narrative approach—an approach that is designed to draw you into the resolution of the mystery.

Here the speaker confuses the date of Josephus' birth, A.D. 37, with the date of the writing of *The Antiquities of the Jews*, which was A.D. 93 or 94.

the Biblical account of Noah's Ark and the Flood. In Genesis 8:4 it says that the Ark came to rest upon Mount Ararat. Second, Flavius Josephus, the Jewish historian, wrote in his history, *Jewish Antiquities*, in 37 A.D., that it had been reported that the Ark had been found on top of Mount Ararat. Finally, more than one thousand years later, in 1300 A.D., Marco Polo wrote in his book called *Travels* that on his way through Turkey to China, he had heard that the Ark was on top of Mount Ararat. For a long time historians had held this information suspect. First, it was difficult to believe that a boat was on top of a mountain; second, all the documentation was hearsay. Proof in the way of verifiable sightings was needed.

Here again a main point is stated differently from what we usually expect. In outline form, the main point would be stated: Actual sightings of the Ark have been reported.

Here and throughout the speech the content is excellent. You should keep one criticism in mind, however. Since the source of this material is important and perhaps necessary for building and maintaining speaker credibility, the speaker should have introduced the sources of the various facts with a statement such as "As Jones pointed out in his book on _____." The speaker presented a good bibliography in his outline of the speech, but he did not introduce enough of the sources directly in the speech.

But these actual sightings did come. On two separate occasions, expeditions on Mount Ararat have seen the prow or side of a large wooden vessel sticking out of the glacial ice pack. First, a Turkish expedition in 1840 sent to Mount Ararat to build barricades against avalanches came back and reported that a large prow or side of a vessel was sticking out of the glacial ice pack. In 1952, more than 100 years later, an almost identical sighting was made by an American oil pipeline mining expedition. This expedition, headed by George Jefferson Green, also found the large prow or side of a vessel sticking out of the glacial ice pack.

ANALYSIS	SPEECH
Still, the examples are good, and the use of the examples helps to gain and hold attention.	Even though these sightings were documented, no one had actually been able to bring a piece of this supposed Ark back for study. And often in history supposed firsthand observations had proved to be wrong. With this goal of getting tangible evidence, Ferdinand Navara, a French explorer, climbed Mount Ararat in 1955, and at an elevation of 14,000 feet, he dug down into the glacial ice pack and found an estimated 50 tons of wood. He was able to bring back some of this wood to France where it was analyzed by the Pre-history Institute of the University of Bordeaux on April 15, 1956. The conclusion of this report said that it was definitely wood, it was white oak, it was more than 5,000 years old, it was covered with pitch, and the wood was hand hewn. The wood was also studied by the Forestry Institute of Research and Experimentation in Madrid, Spain, and they reached the same conclusions. This finding of wood may not appear to offer support for the presence of an Ark until another aspect is considered—this wood was found on Mount Ararat at a height some 300 feet higher than the highest tree in the entire world! Moreover, Mount Ararat itself is 300 miles away from the closest living tree.
Here we get into the third main point, that recently actual material has been brought back from the source.	
The speech continues with specific details.	
I particularly like the way this speech fits together. The audience feels in on the drawing together of the various materials.	
This is an excellent summary. It states the three main points of the speech—points that were only alluded to in the speech itself. Moreover, the rhetorical question and the last statement leave the speech on a high note—a note of mystery and speculation.	So, let's see what we've discovered. Historical documentation dating back as far as 1000 B.C. has said that an Ark or boat rests upon Mount Ararat. Three separate expeditions—one Turkish, one Russian, and one American—have all found something that looks like a boat on

ANALYSIS	SPEECH
Although there are a few problems with this speech (and as you'll discover there are some problems with almost any speech), it is a good one.	top of Mount Ararat. A Frenchman by the name of Ferdinand Navara has actually found more than 50 tons of wood on top of Mount Ararat 300 feet above the highest tree line and 300 miles from the nearest tree. What does this mean? In eastern Turkey, in the area of cold Armenia, on top of a volcanic mountain named Mount Ararat, there rests a very large boat-like object—an object that many believe to be Noah's Ark.

3. PERSUASIVE SPEECH AND ANALYSIS

Open Your Eyes

ANALYSIS	SPEECH
Much of the strength of this speech is a result of the speaker's ability to involve members of the audience personally and get them to feel what she is saying. This opening is a striking example of audience involvement. She does not just tell the audience what it would be like—she has them experience the feeling. The speaker very successfully lays the emotional groundwork for total audience reception of her words.	Would all of you close your eyes for just a minute. Close them very tightly so that all the light is blocked out. Imagine what it would be like to always live in a world of total darkness such as you are experiencing right now, though only for a moment. Never to see the flaming colors of the sunset, or the crisp green of the world after the rain—never to see the faces of those you love. Now open your eyes, look all around you, look at all of the things that you couldn't have seen if you couldn't have opened your eyes.

Speech given in Fundamentals of Speech class, University of Cincinnati. Printed by permission of Kathleen Sheldon.

| ANALYSIS | SPEECH |

Here the speaker begins the body of her speech by telling us about the role of the cornea. Notice throughout the speech the excellent word choice, such as "The bright world we awake to each morning is brought to us by. . . ."

Here again she does not just tell us what it is like but asks us to imagine for ourselves what it would be like *if*. The "rain-slashed window pane" is an especially vivid image.

The speaker continues in a very informative way. After asserting that corneal transplants work, she focuses on the two key points that she wants the audience to work with—the operation works, but it must be done within 72 hours.

Notice that there is still no apparent direct persuasion. Her method is one of making information available in a way that will lead the audience itself to thinking about what effects the information might have on them personally.

In this segment of the speech, she launches into emotional high gear. Still, her approach remains somewhat indirect. Although we

The bright world we awake to each morning is brought to us by two dime-sized pieces of tough, transparent, semi-elastic tissue; these are the cornea, and it is their function to allow light to enter the lens and the retina. Normally, they are so clear that we don't even know they are there; however, when they are scratched or scarred either by accident or by disease, they tend to blur or blot out the light. Imagine peering through a rain-slashed window pane or trying to see while swimming under water. This is the way victims of corneal damage often describe their vision.

"To see the world through another man's eyes." These words are Shakespeare's, yet today it can literally be true. Thanks to the research by medical workers throughout the world, the operation known as a corneal transplant or a corneal graft has become a reality, giving thousands of people the opportunity to see. No other generation has held such a profound legacy in its possession. Yet, the universal ignorance of this subject of cornea donation is appalling. The operation itself is really quite simple; it involves the corneas of the donor being transplanted into the eyes of a recipient. And if this operation takes place within seventy-two hours after the death of the donor, it can be 100 percent effective.

No one who has seen the human tragedy caused solely by corneal disease can doubt the need or the urgency. Take the case of a young stress the importance of directness in language in this speech, the use of "no one" repeatedly through the examples is done by design. Although a more direct method might be effective, in this case the indirectness works quite well.

The real effectiveness of this section is a result of the parallel structure and repetition of key phrases: "no one who has seen . . . human tragedy . . . great joy . . . can doubt the need or the urgency." As this portion of the speech was delivered, the listeners were deeply touched by both the examples themselves and their own thoughts about the examples.

Also note how the examples themselves are ordered. The first two represent a personal effect; the final one a universal effect.

woman living in New Jersey who lost her sight to corneal disease. She gave birth to a baby and two years ago, thanks to a corneal transplant, she saw her three-year-old baby girl for the first time. And no one who had seen this woman's human tragedy caused solely by corneal disease nor her great joy at the restoration of her sight can doubt the need or the urgency. Or take the case of the five-year-old boy in California who was playing by a bonfire when a bottle in the fire exploded, flinging bits of glass, which lacerated his corneas. His damaged corneas were replaced with healthy ones in an emergency operation, and no one who has seen this little boy's human tragedy caused solely by corneal laceration nor the great joy to his young life of receiving his sight back again can doubt the need or the urgency. Or take the case of Dr. Beldon H. Scribbner of the University of Washington School of Medicine. Dr. Scribbner's eyesight was damaged by a corneal disease that twisted the normally spear-shaped cornea into cones. A corneal transplant gave Dr. Scribbner a 20-20 corrective vision and allowed him to continue work on his invention—the artificial kidney machine. And no one who has seen this man's tragedy caused solely by corneal disease, or the great joy brought not only to Dr. Scribbner but to the thousands of people his machine has helped save, can doubt the need or the urgency.

At this point in the speech the audience should be sympathetic

There are many philosophies behind such a gift. One of them was with the problem and encouraged by the hope of corneal transplants. Now the speaker must deal with the listeners' reactions of "That may be a good idea for someone else, but why me?" In this section she offers reasons for our acting. If the speech has a weakness, it may be here. I'd like to have heard a little further development of the reasons or perhaps the statement of an additional reason.

Here she brings the audience from "Good idea—I'll do something someday" to "I'd better act now."

She reminds them of the critical time period and tells them how they can proceed to make the donation. In this section it might be worth a sentence to stress that the donation costs nothing but a little time.

Here the speaker brings the audience full circle. Although she could have used different images, the repetition of those that began the speech takes the emphasis off the images themselves and places it in what the audience can do about those who are in these circumstances.

summed up by a minister and his wife who lost their daughter in infancy. They said, "We feel that a part of her goes on living." Or take the case of the young woman with this explanation: "I want to be useful; being useful brings purpose and meaning into my life." Surely if being useful is important there are few better ways than to donate your eyes to someone who lives after you. But no matter which philosophy you do adopt, I hope each of you will consider donating your eyes to another who will live after you and who otherwise would have to survive in the abyss of darkness. It will do you no good to leave your eyes in your regular will if you have one, for as I mentioned earlier, there is a 72 hour critical period. If you wish to donate your eyes, I would suggest you contact Cincinnati Eye Bank for Sight Restoration at 861-3716. They will send you the appropriate donor forms to fill out, which should be witnessed by two of your closest friends or by your next of kin so that they will know your wishes. Then, when you die and no longer have need for your sight someone who desperately wants the chance to see will be able to.

Will all of you close your eyes again for just a moment? Close them very tightly, so that all the light is blocked out. And once more imagine what it would be like to live always in a world of total darkness such as you are experiencing right now, never to see the flaming colors of a sunset, or the crisp green of the

The last line of the speech is simple, but in the context of the entire speech it is direct and quite moving.

world after a rain—never seeing the faces of those you love. Now open your eyes . . . Won't you give someone else the chance to open theirs?

PRACTICE

Analyzing Communication

1. Using either Interpersonal Communication Analysis Form A (Appendix B-1) or Interpersonal Communication Analysis Form B (Appendix B-2), analyze one of your communication encounters. Select one that occurred during the past day or two so that the dialogue is fresh in your mind.

2. Using the Speech Evaluation Form (Appendix B-6), evaluate a public speech you have heard recently.

*I*NTERPERSONAL *C*OMMUNICATION *A*NALYSIS: *F*ORM *A*

Participants: _____

_____

Apparent purpose of the encounter: _____

_____

Outcome—what was the result? _____

_____

Describe the entire encounter. Use dialogue whenever possible.

_____

On the back of this sheet, list the reasons for success or failure of the communication. Discuss those reasons in terms of presence or absence of various skills.

*I*NTERPERSONAL *C*OMMUNICATION *A*NALYSIS: *F*ORM *B*

Participants: _____

_____

Apparent purpose of the encounter: _____

_____

Outcome—what was the result? _____

_____

Play back the dialogue as you remember it. On the back of this sheet, describe the entire encounter. Use specific dialogue wherever possible. Indicate whether or not various skills were used in the dialogue. Describe their use and consider their relative effectiveness. Check those below that you will be discussing in your analysis.

Message Formation and Response Skills:

☐ Asserting   ☐ Paraphrasing

☐ Dating   ☐ Supporting

☐ Indexing   ☐ Questioning

☐ Describing feelings   ☐ Interpreting

☐ Listening   ☐ Descriptive feedback

Nonverbal Considerations:

- ☐ Environment
- ☐ Self-presentation
- ☐ Body motions

- ☐ Paralanguage
- ☐ Perception checking

Barriers Encountered:

- ☐ Transfer stations
- ☐ Information overload
- ☐ Noise
- ☐ Hidden agendas

- ☐ Defensiveness
- ☐ Inappropriate responses
- ☐ Conflict

GROUP COMMUNICATION
ANALYSIS: FORM A: DECISION

Analysis of group characteristics: _____

_____

Did the group arrive at a decision? Explain. _____

_____

What action was taken as a result of that discussion? Explain. _____

_____

Was the group decision a good one? Explain. _____

_____

Was quality information presented? _____

_____

Were the data fully discussed? _____

_____

Did interim conclusions reflect group discussion? _____

_____

Were conclusions measured against some set criteria? _____

_____

Did the group arrive at the decision by consensus? _____

_____

Did the group agree to support the decision? _____

_____

_____

_____

GROUP COMMUNICATION ANALYSIS: FORM B: INDIVIDUAL

For each of the following questions, rate the participant on a 1 to 5 basis: 1, high; 2, good; 3, average; 4, fair; 5, poor.

	1	2	3	4	5
Preparation:					
Seems to be well prepared	☐	☐	☐	☐	☐
Is aware of the problem	☐	☐	☐	☐	☐
Analyzes the problem	☐	☐	☐	☐	☐
Suggests possible solutions	☐	☐	☐	☐	☐
Tests each solution	☐	☐	☐	☐	☐
Carrying Out Roles:					
As information or opinion giver	☐	☐	☐	☐	☐
As information or opinion seeker	☐	☐	☐	☐	☐
As expediter	☐	☐	☐	☐	☐
As idea person	☐	☐	☐	☐	☐
As analyzer	☐	☐	☐	☐	☐

Carrying Out Roles: 1   2   3   4   5

    As recorder   ☐ ☐ ☐ ☐ ☐

    As tension reliever   ☐ ☐ ☐ ☐ ☐

    As harmonizer   ☐ ☐ ☐ ☐ ☐

    As gatekeeper   ☐ ☐ ☐ ☐ ☐

    As supporter   ☐ ☐ ☐ ☐ ☐

Carrying Out Negative Roles: (For this category a 1, high, would show that the person was not playing that negative role.)

    As aggressor   ☐ ☐ ☐ ☐ ☐

    As joker   ☐ ☐ ☐ ☐ ☐

    As withdrawer   ☐ ☐ ☐ ☐ ☐

    As monopolizer   ☐ ☐ ☐ ☐ ☐

Write an analysis of the person's group participation (two to five paragraphs) based upon this checklist.

*L*EADERSHIP *A*NALYSIS

For each of the following questions, rate the leadership on a 1 to 5 basis: 1, high; 2, good; 3, average; 4, fair; 5, poor.

	1	2	3	4	5
Preparation to Lead:					
Understands topic	☐	☐	☐	☐	☐
Works hard	☐	☐	☐	☐	☐
Shows commitment	☐	☐	☐	☐	☐
Interacts freely	☐	☐	☐	☐	☐
Is decisive	☐	☐	☐	☐	☐
Leading the Group:					
Has group of optimum size	☐	☐	☐	☐	☐
Creates and maintains a suitable atmosphere	☐	☐	☐	☐	☐
Works to develop a cohesive unit	☐	☐	☐	☐	☐
Helps the group form appropriate norms	☐	☐	☐	☐	☐
Has an agenda	☐	☐	☐	☐	☐

Promotes systematic problem solving	☐	☐	☐	☐	☐
Asks good questions	☐	☐	☐	☐	☐
Encourages balanced participation	☐	☐	☐	☐	☐
Refrains from dominating the group	☐	☐	☐	☐	☐
Deals with conflict	☐	☐	☐	☐	☐
Arrives at decisions by means of consensus or voting	☐	☐	☐	☐	☐
Brings discussion to a satisfactory close	☐	☐	☐	☐	☐

Write an analysis (two to five paragraphs) based upon this checklist.

SPEECH EVALUATION

Speaker: _____

Location: _____

Speech Goal: _____

Check your opinion of how well speaker met major criteria:

	Yes	Partially	No
Content:			
Was the speaker prepared?	☐	☐	☐
Did the speaker have specifics to support or to explain major statements?	☐	☐	☐
Was the support well related to points made?	☐	☐	☐
Did material and development meet your ethical standards?	☐	☐	☐

	Yes	Partially	No

Organization:

	Yes	Partially	No
Did the introduction gain attention and lead into speech?	☐	☐	☐
Were the main points clearly stated?	☐	☐	☐
Did they follow some identifiable pattern?	☐	☐	☐
Did the conclusion end the speech appropriately?	☐	☐	☐

Style:

	Yes	Partially	No
Were ideas presented concretely and specifically?	☐	☐	☐
Was the language vivid?	☐	☐	☐
Were transitions used effectively?	☐	☐	☐
Was the language related to audience needs and interests?	☐	☐	☐

Delivery:

	Yes	Partially	No
Was the speaker enthusiastic about the material?	☐	☐	☐
Did the speaker look at the audience throughout the speech?	☐	☐	☐
Was the delivery spontaneous?	☐	☐	☐
Did the speaker use sufficient vocal variety and emphasis?	☐	☐	☐
Was the speaker poised?	☐	☐	☐

Analysis:

Circle your opinion of the speech:

Excellent   Good   Average   Fair   Poor

Using the data from the checklist write on an attached sheet of paper two to five paragraphs of analysis of the speech supporting your evaluation. Also include any aspects of speech setting (size of room, lighting, heating, and the like) or speech audience (size, age, sex, race, attitudes, interests, and the like) that may have affected the speech effectiveness.

THE **C***OMMUNICATION* **C***ONTRACT*

Before reading each of the major parts of this textbook (foundation, personal, group, and public communication), you were encouraged to complete a self-analysis to identify areas of weakness and to write a communication contract. A communication contract should include (1) a statement of your goal, (2) a description of the present problem, (3) a step-by-step action plan to reach the goal, and (4) a method of determining when the goal has been reached.

1. Statement of Goal

After considering the rating scales in the self-analysis section preceding each unit, you may want to improve one or more of your communication behaviors this term. When you have selected a change you would like to make, write your goal specifically. *Example 1:* "Goal: To increase my listening efficiency with my close friends." *Example 2:* "Goal: To look at people more directly when I'm giving a speech."

2. Description of the Problem

Here you describe to the best of your ability the specific nature of that communication problem. *Example 1:* "Problem: Currently when my roommate tries to say something to me, I find myself daydreaming or rehearsing my replies. Consequently, I sometimes miss important points or misinterpret what is being said." *Example 2:* "Problem: Usually when I get up to speak in class or in the Student Senate, I find myself burying my head in notes or looking at the ceiling or walls."

3. A Step-by-Step Action Plan

Read the procedures for implementing a skill or coping with a problem in the sections of the text where the skills or problems are discussed. From these discussions you can decide on the procedures you wish to include in your plan. When you have a plan in mind, write it out in enough detail that any reader could understand your plan. *Example 1:* "Step-by-Step Action Plan: (1) I will consciously attempt to 'clear my mind' when my roommate is speaking. (2) I will learn to use the paraphrasing skill better in order to check the accuracy of my perception of what I have heard." *Example 2:* "Step-by-Step Action Plan: I will take time to practice oral presentations aloud. (1) I will stand up just as I do in class or at Student Senate. (2) I will pretend various objects in the room are people, and I will consciously attempt to look at those objects as I am talking. (3) In the actual speech setting, I will try to be aware of when I am looking at my audience and when I am not."

4. A Method of Determining When the Goal Has Been Reached

Here you will write the minimum requirements for having achieved your goal. *Example 1:* "Test of Achieving Goal: This goal will be considered achieved (1) when I have completed two weeks of listening during which my roommate never has to repeat something for me to get it and (2) when I have internalized paraphrasing to the extent that I remember to do it and do it well." *Example 2:* "Test of Achieving Goal: This goal will be considered achieved (1) when I am conscious of when I am looking at my audience and (2) when I am maintaining eye contact most of the time."

After completing the contract, you should sign it. We would further suggest that you have another person in class witness the contract. (Perhaps you can witness his or her contract in return.) At the end of the term (or at the end of each unit), you can meet with the witness to determine whether or not your contracts have been fulfilled.

Communication Contract

1. Goal:

To look at people more directly when I'm giving a speech.

2. Statement of the problem:

Currently when I get up to speak in class or in Student Senate I find myself burying my head in notes or looking at the ceiling or walls.

3. Step-by-step action plan:

I will take the time to practice oral presentations aloud. (1) I will stand up just as I do in class or at Student Senate. (2) I will pretend various objects in the room are people, and I will consciously attempt to look at those objects as I am talking. (3) In the actual speech setting, I will try to be aware of when I am looking at my audience and when I am not.

4. Method of determining when the goal has been reached:

This goal will be considered achieved (1) when I am conscious of when I am looking at my audience and (2) when I am maintaining eye contact most of the time.

Signed: _____

Date: _____

Witnessed by: _____

*N*OTES

CHAPTER 1

1. Lanna Hagge-Greenberg, "Report on the Liberal Arts Employers Survey, Opportunity for Liberal Arts Graduate." (Indianapolis, Ind.: Midwest College Placement Association, 1979), p. 16.
2. H.J. Leavitt and Ronald A.H. Mueller, "Some Effects of Feedback on Communication," *Human Relations*, vol. 4 (1951), p. 403.
3. John A. R. Wilson, Mildred C. Robick, and William B. Michael, *Psychological Foundations of Learning and Teaching*, 2nd ed. (New York: McGraw-Hill, 1974), p. 26.
4. Paul Watzlawick, Janet H. Beavin, and Don D. Jackson, *Pragmatics of Human Communication* (New York: W. W. Norton, 1967), p. 51.

CHAPTER 2

1. Russell H. Fazio, Steven J. Sherman, and Paul M. Herr, "The Feature-Positive Effects in the Self-Perception Process: Does Not Doing Matter as Much as Doing?" *Journal of Personality and Social Psychology* 42 (1982): 411.
2. In his chapter "Developing a Healthy Self-Image," Don Hamacheck offers a lengthy analysis of the symptoms of inferiority and self-acceptance. See Don Hamacheck, *Encounters with the Self* (New York: Holt, Rinehart and Winston, 1971), pp. 232–237.
3. See Eric Berne, *Games People Play: The Psychology of Human Relationships* (New York: Grove, 1964).
4. S. S. Zalkind and T. W. Costello, "Perception: Some Recent Research and Implications for Administration," *Administrative Science Quarterly* 9(1962):218–235.
5. T. D. Hollman, "Employment Interviewer's Errors in Processing Positive and Negative Information," *Journal of Psychology* 56(1972): 130–134.
6. P. F. Secord, C. W. Backman, and D.R. Slavitt, *Understanding Social Life: An Introduction to Social Psychology* (New York: McGraw-Hill, 1976), p. 76.

CHAPTER 3

1. Blaine Goss, *Processing Communication* (Belmont, Calif.: Wadsworth, 1982), pp. 60–61.
2. *Webster's New World Dictionary*, 2nd college ed. (Cleveland, Ohio: William Collins & World Publishing Co., 1978), p. 414.
3. *Webster's New Collegiate Dic-*

tionary (Springfield, Mass.: G.C. Merriam Co., 1979), p. 334.

4. *Webster's New World Dictionary*, p. 839.

5. W. Nelson Francis, *The English Language* (New York: W. W. Norton, 1965), p. 122.

6. Charles E. Osgood, George J. Suci, and Percy H. Tannenbaum, *The Measurement of Meaning* (Urbana: University of Illinois Press, 1957), p. 36.

CHAPTER 4

1. Mark L. Knapp, *Essentials of Nonverbal Communication.* (New York: Holt, Rinehart and Winston, 1980), p. 184.

2. Albert Mehrabian, *Silent Messages*, 2nd ed. (Belmont, Calif.: Wadsworth, 1981), p. 76.

3. Paul Ekman and W. V. Friesen, "The Repertoire of Nonverbal Behavior: Categories, Origins, Usage, and Coding," *Semiotica*, vol. 1 (1969), pp. 49–98.

4. Julius Fast, *Body Language* (New York: M. Evans & Co., 1970).

5. Edward T. Hall, *The Hidden Dimension* (Garden City, N.Y.: Doubleday, 1966).

6. Edward T. Hall, *The Silent Language* (Garden City, N.Y.: Doubleday, 1959), pp. 163–164.

CHAPTER 5

1. Rudolph Verderber and Ann Elder, "An Analysis of Student Communication Habits," unpublished study, University of Cincinnati, 1976.

2. Ralph G. Nichols and Leonard A. Stevens, *Are You Listening?* (New York: McGraw-Hill, 1957), pp. 5–6.

3. Arthur S. Freese, *You and Your Hearing* (New York: Charles Scribner's Sons, 1979), p. 67.

CHAPTER 6

1. Robert J. Campbell, Norman Kagan, and David R. Krathwohl, "The Development and Validation of a Scale to Measure Affective Sensitivity (Empathy)," *Journal of Counseling Psychology,* vol. 18 (1971), p. 407.

CHAPTER 7

1. John R.P. French, Jr., and Bertram Raven, "The Bases of Social Power," reprinted in Dorwin Cartwright and Alvin Zander, eds., *Group Dynamics*, 3rd ed. (New York: Harper & Row, 1968), pp. 259–270.

CHAPTER 8

1. William Schutz, *The Interpersonal Underworld* (Palo Alto, Calif.: Science & Behavior Books, 1966), pp. 18–20.

2. Stephen W. Littlejohn, *Theories of Human Communication*, 2nd ed. (Belmont, Calif.: Wadsworth, 1983), p. 180.
3. Marvin Shaw, *Group Dynamics: The Psychology of Small Group Behavior*, 3rd ed. (New York: McGraw-Hill, 1981), pp. 228–231.

4. John W. Thibaut and Harold H. Kelley, *The Social Psychology of Groups* (New York: Wiley, 1959), pp. 100–125.
5. Littlejohn, *Theories of Human Communication*, p. 208.

CHAPTER 9

1. B. Sheatsley, "Closed Questions Are Sometimes More Valid Than Open End," *Public Opinion Quarterly*, vol. 12 (1948), p. 12.
2. "As You Were Saying—The Cover Letter and Résumé," *Personnel Journal*, vol. 48 (September 1969), pp. 732–733. This article is a summary of information provided by Harold D. Janes, Professor of Management, University of Alabama. It is also supported by suggestions from up-to-date books and manuals of résumé writing.

3. Selected from Charles S. Goetzinger, "An Analysis of Irritating Factors in Initial Employment Interviews of Male College Graduates," unpublished Ph.D. dissertation, Purdue University, 1954. Reported in Charles J. Stewart and William B. Cash, *Interviewing: Principles and Practices*, 4th ed. (Dubuque, Iowa: Wm. C. Brown, 1982), p. 216.

CHAPTER 10

1. V. H. Vroom and P. W. Yetton, *Leadership and Decision-Making* (Pittsburgh: University of Pittsburgh Press, 1973).
2. Michael Doyle and David Strauss, *How to Make Meetings Work* (New York: Wyden, 1976), p. 126.

3. Robert F. Bales, *Personality and Interpersonal Behavior* (New York: Holt, Rinehart and Winston, 1971), p. 96.

CHAPTER 11

1. John F. Cragan and David W. Wright, "Small Group Research of the 1970s: A Synthesis and Critique," *Central States Speech Journal* 31 (Fall 1980), p. 202.
2. Paul J. Patinka, "One More Time: Are Leaders Born or Made?" in James G. Hunt and Lars L. Larson, eds., *Crosscurrents in Leadership* (Carbondale: Southern Illinois University Press, 1979), pp. 36–37.

3. Marvin E. Shaw, *Group Dynamics: The Psychology of Small Group Behavior*, 3rd ed. (New York: McGraw Hill, 1981), p. 325.
4. Fred E. Fiedler, *A Theory of Leadership Effectiveness* (New York: McGraw-Hill, 1967).
5. Paul Hare, *Handbook of Small Group Research*, 2nd ed. (New York: Free Press, 1976), p. 214.
6. Shaw, *Group Dynamics*, p. 202.

CHAPTER 13

1. Edward E. Crutchfield, Jr., "Profitable Banking in the 1980s," *Vital Speeches*, June 15, 1980, p. 537.
2. Ruth A. Bryant, "Inflation: The Seven Percent Solution," *Vital Speeches*, June 15, 1980, p. 522.
3. Reginald H. Jones, "The Export Imperative," *Vital Speeches*, November 1, 1980, p. 36.
4. Douglas MacArthur, "Address to Congress," in William Linsley, *Speech Criticism: Methods and Materials* (Dubuque, Iowa: Wm. C. Brown, 1968), p. 344.

CHAPTER 14

1. "Fears," *Spectra*, vol. 9 (December 1973), p. 4.
2. Theodore Clevenger, Jr., "A Synthesis of Experimental Research in Stage Fright," *Quarterly Journal of Speech*, vol. 45 (April 1959), p. 136.
3. Larry W. Carlile, Ralph R. Behnke, and James T. Kitchens, "A Psychological Pattern of Anxiety in Public Speaking," *Communication Quarterly*, vol. 25 (Fall 1977), p. 45.

CHAPTER 15

1. John W. Haefele, *Creativity and Innovation* (New York: Reinhold, 1962), p. 6.
2. James Lavenson, "Think Strawberries," *Vital Speeches*, March 15, 1974, p. 346.

CHAPTER 16

1. Wallace Fotheringham, *Perspective on Persuasion* (Boston: Allyn & Bacon, 1966), p. 34.
2. Speech on euthanasia delivered in Persuasive Speaking, University of Cincinnati. Portions reprinted by permission of Betsy R. Burke.
3. Kenneth E. Andersen and Theodore Clevenger, Jr., "A Summary of Experimental Research in Ethos," *Speech Monographs*, vol. 30 (1963), pp. 59–78.

INDEX